OUR PAST PRESERVED

A HISTORY OF

AMERICAN LIBRARY PRESERVATION

1876-1910

OUR PAST PRESERVED

A HISTORY OF

AMERICAN LIBRARY PRESERVATION

1876-1910

Barbra Buckner Higginbotham

G.K. Hall & Co.   **Boston, Massachusetts**

First published 1990
by G.K. Hall & Co.
70 Lincoln Street
Boston, Massachusetts 02111

10 9 8 7 6 5 4 3 2 1

Library of Congress Cataloging-in-Publication Data

Higginbotham, Barbra Buckner.
    Our past preserved : a history of American library preservation,
    1876-1910 / Barbra Buckner Higginbotham.
        p. cm. – (Professional librarian series)
    Includes bibliographical references and index.
    ISBN 0-8161-1932-5
    1. Library materials – Conservation and restoration – United
States – History – 19th century. 2. Library materials – Conservation
and restoration – United States – History – 20th century.
3. Books – Conservation and restoration – United States – History.
4. Libraries – United States – History. I. Title. II. Series.
Z701.4.U6H54 1990
025.8'4'0973 – dc20   90-35860
                                                       CIP

The paper used in this publication meets the minimum
requirements of American National Standard for Information
Sciences – Permanence of Paper for Printed Library Materials.
ANSI Z39.48-1984   ∞™
MANUFACTURED IN THE UNITED STATES OF AMERICA

For Hal and Zeak

Contents

Introduction

Today there is a wealth of literature on library preservation, but little historical information about the people, libraries, and other organizations whose work was the basis for contemporary conservation approaches. A few developments, such as the evolution of mechanized book binding, have been fairly well documented, and a distinct oral history exists among conservators themselves. Nonetheless, the preservation-related thought and activity of the formative turn-of-the-century period have yet to be documented or studied systematically. The bulk of the writing on library conservation addresses application and technology rather than history, probably because the need has seemed greatest in these areas.[1]

The grass-roots nature of early preservation efforts may also explain the absence of historical study. It was 1970 before preservation became the focus of a unit of the American Library Association and was recognized as a subdiscipline of librarianship, as cataloging and reference work had been for decades. It is likely that the long absence of the unifying influence of a national organization and an identifiable leadership inhibited the development of a preservation history. Nevertheless, essays like Pamela W. Darling and Sherelyn Ogden's account of American preservation activity from 1956 to 1980 indicate that contemporary librarians find significance in the preservation events and techniques of the recent past, and occasions such as the establishment by the International Council of Museums of a Working Group on the Theory and History of Restoration point to modern conservators' concern about the lack of a written history of museum and library preservation.[2] Further, since modern libraries maintain on their shelves many books published during the Victorian period, and since (as this book will show) there are striking similarities between contemporary preservation practice and that of our forebears, their solutions may be worthy of our consideration.

Within the last twenty years library preservation has become a distinct discipline with its own curriculum and degree programs. What has often

1

been called "the brittle-books problem" is now a topic of concern not only for the American library community but also for the federal government. Additionally, the press has alerted American citizens to the serious problem of the deterioration of their intellectual history.[3] This book aims to paint a comprehensive picture of preservation thought and activity in turn-of-the-century American libraries, within a larger framework of professional and cultural concerns, in the hope that a historical study of preservation problems and responses will promote further interest and cohesiveness in conservation issues.

It cannot be too strongly emphasized that this book is not a compendium of Victorian preservation techniques. The works of contemporary binding and preservation authorities such as Douglas Cockerell, George A. Stephen, and Joseph W. Zaehnsdorf meet this requirement, are completely illustrated, and can be readily located today; there is no need to replicate them.[4] Although technique is discussed in this volume, no reader of these pages will learn to bind a book. What technical descriptions and evaluations are included are those considered necessary to make clear the general effectiveness of the approaches employed. There was some inconsistency in the use of many preservation-related terms during the period (for example, in the names of various binding leathers); this is not surprising, since many modern conservators differ on the use of certain terms. The generally accepted meanings of the period are used in this text, and the reader is referred to Matt T. Roberts and Don Etherington's *Bookbinding and the Conservation of Books: A Dictionary of Descriptive Terminology* for additional information.[5]

Most broadly, this book explores the circumstances and forces that stimulated awareness of a significant library problem and led eventually to conscious, organized efforts to address it; they establish the Victorian period as the foundation for contemporary American preservation concerns and activities. The subjects of this book are the "public" libraries of turn-of-the-century America – those institutions, whether publicly or privately funded, whose shelves contained quantities of accessible general-interest titles, not repositories dedicated solely to the rare and unique. From the annual reports of these mainstream collections has been drawn a wealth of information about the period's preservation ideas and efforts.

To understand better the significance of the turn of the century as a starting point for the study of preservation in American libraries, some sense of the time's bibliographic concerns and issues is important.[6] The decades that flanked the year 1900 brought great growth in both library construction and the development of library collections. The enormous philanthropy of Andrew Carnegie permitted the building of hundreds of new libraries across the country, contributing to increased interest in library architecture and the development of branch systems in public libraries.

Well-established libraries, such as those of Harvard University and Bowdoin College, the Library of Congress, and the Boston Public Library, enlarged existing space or built anew; smaller city libraries moved from rented rooms in municipal buildings into buildings constructed as libraries. This was also a time of collection building, marked by the development of cataloging codes and classification schemes, as American librarians sought to organize their growing stock.

Library work with children, and a corresponding cooperation between public and school libraries, blossomed during this period. Much was written about a related and rather controversial topic: the role of the librarian in maintaining or even elevating public taste and values. Would open access to collections promote the reading of potentially harmful fiction? Should librarians use circulation and collection policies to shape reading habits?[7] At the Boston Public Library, care was taken to protect children from books that might "inflame their passions or pervert their moral sense."[8]

As the nineteenth century was dying, librarians' concerns about the preservation of their collections quickened. Although American interest in the protection of library materials is as old as American libraries, preservation activities consisted largely of custodial measures before the last quarter of that century. Efforts were made to keep volumes clean and dry, books were bound and mended, penalties were assessed for damage and late returns, and libraries were swept and aired. The Harvard University library went so far as to equip itself with boxes with handles, so that books might be quickly removed in the event of fire.[9]

But by the late nineteenth century the industrial revolution had brought to the shelves of American libraries problems that simple conscientious housekeeping could not solve. Machine binding of books, as well as the use of alum-rosin size and wood pulp in papermaking, had begun seriously to affect the condition of the books in these institutions. Other negative consequences of industrialization, such as the harm done to library materials by artificial lighting, air pollution, and city dust and dirt, were also obvious.

In addition to the effects of industrialization, factors such as collection expansion, increasing levels of publication (and the consequent cheapening of materials and production methods), the aging of collections established mid-century and earlier, and the risks associated with circulating library materials produced preservation awareness, alarm, and action in American libraries. Recognizing the critical importance of conservation, librarians began to take steps to extend the lives of their collections.[10]

Introduction

To produce a portrait of American preservation thinking and technique at the turn of the century, one must examine the years spanning this point. As the birth year of the American Library Association and the American library press (and, by extension, recorded American library history), 1876 makes a practical start.[11] For the first time, American librarians had both a personal and a published forum in which to address issues and exchange ideas. Also in 1876, the Bureau of Education published its report *Public Libraries in the United States of America: Their History, Condition, and Management*, which profiled the library community as the end of the century neared. Its contents, including the chapters "Binding and Preservation of Books" by Librarian of Congress Ainsworth R. Spofford and "Library Buildings" by Justin Winsor, reflected the thinking of America's library leaders.[12]

In 1910 – at the end of the decade before the first World War began – growth, prosperity, and the international exchange of ideas and research began to slow. That year represents the close of the period of initial research into the causes of deterioration in library materials by the U.S. Bureau of Standards and the Royal Society of Arts (London), a period in which librarians proposed the first standards for binding. It also represents a useful break with the next thirty-five year period, during which Harry Lydenberg conducted his work on paper treatment at the New York Public Library, Herman Fussler pioneered in the use of film as a preservation medium, and William Barrow began the research into various aspects of paper permanence and durability that would flower in the 1950s and 1960s.[13]

This book, then, examines American preservation thought, practice, and research between 1876 and 1910. In his book *Presence of the Past*, historian Charles Hosmer says that architectural preservation has become a modern "cultural crusade"; by this he means that American society is actively undertaking the organized and systematic conservation of its historic landmarks.[14] If, like architectural preservation, library preservation can be termed a contemporary cultural crusade, let us then study the period when American librarians first interested themselves in this important issue.

Chapter 1

In the Beginning:
Mission, Ethic, and Training

Before examining the beliefs turn-of-the-century librarians held about the causes of deterioration and the steps they took to protect their collections, it is important to establish their context. How might one characterize preservation interest and activity in 1876 and in the years before? Two events provide interesting insights into librarians' thinking at mid-century.

On 15, 16, and 17 September 1853, delegates from twelve states and the District of Columbia attended the Librarians' Convention in New York City. The invitation to gather for the purpose of "conferring together upon the means of advancing the prosperity and usefulness of public libraries" was issued by a small group of prominent persons, including the librarians of the Boston Athenaeum, the Smithsonian Institution, the Library Company of Philadelphia, Columbia College, and Yale, Harvard, and Brown universities. The conference's topics included Charles Jewett's plan for creating shared cataloging records; periodical and newspaper indexes; classification; the international exchange of duplicate and unwanted library materials; and the distribution of federal documents to libraries. At the time, government publications were sent to members of Congress and "a few favored libraries only"; conference members suggested that these documents be "distributed as to be accessible for reference to all citizens, and at the same time preserved for posterity." At the convention's close, a committee of five was appointed to draft the constitution and bylaws for "a permanent Librarians' Association."[1]

Around the same time, Charles Jewett was collecting data for his survey *Notices of Public Libraries in the United States of America*, which included both narrative and statistical information about 694 institutions. Under the rubric of "public" libraries, Jewett included all those that "are accessible – either without restriction, or upon conditions with which all can easily comply – to every person who wishes to use them for their appropriate purposes." Only personal libraries and those in public schools

5

were excluded, and one might call Jewett's study a precursor of the Bureau of Education's 1876 *Special Report*. In 1849, the year covered by Jewett's survey, there were only fifty-nine libraries in the nation with collections of more than ten thousand volumes. Of these, only five (those at Harvard and Yale, the Boston Athenaeum, the Library of Congress, and the Library Company of Philadelphia) had collections of more than fifty thousand volumes.[2]

Jewett gathered his data by sending out a questionnaire that asked about collection size, special materials (manuscripts, maps, music), budget, staffing, classification, catalogs, service hours, annual circulation, the library building, and whether the library's books had been "injured at any time by insects." Only three of the responding institutions reported problems with pests. Yale's librarian mentioned silverfish but added, "'I cannot discover that it eats much. In my own library at home, two books have been injured by some boring beetle or its larva, (probably a species of anobium,) so that I cannot doubt that books in our public libraries need examination once a year, at least, with reference to this matter.'"[3]

Two South Carolina libraries also complained of insect problems. The librarian of Charleston's Apprentices' Library wrote, "'The old books and those not often consulted, unless bound with Russia leather, are apt to be injured by insects. They may be saved by taking them out every week or two and striking the backs together, also by clippings of Russia leather scattered about on the shelves.'"[4] The Theological Seminary of the Synod of South Carolina and Georgia reported its collection to have been

> much injured by a small shiny moth, which eats off the pasted titles of cloth-bound books, and sometimes by a blackish worm of the caterpillar kind, the product of a brown miller or moth, which eats leather binding. It is also found that in this climate, except in the driest situations, and occasionally even in these, leather-bound books suffer much from mould – English leather-bound books less than American, and French perhaps less than English. One gentleman amongst us has suffered so much from this cause, that he will only have books bound in cloth; and these, if the letters are stamped on the back, without being on a title which is pasted, are injured less by mould and insects than any other.[5]

In the twenty-five years between Jewett's survey and that published by the Bureau of Education in its 1876 *Special Report*, American libraries grew significantly. Of the 3,647 libraries reporting, 266 (versus 59 in 1849) owned more than 10,000 volumes. The number of institutions with more than 50,000 volumes had jumped from five to eighteen, and nine libraries reported more than 100,000 volumes:

Library	Volumes
Library Company of Philadelphia	104,000
Boston Athenaeum	105,000
Yale University Library	114,200
Philadelphia Mercantile Library	125,668
Astor Library (New York City)	152,446
New York Mercantile Library	160,613
Harvard University Library	227,650
Boston Public Library	299,869
Library of Congress	300,000[6]

The *Special Report* contained not only statistical information but also more than thirty essays on various aspects of American library history, management, and philosophy. One of these pieces, Librarian of Congress Ainsworth R. Spofford's "Binding and Preservation of Books," directly addressed the care of library collections; articles by Justin Winsor (Boston Public Library), William F. Poole (Chicago Public Library), and Otis H. Robinson (University of Rochester) touched on the topic. Spofford characterized the importance of preservation, within the larger field of public library administration, as second only to "the selection and utilization of books." His comments covered five different areas: collection management (librarians must periodically examine their shelves for books in need of repair or rebinding); binding economy ("the cheapest binding is that which is done to last, and the most expensive that which the soonest comes to pieces in the hands of the reader"); binding materials (levant morocco was "the only leather likely to give permanent satisfaction"); binding technology (books should be sewn in signatures and not "trimmed all around"); and precautions for readers (who "should not be permitted the vulgar and deleterious practice of folding down the corners of leaves").[7]

In "Library Memoranda," Winsor expressed similar ideas. "Cheap binding is often dear binding. Strong sewing, real leather, and solid board are worth paying for," he wrote. Further, of all binding materials, genuine morocco was the one best able to withstand "foul air and an air heated and vitiated by gas light."[8] In a second essay, Winsor took as his topic the library building. In a section on shelving, he suggested the use of book supports made from "a block of wood" that had been shellacked. Newspapers were to be shelved flat, no more than three volumes to a shelf. Additionally, he wrote that "it is desirable for a large library to have a bindery in the building, which should be amply provided for" in terms of allotted space.[9]

Finally, William F. Poole and Otis H. Robinson, in companion pieces on the administration of public and college libraries, each had a few words regarding the care and safekeeping of collections. Poole advised on the matters of protective book jackets, binding materials, and the dusting of books and shelves, whereas Robinson addressed the broader issue of preservation mission: "[A book] may stand on the shelves a decade untouched, and then, by some event in the literary or scientific world, be called forth and wanted by everybody. For these reasons, and others which might be given, it is generally thought better to suffer a little inconvenience from a mixture of the useful with the apparently useless volumes than to attempt a separation."[10]

At mid-century libraries were small, both in number and size. The information found in the proceedings of the 1853 Librarians' Convention, Jewett's 1849 survey of public libraries, and the Bureau of Education's 1876 *Special Report* combines to produce an interesting picture of preservation concerns and activities at the start of the last quarter of the nineteenth century. Librarians appear to have had some interest in direct causes of damage to their collections (e.g., insects), and the desirability of preserving federal documents is mentioned; however, the major themes are classification, catalogs and cataloging, collection development, and indexing.

It is not surprising that the librarian at mid-century showed only a passing concern with preservation. In 1850 publishers still bound largely by hand. Although deterioration in the quality of book papers had begun to accelerate, most collections were small and grew slowly; no significant number of poorly made volumes had yet accumulated on library shelves and aroused serious concern about library preservation. Twenty-five years later, however, quite a difference in preservation attitude prevailed.

In 1876 many more libraries had been established, and collections were significantly larger. By this time the popular demand for inexpensive literature had begun to take its toll on library collections. While preservation was still not librarianship's primary issue, a clear emphasis on workmanship and materials for binding had emerged. Not all such work was performed with honesty and to a high standard; librarians were advised to engage binders and select materials with care, and to consider the advantages of a bindery located in the library itself. Late nineteenth-century librarians also became aware of the ill effects of artificial lighting and the urban atmosphere, and demonstrated their pragmatism through their concern for dusting and cleaning both the shelves and their stock.

Preservation, as a term and as a concept, was already well established in American library thinking. When the Librarian of Congress wrote about "Binding and Preservation of Books" in the Bureau of Education's 1876 report, he included collection maintenance, binding, and the care and handling of library materials under the umbrella of preservation.[11] The 1878 report of the Astor Library reported that "precautions have been taken for the better preservation of the books upon the shelves, and 1,096 volumes have been bound."[12] Even an advertisement in *Library Journal* for book jackets, adhesive repair cloth, and tissue paper modestly encouraged "all librarians to become acquainted with the articles comprising the 'Holden System for Preserving Books.'"[13] Melvil Dewey appears to have been the first administrator to use the term *preservation* as an actual heading in a library annual report. In 1891, as director of the New York State Library, he introduced a section entitled "Preservation," with the subsections "Binding," "Shelving," and "Building."[14]

There was also a solid sense of preservation mission, stemming from librarians' belief that it was their responsibility to keep collections safe for future generations. While this responsibility was felt in libraries of all sizes and types, it was perhaps strongest in large libraries with a perceived research function. Writing a few years after his retirement as Librarian of Congress, Spofford cautioned that "every librarian or book owner should be something more than a custodian of the books in his collection. He should also exercise perpetual vigilance with regard to their safety and condition." Similarly, the Examining Committee of the Boston Public Library recorded its opinion that "the preservation of property is quite as important as its acquisition," and many libraries concerned themselves with the importance of preserving published scientific research for use by coming generations.[15]

The Library of Congress, Yale and Cornell universities, and the Boston Public Library all felt a responsibility to preserve their complete collections because of their inability to judge which materials future scholars might need. At the Boston Athenaeum, labels were placed in volumes of bound newspapers, asking that readers exercise care, as "future generations of readers have a claim on these volumes, which should be respected."[16] Harvard's librarian spoke eloquently on this subject: "But what the Library once receives and incorporates in its collection, that it becomes responsible for, and should preserve for future reference since there is scarcely a book or a printed sheet that does not record some fact or aspect of current life, and hence possesses its own special interest to the student of human affairs."[17] No matter how inconsequential certain materials might seem to contemporary readers, they should be retained, because "the unconsidered trifles of to-day become the history of tomorrow"; anything the private citizen considers discarding–unwanted books, pamphlets, or magazines–should rather be given to the local library for its consideration.[18]

In developing their collections, public librarians were sensitive to the need to balance the resources devoted to popular and permanent acquisitions. The Cincinnati Public Library attempted to purchase books requested by its readers, while still following "the correct principle of purchasing mainly such works and such editions as give a permanent value to the collection." At the Buffalo Public Library, the librarian reported that "while we have tried to meet the demand for light reading and books on current topics, the gathering and preservation of knowledge in our permanent collection have not been lost sight of."[19]

Despite the existence of a strong preservation consciousness, librarians realized that each institution could not collect and preserve everything. "It might be practicable," wrote Frank Hill, the director of the Brooklyn Public Library, ". . . for libraries within a certain radius to decide upon the different classes of books which they will collect and preserve. Such a plan would not necessarily affect the purchase of any book currently needed, but would make it possible when the pressure for room was felt to weed out from the collections and discard books which had passed from a period of usefulness to one of mere historic interest, because it would be definitely known that elsewhere the books would be preserved." Charles Cutter counseled, "Institutions . . . ought not to spend any part . . . however small, even a few dollars, in binding and storing any thing that will not further their main object–on the chance of being at some time of use." Similarly, the Amherst College librarian advised that libraries exercise a healthy differentiation rather than try to keep and collect all.[20]

From this recognition of the certainty of diversity arose the preservation priority assigned by American librarians to local publications and local history. "In addition to books on one or on a special subject," Frank Hill of Brooklyn continued, "each city might preserve the files of its newspapers and with them all that related to its local institutions, history, etc., thus it would not be necessary for any neighboring libraries to attempt the preservation of such material."[21] It was also recommended that each city collect and protect its own pamphlets, books, and histories; any material relating to the town or any of its citizens should be preserved. The Trustees of the Paterson (New Jersey) Free Public Library made a strong case for this type of collecting in their 1890-1891 report: "Any printed matter relating to the city of Paterson is of value to the Library, such as newspapers, periodicals, pamphlets, reports of churches, asylums, hospitals, &c. These cannot be purchased, as they are not for sale in the stores, but many are undoubtedly laid away on book-shelves as of no value, which would be of great value in a Library where they could be preserved and kept always accessible to students and others interested in the past history of the city."[22] The Boston Public Library preserved such local items as handbills, street ballads, and newspaper clippings as expressions of popular local opinion.[23] Harvard ensured the safekeeping of "various collections of manuscripts, broadsides, scraps, engravings" pertaining to institutional history, as well as "printed accounts, reports, programmes, broadsides, and notices, illustrating the history of the college and university."[24]

Some local libraries also felt a responsibility to preserve state documents and historical material; the Cleveland Public Library added to city and state publications those of, or pertaining to, northern Ohio.[25] The Iowa state librarian requested that the public send her all works of Iowa authors. Someone else suggested that state libraries preserve the periodical material of their own states and that wealthier states assume preservation responsibility for the publications of smaller, poorer states.[26] "The twentieth century has the task of evoking method and order among rather than within libraries," wrote Charles H. Gould, librarian of McGill University. In an article in the *ALA Bulletin* in 1909, he suggested a system within the United States and Canada of regional "reservoir libraries," each of which would "collect and preserve the literature – including newspapers, periodicals, pamphlets – native to or bearing specially on its own region."[27]

Librarians were quite conscious of the potential conflict between the preservation mission and readers' needs. The director of the Brookline (Massachusetts) Public Library wrote, "It is our endeavor to afford every possible facility consistent with the preservation of the Library, to those wishing to borrow or consult the books." Similarly, the New Bedford (Massachusetts) Free Public Library offered that "the greatest freedom in the use of books, consistent with their preservation and proper use, is the policy of the modern library."[28] Perhaps Justin Winsor, Superintendent of the Boston Public Library, was most realistic in his assessment of the difficulty in balancing free public access and preservation: "Two opposing forces are always at work about a Public Library, to afford a severe test of the spirit of its management, viz.: the proper conservatism of those in whose charge it is placed, which endeavors to keep steadily in view the interests of coming generations, for whom as well as for living people the institution is created, and the destructiveness of those people who regard public property as everybody's property, to be used according to individual notices of propriety."[29]

Closely related to preservation mission is the preservation ethic. If this can be understood to include the cautious introduction of new treatments and the use of techniques in harmony with a book's original structure, some evidence of an ethic is discernible at the turn of the century, although it seems chiefly to relate to rare materials. A treatise aimed at owners of fine or rare books counseled against a rash approach to restoration and advised simple repairs; however, "if the old covering is without importance; if, though old, it is some centuries later than the imprint, and is out of touch with the true spirit of the book, (which is not infrequently the case,) here is a book for re-binding." Correspondingly, William Blades, in his 1896 classic *The Enemies of Books*, cautioned against rebinding old books in modern covers; a better approach was to build a case or box for the book and preserve it as it was. A library manual of the period also advised that fine books be repaired rather than rebound, and another writer likened placing a modern binding on an old book to placing "'old wine in new bottles.'" Cyril Davenport of the British Museum, in a lecture before the twenty-eighth annual meeting of the Library Association of the United Kingdom, indicated his belief in the importance of preserving even seemingly minor physical parts of the book, since these might later provide valuable evidence of ownership or craftsmanship.[30]

Spofford advised would-be restorers, before beginning work on a valuable book, to practice first on one of little value.[31] While there appears to have been no awareness of the need for reversibility in preservation treatments, a good example of prudence in the application of new, unproven techniques is the use of various cellulose baths for the strengthening and preservation of manuscripts.[32] In 1910 *Library Journal* reported that scientists affiliated with Berlin's Königliches Materialprüfungsamt, some ten years after the introduction of one such liquid, observed that air and light appeared to alter the preparation and "feared that this decomposition [would] have a deleterious effect on the manuscripts." Further testing of this preservation medium was advised.[33]

Little training for early preservationists existed. This is not surprising, since library education itself was in its infancy (Dewey founded his School of Library Economy at Columbia College in 1887). Alice Kroeger, director of the Drexel Institute Library School, criticized authors of library textbooks for giving little notice to the proper care of books. "Text-books on library science," she wrote, "apparently do not consider the subject worth mention, believing possibly that such elementary matters are understood by all." Likewise, Arthur L. Bailey, chairman of the American Library Association's Committee on Bookbinding, faulted library schools for their scanty attention to binding instruction. While some schools arranged tours of binderies for their students, "it is doubtful if many library school graduates have a proper appreciation of the importance of the subject or can recognize good bindings when they see them." Only one school had "a special binding plant for the use of its students," and no institution devoted more than eight hours to the topic.[34]

Still, library schools did provide some preservation training. Dewey announced his intention to educate Columbia College students in "heating, lighting, and ventilating book- and reading-rooms," as well as "binding, leathers, sewing, lettering, . . . repairs, etc." In 1900 a course in library handicraft (largely bookbinding) was offered at the Colorado State Normal School, where students learned to sew, repair, recase, and make pamphlet binders and book covers. The summer library training school at Winona Lake, Indiana, required that students purchase a kit (including copyrighted instructions) for making book repairs.[35]

The New York Library School at Albany offered a course in bookbinding and published a list of items students had to acquire, including a press, sewing bench, hammer, knives, bone folders, and mill board. A syllabus was published for Columbia University Teachers College's bookbinding course, which covered "the construction of boxes, portfolios, desk-pads, note- scrap- and guest books, rebinding of old books and magazines and a full course in library mending." In an ambitious effort, the senior class of the Department of Library Economy at the Armour Institute of Technology, Chicago, prepared a series of papers taking a book from selection to discard; several of these "practical" papers addressed binding and repair and were later presented as a special program before the fifth conference of the Wisconsin State Library Association in 1896.[36]

Although preservation was not the clearly defined functional area of librarianship that it is today, American librarians had a clear sense of the importance of preserving their collections as the turn of the century approached. There is considerable evidence that many institutions aimed to build libraries of permanent value and to keep their collections safe for the use of future generations. An incipient preservation ethic is also observable in that period. Most persons performing preservation work learned their craft on the job, from more seasoned menders and binders. From a stage thus arrayed begins this history of preservation in turn-of-the-century American libraries.

Chapter 2

The Environment as Enemy

American librarians were acutely aware of the many environmental forces working fatal mischief on their shelves. Spofford advised, "The books of every library are beset by dangers and by enemies. Some of these are open and palpable; others are secret, illusive [*sic*], little suspected, and liable to come unlooked for and without warning."[1] Like many of his colleagues, he numbered excessive heat and damp among these dangers, as well as the by-products of gaslight.[2] In 1892 the Boston Public Library reported the discovery of 3,000 volumes whose bindings crumbled at the touch and had to be sent quickly to the bindery; their state of deterioration was ascribed to overheated rooms and the library's use of coal gas for illumination.[3]

Air pollution, sunlight, and dust were also judged harmful to library materials.[4] The secretary of the Andover Theological Seminary, writing to *Library Journal*, ended his letter by asking, "Is not a dark room, with the temperature not above forty degrees or fifty degrees, and only moderately dry, the best condition for the preservation of books and paper?"[5] While one librarian commented with resignation that some environmental conditions were almost impossible to remedy, an optimistic colleague cataloged the steps taken in designing the book stacks for the new Library of Congress in order to avoid as many of these ills as possible. The new area would be characterized by even temperature, good ventilation, the absence of dust, and security from damp.[6] In summary, "It may be said that the better adapted a room is for human occupation, the better it is for the books it contains."[7]

Perhaps dust was the simplest and most visible of these several environmental plagues. The librarian of New York's Young Men's Christian Association noted, "A great enemy of fine books is dust."[8] William Blades also included dust among books' foes, but William F. Poole, director of the Chicago Public Library, disagreed. Reviewing Blades's *The Enemies of Books*, and in a typically critical mood, Poole commented:

We are inclined to class "Dust and Neglect" among the friends and preservers, rather than among the enemies of books. Dust is no injury to the body or paper of a book, and if it be dry, and not filled with such soot as we have in Chicago and other western cities, it is not injurious to the bindings of books. It at least keeps them from being handled. That we have so many fine copies of the "incunabula" or "cradle-books" of the fifteenth century, clean and immaculate as when they came from the presses of Gutenberg, Wynkin de Worde, and Caxton, must be credited to dust and neglect. With the dust of centuries upon them they have been neglected and lost sight of in old monkish libraries.[9]

Nonetheless, librarians seem to have agreed with Blades rather more than Poole, and they made considerable efforts to keep the materials in their care dust-free.

Air pollution was also a serious problem for urban libraries. Most cities' chief fuel source was coal, which produced soot that drifted into library windows and settled on books. "Wherever soft coal is burned as a principal fuel, a black, fuliginous substance goes floating through the air, and soils every thing it touches. It penetrates into houses and public buildings, often intensified by their own interior use of the same generator of dirt, and covers the books of the library with its foul deposits."[10]

The Boston Public Library reported that city smoke from the burning of soft coal menaced its collections. Harvard's librarian characterized Cambridge's air as increasingly smoky; the library's three-quarters of a million volumes were "soiled by the tenacious griminess of soft-coal smoke . . . different from the coating of ordinary dust that a breath displaces."[11] At the 1893 Chicago conference of the American Library Association, St. Louis librarians complained bitterly of the harm soot and sulfur did to the books in their libraries; Frederick Crunden, director of the St. Louis Public Library, described "janitors going around every day gathering up soot by the shovelful."[12] As someone else correctly observed, books in rural libraries, owing to the "purity of country air," fared better than their city cousins, which became coated with the "fearfully greasy compound" common in urban areas.[13]

Nineteenth-century librarians also understood the injury that both heat and frequent or rapid temperature shifts could do to their collections, and attempts were made to regulate the library environment in order to avoid extremes and fluctuations. In designing their buildings, librarians weighed the requirements of both people and books. Indeed, popular thought held that books and people could be comfortable under fairly similar conditions; as Poole pointed out, "Books cannot live where men cannot live."[14] Libraries with combined shelving and study space aimed at maintaining a constant temperature of sixty-eight to seventy degrees. At the St. Louis Public Library, the thermostat was set so that steam came up whenever the temperature in the library dropped below seventy degrees and shut off when it rose a degree or two above that level; the heat in the Boston Athenaeum was regulated in the same way.[15]

When libraries were built with separate stack and reading areas, shelving space was typically kept cooler than public rooms.[16] The Worcester County (Massachusetts) Law Library maintained separate stack and reading rooms; "books do not need so much heat, light or ventilation as do readers, and the combination is sure to be bad for both readers and books." The Pittsburgh Carnegie Library was even more advanced, with a separate core of central stacks equipped with sealed windows and an air-washing system.[17]

Libraries with high ceilings and tall book stacks were particularly vulnerable to the ravages of heat, which caused books to lose "flexibility and toughness," transformed them into dust, and desiccated, shriveled, and warped them.[18] The New York State Library was alarmed to discover temperatures of 145 degrees near the top of its forty-eight-foot-high ceiling, and similarly damaging temperatures were reported in other libraries. Spofford stated that the books in the higher galleries at the Library of Congress "will almost burn your hand"; at the Minneapolis Public Library the heat in the upper halls was "oftentimes unbearable to readers, and caus[ed] injury to the books." Poole estimated that temperatures of sixty-five degrees on the floor of a high-ceilinged library room meant that books shelved near the ceiling suffered temperatures of 140 degrees.[19]

In these large, domed buildings, constructed so that books spiraled up the walls of a great hall while readers studied at tables below, it was almost impossible to separate books and people. The Peabody Institute in Baltimore was housed in a building designed in typical great-hall style. Eventually, separate reading rooms for the public were established so that the upper hall area and its books could be kept at a temperature friendly to library materials but far too cool for the public seated at tables sixty-one feet below.[20]

Although many continued to believe that the by-products of illuminating gas caused leather bindings to deteriorate, by 1890 there was some recognition that in fact the heat generated by gas, more than the derivatives of combustion, was the feature of gas that most damaged library materials.[21] Librarians also realized that heat induced dryness, and both of these factors were often mentioned as twin culprits in the deterioration of library materials.[22] Additionally, heat hastened the damage done by the acidic residues that modern tanning methods often left behind, and encouraged the presence of insects injurious to books.[23] As for the harmful effects of low temperatures, one librarian asked, at a discussion during the 1881 conference of the American Library Association, whether extreme cold was as bad for books as extreme heat. Justin Winsor responded that although cold stiffened glue and could thus cause bindings to crack when books were handled, all in all it was not so damaging as heat.[24]

Significant temperature fluctuations also injured library materials, often causing them to dry and crack. Lowering temperatures when the library was not in use represented a false economy, because "the violent alternations of temperature are injurious to the books."[25] One of the most striking accounts of the ill effects of temperature shifts comes from the annual reports of the Redwood Library (Newport, Rhode Island), which in 1898 warmed the reading room but had no heat of any kind in its stacks. While the ceilings in the stack room were too high to heat the space for readers' browsing comfort, the librarian pleaded, "for the sake of the health of the Library staff . . . as well as for the preservation of the books themselves, it should be kept above freezing. Last winter the temperature of the Stack Room ranged at about twenty-eight degrees for weeks at a time. Between freezing and thawing in one part of the Library, and being slowly calcined in another, the books stand a very good chance of being irretrievably injured." The following year, radiators that kept the temperature at about forty-five to fifty degrees, rather than permitting it to drop below freezing regularly, were installed.[26]

Unquestionably, more was written about the injuries done to library materials by gaslight and its by-products than any other cause of destruction. The New York and St. Louis Mercantile Libraries, the Providence and Buffalo Public Libraries, the Manchester (New Hampshire) City Library, and even small public libraries lamented the deteriorating effects of gas.[27] In the Bureau of Education's 1876 report, Winsor warned that gaslight was "very detrimental" to leather bindings; the U.S. Department of Agriculture advised that paper be kept out of gas-lit rooms;[28] library literature was peppered with similar general warnings.[29]

Most librarians believed that sulfurous residues produced by coal-gas combustion settled on library materials, hastening their disintegration.[30] Still, a few thought that since the shelves of libraries that had never known gaslight (or perhaps any type of artificial lighting) were also filled with fragile, crumbling books, there must be other guilty forces.[31] Many scientists and librarians, both in the U.S. and abroad, conducted experiments and research in an attempt to analyze the seemingly destructive effects of gaslight in libraries; this research was thoroughly reported in the American library press. In 1842 Professor Michael Faraday studied the impact of illuminating gas on leather bindings in London's Athenaeum Club Library and advanced the "sulphur in gas" theory, which became quite fashionable in library circles. Ten years later, Frederick Crace Calvert, a chemist in Manchester, England, conducted research that led him to believe that fumes from burning gas "aggravated rather than originated" leather deterioration; unfortunately, his theory attracted little attention.[32]

In 1854 Dr. Henry Letheby reported to London city authorities that the products of coal-gas combustion harmed library bindings; they caused leather, paper, cotton, and linen to rot.[33] Similarly, both William R. Nichols, a professor at the Massachusetts Institute of Technology, and scientist A. H. Church believed that bindings deteriorated because they absorbed sulfurous coal-gas fumes.[34] At the 1877 Conference of Librarians in London, Guillaume Depping, a Frenchman, suggested that a committee of librarians and chemists be formed to investigate the true causes of leather deterioration. Since some believed it to be gas, others heat, he thought that "the opinion of scientific men should be taken"; however, no action occurred.[35]

Another ten years passed, and C. J. Woodward conducted his experiments at the public library in Birmingham, England. He concluded that burning gas caused a moist film of sulfuric acid to form on books, and that the acid sank into the bindings as the moisture evaporated, causing them to disintegrate.[36] In 1900 the Royal Society of Arts, London, appointed the Committee on Leather for Bookbinding. In its analysis of "the durability of leathers now used for the purpose of binding books," the committee concluded that the fumes of burning coal gas had the most negative effect on leather bindings. The results of a survey sent to a number of British librarians showed that they also believed gas fumes to be the number one cause of such deterioration.[37] Another committee of the Royal Society of Arts, studying the causes of paper deterioration, reported that the fumes of burning gas also contributed to this problem.[38] Following this same thinking, the Sound Leather Committee of the Library Association of the United Kingdom (LAUK) recommended that librarians avoid shelving their collections in gas-lit rooms.[39] While Arthur D. Little (like Calvert before him) challenged the weight given by other scientists to the role of gas in the deterioration of library materials (in a well-ventilated room, he believed that its effects would be rather small), the popularity of the theory continued until electric lighting became so common that it rendered the issue unimportant.[40]

Moisture or high relative humidity ("damp," in the vernacular of the time) was another assailant of library materials and their components, including paper, leather, paste, and cloth.[41] The covers of books exposed to damp were often "'foxed,' discolored and mouldy"; paper was weakened and made more susceptible to bacteria and pests, as excess moisture softened and made more palatable the starch, glue, and sugars insects liked to eat. Dampness also engendered mildew, which destroyed paper.[42]

Even the public recognized the dangers of excess moisture. In Dover, New Hampshire, the townspeople were concerned that the new rooms planned by the library board "would be more or less damp and cause ruin or injury to the books"; in response, the trustees pledged that the "proper preventions and safeguards" would be taken to avoid this problem.[43] The Nebraska state librarian complained that "lack of ventilation, dampness and mold are fast converting ... valuable books into food for the furnace – rather expensive food."[44] At Harvard, early records of the college were "discolored and rotted by damp."[45] In 1896 the directors of the Redwood Library recommended to the proprietors that the cellar walls and floor be cemented; because of dampness, the space could not be used. Three years later, the directors reported with alarm that water accumulating in the cellar was endangering the fire in the furnace and that "repeated dampness is a source of injury to the books in the Library above."[46]

Crowded libraries were often forced to shelve portions of their collections in basement space – space notoriously susceptible to dampness. In 1886 the Providence Athenaeum designated the east room in the basement for maps and bound newspapers. The space was furnished with a case in which the library's many illustrated books were housed. Later, however, because of dampness, these valuable materials were removed to the director's office.[47] The Boston Public Library, forced to shelve its newspapers in an "out-of-the-way, half-lighted, damp and dingy basement," termed these conditions "discreditable."[48] Likewise, the Forbes Library in Northampton, Massachusetts, recorded that "every year valuable sets have been added to the store in the basement, where these are submitted to conditions of dampness, dust and inconvenience which results, or will in time, to serious injury to these books."[49]

The Library of Congress particularly condemned its basement newspaper stack space, characterizing it as "wholly unsuitable" and "damp at times."[50] Some libraries, such as the Dedham (Massachusetts) and Detroit Public Libraries, reported having taken steps to prepare basement shelving areas so that dampness could not creep in and damage the materials shelved there. Others resisted any suggestion of the use of basement space; as the Rhode Island state librarian commented, "The ignorance displayed by such advice is unworthy of a reply."[51]

Librarians guarded against dampness in several ways. They attempted to keep books on open, dry, airy shelves; in arid weather, windows might be left open but screened in some way, to obstruct dust.[52] Books kept in closed cases or safes, where the lack of circulating air could promote mold and mustiness, were examined from time to time; "otherwise they may be destroyed by dampness even while it is thought that they are most carefully guarded."[53] It was said that a saucer of quicklime placed near bookcases and changed every two to three days protected volumes from dampness by absorbing any excess moisture in the air.[54] Since stone walls could hold moisture and transfer it to books on abutting shelves, it was thought a good idea to batten exterior walls and to run shelves at a right angle to interior walls, with the ends twelve to eighteen inches away from the wall.[55] It was also recommended that libraries not be built directly on the ground; their basements should be raised and windowed.[56] Books that had been exposed to dampness were to be wiped and placed in sunlight, or in front of a fire, for a short time; for thoroughly damp volumes, every page might need to be wiped and the book then spread open to dry.[57]

No one doubted that daylight faded and injured library materials; the more directly and strongly it shone on them, the stronger the effect.[58] One scientist noted, "A week of sunshine is enough to make a yellow journal brown and brittle . . ."[59] Finding that sunlight damaged leather bindings, the Royal Society of Arts conducted experiments in which they shielded leather samples with colored glass. They discovered that the ill effects of daylight were greatly minimized by panes tinted yellow, olive, or orange. Similarly, a binder from the Detroit Public Library felt that red, yellow, and green glass could be used advantageously to shield books from direct natural light.[60] Many libraries installed shades or blinds to protect their materials from sunshine.[61]

Among the pests chronicled by library literature, rodents were the most neglected. Spofford noted that mice gnaw books and that "a good library cat or a series of mouse traps, skilfully baited, may rid you of this evil." The librarian of the U.S. Department of Agriculture recommended that library floors be laid on cement, thus protecting the building against rats and mice.[62] While there is little mention of insects in the annual reports of American libraries, a great deal was published about those said to feed on library materials and their components. The fascination of the library press with such pests is difficult to explain. Perhaps insect infestations were more common than internal library documents indicate, and librarians felt more comfortable addressing this slightly unsanitary topic in impersonal journal articles rather than in their own annual reports.

Books and periodicals described all manner of beetles, moths and their larvae, book lice, cockroaches, silverfish, and termites, which might attack book covers, gnaw paper for use in building their webs, devour glue and pasteboard, and attack the starch present in paper and cloth.[63] Librarians and scientists were often almost poetic in addressing this topic. In his modest book *Facts about Bookworms*, J. F. X. O'Conor, a Jesuit who was first the librarian at Francis Xavier's College, New York City, and later at Georgetown University, wrote, "A strange truth it is, that the same material that supplies food for the spiritual intellect of man should also supply food for one of the tiniest creatures in God's creation." A 1908 issue of *Scientific American* asserted that "more books and manuscripts have been destroyed by insects than by fire, water, rats and mice combined"; however, it is very doubtful that this extravagant statement could be documented.[64] One author whimsically suggested that while books by "authors whose works had stood a century of ups and downs of popular favor" might be exempted, in all other cases the bookworm might be viewed "as a humble benefactor, working day and night and reducing the mass of printed works by bores and dunces as fast as it can."[65]

Though perhaps not the most destructive insects in American libraries[66] (that honor probably belongs to the common cockroach), bookworms certainly attracted the most attention–though no one was quite sure what sort of creature the bookworm was. Some thought it to be the cigarette, or drugstore, beetle (*Sitodrepa panicea*); others said it was the grub stage of certain caterpillars; still others thought the bookworm was no one insect, but rather the larval form of a number of beetles (probably various Anobiid) or moths.[67] One author, identifying at least eleven different groups of bookworms, concluded, "It is not necessary to say that none of these bear any resemblance in any period of their existence to worms, and that the term bookworms is a misnomer. The word has become so firmly fixed in literature, both in its figurative and literal sense, that its misuse will no doubt continue."[68]

What sort of damage was indicative of bookworms? Often the outside of a leather binding would appear to have been peppered with shot or pierced repeatedly by a needle; upon opening the cover, one would find twisting and turning tunnels and passages bored into the text block.[69] Some librarians believed that while books with worm holes might be found in American libraries, the insects themselves were no longer living and the damage was old. It was popularly thought that bookworms did not care for modern library materials, owing to the makeup of contemporary papers, which contained clay, bleaches, plaster of paris, and so forth.[70] Nonetheless, there were some discoveries of living, chewing creatures; in fact, some librarians made pets of them, studied and drew them, and described their appearances in almost photographic detail.

Massachusetts librarian Samuel Green discovered live vermin in books acquired from Florida. After sending them to Samuel Garman of the Museum of Comparative Zoology, Cambridge, he learned that some of the insects were larval beetles, popularly called bookworms.[71] Anna Tyler described the discovery by a class of library school students at Pratt Institute, Brooklyn, of a live bookworm in a sixteenth-century vellum-bound book and their attempt to keep it alive and study it. She also reported that the Library of the College of Physicians in Philadelphia and the Cornell University Library had found living bookworms in their collections.[72] On more than one occasion, binders sent live bookworms to William Blades, who attempted to feed and study them; one lived for eighteen months but never metamorphosed. Another Englishman, the librarian at Stratford-on-Avon, described his pet bookworm. Kept in a jar and fed, it grew from one-fourth to three-eighths of an inch.[73]

O'Conor gives the fullest of all descriptions of encounters with living bookworms. While at Georgetown University, he found a bookworm (it was "covered with bristles and looked for all the world like a tiny hedgehog"), which he first exhibited to the university president and subsequently fed and studied under a microscope. The bookworm (or worms – it is unclear how many he found) ate paper placed in its box and was identified as "Dermestes Lardarius, or larvae of the brown beetle." At the president's suggestion, O'Conor took his pet to Spofford at the Library of Congress, who sent it to Spencer F. Baird, U.S. Commissioner of Fish and Fisheries, who in turn relayed it to C. V. Riley, Chief, Division of Entomology, U. S. Department of Agriculture, for his examination. Over the course of his career, O'Conor found over seventy-two examples of various insects, living or dead, in books; he concluded that no one else had seen more specimens or studied the bookworm more diligently.[74]

Spofford correctly pronounced cockroaches a more serious American problem than bookworms, and Blades agreed.[75] Variously called cockroaches, Croton bugs, or domestic black beetles, roaches were noted to be bold, "fearing neither light nor noise, neither man nor beast."[76] Cockroaches were especially injurious to cloth bindings, enjoying the starch and sizing they contained. They also fed upon gold lettering, which contained albumen.[77] Another American library pest was the silverfish, which liked dark, damp corners and also fed on the starches, glue, and sizing found in book cloths and labels.[78]

Termites, recognized as a potentially serious problem in warm or tropical climates,[79] were not of grave concern to American librarians. It is interesting that the only two references to termites and their destructiveness relate to New England libraries. An 1886 article in the *Boston Weekly Transcript* marked termites (or white ants) as particularly dangerous because they avoided light and worked in the dark. The author advised that buildings be protected from this menace by thoroughly removing tree stumps before cellar floors were laid and by keeping flowers, shrubs, and ivy well away from building walls. The Massachusetts State House, where valuable papers and archives were stored, was already infested with termites, and it was urgent that funds be appropriated to follow their trails from the basement throughout the State House so that all infestations might be identified and treated.[80]

In her 1908 annual report, F. Mabel Winchell told a chilling tale of the Manchester City Library's grim contest with termites. Late in March, library staff discovered that some materials lying atop a basement packing case were riddled with holes and "alive with tiny white animals." They were quite surprised when an authority identified them as termites; they had thought these insects were confined to tropical climates. Next, staff discovered that the termites had already eaten through the basement floor, through the packing case and its contents, and into the books on top of the case. They were also thriving in other packing cases, where they had "demolished beyond recognition" newspapers, pamphlets, and leather bindings. Even after the basement was fumigated with formaldehyde, the termites were "as lively as ever."

The basement floor and wooden wall sheathing were torn out and a cement floor laid; all the basement shelving was placed on bricks. Oak posts supporting the main part of the building were replaced, and the basement woodwork, all of which was infested, was torn out. By late August, the library believed all its work had been completed. Then, "one day in the fall we heard a cracking of timbers followed by a great rumbling and rush of coal. One of the uprights of the coal bin had been so eaten that it had given way and the bin being full to the ceiling, poured its coal out into the cellar in a small avalanche." Staff now believed the termites to also be present in the beams of the main floor. Word of the library's experience traveled, and termites were discovered in many other Manchester buildings. The library responded by developing an exhibit to alert people to this danger; it also compiled a bibliography on termites.[81]

Much was written about numerous ways of destroying or deterring insects. Some of the recommended preparations, such as the chemical group pyrethrums, are still used as low-toxicity insect poisons, but the effectiveness of many of the treatments is questionable. Some, depending on strength of application, may actually have been harmful, and there is little evidence in library documents of broad application of the more extravagant techniques. The general methods that were recommended included exposing insects to poisonous vapors, sprinkling shelving and books with toxic powders, and treating books or their components in various ways.[82] Among the many substances whose vapors reportedly killed insects were benzine, carbolic acid, hydrocyanic acid, burning sulfur, carbon disulfide or bisulfide, chloroform, naphthalene, camphor, creosote, and oil of eucalyptus.[83] The more volatile and deadly of these, such as benzine and carbon disulfide or bisulfide, were to be placed, with the books, in airtight containers.[84] Less combustible substances, such as naphthalene, camphor, creosote, and oil of eucalyptus, could be wrapped in paper or absorbed with a sponge and placed alongside books in cases or on shelves.[85]

While one scientist advocated sprinkling books with benzine, this use of a highly explosive chemical appears to have been unusual.[86] A few of the recommended substances carried with them certain cautions: fumigating with burning sulfur would not kill insect eggs; too much chloroform could harm the books themselves.[87] The St. Joseph (Missouri) Free Public Library reported that "a fumigating room is provided in the receiving or unpacking room, near the entrance at the east side. This has a flue or duct to the roof, and works well."[88] Another librarian advised that bindery returns be unpacked and examined outside the building before being admitted to the library.[89]

Among the powders with which books and library shelves might be safely treated were pyrethrum (one could sprinkle it about in the evening and sweep up dead roaches in the morning), borax (reported by one librarian to be rather ineffective), pulverized alum and pepper, camphor and snuff, camphor and bitter apple (colocynth), camphor and tobacco, or snuff alone.[90] Most treatments were to be repeated every few months; instead of powders, at least one scientist recommended placing dishes of mercury around the library, to attract and kill insects.[91] Mixing book pastes with alum, colocynth, arsenic, corrosive sublimate, naphtha, benzine, and other poisons was recommended as another way in which insects might be discouraged.[92]

Varnishing books was also said to protect them from cockroaches; corrosive sublimate (mercuric chloride) or spirits of wine (alcohol) might be added to the varnish for additional effectiveness.[93] Some thought that rubbing petroleum jelly (commonly called by the trade name vaseline [uncapitalized]) on the edges of the text block warded off insects; others recommended rubbing books with a woolen cloth dipped in powdered alum and washing bookshelves with sulfate or acetate of copper.[94] One of the mythic qualities of russia leather was its ability to repel insects, said to dislike its distinctive smell; those who persisted in this belief recommended interfiling russia-bound volumes throughout the collection.[95] Perhaps the most sensible counsel for preventing insect infestations was to review the shelves periodically, dust the books, and examine them for evidence of problems.[96] The noted bookbinder Joseph Zaehnsdorf believed that bookcases built of cedar, cypress, mahogany, sandal, and dry oak would discourage insects; the woods were hard and had distinctive smells, so insects did not like to "pierce" them.[97]

Several intriguing descriptions of insect traps exist. One such device involved a notched box inverted on a plate on which a sheet of paper spread with paste has been placed. When the insects entered through the notches they were trapped in the paste and "destroyed at their own banquet." Another consisted of a glass baited with flour, with thin wooden sticks running from the floor to its rim; once a roach or other insect crawled up and fell in, it could not climb out again.[98] Still another method called for placing saucers of lard and water around the library; insects, presumably attracted into the saucers by the lard, could not escape these watery, greasy traps.[99]

Suggestions for ridding books of insects included scraping and brushing the volumes and applying heat, either by baking them in an oven (being careful not to burn the leather) or placing them in watertight boxes immersed in hot water.[100] At the Congress of Librarians held in conjunction with the Paris Exposition of 1900, two prizes–one of a thousand francs, the other of five hundred–were offered for studies on methods of preserving books from insect "agents of destruction." Twenty-three essays were submitted, and the prizes were claimed by an Austrian chemist and a French professor.[101]

In the end, vigilant custodianship was American librarians' only real tool against the ills of dust, dirty air, temperature, moisture, and insects. A sophisticated understanding of the causes of decay, as well as the preservation techniques this understanding would generate, were to be part of the future. For the present, librarians concentrated on using the best method at their disposal–effective housekeeping–to address those external sources of ruin they could perceive, comprehend, and, after some fashion, remedy.

Chapter 3

The Library Building:
A Collection's First Defense

Because the library building itself was any collection's most fundamental source of security, its design, mechanical systems, maintenance, and protective qualities were key to the preservation mission. The latter part of the nineteenth century was a time of great building for libraries, and one institution's experience illustrates how preservation concerns influenced decisions about location, design, construction, protection from fire, ventilation, and lighting.

Between 1876 and 1894, the Boston Public Library campaigned for, designed, and built a new library building. Preservation issues influenced all these phases of activity. In its 1876 report, the Examining Committee called attention to the existing building's poor ventilation and the associated decay of materials shelved in the upper hall. A study of the ventilation system was recommended, and the need for new wings to house documents and newspapers was cited. By 1877 the librarian, Justin Winsor, and the city architect were planning for an addition; a year later, with the ventilation problems no better and crowding more severe, the Examining Committee recommended instead that a new building be erected, on a new site. At the current location, in the city's commercial area, the library would never be safe from fire; further, a new building could be constructed according to modern architectural principles more favorable to the preservation of the collections.[1]

The library's 1879 report dramatically underscored the existing building's vulnerability to fire: it was surrounded by frame structures. The precautionary steps of covering certain inner doors with metal and hiring a police officer to patrol the library each night were taken. Over the course of the next seven years, land for a new building was acquired, and the cornerstone for a McKim, Mead, and White structure was laid at Copley Square. The new library was to be built with ninety windows, augmented by electric lighting; each stack story was to be separate from

27

every other one, to guard against the spread of fire. At last, in 1896, the library's annual report noted that everyone acquainted with the value of the collections was pleased to have seen their removal from the old building to the new.[2]

During this same period, many other libraries voiced concerns about their buildings' designs and mechanical systems. A popular topic of debate was the traditional great hall style of library architecture, which some modern librarians (notably William F. Poole) were vigorously challenging.[3] Poole thought that libraries with sky-reaching galleries "have been constructed chiefly for show and architectural decoration, and with little reference to the preservation of the books and the convenient administration of the library."[4] In describing to the Chicago press his plans for the Newberry Library, he cited the ill effects of great hall design, with its high galleries and skylights: the heat that accumulates near the ceiling "shrivels up the covers and loosens the leaves, leaving the books mere wrecks. The attendants who go to the upper shelves are covered with a fine red dust, the ashes of leather bindings."[5] Polluted air that accumulated near the tops of high-ceilinged rooms also injured materials shelved there, and large open galleries permitted fire to spread rapidly. Poole concluded that the creation of a number of individual rooms with low ceilings reduced these hazards.[6]

Not everyone agreed with Poole. In a discussion following Poole's delivery of a paper, one librarian pointed out that the cost of land made shelving all books on ground level objectionable. Winsor joked, "We are undergoing in America a revolution of ideas in this matter. We are substituting packing-rooms for show-rooms."[7] Nonetheless, librarians took the issue seriously enough that *Library Journal* published a lively exchange on the topic as it related to the design of the new building proposed for the Library of Congress.

In a paper presented before the 1882 conference of the American Library Association, Poole reported that he, Spofford, and other librarians strenuously objected to a plan already put forward for the new building. It called for galleries even higher than those in the current library (five stories versus four); the heat in their upper reaches would be enormous and injurious. In the ensuing discussion, Karl A. Linderfelt of the Milwaukee Public Library called for a resolution protesting the design for the new building; a committee that consisted of Linderfelt, Poole, and Lloyd P. Smith (Library Company of Philadelphia) was appointed to study the matter. As a result, a resolution was passed, asking that more modern concepts be developed for the "safety of the books," among other reasons; the existing plans were said to be outmoded and to "embody principles of construction which are now regarded as faulty by the whole library profession."[8]

Apparently, Poole himself proceeded to develop some designs for the new Library of Congress building, following his own idea that a library should have numerous low-ceilinged rooms. A year later, in a discussion at the 1883 conference of the American Library Association, a letter from Spofford (who disliked Poole's plans for the building's interior) was read. "I am not willing," the Librarian of Congress wrote, "to have the interior plans of a library building of national importance dwarfed to the dimensions of a prolonged series of packing-boxes." He went on to say that the national library needed "a grand central hall, sufficiently impressive in height and proportions to show at once, by its well-lined walls, the wealth of its literary stores, and to appeal to public taste as something worthy of the country."[9]

Although Spofford was absent, and thus no real debate could take place, Poole did not hesitate to strongly reiterate his own views. He reminded his colleagues that at the time of the Washington, D.C., conference, Spofford had shared their distress at the damage done to library materials by heat collecting in high galleries, and accused Spofford of reversing himself. He went on to say that visitors to the nation's capital who wished to view memorials should see the Washington Monument and the Capitol, and let the national library be constructed for "the quietude of readers, and safety of the books." Dewey, slightly off-target but probably speaking politically rather than practically, supported Spofford. "The United States can afford coal to warm a beautiful hall," he said, "and runners enough to get all the books promptly."[10]

The question of building location also interested librarians, and it provides a good example of the inherent conflict between the convenience of readers and the preservation of library collections. While there was some sentiment that public accessibility should be the principal consideration in deciding where to erect a building and that libraries should therefore be built in the hearts of population centers, most librarians agreed that their buildings should be sited as far as possible from dusty streets, flammable frame structures, and urban smoke.

Spofford suggested that libraries be constructed with large yards around them, separating them from the dust of the road; "where the library is already located immediately on the street, a subscription for sprinkling the thoroughfare with water, the year round, would be true economy."[11] Both the public libraries of Bangor, Maine, and Paterson, New Jersey, hoped to erect new buildings away from busy streets, in quiet, clean areas far from city traffic centers; modern readers will find it ironic that the public libraries of New York City and Boston were listed as examples of libraries so situated.[12] Another motive for isolating the library was to protect it from flames. Many libraries were quite conscious of the danger of being surrounded by wooden buildings and coal sheds in a crowded commercial section of the city.[13] Finally, libraries might suffer less from the pollution of city smoke if located outside the local center of business.[14]

Librarians also considered the impact of their buildings' mechanical systems, although in some cases these arrangements were quite primitive. A few libraries were heated with open fires. The trustees of the Fletcher Free Library in Burlington, Vermont, observed that "on windy days, the stoves fail to keep the place warm enough for comfort and health. The coal-dust and ashes from them are a serious injury to the books, and readers in the library room would be much better accommodated with freer space and a better climate by their removal."[15] All in all, steam heat was the method of choice. Dewey's Readers' and Writers' Economy Co. recommended its Economy Steam Heater over hot-air furnaces, and the Cincinnati Public Library reported that laying steam pipes beneath marble floors warmed the building yet did not overheat books on the top shelves of the bookcases above.[16]

Dewey liked low-pressure steam heat better than fireplaces, stoves, and hot-air furnaces because it was less likely to cause a fire and generated no dirt and dust.[17] In their 1899 annual report, the trustees of the Redwood Library (Newport, Rhode Island) rated the introduction of steam heat as the year's most significant accomplishment. Previously, the library had been heated with large stoves; the new system would not only keep the public warm but "the fine ashes and dirt from the stoves, so detrimental to the books, [have] also been got rid of."[18] That same year, the town of Brookline, Massachusetts, planned to heat the public library, the high school, and the grammar school with steam from a new central plant. The library's trustees noted that while this system would benefit the books' bindings, it would be more costly.[19]

The need for adequate ventilation was another recurring theme, and the librarian's choice was either open windows and skylights or special ventilation shafts. Some illuminating gas jets, designed with twin tubes running from lamps on library counters to the building's exterior, were self-ventilating. One tube brought in cool outside air; the other carried away the hot, foul air emitted by the lamp.[20] Effective ventilation was desirable for a number of reasons. It allowed heat and impure air injurious to library materials to escape the building, helped prevent the formation of mold and mildew, and created a healthful atmosphere for readers.[21] Of these, allowing the harmful by-products of burning illuminating gas to escape was paramount; books in gas-lit libraries with capable ventilation systems were in better condition than those in similarly lit buildings with faulty air circulation.[22]

Like the issue of library location, library lighting illustrates the conflict between the convenience of the reader and the preservation of the collections. Readers required light by which to read, while books were best served by a low-light environment. Still, by protecting their books from direct sunlight and choosing their source of artificial lighting wisely, librarians could serve their clients' needs with no great harm to the materials in their care. Some nineteenth-century libraries had no artificial lighting of any kind; they depended upon windows and skylights, and on winter days when dusk came early, they simply closed. Such libraries included the Boston Athenaeum and Harvard College. In 1889 Justin Winsor, listing six reasons that Harvard's library building was inadequate, included among them the lack of sufficient lighting: "The deprivation of the use of such reading room facilities as we have during the long evenings of the months from October to March – being the larger part of the College year – is generally thought to occasion a great abridgement of opportunities for the students. The present building has no means of lighting it artificially."[23]

While these unlit libraries escaped the deterioration caused by some types of artificial lighting, it was still important that their collections be shielded from the direct rays of the sun, which, while providing their only illumination, also faded and weakened the volumes they housed. William I. Fletcher, the librarian of Amherst College, suggested that "large side windows let too strong a light upon the books near them, to their decided injury. Roof light is not available in the lower part of a high building, and in the upper part it is accompanied by roof heat." Fletcher proposed that libraries be built with large numbers of windows six to eight feet high, placed at the tops of the building's walls; this would provide for a quantity of safer, diffused (rather than direct) light.[24]

Influenced by the Royal Society of Arts' research, which cited "excessive sunlight" as one of the causes of the deterioration of leather bindings, Bernard Green, Superintendent of Buildings at the Library of Congress, designed special blinds for the windows in stack areas that received a great deal of direct sunlight. These vertical blinds were made of metal and could be adjusted at any angle, within ninety degrees, by means of an electric motor operated by a button that controlled multiple blinds. "The great number of the windows, some six hundred, required special mechanical control of the shades, and they are now operated conveniently and in a moment in separate sets of about 150 windows each by any attendant in the stack."[25]

The research of the Royal Society of Arts' Committee on Leather for Bookbinding indicated that the harmful effects of the sun were counteracted when light passed through windows tinted yellow, olive, and orange, and committee members "strongly recommended that library windows exposed to direct sunlight should be protected with suitable coloured glass."[26] However, there is no indication that libraries in England or the United States adopted this practice.[27]

While the lack of artificial lighting may have been an annoyance for readers, an environment in which library materials were both shielded from the rays of direct sunlight and spared the effects of open-flame or electric lighting was doubtless beneficial to them. Although most libraries used either gas or electric lighting, there are some examples of other types. In 1885 the Hobart College Library was almost completely destroyed in a fire attributed to a kerosene lamp. In 1899 the Providence Athenaeum, largely lit by gas and electricity, mentioned the need to introduce electric lighting "at the reading desks where kerosene is now used with its attendant dangers and disagreeable scent."[28] The Brooklyn Mercantile Library, having abandoned gas lighting for oil out of "financial necessity," reinstituted gas in 1883 after an overturned oil lamp nearly caused a serious fire; the use of gas added another $1,000 a year to the library's operating expenses.[29] In his 1887 report, Melvil Dewey cited the need to bring electricity from Columbia College's new library building into the old one, where oil hand lamps were in use during the evenings; he feared fire.[30]

Gaslight, more popular than any other type until the introduction of electricity, was inimical to library collections in several ways. It emitted considerable heat and produced unpleasant vapors and gritty deposits; in the absence of superior ventilation, the by-products of illuminating gas settled on and damaged library materials. Nonetheless, until late in the nineteenth century, most libraries that were artificially lit were illuminated with gas.[31] It is fair to note that not all gas lamps were equal, and some were certainly better designed than others in terms of burning cleaner and cooler. The Wenham, a regenerative burner, and the Welsbach, an incandescent one, were among the models preferred, because their combustion was more complete. The Welsbach was patented in 1886, after the beginning of the use of incandescent electric lighting; it enjoyed some popularity because it compared favorably to electricity in terms of cost.[32] Blades recommended a burner he termed a "sun-light," because its fumes were carried away through tubes into the outside air. Others were critical of the sun-light; books on tables under its burners were found "spotted with dirty water, formed by condensation in the tubes and dropped down from thence. When there was a high wind the soot accumulated in the sun-lights was blown down, covering everything in the room."[33]

In 1879 electric lamps were installed in the British Museum Reading Room, and American librarians followed with interest the first important introduction of electric light in a library.[34] There were many reasons to prefer electric lighting over gas or other open flames. It eased ventilation problems because it produced no polluting and harmful by-products.[35]

Electric lighting was cool, and there was no associated heat build-up;[36] it did not yellow paper as quickly as gaslight.[37] Finally, electricity presented much less danger of fire than did gas.[38] From citing benefits such as these, libraries across the country either praised their electric lighting systems[39] or spoke of the need to introduce electricity.[40]

In suggesting to the city's board of supervisors that gaslight be replaced with electric, the trustees of the San Francisco Public Library pointed out that "enough could, without doubt, be saved in the preservation of books to pay the difference in the cost of the electric light."[41] The trustees of the Springfield (Massachusetts) City Library Association pointed out that electric lighting "has ceased to be regarded as an experiment, its value having been thoroughly tested, and its superiority to gas for many purposes, established. It is certainly preferable to gas as regards smoke and soot, and it neither vitiates the atmosphere [n]or essentially increases the temperature."[42]

Several libraries improved their initial installation of electric lighting. At the New Bedford (Massachusetts) Free Public Library, the trustees appealed to the city for funding to replace arc lamps with incandescent ones, because "the particles of red-hot carbon which often drop from the lamps are a constant source of danger from fire, and within a few months a fire started by the dropping of such sparks on an umbrella was rendered harmless by the chance presence of the librarian on the spot at the moment when the blaze broke out."[43] Queens Borough (New York) Public Library found tungsten lamps cheaper than other types, and installed them in its branches. The Silas Bronson Library in Waterbury, Connecticut, switched from carbon filament to tungsten lamps and was thus able to burn more lights for less money.[44]

There were cost considerations associated with the introduction of electric lighting, which was generally more expensive than gas. The Omaha Public Library reported that gas for a six-month period cost $143.50, whereas electricity, at $419.29, cost about three times as much. The New Haven (Connecticut) Free Public Library found that it could save $600 per year by using gas rather than electricity. The Springfield (Massachusetts) City Library Association initially estimated that electric light would cost about one-third more than gas; later, it decided the cost of the two lighting types would be about equal.[45] Melvil Dewey believed that after an electrical plant was paid for, it was less costly to use electricity than gas; he, Poole, and other librarians praised the Edison incandescent light.[46]

Despite the many benefits of electric lighting, libraries sometimes chose gas over electricity because of its lower cost. The St. Joseph (Missouri) Free Public Library was wired for electric light, but because the local gas company's franchise required it to supply the library with gas free of charge, the library used gaslight. On special occasions, such as the building's opening, both gas and electric lighting were used, "and the effort [was] striking."[47] There are a number of examples of libraries returning to gaslight, having found electricity beyond their means. In 1895 the Newark (New Jersey) Free Public Library, as an economy measure, replaced fifty-five electric lights in the entrance hall and reading room with twenty-two gas burners; the overall cost of library light declined from $308.60 in November 1894 to $213.84 in November 1895. The Omaha Public Library returned to gas for similar reasons, and the St. Louis Public Library installed Welsbach burners in place of electric lamps in its reading room.[48]

Even when a building's mechanical systems were fairly sophisticated, in order for the library to play its proper preservative role, considerable energy was devoted to housekeeping, and every librarian still faced the traditional hand-to-hand combat with dust and dirt. In an anonymous 1886 letter to the editor of the *Indianapolis Journal*, a reader who signed himself "R. D." complained:

> A visit to our public library, not long since, disgusted me in toto. The air was dreadful – like that found by Bill Nye in sleeping cars – "the same air that had been used before the war;" and the room was decidedly and unequivocally dirty, there being enough soil deposit before the delivery counter to have made a good respectable cow-path. The book which was put on my card was also filthy, actually looked small-poxy, and for that reason was carried home at arm's length and returned without reading. Now, am I too particular to live, or are these conditions unavoidably connected with public libraries?[49]

The librarian took issue with R. D.'s letter, while denying none of the charges. Although readers dirtied the library's books, he said, "that is what they are there for." He pointed out that the library was too small for the number of people who used it, so that bad air inevitably built up over the course of the day. Further, there was never more than a day's accumulation of dirt on the floors, as they were cleaned every evening after nine o'clock, when the building closed.[50]

At the Brookline Public Library, "the rooms of the library . . . [were] carefully kept in excellent order, and constant war upon dust and dirt ha[d] been maintained throughout the year with brush and sponge, attaining thereby the happy result of freedom from these natural enemies of library economy."[51] The Boston Public Library was thankful when the city's coal strike ended and there was a return to burning hard coal; the soft coal had left deposits of soot all around the library, necessitating extra cleaning.[52]

Unfortunately, not all librarians were so vigilant. In a *New York Sun* editorial, the terrible conditions of the City Library ("the collection of books that has been gradually accumulating ever since the foundation of the city, and that is now shelved in the City Hall, over the police station") were described and decried. The room, shelves, and walls were said to be filthy, and dust was everywhere; "great piles of books, dust-covered and in ragged wrappers" were piled about. It was noted that both the positions of librarian and assistant were patronage jobs.[53]

Many libraries, particularly the larger ones, employed janitors. In 1895 the Providence Athenaeum reported that the janitor had begun to work full-time, with the result that the building and books were much cleaner. In the 1907 annual report of the Andover (Massachusetts) Memorial Hall Library, the janitor's name appears alongside the names of the trustees and librarians; the expenditure for the janitor's salary and cleaning materials was $629.15. At Bowdoin College, the custodial function was so important that the librarian planned to train the janitor for the new building himself.[54]

Librarians took a number of steps to keep their buildings clean and dust-free. Carpets, except for small ones that might be removed easily for cleaning, were inadvisable; they collected dirt and attracted moths.[55] In most libraries the collections were dusted annually, if not more often.[56] Still, not everyone agreed that frequent dusting was desirable. In 1879 the Silas Bronson Library recorded that "the annual dusting of the books was this year omitted, not for want of time but because the severe handling to which the books are subjected in the process of dusting is far more injurious than the dust itself, and it should be resorted to as seldom as possible."[57]

In different libraries, dusting was done by different types of staff. Dewey felt it important to employ "one who understands dusting books" for the work. The Providence Athenaeum was perhaps following his advice when "in consequence of the extremely dusty condition of the books and shelves, a competent man has been set to work dusting and cleaning." Likewise, the Cleveland Public Library reported that "a competent person has been engaged whose duty it is to keep books and shelves free from dust."[58] Some libraries used their general custodial staff to dust the collections. Apparently, in the University of Michigan Library, the janitor dusted one floor a year, so that the books on each of the three stack floors were dusted every third year. At the Atlantic City (New Jersey) Free Public Library, the librarian complained that janitors were spending so much time going to readers' homes to follow up on overdues that the dusting was being neglected.[59]

Many libraries, however, differentiated between book dusting and other custodial tasks. Book cleaners, as those who dusted were often called, seem to have been a more specialized and skilled group of workers. The names of the five book cleaners of the Cincinnati Public Library are listed in the library's 1907-1908 report; further, the death of one of the cleaners is noted. The Lawrence (Massachusetts) Free Public Library petitioned to hire extra help to dust its books and shelves, pointing out that dusting was not properly part of the janitor's work. The superintendent of the capitol of the state of New York assigned special book cleaners to dust the New York State Library's collections.[60]

In 1876 the Ohio State Library reported that it paid $200 for the expenses of dusting every book in the main library and most of the ones in the documents room. As collections grew, dusting became a costly proposition. In 1908 the annual cleaning of Harvard's books took four men three months; the librarian noted that dusting "is a constantly increasing, but apparently unavoidable, item of expense."[61]

There were several schools of dusting; some librarians preferred cloths, others brushes, others "clapping," and still others dusting machines.[62] Clean, soft cloths were thought by their proponents to be nonabrasive and gentle to bindings; sometimes the cloths were sprayed with a little water to decrease the scattering of dust.[63] Advocates of brushes recommended holding a book tightly closed while brushing its top; some thought the brush should be hard, others soft. One librarian recommended brushing books over a table with wet sawdust beneath it; presumably, the sawdust absorbed the dust.[64] Clapping called for simply slapping two books together so that the dust flew off both.[65] The Grand Rapids Public Library cleaned its books, before moving into a new building, by clapping them together over tubs of water placed near open windows, then opening each volume and fanning its pages so that any loose items fell out.[66]

Some librarians favored mechanical means of dusting. The Cleveland Public Library asked that either another duster be added to its staff or dusting equipment be acquired. A "book-dusting machine" invented by J. F. Langton of the St. Louis Public Library was described in *Library Journal* in 1904. It consisted of a motor that sucked air in through a hose and blew it out the other end at four pounds of pressure. The resulting blast blew dust off books and into "a wet blanket hung in a travelling frame of flannel."[67] The vacuum cleaner, however, whether portable or installed as a central unit, was the most popular mechanized duster.

In 1908 Harvard tested a new machine, plugging it into electric light sockets and pulling it between the rows of stacks. Tests showed that while the machine scattered less dust than manual methods, it was not much faster. Also, the brush had to be wielded with care, lest older bindings be damaged. Using the vacuum cleaner was more tiring for staff than holding a cloth. The initial cost of the machine was high, and the cost of the electricity a continuing one. Harvard concluded there was no real advantage to mechanical book cleaners.[68]

Most libraries had more positive experiences with vacuum cleaning. At the John Crerar Library in Chicago, staff found that vacuuming saved time over manual dusting and did a thorough job. Delicate books could be better dusted with the vacuum method, and there were special attachments for volumes with gilded edges.[69] At the Boston Athenaeum, vacuuming was thought to be faster than dusting by hand, but the problem of disturbing readers needed to be addressed. The Brooklyn Public Library bought a vacuum for its Montague Branch and reported full satisfaction with its performance; the Chicago Public Library was also pleased with a machine it purchased.[70] The Fitchburg (Massachusetts) Public Library and the Wilmington (Delaware) Institute likewise found the results they obtained with vacuum cleaners to be excellent. At Wilmington, time was saved by vacuuming the books as they stood on the shelves rather than removing them on trucks to another area of the building.[71] As the director of the Grand Rapids Public Library put it, "Vacuum cleaners for libraries are no longer an experiment."[72]

A few institutions, including the public libraries of Boston, Cincinnati, Providence, St. Joseph, and St. Louis, actually installed vacuum cleaning systems.[73] The Cincinnati library's consisted of rubber hoses connected to standpipes, which were in turn connected to basement vacuum pumps. In St. Louis a feed pipe ran from a five-horsepower basement motor with two compressed-air tanks and an air compressor, to every floor in the building. Rubber hoses attached on each floor blew dust off the books and into an attached funnel. The New Hampshire State Library installed a pipe so that it could be connected to the state's vacuum cleaning plant.[74]

Libraries also needed protection from disaster, and nineteenth-century buildings were often more vulnerable to flood and fire than their modern counterparts. American librarians were vigilant against water, chiefly as it came from leaking roofs and skylights. In 1876 the Providence Athenaeum made $250 worth of repairs to its roof, including the replacement of some water-damaged flooring. In a word of apology to the library's proprietors, the directors wrote: "The Directors always regret any necessity which occasions the diversion of a considerable amount of money from the increase and care of the library, for after all, the maintenance and growth of the library form the grand object of the institution. The expenditures of the past year, here referred to, though not directly for books, are yet very intimately connected with the safety and well being of the library. The books on our shelves are never secure from injury while water is liable to drop from leaks in the roof. . . ."[75]

The directors of the Redwood Library pointed out to their proprietors occasions when drips (owing to a roof "not impervious to water") injured books and wet, crumbling ceiling plaster showered down upon them. At the Fletcher Free Library in Burlington, Vermont, the roof also leaked;

with every rain, the books in the galleries were badly wet. The librarian and his assistants routinely used pans and pails to catch the intruding rainfall, but they feared the damage rains could do when the library was closed. On one teeming Sunday, the librarian visited the library and mopped up before attending church.[76] Similarly, Maine's state librarian used dishes to catch rain leaking into the library. During serious storms, the building was deluged. The librarian wrote, "It becomes almost impossible to keep the books from getting wet, and sometimes a nice volume becomes damaged and spoiled. I sometimes find great difficulty in keeping the Ten Commandments in anything like an unfractured condition. I feel like breaking the whole lot. Now I do not object to the work or the watching, but it seems to me that the Librarian could be better employed in the discharge of those duties that naturally and necessarily belong to him."[77]

There were no significant floods affecting libraries, either in the United States or abroad, between 1876 and 1910. Fires, however, were several and well-publicized; there were numerous opportunities for blazes in American libraries. In an 1893 survey conducted by Reuben B. Poole, eleven out of fifty-six responding libraries had experienced fires.[78] Among those struck by flame were the Library of Congress; the libraries of Harvard University, Hobart College, Johns Hopkins University, and Trinity College; the Chicago Historical Society; three Minnesota libraries (those of the state capitol, the historical society, and the supreme court); and the public libraries of Chicago, Milwaukee, Paterson (New Jersey), and Lowell and Marlborough (Massachusetts).[79] Often, the damage done by smoke and the water used to fight the fire was greater than that done by the blaze.

While each of these disasters was tragic (Marlborough's entire history in books, paintings, and photographs was lost); the Paterson Free Public Library occupied a new wing on 4 June 1901, only to have the entire library destroyed by fire on 9 February 1902), in many ways the Bangor Public Library's experience with fire is one of the most poignant. In 1893 firefighters battling a blaze in a neighboring block soaked several thousand books in the Bangor library; it was a number of days before the library could reopen. On 1 August 1896, a Saturday evening, fire broke out in the building the library occupied, one floor below it. Fortunately, stores were open late that night and the fire was seen and brought under control. In his annual report for that year, the librarian pleaded for a separate, fireproof library building.[80]

In the Bangor librarian's report for 1910 is the story of another narrow escape from fire. The blaze occurred during library hours and was confined to the store in which it started, located in the same building as the library. Again, the librarian described the need for a fireproof library, but no action appears to have been taken. Tragically, the text of the 1910 report is prefaced with this note: "Since these reports were written, the Library with its contents was totally destroyed by the great fire of April 30, 1911."[81] Unfortunately, Bangor's experience was not atypical.

The fires that received the most attention in the American library press occurred both at home and abroad and often generated a flurry of preservation concern. In 1879 the Free Public Library of Birmingham, England, burned; one of its most significant collections was a Shakespearean one. One *Library Journal* article warned that the fire must make American librarians vigilant; in another, Poole suggested that the Chicago Public Library, and perhaps others in nonfireproof buildings, could learn a lesson from the Birmingham experience. Next, *Library Journal* published an article about fire prevention that was said to have been prompted by the Birmingham fire. Another librarian, writing a brief history of the destruction of libraries by fire, said he had been inspired by the British blaze. Spofford pointed out that Birmingham lost many treasures that even insurance payments could not replace. At the Boston Public Library, news of the Birmingham fire led to the hiring of a night watchman to patrol the building.[82]

On 26 January 1904 fire destroyed many of the treasures of the National Library of Turin; however, a positive outcome of this destruction was that it raised the consciousness of the Italian government about the need for fire prevention in libraries. Italy subsequently conducted a survey to ascertain the real conditions (with regard to susceptibility to fire) in thirty-one government libraries. One scholar pointed out that if photography could be used to reproduce unique library materials, fires such as the one that destroyed the Turin library would be rendered less drastic. Articles about ways to restore burned, water-soaked books were written, describing the techniques used after the Turin blaze.[83]

In this country, fires at the Philadelphia Mercantile Library (1877) and in San Francisco were well covered by the press. In Philadelphia, the flames resulted from the collapse of the wall of a neighboring building onto the library's roof. Articles about book-drying techniques and fire-prevention methods for libraries followed this fire.[84] In San Francisco, as a result of the 1906 earthquake, not only the public library but also the Mechanics' Institute, the Mercantile Library, the Sutro Library, and the Stanford University Library burned. Unfortunately, the design of the public library seems to have promoted the fire's spread. Librarians were conscious of the increased value of California's remaining unharmed collections, as well as the importance of taking all possible preservation precautions with these surviving libraries.[85]

Libraries of all types (but particularly those in wooden buildings) aspired to fireproof quarters.[86] The trustees of the New Bedford Free

Public Library were eloquent in their plea: "The library now contains nearly One Hundred Thousand volumes besides valuable pamphlets, rare engravings, and other choice literary and artistic treasures. These belong to the people and are dedicated to the people's use as a great, free, popular university. How priceless the possession! How irreparable the loss! We again call your attention to the fire hazard always threatening this building and its contents. Can New Bedford longer afford to take the risk?"[87]

In describing the Watertown, Massachusetts, library's need for a permanent, fireproof home, the librarian first quoted Milton on the need for a "good book," then added: "But a good book to be useful must be protected, made accessible, preserved."[88] Because fire was an ever-present threat, the Library Committee of the Reynolds Library in Rochester, New York, decided that there was little harm in being guided solely by the public's taste in spending its book budget:

> While this method of growth may not be ideally the most perfect and symmetrical, it is still in many respects the most satisfactory and useful. As long as the library is located in its present quarters it is certainly a question whether it is wise to expend a large sum of money in the purchase of books which do not seem at present to be demanded by the reading public. If our books were secure from the possible danger of fire, this economical policy might not be as defensible as it is under our present circumstances. As we are now situated, it seems to the committee more discreet to keep our accessions as close to the public requirements as possible.[89]

Not only did a fireproof structure protect the library's materials, but it was also seen as a means for attracting gifts, thereby increasing the collections.[90] The Philadelphia Free Library, housed in rented space, believed it would never attract gifts like those given in New York City and Boston until it had a dedicated, fireproof building. In 1887 the St. Louis Public Library reported that it could have secured a valuable medical collection, if only its building had been fireproof.[91]

How were buildings made safer against fires? It was advised that book space and office space not be mixed; the more rooms, the less opportunity for fire to sweep an entire collection. Watchmen should patrol the facility at night.[92] In Reuben Poole's survey of fifty-six libraries with a total of 5,231,529 volumes (one-sixth of the total library collections in the United States, according to the Bureau of Education's 1892 report), forty-five occupied their own buildings, and nineteen of those buildings were reported to be fireproof (that is, built of brick or stone). One prominent insurer gave his criteria for a "standard," or reasonably fire-resistant, building: all iron beams must be enclosed and protected; brick was "the safest material" with which to build; windows and doors should be covered with tin; electric lighting was preferred to gas.[93] Among the libraries reporting fireproof construction were Yale University, the Detroit and Syracuse public libraries, and Columbia College.[94]

Unfortunately, not all construction touted as fireproof actually was. Indeed, *fireproof* was a relative term. Some materials initially thought to be fireproof (iron, granite) later proved not to be. In San Francisco, fires following the earthquake destroyed fifty-four supposedly fireproof buildings. The Boston Public Library's building was thought to be fireproof when erected, but by 1879 fires in similarly constructed buildings in Boston and Chicago shook that belief.[95]

Whether or not contemporary fireproofing techniques were completely effective, they certainly helped. Buildings made of stone, brick (especially certain types of fireproof brick), and concrete were more secure than those built of wood.[96] In addition, many libraries installed metal or concrete fire shutters, fireproof roofs and floors, and even fireproof partitions or walls to prevent the spread of fire from one area of the library to another.[97] Electrical wiring was run in conduits, interior wooden doors were covered with iron or tin, and iron or steel supporting columns were encased.[98] The Boston Athenaeum, Providence Athenaeum, St. Louis Mercantile Library, Boston Public Library, Bowdoin College Library, and Chicago Public Library all took some of these measures, attempting to make their collections safe from fire.[99]

A number of libraries owned, or planned to install, separate fireproof vaults for costly or unique materials.[100] The Indiana State Library kept valuable items in an asbestos-lined steel compartment; at the New York State Library, Dewey proposed that a fireproof safe or room be provided for important materials until a fireproof building could be built.[101] In response to the public library fire in Birmingham, England, one person suggested that "treasures which no insurance money can replace be kept on a ground floor, in cases resting upon wheels, and set upon a tramway of stone or iron running into the open air through a door or doors which it would be easy to make secure when closed, yet handy to open on occasion. A chain extending to the outer door would allow the cases to be drawn out of danger in a very short time, and a slight inclination of the tramway would make this easier."[102]

Librarians employed many methods of fire prevention. It was thought that books packed tightly on shelves would burn more slowly; Reuben Poole noted that piling books up on the floor (as was the practice in the overcrowded Library of Congress building) was like creating firewood.[103] A few libraries conducted fire drills for staff or gave them formal instruction in fire procedures. Electric lighting was safer than lighting by gas or other open flames; at the Boston Athenaeum, as a further precaution, the flow of electricity to the building was cut off daily, from 6:00 P.M. until 8:00 A.M.[104]

By 1907 each department in the Boston Public Library had a fire alarm box, the fire department regularly inspected the building, smoking was not permitted, and a watchman patrolled the stacks. Similarly, at the Worcester (Massachusetts) Public Library, a janitor was present after closing time, and the Astor Library (New York City) building was inspected every night. Reuben Poole's 1893 survey of libraries' protection against fire showed that forty of the fifty-six responding libraries had a watchman.[105] At the Providence Athenaeum in 1904, the Committee on Building and Grounds reviewed the library for fire precautions and recommended that the library invest in 325.00 worth of fire-detection equipment and an "annual charge for supervision and maintenance" of $48.00; the board agreed to consider the proposal.[106]

Fire-extinguishing techniques ranged from the simple to the elaborate. Rooms might be equipped with hydrants, hand pumps, and buckets. The Worcester Public Library had a standpipe with a hose attached to it on all four floors of the building, plus buckets filled with water. At the Astor Library, the north side of the building had an iron standpipe and a fire ladder by which water and firemen, respectively, could reach the roof from the yard.[107] Most libraries had automatic fire extinguishers. One of the most unusual extinguishing devices was manufactured by the British firm Lawes and McLennan. It consisted of piping with many holes, placed along the cornice of each room and connected to the library water supply. When fire burned through a linking cord, water sprayed out into the room.[108]

Because of the late nineteenth century's emphasis on library construction, it is not surprising that librarians, as they planned buildings that in many cases would be the first single-purpose structures their collections had ever occupied, considered the preservation implications and opportunities present in the library building. An emerging profession's popular self-concept as a field of library economy also promoted an interest in matters related to the care of collections through efficient building maintenance. The building and its systems and maintenance were considered the collections' first defense, just as they are today.

Chapter 4

Precautions for Readers

In 1898 a British librarian commented on the efforts made by his American counterparts to persuade readers to care properly for books in their possession: "in America, great pains are taken to appeal to the better feelings on this point."[1] Certainly, he was correct: the proper handling of the collections was another popular preservation approach in the late nineteenth century. A librarian from Ashtabula, Ohio, described the list of "commandments" he had compiled for patrons, counseling them how to treat the books charged to them.[2] Many libraries either stamped or labeled books, maps, and other materials with cautions for readers, the general sense of which was "handle with care."[3] At the Boston Athenaeum, this admonition was placed on all volumes of bound newspapers:

Handle with Great Care

1. The paper on which newspapers are printed is generally of poor quality and grows brittle with age.
2. Most newspapers are difficult or impossible to replace if worn or injured, and, unlike other publications, they will never be reprinted. Only a very small number of copies exist anywhere.
3. Future generations of readers have a claim on these volumes, which should be respected.

Therefore, handle carefully.[4]

Other libraries used bookmarks to convey similar suggestions.[5] There is also evidence that staff spoke personally with patrons about the proper care of books. At the Boston Athenaeum the attendant in the art room often asked readers to turn leaves more carefully, as well as to refrain from leaning against the edges of large books and touching engravings; "he takes advantage of this to give to all newcomers and often to repeat to habitués a number of cautions on the proper treatment of fine books."[6]

Librarians also believed that they could indirectly inspire the reader to care for books by keeping the collections clean and in good repair. Inversely, circulating books that were dirty, mutilated, or in need of rebinding encouraged a lack of respect for library materials; a book in good condition was "a civilizing influence."[7] A librarian from the New York Public Library advised that "the only thoroughly successful means of securing respect and good care of library books is for libraries to maintain higher standards of excellence in respect to intelligent repairing and binding, to discard promptly a book which is to any extent mutilated or which is so soiled as to make it seem unwarrantable to ask a boy to wash his hands before touching it."[8]

Careless handling was ranked by one librarian among the four major reasons books wear out. Another librarian wrote, "Books are neither card-racks, crumb-baskets, [n]or receptacles for dead leaves. Books were not meant as cushions, nor were they meant to be toasted before a fire."[9] The Manchester (New Hampshire) City Library believed that greater care on the part of readers would save the library much trouble and expense, "as it is not the reading of the books that injures them, but the careless handling."[10]

Librarians, however, seemed to vary considerably in their assessment of the ways in which readers treated books; perhaps there were questions of individual personality and perception. Year after year in her annual report, the librarian at the Brookline (Massachusetts) Public Library deplored the carelessness with which materials were treated, quoted potential punishments from the state laws of Massachusetts, and even prosecuted guilty patrons. But nearby at the Boston Public Library, Justin Winsor wrote that while some people "regard public property as everybody's property, to be used according to individual notions of propriety," readership continued to increase and the collections enjoyed "remarkable immunity from loss or irremediable injury"; he concluded that the library staff must be doing a good job in inspiring the popular conscience.[11]

Librarians agreed that readers should not open books face down on tables; to do so abraded and dirtied their pages. Likewise, patrons should be careful not to lean upon the edges of books they were reading, permit a cover to dangle over the table's edge, or drop a book on the floor.[12] Piling open books on top of each other rumpled and soiled the pages; removing books from the shelves by pulling at the headcap often tore the back, whereas "a slight pressure of the books on either side of the one desired will enable the reader to grasp the book half way down, and thus avoid any strain on it."[13]

Readers were also asked to refrain from wetting their fingers to turn pages, or turning down corners to mark their places.[14] Bookmarks were often furnished free of charge to discourage the latter practice, which librarians variously termed "deleterious," "vulgar," and "pernicious."[15] The director at the Lawrence (Massachusetts) Free Public Library reported the additional problem that "many books are injured by being taken into the mills and read surreptitiously, when the operative is supposed to be working. This accounts for so many coming back thoroughly saturated with grease, or tinged with aniline dyes." Similarly, another library reported that there was "more indication of injury from unwashed hands than from deliberate mischief."[16] Accordingly, readers were encouraged to wash their hands before handling books; the St. Louis Public Library installed a lavatory for this purpose.[17]

The same gratis bookmarks that discouraged the public from turning down page corners also helped deter them from writing in books.[18] The Boston Public Library commented: "In general, persons using the Library treat the books as carefully as they would their own property. There is, nevertheless, one matter to which the public attention should be directed, and that is to the selfish but not uncommon habit – due, probably, to the thoughtlessness or vanity of a certain class of readers – of underlining passages and making pencil comments in margins. Offenders in this respect seem to forget that such marks deface the pages, and annoy sensible readers."[19]

Placing foreign objects in books could also injure them. Readers were advised to put nothing thicker than a sheet of paper between the pages of a book, to avoid using pencils as bookmarks, and never to place letters, cards, or the like in books; to do so weakened the binding and, if the objects were thick enough, could break the book's back.[20] Further, one should not combine dining and reading; "butter, also marmalade" were listed among the foes of books, and one librarian warned of the "careless damage, which may be occasioned by . . . morsels from a furtively eaten sandwich."[21]

Tobacco smoke was often included among the causes of decay in leather bookbindings. Coupled with the damage a careless person's cigarette ashes could do to a book and the danger of fire, this consideration led many libraries to ban smoking or to limit it to a particular area. At Columbia College, the trustees passed a resolution "that the chief librarian be directed strictly to enforce the rule of no smoking in the rooms or corridors of the library building."[22] A few libraries placed certain restrictions on their readers' use of valuable materials. Some permitted only the use of pencil (versus ink) and prohibited the tracing of illustrations or the use of compasses for measuring diagrams. Spofford suggested that readers be permitted to examine only one folio book at a time, to prevent their opening one atop another.[23]

Adult readers were not librarians' only targets for edification. There was a common conviction that children, although inherently careless, could be taught to handle books properly. William Blades was particularly pessimistic about children's approach to books; "children," he said, "with all their innocence, are often guilty of book-murder." They enjoyed (according to Blades) tearing out pages, as well as pushing in and pulling out the books on lower shelves, while sporting "mouths full of candy and sticky fingers."[24]

In the 1890s Linda Eastman formed a club, called the Children's Library League, at the Cleveland Public Library (where she subsequently became director). The purpose of the club was to encourage children to care for books and to promote a sense that they and the library staff were partners in this effort. The group's motto was "Clean hearts, clean hands, clean books." It was patterned after Colonel Waring's Street-Cleaning League of New York, on the popular principle that the most successful reforms begin with children. Each member signed the following agreement:

> We, the undersigned, members of the Library League, agree to do all in our power to assist the librarian in keeping the books in good condition. We promise to remember that good books contain the living thoughts of good and great men and women, and are therefore entitled to respect. We will not handle any library book roughly nor carelessly, will not mark it, turn down leaves, nor put anything into it thicker than a slip of paper. We will also do all in our power to interest other boys and girls in the right care of books, and will report all books which we find in bad condition.[25]

Bookmarks expressing these convictions were also distributed.

Miss Eastman found that after the league was formed, children's books were returned cleaner than previously. Further, she reported, "these results have also extended to the larger number of books used by adult readers, thus proving that there is no surer way to create a sentiment in a community than to enlist the sympathy of the children."[26] Writing about her experiences in *Library Journal*, she reported that "dirt is at a discount; it is noticed that many more children than formerly now stop to choose the cleanest copy of a book." Children also reported soiled and torn books to the staff so that these could be cleaned and mended, and on inclement days routinely wrapped up their books with paper provided by the library, "which saves many a book from a mud-bath on its way to or from the library."[27]

The Cleveland Library League inspired many similar associations across America. Among the public libraries with children's leagues were those of Providence, Evanston (Illinois), Braddock (Pennsylvania),

Minneapolis, and West Bay City (Michigan).[28] Even those libraries without formal clubs did much to engender in children a protective spirit toward library materials. Children were taught simple things, such as how to open, handle, and reshelve a book.[29] To emphasize the labor involved in book making, talks were presented on the arts of printing and binding; presentations on the proper care of books were given in the schools.[30]

Some libraries invited children to participate in the cleaning and mending of books. At the Oconto (Wisconsin) Public Library, a Saturday cleaning party was held; fifteen attendees cleaned five books each, and another party was planned. A librarian at the Medford (Massachusetts) Public Library, at one boy's request, taught the child how to make minor book repairs. When asked by another child what he was doing, he replied, "'Helping, I hope.'"[31] Care labels were pasted into children's books, and paper covers were distributed on rainy days. One library mounted a display of mistreated books.[32] Librarian Caroline Hewins wrote a poem, popularly known as the Goop verse, that was prominently posted in many libraries across America:

> *The Library Goop*
>
> The Goops they wet their fingers
> To turn the leaves of books,
> And then they crease the corners down
> And think that no one looks,
> They print the marks of dirty hands,
> Of lollipops and gum,
> On picture-book and fairy-book,
> As often as they come.
> ARE YOU A GOOP???

The Democrat Printing Company of Madison, Wisconsin, printed the Goop verse "attractively on heavy green cover paper, 11 x 14 inches, suitable for posting"; it could be purchased at a cost of fifteen cents. The H. W. Wilson Company also printed the little poem on three-by-five-inch sheets of paper "for advertising purposes."[33]

Bookmarks, popular educational tools in the children's rooms of libraries, often carried suggestions about the care of books. In 1906 the senior class of the New York Library School produced a bookmark with the following verse by Annie T. Eaton:

> You are old, little book, the small boy said,
> Yet your pages are still clean and white,
> Your covers are stiff and your corners are straight,
> Do you think at your age it is right?

In my youth, said the book, I came into the hands
Of children who handled with care,
They opened me gently, their fingers were clean,
My margins they kept clean and fair.

They never used pencils as bookmarks or tried
To pull me apart in their strife,
With such care and treatment my strength and my looks

Will last me the rest of my life.[34]

While this verse was popular and used in a number of libraries, the most-used bookmark in American libraries was the Maxson bookmark, developed by the Reverend Henry Doty Maxson of Menomonie, Wisconsin, for the Mabel Tainter Memorial Library of that city. Instead of verse, the Maxson bookmark carried prose delivered from the point of view of a book, asking the child not to handle it with dirty hands, leave it in the rain, write in it, and so forth. For example: "'Whenever you are through reading me, if you are afraid of losing your place, don't turn down the corner of one of my leaves, but have a neat little Book Mark to put in where you stop, and then close me and lay me down on my side so that I can have a good, comfortable rest.'"[35]

Like their counterparts in the general library, children's librarians believed that their readers learned much about the correct way to treat books by observing the library staff. The presence on the shelves of tattered books encouraged careless treatment; soiled books should be withdrawn from circulation and the shelves kept neat.[36] Many libraries had washrooms, where children were required to clean their hands before using the library. Even if there was no washroom, children were expected to exhibit clean hands before they were permitted to handle books.[37] The Menasha (Wisconsin) Public Library issued cards headed "Clean Hands, Clean Cards, Clean Books," to its young patrons; each time a library book was returned in good condition, a stamp was placed on the card. After ten stamps, the child would receive a picture; after ten pictures, the reward was a library badge or button. The practice at the Newark (New Jersey) Free Public Library was to send children with dirty hands home, after stamping their cards with "hands." Still, the library did have two washbasins "to which are sent a few boys, to whom it seems wiser to give a book on the day they ask for it."[38]

Despite the emphasis librarians placed on their readers' handling of the collections, it seems likely that nineteenth-century library users were no more abusive than those of today. If turn-of-the-century librarians pressed the proper treatment of library materials somewhat more than we do now, it was probably because their only available preservation approach was the protection of the physical item. This theme of care continues in the next chapter, which covers the ways in which staff prepared the collections for the readers' use.

Chapter 5

The Preparation and
Maintenance of Library Materials

From the time a volume entered the library, throughout its life as a part of the collection, the staff did many things to ensure its continuing vitality. Librarians examined new books carefully to be certain they were complete and sound before adding them to the collection. Before the library's label or stamp was affixed, each title was collated page by page and checked for defects such as duplicate, missing, incorrectly folded, or torn pages, since dealers and publishers would replace imperfect volumes free of charge.[1] To make a new book flexible and less likely to break at the back with rough handling, staff would open it in a number of places before putting it on the shelf. First the book's spine was laid on a smooth surface. Then the front and back covers were lowered while the text block was held in the hand. Alternating from front to back, a few pages at a time were opened and gently pressed down until the center of the book was reached. Cedric Chivers, probably the period's most innovative commercial binder, noted that a trained person following this method could open two hundred books in a half hour.[2]

To spare the volume accidental injury at the hands of an eager reader, unopened leaves were slit with a smooth, flat ivory knife held parallel to the edge of the book.[3] Fine-grade sandpaper was used to smooth the rough edges.[4] Other accessioning practices, such as perforating, stamping, or embossing signs of ownership on plates and pages, were less salutary; however, it seems that protecting the book against theft had a higher priority than preserving it from the marring effect of property indicators. Title pages, plates, portraits, maps, and illustrations were usually stamped; the Howard Memorial Library in New Orleans routinely stamped the eighty-seventh page of every volume.[5] Thus prepared, the new volume was sent for cataloging, where librarians sometimes used a "snake" – a half yard of wide, doubled ribbon that had been filled with shot and stitched closed – to hold the book open gently and thus help them avoid leaning on its edges.[6]

Whether to place protective jackets (generally made of paper) on the books in one's collection was a controversial matter. Those who disapproved had many reasons: a book's sewing typically gave out before its covers, so what use was a paper jacket in prolonging the life of the book? Further, shrinking and expanding with the weather, paper jackets could place stress on the book's binding. If the paper jacket were pasted to the inside covers of the book itself, the book was defaced; if it were not pasted down, it rubbed against the binding, abrading it. A tight jacket might strain the binding. Finally, applying jackets was costly and took a great deal of staff time, and the shelves in libraries where most of the books were covered looked monotonous and uninteresting.[7]

Nonetheless, book jackets had their defenders. Jackets kept the book's own binding clean; smells and dirt could be discarded along with the paper cover. In a library with little money for rebinding, jackets could make shabby books more attractive.[8] A library might choose to cover only certain types of books, typically those that enjoyed the greatest use, such as children's books and fiction. Some institutions covered fine bindings; one covered all books it did not intend to rebind. The University of Michigan Library reported that it put paper jackets, at fifteen cents each, on about one-third of its collection, but gave no indication of the types of books that were covered.[9]

Paper was the chief material from which protective book jackets were made.[10] In 1879 the ALA Cooperation Committee announced its intention to stock two types of book-covering paper; it recommended that libraries vary the color of paper with the type of reader. A borrower assessed as genteel might receive a light-colored jacket, whereas a working-class patron would get a darker one less likely to show dirt.[11] At the Brooklyn Mercantile Library, books received a cover of "smooth light-brown paper"; the Newark (New Jersey) Free Public Library used red-rope manila paper or brown hardware paper.[12]

In Louisville, Kentucky, the public library provided readers with a manila envelope, eight inches by ten inches, to protect books in circulation. On one side the rules of the library were printed; on the other was an advertisement for the local firm that provided the library with five thousand envelopes free of charge.[13] The Brookline (Massachusetts) and Queens Borough (New York) public libraries used vellum de luxe book cloth for jackets; it came in many colors, wore well, and needed to be replaced less frequently. The Haverhill (Massachusetts) Public Library used a similar product, art vellum binder's cloth; while it cost more than paper, it was more durable, soiled less quickly, and required less labor to apply.[14]

Though most book jackets were homemade affairs, there were several commercially available products. The Holden System for Preserving Books included book jackets, guaranteed to last one year of "public school wear." The jackets were said to be adjustable, waterproof, germproof, and to wear like leather. F. Van Everen of New York City marketed Adjustable Book Covers, which came in three sizes and were made of manila paper. Stronghurst Manufacturing sold a jacket called the Twentieth Century Book cover; one size adjusted to fit any book, and the jacket came in two parts, which were to be laced and glued together.[15]

Some libraries, like the Boston Public Library, replaced book jackets after every circulation; the Watertown (Massachusetts) Free Public Library replaced paper jackets after every tenth circulation. Other libraries appear to have reviewed the jacket's condition upon its return and replaced it as need seemed to indicate. The Fletcher Free Library in Burlington, Vermont, reported that the average number of circulations a book would withstand before its jacket needed to be replaced was three.[16] Staff time and the cost of the jackets appear to have been the major factors in determining the frequency of replacement.

Most librarians recognized the value of providing some sort of protective wrapping for books that went out on rainy or snowy days and encouraging patrons to wrap volumes which they returned in bad weather. At the Oxnard Public Library in Ventura County, California, books were wrapped on wet days, or if the staff suspected they were to be placed on the floor of a buggy. In Poughkeepsie, New York, the librarian recommended fining patrons fifty cents to one dollar for returning books unprotected in inclement weather.[17] On damp days, library staff often placed wrapping paper, old newspapers, or used envelopes on circulation counters, where readers could help themselves.[18]

When books were not in circulation, the cases that held them provided support and protection. In the last quarter of the nineteenth century, standard library shelving was unknown. There was wooden shelving and metal shelving, shelving with doors or curtains, and shelving that lacked these accessories. As one librarian said with resolution, "All books cannot be housed in iron safes; we must be content to see most of them ranged on shelves, with or without a glass front, and to know that they are still liable to damage from fire, water, dust, or foul air."[19] Nonetheless, certain features were considered desirable in library shelving and its placement.

Shelving was commonly kept away from open flames or other sources of heat, such as fireplaces, heaters, and heating or hot water pipes. To protect books from injury and to facilitate cleaning, the bottom shelf was typically placed four to six inches above the floor.[20] All shelf surfaces were to be smooth, to avoid attracting dust and abrading the books. Adjustable shelves were considered a good idea; entire shelves could be removed in the event of fire, and shelves could be moved up or down to accommodate books of various heights.[21] An advertisement for The Boston Stack, manufactured by the Boston Shelving Company, stressed "strength," "free circulation of air," and "little surface to catch dust" as the important qualities of its product. Rigid support and smooth surfaces were among the requisites that an engineer listed for the stacks in the new Library of Congress building, which was to house over four million volumes.[22]

There is considerable evidence in the American library press that British libraries favored attaching leather or cloth "falls" to their shelves (some institutions substituted blinds). In some cases, these curtains were kept lowered at all times, unless a reader or staff member was perusing the shelf; this protected the books from dust and light. It was more usual, however, that such curtains were lowered while the library was being swept or dusted. Although Cutter recommended that "hangings of grass cloth" be placed on shelves, and both Samuel Green and Melvil Dewey suggested that shades could be used to shield books from light and dirt, there is no indication that curtaining shelves was a common practice in American libraries.[23]

Some libraries preferred shelving with doors, especially for rare and valuable materials; in theory, such cases provided security and shielded materials from dust.[24] Enclosed bookcases had their detractors, however, who believed that the doors kept out light and air, thus promoting mildew, mold, and decay. Bernard Green described such cases as "contrived to hold and hide indefinitely whatever got into them, especially dust, litter, and musty odors." Another librarian described "glazed cases" as suitable only for plants. One library noted that dust still crept into its enclosed shelving, so that the annual library cleaning remained imperative.[25] Librarians who considered doors essential for security were advised to choose wire over glass; it was also recommended that materials in closed cases be aired from time to time, and the shelves cleaned.[26]

Folios and other oversize volumes needed special shelving. Very large books should lie flat ("'like fallen warriors, on their sides,'" as one person put it), no more than three to four per shelf, in order to prevent scraping the bindings of some volumes while removing those on top of them.[27] A number of libraries used flannel, leather, or carpet to cover folio shelves, as further protection for bindings.[28] Sliding shelves, which pulled out toward the reader for ease of access, were preferred over stationary ones. At the St. Louis Public Library, gas-pipe rods covered with velveteen were used to construct roller shelves. The Indianapolis Public Library employed a "latice-work [*sic*] frame which slips backward and forward," and Dewey used something called the Taylor Sliding-drawer.

Counter-height shelving was preferred, so that the top might be conveniently used as a shelf for consulting heavy volumes. For libraries wishing to shelve large, heavy volumes upright, binder Cedric Chivers invented a device he called a shoe – actually a pasteboard enclosure or brace that fit over the lower fore-edge of the text block, inside the covers, to prevent the pages from sagging and pulling on the upper part of the back. Another similar device was almost like a slipcase whose sides fit between the text block and the covers rather than over the covers; it protected and supported all three exposed edges of the book.[29]

Special tables were sometimes provided for the examination of oversize, illustrated, or rare volumes. At the Lenox Library (New York City), materials were given to readers on cloth-covered tables; Harvard wanted its new library building to have a special room with broad tables for the use of large illustrated volumes. Spofford recommended adjustable stands for folios, so that frequent shifting of the volume's position or angle might be avoided. Perhaps he referred to something like the Perfection Adjustable Book Table (in use at New York's YMCA library), whose top adjusted to various angles and whose lower edge kept books from slipping to the floor. The table's surface could be raised or lowered; its base consisted of an iron rod atop four legs.[30]

The best material from which to build library shelving was warmly debated. Wooden shelving had its pluses and minuses. Those concerned about fire eschewed wood in library interiors – even so-called fireproof woods.[31] The Springfield (Massachusetts) City Library discovered that cheap softwood shelves in some areas of the building were disintegrating, wearing the bindings of the books with their rough surfaces, and shedding a fine, dustlike powder.[32] But many librarians felt that wood shelving was less harsh and abrasive to bindings than metal. The British Museum, after installing iron shelving, found it necessary to cover both the shelves and standards with leather. Poole pointed out that if one's building were built along fireproof standards, it would make little difference whether the shelving was wood or metal. On the other hand, if the library were not fireproof, the presence of iron shelving would make little difference in a blaze, "for it is quite as wel [*sic*] that books should be burnt, as fried on a gridiron. Your books ar [*sic*] lost in any event – if not by fire, then by smoke and water." William I. Fletcher also believed that metal shelving offered little or no protection in the event of fire; as much damage was likely to be done by the warping of iron shelves as by the burning of wooden ones.[33]

Still, as the decades progressed, there appears to have been a preference for metal shelving. Harvard set the example in 1877 by building the first iron stack; later, steel predominated. In 1898 the Redwood Athenaeum (Newport, Rhode Island) praised its new steel stack, which was superior to the old wood shelving in many ways: it was more open, permitting better ventilation; the shelves could be adjusted; books were less subject to mildew, and there were no dark corners to shelter insects, especially the silverfish that had injured books in some "bin-like wooden cases." The Somerville (Massachusetts) Public Library's new building offered steel stacks, constructed so that air could reach every shelf.[34]

At the library in St. Joseph, Missouri, the shelving of the Art Metal Company was installed (1901). The Providence Public Library used a marble and "japanned steel" stack in its new building. Corners and angles were kept to a minimum to prevent the accumulation of dust and facilitate cleaning with a damp cloth.[35] According to Bernard Green, the stacks designed for the new Library of Congress building and constructed by Snead Iron Works of Louisville, Kentucky, represented ten years of thought. The shelves were of smooth white marble; there was a slit or opening every four to five inches in each range end, to admit air and light. Every part of the stack that the books touched had been smoothed and coated with magnetic oxide of iron to protect it from rust and corrosion and eliminate the need for painting. The stack manufactured by the Library Bureau during this same period was similar; built of steel, it possessed either steel or wood adjustable shelves. Both were nonabrasive, but those of wood would not collect moisture in warm weather, as metal shelving did.[36]

There was some talk of developing fireproof shelving materials, as well as protective fireproof boxes for valuable books; however, little if anything appears to have been achieved in either area. In July 1884 a number of distinguished bookmen (including the binder Joseph Zaehnsdorf) gathered in the English garden of Bernard Quaritch, where a bonfire was built and three volumes "of legal character and little worth, and therefore doomed heretical by such a tribunal," enclosed in different types of "'pull-off'" cases, were roasted. "After half-an-hour's intense suffering, the victims were hauled out, and by-and-by extracted from their ruined coverings." A book in a tin-lined case with no air holes suffered no damage from the flames, but some from contact with the hot tin. The second case, one "of the usual kind" (probably a Solander box[37]), which also had no air holes, kept its book intact and unhurt. The volume in the third case, which was exactly like the second but drilled with air holes, suffered the most, as both fire and water entered the case. However, since the damage was not too great and since air holes were viewed as beneficial while the book simply sat on the shelf, the third case was deemed the best.[38]

Although the story of the experiments in Mr. Quaritch's garden represents a fascinating and curious moment in library history, there is no evidence that slipcases or boxes were widely used for fire protection. Also, the Solander box pierced with air holes seems not to have supplanted the ordinary Solander box. Equally intriguing (and ultimately unproductive) were discussions of the possibilities of the use of uralite, an incombustible mineral mined in the Ural Mountains, for library and museum shelving.[39]

Woods that had been chemically treated, coated with so-called fireproof paints, or covered with fireproof materials were marketed as fireproof wood. In 1902 Edward Atkinson, President of the Boston Manufacturers Mutual Fire Insurance Company, solicited samples from six companies supplying what they described as fireproof wood for library and museum shelving. Three of the six responded, and in the resulting tests all the woods burned. Atkinson concluded, "The claim that any such wood is 'absolutely incombustible' is without any warrant in fact. The chemical treatment works in some measure as a fire-retardant."[40] There is no indication that supposedly fireproof woods caught the attention of American librarians, who by the time of Atkinson's experiments were largely committed to steel shelving.

Collection maintenance, which could be said to begin at the moment a book was returned to the circulation counter, was another important method of caring for library volumes. Before being sent for reshelving, every book was examined for loose leaves or plates, torn pages, dirt, and folded page corners.[41] At the Providence Athenaeum the "Regulations of the Library, Reading Room, and Other Rooms" required the librarian to "examine each book on its return to the Library, before it is permitted to be taken out again, or is replaced on the shelves for the purpose of ascertaining whether any injury has been done to the same, . . . to turn up all leaves that have been turned down, and to place in their proper position all maps or plates that may have been wrongly folded, to preserve in proper order all books, pamphlets, charts, etc., before permitting them to be used."[42]

Additionally, librarians were periodically to examine their shelves for materials in need of care. In the Bureau of Education's 1876 *Special Report*, Spofford counseled librarians to go through their collections at intervals and identify books requiring repair or rebinding. Such was the practice in many libraries: the Newark Free Public Library regularly reviewed its shelves for books needing attention. In Council Bluffs, Iowa, there was an annual inspection of the shelves. The public libraries in Dayton, Queens, and St. Louis all routinely surveyed the stacks for volumes wanting mending or rebinding.[43] Many other libraries reported conducting collection condition surveys as special projects – perhaps in a given subject area, or in preparation for a move to a new building.[44]

Librarians attempted to avoid overpacking their shelves. Crowded shelves made it difficult to remove or reshelve books and increased wear on bindings. Unable to slide back the books on either side of a desired volume to remove it properly from the shelf, readers were tempted to grasp the book at the top of the spine, often tearing the headcap. As one librarian remarked, "no book ought to be squeezed or even coaxed into its place: they should move easily both in and out."[45]

Unfortunately, not all libraries enjoyed sufficient growth space, and overcrowding was frequently a problem. The libraries of Cooper Union, Harvard University, and Cincinnati were forced to shelve two and three volumes deep in some areas, and this squeezing caused injuries to the collections. The Iowa state librarian remarked that such shelving practices were followed "at the risk of ruining the bindings and killing or maiming the person who attempts the dangerous ascent of short ladders and narrow shelves to reach [the books]."[46] Some libraries, like that of the Peabody Institute in Baltimore, had sufficient space to expand the collections and eliminate overcrowding. In his 1876 report, the institute's president noted, "I find that many bindings have been injured by packing the books too closely into the cases, the sides having been rubbed and tops often torn in taking them out. I have had the whole library examined, and the books loosened on the shelves where they were too tightly packed." Other libraries, like Providence Public, were able to solve such problems when a new building allowed books to be shelved "with suitable allowance of space, instead of crowding them two or three tiers deep, or wedging them in, one above the other." [47]

Another by-product of insufficient shelf space was fore-edge shelving. Although the Evansville (Indiana) Public Library reported purposely shelving all books on the fore-edge and very close together,[48] most libraries tried to avoid this practice. The Bureau of Education's 1876 *Special Report* advised that "turning books downward upon the fore-edge is another injurious practice, which deteriorates the solidity of the binding." Another librarian, while acknowledging that fore-edge shelving saved space, noted: "My experience leads me to fear the ruin of the back, especially of the larger and heavier books. When standing on the front edge, the weight of the book, unless closely packed, falls on the back, and after a time that falls in and becomes loose. My experience also leads me to fear sad warpings of the covers where a part of the books are not on the shelf."[49]

In every library, book supports formed an essential part of shelf maintenance. In fact, the merits of various supports were debated at length in the pages of *Library Journal* and other popular bibliographic periodicals. Melvil Dewey summed up the virtues of book supports in this way: "Little devices of this kind . . . preserve the books from injury, [and] are good investments for the poorest libraries." Supports kept books standing upright on partially filled shelves, thus preventing the bindings from listing, warping, or straining.[50] In terms of model or style, the choices were almost limitless; many local libraries' inventions were eventually marketed nationally.

The simplest choices were wood blocks and their variations (sand-filled zinc blocks, iron blocks) or paper-covered bricks. Blocks of wood were cheap and easily labeled, and it was unlikely that staff or readers would "knife" books on their broad surfaces. The same virtues belonged to bricks, except that Dewey found them hazardous to readers' toes when they tumbled off the shelves. Regrettably, both blocks and bricks occupied considerable amounts of valuable shelf space and often were not tall enough to support large volumes. Sometimes wood blocks were too lightweight to hold up heavier books.[51]

Libraries began to design and produce more elaborate book supports. Again, Dewey's comments are of interest: "Scores of devices have been made, tried, and rejected as not worthy [of] adoption, . . . unsightly on shelves, taking up room needed for books, heavy, bulky, clumsy, with springs constantly getting out of order, adapted to only one use or to only one thickness of shelf, and too expensiv [*sic*] for wide use. The want has led to many efforts to supply it."[52] The Massey book support, named for its inventor, A. P. Massey, librarian of the Cleveland Library Association, consisted of "an iron casting, a thin black walnut book, and two screws"; the wood piece rested flush against the front cover of the last book on the shelf, and its iron casting screwed onto the shelf's lower edge, adjusting to fit any shelf thickness. Dewey liked the Massey support because it possessed "no springs or delicate parts to get out of order" and was easy to attach, remove, or slide as more books were added to the shelf. Still, it was sturdy when stationary and could be obtained at a cost of fifteen cents each, $10 for one hundred, or twenty-five cents for a single sample.[53]

In 1878 the ALA's Cooperation Committee evaluated the Economy book support, manufactured by Dewey's Library Bureau. The Economy (also called the Library Bureau book support) consisted of a single thin sheet of iron, with both a front and a rear tongue extending from it at right angles. The rear tongue slid under the bottom edges of the last few books on the shelf, the thin sheet of iron rested against the front cover of the last book, and the front tongue extended toward the shelf's end. The committee liked the Economy because it had no moving parts, springs, screws, or joints. It was thin and occupied little space on the shelf. Less space was required to store extra stock, as the supports nested together. "The only fault in it is that careless boys may crowd a book astride the iron plate, thus injuring the leaves." The Economy (whose descendants populate modern library shelves) sold for twenty-five cents each, and a free sample was available; in 1890 the Astor Library (New York City) ordered a thousand.[54]

Another popular support was the Crocker book brace, patented and manufactured by the Reverend Henry Crocker of Bristol, Rhode Island. It consisted of a thin, flat piece of beechwood that rested against the front cover of the last volume on the shelf. A narrow, adjustable steel strip, attached with screws to the block's outer face, extended above the block and pressed tautly against the bottom of the shelf above, acting as a spring and holding the contents of the shelf firmly in place. Crocker offered fifty of the braces for a sixty-day free trial. Charles Cutter of the Boston Athenaeum and Reuben A. Guild, the Brown University librarian, praised the Crocker support, and Dewey's Library Bureau recommended it over the Massey and Economy products. At the Pratt Institute, the Crocker replaced the Library Bureau supports for use in the reference department; unfortunately, however, the Crocker scratched the shelves.[55]

There were other book supports in addition to these three most successful ones. The Boston Public Library's support, also commercially available, was a three-cornered block of wood. The Yale University model, made of either japanned steel or steel and wood at $16 or $25 per hundred, respectively, was almost identical in design to the Massey. The Mason book support, which originated in Great Britain, was a near twin of the Library Bureau's Economy model. The Lowell book support, made by Concklin and Company of Lowell, Massachusetts, worked, like the Crocker, on a spring principle. J. N. Larned of the Buffalo Public Library offered the wire Buffalo Book Brace, which had limited commercial success because its use required grooved shelving. The Newton (Massachusetts) Free Library also marketed its own invention at the bargain price of fifty to eighty cents a dozen, depending on the size selected.[56] Undoubtedly, the list could be longer still.

In addition to protecting volumes while they were on the library's shelves, staff also took pains properly to pack books meant for shipping. Melvil Dewey suggested that pamphlets be mailed flat in envelopes, not rolled.[57] The Harvard library noted that it often refused interlending requests if an item "is thought too valuable to be exposed to the dangers of travel."[58] Most libraries used sturdy boxes, sometimes specially made, to transport their collections. The boxes might be lined with paper, then the books themselves individually wrapped in paper. Empty spaces would be filled with crushed paper, and the books would be packed tightly to prevent them from being injured by knocking about.[59] In 1907 the Los Angeles Public Library switched from bags to boxes for transporting books to the schools, noting that the bags destroyed more books than did careless patrons.[60]

The Iowa Library Commission provided instructions for the care of the shipping crates used with the state's fifty-volume traveling libraries. These boxes, in which the books would also be returned to the State Library, were to be kept "in a safe, dry place." The State Library of New York enclosed notices in shipments it made to other institutions, requesting that the books be returned in the same container in which they had arrived. Library staff found that this prevented the "carelessness that sometimes sends a book back in a thin paper with a string around it, to the permanent damage of the cover."[61]

Through shelving and maintaining the collections, the library staff cared for the volumes in their keeping. Because late-nineteenth-century publishers' editions were often flimsy, special importance was attached to these activities. By the turn of the century, although standard shelving did not yet exist, there was general accord about the materials and qualities preferred in book stacks. Certainly, what one might term the small-appliance debates – those centering on book jackets and book supports – reveal as much about the nineteenth-century American librarian's concept of the responsibilities of the profession as they do about his or her sensitivity to preservation issues.

Chapter 6

Binding:
Its Importance and Economics

Between 1876 and 1910, binding was the principal preservation technique
in American libraries. Because the period's only preservation option was
the protection of the artifact, and because books came to libraries either
unbound or clad in cheap, insubstantial publishers' bindings, librarians
had no choice but to make a strong intellectual and financial commitment
to binding. It is useful to recall the quotation of Ainsworth Spofford (from
the Bureau of Education's 1876 *Special Report*) that appeared in the first
chapter: "Next to the selection and utilization of books, there is no subject
more important in the administration of a public library than the binding
and preservation of the volumes." Other librarians felt as strongly as he,
and preservation and binding were strongly joined in the minds of this
period.[1]

When Reuben B. Poole declared, "the purpose of bookbinding, it has
been well remarked, is 'to permanently preserve the best and noblest
thoughts of mankind,'"[2] he was paraphrasing Spofford in *A Book for All
Readers*: "When it is considered that the purposed object of bookbinding
is to preserve in a shape at once attractive and permanent, the best and
noblest thoughts of man, it rises to a high rank among the arts. . . . And the
ideal of every librarian should be so to care for the embodiments of
intelligence entrusted to his guardianship, that they may become in the
highest degree useful to mankind. In this sense, the care bestowed upon
thorough and enduring binding can hardly be overrated, since the life of
the book depends upon it."[3]

Other librarians also linked binding and preservation. In the Indiana
State Library, "the chief object of binding is durability and preservation."
Likewise, at the Alameda (California) Free Library, "not only does
rebinding enhance the exterior appearance of the books but it preserves
them." The authors of the "A. L. A. Library Primer" acknowledged, "Binding
a book means not only covering it, but preserving it."[4] The Trinity College

librarian noted that binding kept the leaves clean and protected the text block from curling and twisting, and Bowdoin College planned to bind "all printed matter worthy of preservation," as did the New Hampshire State Library.[5] To Edward F. Stevens, the Pratt Institute's new librarian in 1910, go the honors for the most vivid description of the significance of binding: "When books are marshalled in the people's service into the ranks of a public library's army, the warfare that ensues is an actual hand-to-hand fight for the survival of literature, less indeed with the traditional 'enemies of books' than with their supposed friends. So the bindings of books, preparatory to the conflict, have become highly developed forms of the protective device, calling to mind the extreme elaboration of the art of the armorer in the early sixteenth century."[6]

Another indication of the presence binding had in the nineteenth-century library consciousness was the number of surveys taken on the topic. The American Library Association's Committee on Bookbinding and Book Papers sent out numerous "circular letters" seeking information from librarians on topics ranging from in-house binderies to their interest in paying an extra dime for an especially sturdy library binding. The committee also surveyed publishers about their willingness to improve binding techniques.[7]

The ALA Committee on Library Administration canvassed librarians about the durability of different publishers' bindings. The Newark (New Jersey) Free Public Library's John Cotton Dana sent out an extensive questionnaire requesting information on sewing practices, binding materials and costs, and the "'life histories' of books and bindings, to be answered from the library's bindery records." The Wilmington (Delaware) Institute mailed a form letter to thirty libraries of similar size, soliciting data on the average number of circulations a book enjoyed before being rebound. The Iowa Library Commission asked that librarians send reports on this same topic, with the titles arranged by author, title, and publisher.[8] Across the Atlantic, British librarians were just as actively using circular letters to collect information on binding materials and practices. Their work, including the many surveys published by the Royal Society of Arts and the Library Association of the United Kingdom, was followed with interest by American librarians.[9]

Quite a lot was spoken and written about the librarian's role in binding. It was necessary that he or she learn much of the "binder's art," as Winsor called it in the Bureau of Education's 1876 *Special Report*, in order to avoid becoming the victim of poor workmanship and inferior materials. Those unfamiliar with the technical aspects of binding would be "undiscriminating bargainers," unable to recognize the difference between superior and substandard craft.[10] Librarians were to give strict written instructions or specifications to binders and to ascertain, when the work was returned, that these had been followed.[11]

Late-nineteenth-century librarians needed not only this basic technical knowledge but also a sophisticated understanding of the use to which their collections would be put and the appropriateness of other preservation options.[12] The decision to rebind was a decision to reselect the title for the collection and thus to commit further library resources to processing, housing, and caring for it. For this reason, "a book should never be rebound merely because it happens to be in the library. Before rebinding, a librarian should consider carefully whether the book is of enough value to warrant the expense."[13]

John Cotton Dana recommended that such decisions be made thoughtfully and only after a number of alternatives had been considered. He suggested that librarians ask themselves these questions: Is this the only copy of the book? Is the title still popular? Should people be encouraged to read it? Has the book been superseded by more recent material? Does it have historical value? Which is cheaper to process, a rebound book or a replacement? Which would last longer? Should the book be mended instead? Or will that prevent its being rebound at a later date?[14] Often, a worn volume could be replaced more cheaply than it could be rebound.[15] Thinking along the same lines as Dana, Frederick Crunden, director of the St. Louis Public Library, suggested that binding decisions called for "judgment based on knowledge of wearing qualities of different kinds of bindings, on the sort of usage the book is likely to receive, the amount of wear left in it, and the cost of a new copy." The person making such decisions should be someone of "knowledge, experience, and judgment" who would also consider the advisability of discarding the book, repairing it, or simply sending it back to the shelf.[16]

As one studies the literature of this period, five principles of binding economics emerge, though no one characterized them as such at the time. First, never compromise on the quality of binding materials. Winsor observed that "cheap binding is often dear binding. Strong sewing, real leather, and solid board are worth paying for." Spofford cautioned that low bids from a binder often meant inferior leather, thin, spongy boards, cheap thread and glue, "and other devices resorted to by every mechanic who has to make a cheap job pay." A librarian should deal with an experienced, trusted firm and be willing to pay fair prices for binding.[17] Further, since labor was the principal part of any binding's cost, there was little economy in choosing cheap, inferior materials.[18]

Second, the librarian should choose a binding based on the use the book will receive. "Ephemeral publications which are not expected to be used or kept more than a year or two years at the outside" should be bound with thrift.[19] Douglas Cockerell advised dividing books into three categories: valuable books, to be given the best possible binding; books of "permanent interest" but without artifactual value, to be bound strongly but for which "the best and most careful work would be too expensive"; and books of temporary interest, which could be bound very inexpensively.[20]

Third, librarians were advised to bind well initially. One reason was that every rebinding, with its associated trimming, scraping, and resewing, injured the book, and repeated rebindings ruined it.[21] Also, an initial sound binding was more economical in the long run, as it often eliminated the need for subsequent rebinding. The librarian of the Seattle Public Library remarked, "I have never wavered in the belief that . . . the most careful binding would be the cheapest in the end."[22] Someone else suggested that the initial expenditure of an extra twenty percent on a binding served as "insurance against further expense" (that is, rebinding). The Pratt Institute's librarian pointed out that binding well the first time not only saved the cost of later rebinding but also the associated staff time.[23]

A fourth principle of binding economics was to rebind before the book (chiefly its folds) became so worn or broken that rebinding was no longer possible.[24] Finally, the binding should be suited to the physical characteristics of the book itself. Popular fiction and certain other volumes should not be given expensive, sturdy bindings that would long outlive the inferior paper on which the books themselves were printed.[25] Paper type, quality, and weight, as well as the available inner margin, also governed decisions about choice of sewing and binding style.[26]

Libraries generally used about one-third of their book budget for binding. In 1899 the Boston Athenaeum spent $8,004.42 on books and $2,727.83 on binding. As machine-bound books began to accumulate on American library shelves, binding bills grew. In their 1898-1899 report, the board of the Silas Bronson Library in Waterbury, Connecticut, ruefully remarked, "The cost of rebinding grows larger each year, but a maximum must some day be reached."[27]

A few fortunate libraries, among them the Boston Athenaeum, the public libraries of Buffalo and Louisville, Kentucky, and the Trinity College Library, appear to have had binding funds adequate to their needs. The Boston Athenaeum reported that "the funds are sufficient for all reasonable demands in this department of work."[28] A larger group of institutions, however, found their binding budgets inadequate. In 1904 the Springfield (Massachusetts) City Library indicated that it had insufficient money to keep up with binding, and in 1899 the New York Society Library needed a special sum of $1,000 to rebind newspapers and periodicals threatened with the possibility of injury.[29] Shabby books and periodicals were often withheld from use until they could be rebound.

The Queens Borough (New York) and Boston public libraries are excellent examples of libraries whose resources for binding seldom fully met their needs. In 1908 the Queens Borough trustees indicated that the contents of the library shelves were quite shabby because there had not been enough binding money in previous years. That year 7,995 volumes were rebound, and 15,500 candidates for binding in the next year were identified. When 1909 came, however, only 5,218 volumes could be treated. In 1910 funds were supplied for the remaining books that had been set aside in 1908; because of the size of the order, the library got "special terms" for the work, at about fifty-seven cents a volume.[30]

In 1891 the trustees of the Boston Public Library pointed out that "the question of the binding of books is becoming each year more serious." In 1890 the library owned 536,027 volumes but spent only $2,902.34 on binding. The books first placed on the library's shelves in its early days "seem[ed] to have reached the limit of serviceableness almost simultaneously and all need[ed] attention at once." The trustees asked for a special allocation of $6,000. Eight years later, in 1899, this money had still not been allocated. The trustees asked the mayor for a special expenditure of $30,000 for delinquent binding, $10,000 of it to be granted that year. Instead the library received a decrease in funding of $10,692.26. The following year, $10,000 of the $30,000 special request was granted; the remainder was to come in two more annual installments. But by 1908 the trustees were again seeking a special allocation for deferred binding, this time $2,500; without these funds, they noted, many books would have to be withdrawn from circulation.[31]

As unfortunate as these libraries' circumstances might seem, a surprising number of institutions appear to have had no funds whatsoever for regular binding. In 1894 the librarian of the Alameda Free Library pointed out to the trustees the need to do considerable rebinding. "I would therefore call your attention to the urgent advisability and necessity of asking that a special appropriation be included in our next apportionment, to meet the expense of placing the volumes of the Library in such conditions as prudent economical considerations demand." The librarian of the General Theological Library (New York City) in 1875 listed three items in "The Wants of the Institution" section of his annual report: a larger book budget, a new facility, and "a fund for binding of books. Such a fund is, perhaps, the last to be created, but it is of about the first consequence." Unfortunately, this plea was repeated throughout the next twenty-five years.[32] In 1901 the Bradford (Pennsylvania) Carnegie Public Library deferred the purchase of any new books in order to spend $442.70 on binding, although this sum still was not adequate; two years later, the librarian suggested that gifts from the public would help address binding needs.[33]

The Pennsylvania and Washington state libraries also sought binding budgets. In 1888 Pennsylvania's librarian pointed out that the New York State Library received $2,000 a year for this purpose and that preservation of Pennsylvania's collections demanded a similar sum; the state binder would not perform the work because he was reimbursed at eighteen cents a volume, and the library's binding would cost three to four times that amount. In requesting a binding budget for his library, the Washington state librarian suggested that the legislators, in considering the annual expenses of the library, remember that many books are bought in paper covers.[34]

Throughout the entire period of this study, the Redwood Library and Athenaeum (Newport, Rhode Island) apparently had no regular binding allocation and depended chiefly on the kindness of various donors. In 1878, 1880, 1884, and 1900 the directors made several appeals for funds to the proprietors; an endowment whose interest would be used for binding was favored.[35] Meanwhile, records of small gifts for binding appeared in every report. In 1879 two women gave $50 and $12, respectively, for binding; in 1882 Miss Maria Anderson gave $100 to bind 100 periodical volumes, and a clause in the will of a past president of the library specified a sum for acquiring "medical, classical, or historical books . . . and in keeping in repair the books embraced in the said collection."[36] In 1885 a friend of the library paid for the binding of thirty-six periodical volumes and sixty-seven monographs; in 1902 A. B. Emmons funded the binding of twenty-three volumes of the *Nation*.[37] Between 1886 and his death in 1902, Henry G. Marquand, one of the directors requesting a binding fund from the proprietors, consistently made small gifts for this purpose, ranging from as little as $80 to as much as $300. Mr. Marquand was a most welcome benefactor.[38]

Because deficiencies in the materials from which books were made was a topic so little understood (and one for which the remedies were few), and because publishers' case-made books withstood so few circulations, librarians directed their attention to preservation approaches that addressed the external book, thus establishing binding as the major preservation method in turn-of-the-century American libraries. The librarian who wanted quality workmanship and materials needed a fair amount of technical knowledge. Also, because economy in binding involved matching construction and materials to the use the book would receive, he or she also needed an understanding of the title's place and purpose in the collection and, by extension, a clear picture of the scope and mission of the library. Such concerns contrast markedly with those discussed in previous chapters and are consistent with the professional responsibilities perceived by present-day librarians.

Chapter 7

Binding Materials: Costs and Choices

Most library volumes were bound in cloth or leather; there was an impressive array of each from which to select, and many opinions as to the best and worst choices.[1] Many of the terms used for binding leathers and cloths had no precise technical definitions; they were used at the discretion of the binder or vendor to enhance the appeal of the product. Libraries often tried a variety of materials before settling on the one or ones they found most suitable. The broad experimentation conducted at the Newark (New Jersey) Free Public Library and the Springfield (Massachusetts) City Library exemplifies the curiosity and inventiveness shown by American librarians in evaluating different cloths and leathers for their two most important qualities: permanence (the ability to retain strength while aging) and durability (the capacity to stand up under use).

In 1891 the Newark library bound or rebound 2,070 volumes in buffing, and eighty-one volumes "in a better quality of leather." Two years later, 470 books were bound in American russia (cowhide), and 1,152 in split leather; at the time, the library owned between forty and fifty thousand volumes. Early in 1902, with John Cotton Dana as librarian, Newark decided to do no more binding in leather. Instead it tried cloths such as art canvas, art vellum, and English linen. Before the year's end, however, the library settled on cowhide with art vellum sides for heavily used titles and English linen with art canvas sides for more permanent but less-used volumes. By 1903 English linen, art vellum, and art canvas had been superseded by imperial morocco cloth (a fabric that imitated morocco, the finest binding leather); it was perceived to wear better than its predecessors. Morocco leather was in use for high-demand works of nonfiction (such as reference books and indexes), and three hundred volumes were sent to England for binding in pigskin.[2]

In Springfield (where Dana was the librarian from 1898 to 1901), skiver (split sheepskin) was the material of choice at first, but the books shortly wore out. Next, "a zinc back and heavy wire" were used; this binding held up well but was "very clumsy." Split cowhide followed, and then full canvas, which "soiled badly." By 1901 art vellum or Holliston cloth was in use, plus Cedric Chivers' duro-flexile binding, which was probably half pigskin.[3]

Then as now, cost was among the many factors influencing the choice of binding materials.[4] Morocco leather (here used broadly to mean any vegetable-tanned goatskin) was by far the most expensive, ranging in price from about $42 to $60 per dozen for large, fine levant skins to as little as $18 a dozen for cheaper grades. Dewey estimated that the cost of skins in the mid-range worked out to about forty cents per square foot. Proponents of morocco felt its use represented a good investment; a book covered in it would probably not require rebinding.[5] Less-durable persian leather (the vegetable-tanned hides of hair sheep; variously called persian calf, persian morocco, or bock) cost $6 to $12 per dozen skins; these skins were smaller than those of true morocco.[6] Pig (with each skin two to four times the size of a morocco skin) cost between $7 and $11 per hide; it was thick and sturdy.[7] Among the less durable leathers, American russia and calf were nonetheless quite expensive at $42 to $66 and $21 to $29 per dozen skins, respectively. Roan (a close-grained sheepskin) was more reasonably priced ($8 to $11 per dozen hides), and skiver cheaper still ($5 to $9 per dozen).[8] Half-binding in ordinary sheepskin – that is, using it to cover only the spine, part of the sides, and the four corners of a book, with a cheaper material such as paper or cloth for the rest – was reportedly one and a half to two cents cheaper per volume than binding in russia.[9]

Cloths were considerably less expensive than leathers. Linen buckram could be purchased from Winterbottom of Manchester, England, for fifty-five cents a square yard; the same quantity of cotton buckram cost forty to fifty cents.[10] Duck cost ten to twenty cents a yard, and canvas and art canvas about the same amount; cotton and linen book cloths were also at the bottom of the price scale at twelve to twenty cents per yard.[11]

Cost was an important consideration in choosing binding materials, and librarians often kept costs low by reserving leather and cloth for the parts of a binding that would receive the most wear – the spine and corners – and covering the sides, or boards, with cheaper material. Paper, for instance, was frequently used to cover the sides of a volume, while more durable leather or cloth was used to cover the spine.[12] Besides being less expensive than cloth or leather, paper did not fray or attract dust. It was easier to replace when dirty or worn (new paper was simply pasted on top of old), and readers could more easily remove books with low-friction paper sides from the shelves.[13] The imitation leather with which the Newark Free Public Library and other institutions covered the boards of some volumes was probably paper coated and stamped to resemble leather. Spofford criticized it for its lack of smoothness and durability.[14]

Librarians and binders who wished to use leather could choose among many products prepared in many ways. Though there was considerable discussion about which sort of leather was the worst, and many different ideas about how to rank those in the middle of the scale, morocco was unquestionably at the top of everyone's list. One librarian testified that the books in his collections taught the lesson "that time alone can teach" – that "no leather of recent manufacture except for the most expensive morocco is fit for bookbinding."[15] There were several types of morocco, a general term for any vegetable-tanned goatskin, though most of the tanning was done with sumac. Levant (so called because it came from the eastern Mediterranean) was considered the best type of morocco and was the most costly. Many excellent moroccos were also manufactured in Germany, Switzerland, and Norway, and cape morocco was so named because originally it came from goats (or, some say, hair sheep) native to South Africa, perhaps near the Cape of Good Hope. Unfortunately, not all leathers with the word *morocco* in their names were the genuine article; most references to turkey morocco probably apply to a leather made from calfskin, and so-called Hausman morocco may also have been calf.[16]

Among the many qualities that made genuine morocco so desirable were its ability to resist the effects of heat, foul air, and illuminating gas; it was also flexible, durable, and resistant to stains, scratches, and moisture.[17] For all these reasons, morocco was considered a highly cost-effective binding material; though initially expensive, it typically outlasted cheaper leathers by a factor of three.[18] Nonetheless, because of its cost few libraries could bind exclusively in morocco. Books that received this covering were typically destined for heavy use and hard handling; reference materials, oversize or heavy volumes, and fine books were also often bound in morocco.[19]

Believing the spine to be the part of the book that experienced the greatest amount of wear and stress, many librarians bound in a style called half-morocco and thus obtained the strength and durability of morocco at a lower cost. The spine and part of the sides of the book, as well as the four corners, were covered in morocco, and the remainder of the sides in a cheaper material such as paper or cloth.[20] Half-binding in morocco was considered superior to full binding in cheaper leathers such as russia and sheep. While not quite so strong as full morocco, it cost about half as much and was well suited to all but the most heavily used reference materials.[21] Among the institutions that bound in half-morocco were the New York State Library, Brooklyn's YMCA Library, the John Crerar Library (Chicago), the Columbia College Library, the Library of Congress, and the public libraries of Peoria, Illinois; Boston; Newark; St. Louis; Cleveland; and Waterbury, Connecticut.[22]

Persian morocco (sometimes called bock) was a misnomer. While some leather so named may have come from a small Indian goat, most of it was actually the vegetable-tanned skins of Indian hair sheep. Smaller, finer skins were more likely to be goat; larger ones, sheep.[23] Unfortunately, persian was often sold to unsuspecting librarians as morocco; despite its impermanence, it was also fairly expensive.[24] Persian was generally prepared with catechols (a class of condensed, astringent vegetable tannins), and experience showed that after about ten years, "red decay" set in. Additionally, sunlight faded persian, and heat embrittled it.[25] Nonetheless, persian was sturdy during its lifetime, making it suitable for binding materials to be kept no more than a few years, such as works of popular fiction.[26]

Pigskin, especially in half-bindings, was another strong, popular binding leather, ranked second only to morocco by noted binder Joseph Zaehnsdorf. It was attractive and could be tanned into a very strong leather that was resistant to "atmospheric influences."[27] Pigskin was quite thick, not so pliant as other leathers, and thus somewhat difficult to work with; placed on little-used materials, it eventually became brittle.[28] For these reasons, it was best suited for binding large, heavy, and frequently handled books, such as reference works.[29]

While pigskin may have been somewhat more popular in England, British bookbinder Cedric Chivers, who served hundreds of American libraries, routinely used half-pigskin "guaranteed free from acid" for his special library bindings.[30] Sealskin promoted by Douglas Cockerell, the Library Association of the United Kingdom's (LAUK's) Sound Leather Committee, and the Royal Society of Arts, was also used in Great Britain. Like pigskin, it was very tough and strong, yet much more flexible because of its considerable oil content. Its expense and limited availability prevented wide adoption, however, and there is no indication of American acceptance of seal.[31]

Although librarians agreed about the strengths of morocco, persian, and pigskin, and there was some consensus about which leathers were the poorest and least desirable, there was a middle group of leathers in which no clear-cut preferences emerged. Justin Winsor preferred russia over calf. A Boston bookbinder thought calf was better than cowhide. Blades believed that russia deteriorated more quickly than calf. Another librarian placed calf over roan, and the LAUK's Sound Leather Committee ranked calf ahead of all binding leathers except morocco, pig, seal, and sheep. Edward B. Nicholson of the Bodleian (the main library at Oxford University) told American librarians that russia, calf, and roan were all equally unacceptable; "no librarian with any knowledge of these leathers,

and any regard for the future of his library, will ever think of using them."
In light of these many opinions, it seems best to examine the qualities of
these leathers and the uses to which each was generally put.[32]

Calf was a very attractive smooth leather, often placed on elegant,
little-used books and books in private libraries. Perhaps because of
tanning methods, and perhaps because it was the skin of an immature
animal, calf was not strong and did not wear well.[33] Not only did it soil
and scratch easily (resulting in higher labor costs in the bindery and
greater waste), but calf bindings often cracked at the joints; the covers
could break away from heavy volumes sitting on the shelves, simply from
their own weight. Calf crumbled with exposure to foul air and thus had a
life span of only a few years in urban libraries.[34]

Cowhide, despite the fact that it too developed "red rot" and generally
lasted less than a dozen years,[35] was a favorite American binding leather
for popular materials (especially in half-bindings, combined with paper or
cloth sides) and heavy books. The ALA's Bookbinding Committee
recommended cowhide for fiction and juvenile books.[36] Among the
libraries doing full or half-binding in cowhide were the Library of
Congress, the New Hampshire State Library, and the public libraries of
Washington, D.C., San Francisco, Newark, and Wilmington, Delaware.[37]

Russia leather was a shaved, willow-tanned cowhide. It was treated
with birch bark; this tanning method, thought to have originated in Russia
(hence the name), gave it a distinctive odor. Russia was generally dyed in
dark colors. Sometimes similarly tanned horse, goat, calf, or sheep hides
were also called russia.[38] Russia was largely condemned; susceptible to
both light and heat, it tended to break at the joints, crumble, and decay.[39]
American russia (an imitation of genuine russia) was produced either from
cowhide or the hide of the American buffalo. It appears to have been a
much sturdier and better-liked leather (though it also had a limited life)
and was used in many American libraries.[40]

Buffing, a leather derived from splitting cowhide, was the inner side of
the skin.[41] Because of its thinness, it lacked strength and was particularly
vulnerable to heat and pollution. While everyone recognized buffing's
impermanence, there was disagreement about its suitability for popular
titles. Some librarians believed that it would last as long as the poor-
quality paper on which novels and children's books were printed and was
therefore adequate; others thought it was too weak to withstand the hard
wear such materials typically received.[42] At one time or another, the
public libraries of Jersey City (New Jersey), Seattle, San Francisco,
Portland, Oregon, and Newark used buffing for part of their binding.[43]

Roan was a close-grained, vegetable-tanned sheepskin, often colored
and finished in imitation of morocco. Originally roan, like morocco, was
tanned with sumac; later, many other vegetable tannins were used. One

authority referred to roan as the cheapest leather one might satisfactorily use.[44] Roan varied in quality, largely because of the different tanning methods used. Good roan had a grained, hard-finished surface yet was soft and flexible; poor roan was smooth, spongy, and easily scratched and split. Many librarians and binders believed that a quality roan was equal to cowhide in strength and permanence (lasting about ten to twelve years). But like most of the aforementioned leathers, roan succumbed to the effects of heat and gas and was most appropriate for books not intended as part of the permanent collection.[45]

It was very difficult to find any librarian with a kind word for sheepskin. Although Justin Winsor preferred it over russia and calf, he represented a minority: sheep was condemned by the Office of Education's 1893 annual report (a collection of library papers prepared to supplement the 1876 *Special Report*), the U.S. Superintendent of Documents, the Royal Society of Arts, the Library of Congress, and the Boston Public Library.[46] Sheepskin crumbled or split in a heated, impure atmosphere more quickly than any other leather. Librarians vividly described their experiences with this leather, which "crumbles into dust at the touch" and "is reduced to a powder (sometimes occasioning explosions) by the action of gas and heat." Henry Evelyn Bliss termed sheepskin "the worst fraud known to the trade"; the Worcester County (Massachusetts) Law Library called it "without a doubt, the worst covering put on books at this time."[47]

The expense and continuing growth of law sets and government reports, which could fill shelf upon shelf in a library, made the vegetable-tanned sheep commonly used to bind them a particular source of complaint. "Law sheep" was dry, soft, and began to crumble in only a few years. The New York State Library found itself in a position common to libraries across America: books in their law sets were deteriorating from age rather than use. Still, new volumes in the same titles were being bound in the same material.[48]

This state of affairs prompted the Congressional Committee on Printing to seek from librarians "an expression of opinion regarding the material to be used in binding Government documents." According to law, leather-bound sets had to be bound in sheep; those wishing to protest were instructed to write their representatives in Congress. Similarly, William L. Post, the Superintendent of Documents, asked librarians to express to government agencies their opinions about sheepskin bindings. "My idea," he said, "would be voiced in the language of most librarians in the Association, that there could be nothing worse than sheep bindings, and if we can possibly change to a good class of cloth or buckram, we will be doing a good thing for the librarians, and will certainly be doing a good thing for Uncle Sam, because we will be saving about $150,000 a year."[49]

If sheep was bad, skiver was worse still; it was considered by many to be the most inferior of all binding leathers. It was weak, its surface was poor and fragile, and it split or decayed in a short time.[50] In 1886 the Columbia College Library reported having abandoned it in favor of cloth; skivers, it was found, "soon wore to ragged edges, [and] were from the first cheap and ugly." Nonetheless, some libraries (among them the San Francisco Public Library) used skiver for thin books, "fiction and other cheap literature."[51]

Vellum and parchment were seldom used in general library collections. Neither was technically a leather, because the method of producing them did not include tanning.[52] Vellum warped, cracked, and cockled as a result of temperature variations, heat, and dryness; additionally, it was embrittled by light, and its whiteness made it difficult to keep clean.[53] For these reasons, it was seldom found in circulating collections and was most often used for binding little-used, lightweight materials.[54] Likewise, parchment was recommended for books that received light use.[55] It was difficult to work with because it was elastic when damp and had to be lined; however, it did not crack as vellum did. In general collections, it was most frequently used to cover and protect the corners of a volumes' covers.[56]

As the nineteenth century progressed, librarians grew increasingly wary of leather as a primary binding material. Like all library materials, leather-bound volumes were negatively affected by the environmental forces mentioned in chapter 3 (dust, light, heat, dampness, and the residues of illuminating gas).[57] However, leather suffered further from certain internal sources of deterioration. As John Cotton Dana observed, "Leather has within itself that which leads to its own destruction."[58] Though librarians at home and abroad recognized the seriousness of the leather problem, it was the British who first formally tackled it.

Perhaps because English collections were older or larger, the British took action more quickly than their American colleagues. Bookbinder Douglas Cockerell described the common concerns that led to the Royal Society of Arts' investigation of disintegrating leather bookbindings. The puzzling and inexplicable juxtaposition on library shelves of crumbling and intact leather volumes led binders and librarians to suspect that the deteriorated bindings possessed characteristics that led – perhaps in conjunction with negative atmospheric forces – to their decay. As a binder, Cockerell worried "that it might be possible that the leather I was using for the repair of the backs of perished bindings might wear no better than that which it replaces." The three common theories that attributed leather decay to dampness, heat, or illuminating gas no longer seemed sufficient when damaged bindings were also found in libraries free of these hazards.[59]

In 1877 at the Conference of Librarians in London, a proposal was made to establish a committee of librarians and chemists to study the problem of disintegrating leather-bound library collections, but no action was taken.[60] Later, the matter was discussed at several meetings of the IAUK. In 1899, a meeting of interested persons was held at the Central School of Arts and Crafts in London, and a committee was formed to study the issue and "to encourage the production of sound and durable leather for bookbinding." After several meetings, the group concluded that the matter was too large to be effectively dealt with by an informal body and petitioned the Royal Society of Arts to assume the investigation. In February 1900 the Committee on Leather for Bookbinding was appointed; when it first met on 3 May 1900, two subcommittees were formed. The first was "to visit a selected number of libraries and to ascertain the comparative durability of the various bookbinding leathers used at different periods and preserved under different conditions," and the second was "to deal with the scientific side of the matter, to ascertain the cause of any deterioration noticed, and, if possible, to suggest methods for its prevention in the future."[61]

The committee's report was submitted on 17 June 1901 and printed in the *Journal for the Society of Arts* on 5 July 1901. At the same time, the committee, having been reappointed, decided that the report should appear in a more permanent form, with color illustrations and leather samples. This publication was underwritten by the Leathersellers' Company; the work was reorganized and certain parts of the original report rewritten. Meanwhile, Cyril Davenport of the British Museum and E. Wyndham Hulme of the Patent Office were independently studying "the question of the deterioration of binding leathers." In 1904 they sent a circular to English librarians on the topic, suggesting the formation of "a united action" in obtaining better leathers, the publication of a handbook on the topic, and the employment of someone to whom samples of leather might be submitted for testing. Subsequently, the IAUK appointed Dr. J. Gordon Parker as leather analyst to the association, with an established fee schedule.[62]

Both the Royal Society of Arts and the IAUK found clear evidence of premature decay in modern leather bindings. Some leathers appeared to be fairly shelfworthy until around 1860, but after that date all leathers seemed to worsen.[63] Beyond the usual unfriendly atmospheric influences, it seemed that these problems were attributable to the tanning and coloring processes used with modern binding leathers, as well as the mechanical procedures sometimes employed in graining, paring, and splitting skins.

One of the findings of the Royal Society of Arts was that certain acids used in the tanning process (i.e., the conversion of hides to leather) negatively affected binding leathers.[64] One librarian, having studied the society's report, concluded that "leather as made at present contains within itself the elements of decay." While some animal hides possessed qualities that made for better leathers, such as close graining, the Committee on Leather for Bookbinding believed that even sheepskin ("although not as close in texture as morocco and calf") could be made into a decent leather if properly tanned.[65] Put another way, sound leather was not necessarily a particular type of skin, but rather one prepared in certain ways.[66]

A Dubliner is credited with having introduced sulfuric acid into the tanning process around 1768. The public's growing demand for books made the slower, more stable tanning methods of the past impractical. Leather manufacturers no longer found it cost-effective to pack leathers for months between layers of tanning materials while tannic acids slowly soaked in. As the book-production industry grew, faster ways of tanning were needed; the use of sulfuric acid greatly shortened the process while also reducing opportunities for bacterial injury.[67] Unfortunately, the leathers produced by these modern tanning techniques were not then thoroughly washed, and residues of sulfuric acid remained. As heated library atmospheres dried out the typical binding's 15 percent water reserve, these residual acids became concentrated enough to destroy the leathers.[68]

Modern tanning methods involved either mineral or vegetable materials. Chrome tanning (a mineral process) could leave residues of sulfur in leathers; when these combined with moisture, "a slow oxidation of the sulphur [sic] to sulfuric acid" occurred, and deterioration resulted.[69] Modern vegetable tanning was of two types: one using catechol tannins, the other pyrogallols. While the pyrogallols were considered fast tanning materials, they typically produced fairly long-lived leathers; among the sources of pyrogallols were sumac, algarobilla, galls, divi-divi, myrabolans, oak, and chestnut.[70] On the other hand, leathers tanned with catechols (obtained from hemlock, larch, spruce, quebracho, pistachio, mangrove, gambier, turwar bark) developed "red rot" and crumbled with exposure to light and air.[71] Of all the sources of catechols, turwar bark (generally used to tan so-called persian morocco) was considered the worst.[72] Librarians and binders also believed that overtanning (whatever the tannin employed) and retanning (a process routinely performed on leathers imported from India, Australia, and New Zealand, which typically arrived only "rough tanned") were very injurious to binding leathers and promoted their early deterioration.[73]

Librarians observed that colored binding leathers deteriorated more quickly than natural ones. The bindery foreman at the Boston Public Library noted that through the addition of dyes, leather "can receive no benefit, but rather some harm"; olive and light brown colors seemed to hold up best, blacks and dark greens to disintegrate most quickly.[74] Another reason for preferring natural or lightly colored leathers was that only the best-quality skins were so treated; poorer quality hides and those with obvious imperfections were generally dyed darker colors to mask their flaws.[75]

Acids used in the dyeing process (which "no amount of washing" would remove) also contributed to the early decay of binding leathers. A Hartford binder found that black sheepskin and skiver rotted early; "the cause is supposed to be the acid which is used to set the color."[76] Tests performed by the Royal Society of Arts found that calf tanned with oak bark still contained free sulfuric acid, which had been used as a brightener in the dye bath. In further testing, such leather was shown to deteriorate much more quickly than that which was acid-free. Even lengthy washing of the acid-brightened calf could not completely remove this substance, which "appear[ed] to dissolve in the leather and [adhere] most tenaciously to the fibres."[77] Acids found in bleaches were another principal cause of decay associated with the coloring process. Leathers were commonly bathed in weak sulfuric acid to whiten them before coloring them, although harmless acids (e.g., formic, acetic, lactic) were equally effective and could be washed out.[78]

Binding leathers were also weakened by mechanical means. The artificial graining of leather, achieved by rolling or crushing it between heated embossing plates, not only injured the skins but was frequently done out of a desire to defraud. This process enabled the unscrupulous leather seller or binder to offer unsuspecting clients sheep, skiver, roan, and other poorer leathers as if they were morocco. Henry Evelyn Bliss drolly referred to this shoddy business practice as "a 'skin' in every sense of the word."[79] The heat used in the graining process dried the leather and reduced what strength it had, while the crushing and pounding of the plates flattened and destroyed the fibers, causing the leather to lose its elasticity.[80]

Unduly paring or overstretching leather also contributed to its deterioration. Joints pared too thin broke more quickly. J. Gordon Parker pointed out that paring away one quarter of a skin's thickness caused the leather to lose 60 percent of its total strength. The Royal Society of Arts recommended that rather than shave or pare large, thick skins to suit smaller books, one should use a small, naturally thin skin. Splitting skins horizontally, so that only the top or bottom layer was used in the binding, was also ill-advised because it cut the skin's network of fibers, weakening it considerably.[81]

Leather continued to play some role in the binding program of almost every American library, but because of its cost and frailties, few libraries used it exclusively. Leathers were chiefly recommended for books expected to receive considerable wear (e.g., fiction and juvenile titles) because they held up better than cloth under heavy use.[82] However, cloth was often considered superior to lesser-quality leathers. In 1895 the Boston Public Library was binding almost entirely in cloth, uncertain that even "good leather" was "tolerably sure to last for twenty years." While excellent leathers were still available at high prices, librarians unable to pay top dollar were better served by cloth.[83]

There is evidence that more and more libraries were turning exclusively to cloth. By 1905 the Indiana State Library followed the not uncommon practice of using leather only to match volumes in continuations (Dana puzzled that librarians used leather even to this limited extent, especially when earlier volumes in the same sets were deteriorating).[84] In 1908 the ALA's Committee on Bookbinding recommended that leather be avoided for all but the most heavily used books "until more specific points can be determined after much time and experimentation." Further indication of the lack of confidence in leather as a binding material came from the LAUK's Sound Leather Committee, which reported that many leather manufacturers "are desirous of removing the distrust which at present exists with regard to leather, and to reinstitute this article as being the standard and natural covering for books."[85]

For at least one librarian, the overtures of the leather manufacturers came too late. He wrote that since "the chemistry of leather is little understood," yet "the effect of the modern system of the treatment of binding leathers is evidently radically unsound," and "the tanner declines to be held responsible for the permanency of his wares, the conclusion appears to be irresistible that for the present the use of leather should be laid down for some cheaper and more trustworthy material." Yale's librarian agreed: "From past experience, we lean strongly to discarding the use of leather, especially of domestic origin. The cost of obtaining properly tanned leather, which will probably outlast a reasonable number of years, even if little handled, has been found almost prohibitive."[86]

Book cloths had been used as binding materials in American libraries since around 1825, just a few years after their introduction in England. Throughout the nineteenth century, English cloths were the standard in American use, and those sold by Archibald Winterbottom & Sons of Manchester, England, were very popular. In 1883 Interlaken Mills in Providence became the first U.S. company to manufacture book cloths; its plant was in Arkwright, Rhode Island. A short time thereafter, Joseph Bancroft & Son of Wilmington, Delaware, also entered the book-cloth market. An important Bancroft contribution was the development of its number 666 cloth, selected in 1908 as the standard cloth for binding government publications.[87]

In 1893 Holliston Mills of Norwood, Massachusetts, began to offer its book cloths for sale. Still, book cloth was "essentially a starch-filled muslin cloth giving a fair amount of satisfactory wear"; colors usually ran when the cloth was wet. In 1895 the Fabrikoid Company of Newburgh, New York, produced a water-resistant cloth, and soon a second company in Newark, New Jersey, began marketing a waterproof cloth under the trade name Keratol. Both types of cloth – the original and the water-resistant – were popular, particularly for rebinding, and by 1900 American-made book cloths predominated in American libraries.[88] In 1896 the Wilmington Institute (one of many libraries experimenting with various binding materials) reported its use of Bancroft's book cloth for fiction and juvenile books at a savings of twenty cents a volume over American russia; the cloth wore well and was attractive.[89]

Just as there were many leathers from which librarians might select, there were numerous book cloths. The same experimentation that took place with binding leathers also occurred with cloths as librarians sought sturdy materials that would resist decay and withstand hard use. In making their selections, librarians attempted to practice good binding economy by matching cloth quality to the value and intended use of a given book. Early book cloths were not as satisfactory as the water-resistant ones produced nearer to the turn of the century; they tended to absorb moisture, retain dust, warp, and even shrink. Water streaked or ruined them, light-colored ones dirtied easily, and they were not easily cleaned. Lightweight cloths tore and frayed, and even sturdier cloths, when used on the spines of books, did not withstand wear as well as most leathers.[90]

On the other hand, book cloths had qualities that librarians found inviting: they were not affected by heat and pollution, and they did not eventually crumble, as did almost all leathers except morocco.[91] Lamenting the shelves' decaying leather bindings, an Indiana librarian commented, "It is also apparent that even the poorest quality of binder's cloth will outlast the larger portion of all leather used in bookbinding." In Massachusetts, another librarian agreed: "A cloth binding will stand on the shelf under the influence of gas, light and superheated air for years in good condition." At the Seattle Public Library, where book cloths had replaced leather not only because of their lower cost but because they did not decay and require replacing, the librarian wrote, "The investigations of experts and the experience of libraries seem to prove that no leather now available for the binding of books will stand the disintegrating effects of time, heat, gas, and sunshine to which library books are more or less subjected."[92]

Since many book cloths lacked the durability of leather yet possessed the permanence that leathers generally lacked, it is not surprising that they were often used in different ways in a library's binding program. Cloth was good for books used infrequently, books a library wished to retain indefinitely,[93] and medium-sized and small books, which did not require the support provided by leather's greater strength.[94] After 1900, however, as binding cloths began to improve in durability and water resistance, some libraries turned to cloths for all their binding needs. By 1908 the Yale University Library bound all but its unusually valuable books or books of great beauty in cloth. In 1902 the Newark Free Public Library also had forsaken leathers in favor of an array of book cloths.[95]

Canvas and duck were strong, popular fabrics – plain, closely woven, and typically made of cotton. Duck was reputedly the more durable; canvas, slightly more attractive. Like many cloths, canvas dirtied easily and absorbed grease.[96] It also outwore leather, cost much less, and was unaffected by atmospheric problems.[97] Canvas was a frequent choice for binding large folio volumes and other heavy books.[98]

For sheer strength, duck was the librarian's best choice. Although it was repeatedly cited for its ugliness, showed dirt quickly, did not readily accept gold lettering, and clung to the books shelved on either side if it, duck was nonetheless "generally conceded to be the most durable and most economical material" available for binding.[99] Duck possessed, "like the ugly duckling of fable has for those who have eyes to see, the highest beauty, in this case, the beauty of usefulness."[100] The Boston Public Library used duck for elephant (oversized) folios, attaching straps to their backs with copper rivets so that the books could be pulled off the shelves by the straps, not by their spines. The Brooklyn YMCA Library used duck for volumes that would receive hard use, and the New Haven (Connecticut) Free Public Library bound both quartos and folios in duck. In St. Louis, duck was the material of choice for reference books and all infrequently handled materials. By 1905 the Connecticut State Library bound almost exclusively in duck, and the Library of Congress used duck whenever durability was the first quality sought.[101]

Linen and art linen (the latter was impregnated with sizing) were rugged binding cloths used in much the same way as canvas and duck. Because these fabrics frayed with hard use, they were suitable for heavier, less frequently used volumes, pamphlets, or books (e.g., novels and juvenile titles), which would be ready for the trash heap by the time their covers wore out because of the poor quality of their paper or the hard use their pages received.[102] In some cases, linen was used for the covering of a book's spine, and lighter-weight cloths for the front and back covers.[103]

These linens, like duck and canvas, were not attractive in finish and color. Nonetheless, their qualities of permanence and economy made them appealing to many librarians. In 1895 the Boston Public Library was binding almost exclusively in "grayish brown cotton duck or grayish white linen." In his annual report for 1908, Yale's librarian wrote, "At present, we are using large quantities of various kinds of linen fabrics, importing much of it from Europe. Barring books of unusual value and beauty, we incline to the use of strong and simple bindings, with clear and prominent lettering."[104]

At the second conference of the American Library Association, held in New York City in 1877, Justin Winsor spoke of a note he had seen in an English newspaper about a new binding material called buckram. Unable to locate samples, he had written to Edward B. Nicholson (then at the London Library), asking his opinion of buckram and seeking more information on this new material. Nicholson mailed samples to Winsor and gave buckram an approving report: it was "more durable for binding than leather, and not subject to certain effects that are produced on leather bindings under unfavorable conditions."

Winsor informed his colleagues that he had arranged to have some buckram imported, but Dewey cautioned that while he believed "buckram was to be the coming binding . . . a little more experience was needed before recommending it." Goat, at present, should still be the ALA's recommendation. Winsor characterized buckram as "a stout linen cloth, which, being sized and rolled through hot cylinders, becomes almost as hard as vellum." ALA members hoped that "a strong linen fabric in place of the muslin in common use would give the durability of leather without the expense"; the Co-Operation Committee was to consider this new material and report to the membership.[105]

Nicholson, one of buckram's biggest proponents, preferred this newer cloth to leathers and other cloths as well – it was sturdier, resisted wear, and was not affected by heat. It cost about 25 percent more than other cloths, and there was a 40 percent American import duty. Still, it was cheaper than half-calf. The buckram used by Nicholson and imported by Winsor was manufactured in Scotland and dyed in eight different colors.[106] (Ten years later Dewey noted that all buckram used in the U.S. was still imported; U.S. book-cloth firms did not manufacture it.)[107]

Buckram's initial glow began to dim rather quickly. Three years after his initial correspondence with Winsor, Nicholson retracted his unequivocal support of buckram. Further experience had proven that it did not hold up well under heavy use, that most colors of buckram (as well as the fabric glaze itself) faded, and that the fabric stained; he restricted his recommendation to use on large, little-used books.[108] American librarians shared Nicholson's revised opinion; through their own use of buckram they discovered that it discolored, tended to embrittle, did not readily accept lettering, and was difficult to work with.[109] While U. S. librarians continued to believe that "the great thing wanted in bookbinding is to reduce the use of animal matter to a minimum, and to extend the vegetable," buckram was not the cure-all for which librarians had hoped.[110]

Nonetheless, buckram was strong and resistant to heat and decay; it had its uses and its users. The Astor Library of New York City found that its linen buckram wore better than duck. Buckram was better than sheep for binding law materials (Bancroft's number 666 cloth was also called "legal buckram"), and the Detroit Public Library used buckram for the books expected to receive the most wear. The New Orleans Public Library bound less-used titles in buckram.[111] There is considerable evidence that buckram had improved significantly in quality by 1900. After that date, a number of libraries (including the libraries of Johns Hopkins University and the Cooper Union, the Worcester County Law Library, the Iowa State Library, and the public libraries of Washington, D.C., Brockton, Massachusetts, East Orange, New Jersey, Grand Rapids, Providence, St. Louis, and Detroit) begin to report their satisfaction with buckram bindings.[112] By 1909 the ALA's Committee on Bookbinding had given buckram its recommendation for use on large, occasionally used reference volumes.[113]

Art canvas was another fairly heavy book cloth. Although secondary in weight to canvas and duck, it had the advantage of a much more attractive finish. Art canvas was used for the same types of materials as was buckram (less-used, light- to medium-weight volumes).[114] The public libraries of Washington, D.C., Newark, and Seattle used art canvas, as did the Indiana State Library. The grade used at the Seattle Public Library, manufactured by Interlaken Mills, may have been a finer one; used to bind fiction, it was reported to be "stronger than leather, more durable than any but the best."[115] Art vellum was a much lighter book cloth, again with an attractive finish. It was often used for smaller, lightly used materials and was part of the binding programs at the Springfield City Library and the Washington, D.C., Public Library.[116]

Yet another popular lighter-weight fabric, imperial morocco cloth, was typically used in full bindings for lightly used titles or for the sides of more heavily used volumes with leather spines. It was used in the Newark, New Haven, East Orange, and Seattle public libraries, and recommended by the ALA's Committee on Bookbinding.[117] Holliston cloth (manufactured by the Holliston Company) and Keratol were two more lightweight book cloths, also used for smaller, lighter books or to cover the sides of larger books.[118] (The Holliston Company manufactured a range of book cloths, including a buckram and other heavier-grade material.[119])

Out of this extensive experimentation with various binding materials emerged an interest in setting standards that librarians could require binders to follow. The Congressional Committee on Printing sought the assistance of librarians, long unhappy with sheepskin as a binding material for federal publications, in identifying a better solution. In its report for 1908, the ALA's Committee on Bookbinding described the meeting held on 1 June of that year in Washington, D.C., to discuss the binding of government documents – the meeting that resulted in the designation of Bancroft's number 666 cloth, or "legal buckram," as the fabric of choice. The meeting was called by the secretary of the Printing Investigation Committee. Present were the chairmen of the ALA's committees on federal relations and bookbinding, three representatives from the Library of Congress, the director of the Washington, D.C., Public Library, the public printer, the superintendent of documents, the chief of the Bureau of Standards, and other government experts. Tests performed by the bureau on twenty-three book cloths manufactured by three companies were reviewed. Each cloth had been subjected to "very severe physical and chemical tests," then ranked on how well it withstood them. The qualities on which the materials were judged included "tensile strength, the wear received in handling or shelving, the ability of the cloth to withstand folding, color, and the attack of water bugs."[120]

Three cloths emerged as nearly equal in quality, but the librarians present at the meeting agreed that one of the three was superior to the others. The Committee on Bookbinding was certain that this cloth (unnamed in its report) would be the one chosen to replace sheepskin for binding federal documents. Further, the committee concluded that "the result of this conference will be more beneficial and more far-reaching than at first appears. . . . Not only will government documents be clothed respectably, but all library bindings where cloth is used will be immeasurably benefited. Heretofore, book cloths have had to be accepted more or less on trust. As soon as the specifications have been formulated, librarians can bring immense pressure to bear on manufacturers to give us cloths that will stand severe tests."[121]

Less than a year after its report, in March 1909, the Committee on Bookbinding used the pages of *Library Journal* to print the book-cloth standards that had since been developed and published by the U.S. Bureau of Standards. Librarians were encouraged to supply binders with copies of these standards and to insist that the cloths used to rebind their books meet them. For a small fee, the bureau's personnel would perform tests on samples forwarded by librarians and determine whether the cloths met the standard. A pamphlet describing the tests to which the samples would be subjected was available free of charge.[122]

During this formative period in American library bookbinding, few libraries bound every volume in the same material. Instead, attempts were made to match the material to the use a given book might receive, and experimentation with different leathers and cloths was common. While top-quality leather was almost unbeatable in terms of permanence and durability, book cloths gained the field as the nineteenth century progressed, because of their low cost and ability to survive in overheated library rooms. As book cloths improved in quality and as standards for their manufacture were established by the U.S. government, American librarians were free to turn their attentions to the binding process itself.

Chapter 8

Hand Binding

During the late nineteenth century, libraries did the greater part of their binding by hand. In contrast, publishers did their binding by machine, except in the case of certain very fine volumes. In choosing from the many options for constructing and sewing bindings for books that arrived in paper covers or required rebinding, librarians focused on strength, solidity, and flexibility, the three most important qualities any binding could possess.[1]

Ainsworth Spofford gave a concise description of taking a book apart (also known as taking it to pieces, taking it down, pulling it, or disbinding it) in preparation for rebinding. If the tapes or cords were not laced into the boards, and if the book was bound flexibly, with the sewing supports resting above and against the backs of the signatures rather than recessed into the paper, the cover could be pulled off with ease. Otherwise it was necessary to cut the volume at the joints (the junctures of the book's spine and its boards) in order to remove the covers. If the leather covering the spine was glued to the backs of the signatures, it was soaked in water until it separated from the text block. Next, the signatures were taken apart by cutting the cords or tapes to which they were sewn, and all threads and glue that remained were removed from them. Finally, the book was pressed for about eight hours. Intermediate steps often included mending and collating the pages.[2] Then the volume was ready to be rebound.

Librarians discussed and documented every aspect of hand binding: collating, folding, sewing;[3] the procedures of endpaper construction, gluing and lining, rounding and backing the spine of the book,[4] cutting and fitting the boards,[5] working and attaching the headbands,[6] and burnishing, sprinkling, or gilding the edges;[7] and finally, covering the boards with leather, cloth, and paper, or (for casebound volumes) case making and casing-in.[8] In the press, the most popular topics were guarding, sewing, attaching the text block to the boards, and the matter of hollow versus tight backs.

"Guarding" meant pasting a strip of cloth or paper around the inner edge of a sheet, plate, illustration, or signature to provide a hinge that could be sewn. In good library binding, the first and last signatures of the book (the ones that received the greatest strain in opening and closing) were routinely guarded; the ALA Bookbinding Committee recommended this practice.[9] All signatures that were damaged or broken at the back were also to be guarded before being resewn.[10]

There were two ways of attaching a single sheet, plate, or map within a binding. Sometimes, the inner edge of the sheet was simply pasted, or "tipped," onto the page immediately following it. Not surprisingly, librarians objected to this practice; the sheet did not become an integral part of the bound volume and could easily be detached and lost.[11] A better method was to guard the sheet or illustration as described above, wrap the guard around the adjoining signature, and sew through the guard when the signature was sewn.[12] Instead of guarding plates and illustrations, some librarians had binders mount them on muslin, cambric, or other lightweight fabric, especially if they were folded. The inner edge of the cloth could then be wrapped around the adjoining signature, just as a guard would have been.[13] Another approach, used with fine, valuable, or heavily illustrated books, was to remove all plates and bind them together separately.[14]

Of all the steps in hand binding, sewing was considered the most important, for it was the sewing that held the sheets and signatures together as a unit. As Spofford wrote, "No book can be thoroughly well-bound if the sewing is slighted in any degree."[15] Similarly, Cyril Davenport advised that "when a book was properly sewn with perfect bands ... it was practically ensured from harm for all time. The leather of the back might wear away, but the bands would still hold the book together."[16] To a great extent, the sewing determined the book's strength and flexibility; the sheets were to be "firmly and permanently secured, and yet the volume when bound must open flexibly and freely."[17] Strong, durable thread was critical. Irish linen was the best, and Hayes and Barbour were the two most popular manufacturers.[18]

Librarians and binders attempted to suit the sewing style to the book in hand. The book's weight, paper, and covering material (leather, cloth) were all considered by Gilbert D. Emerson, a Philadelphia binder who served libraries across America; further, this "Representative American Library Binder" was willing to take sewing instructions from his clients – whether always to oversew, never to oversew, to oversew as a last resort, and so forth. In its in-house bindery, the Peoria (Illinois) Public Library also made sewing decisions to suit the characteristics of the individual book. A volume's size and weight were considered in determining both sewing technique and the number of cords or tapes to employ.[19]

Hand binding called for sewing the signatures of a volume onto cords or tapes, either "all along" ("one sheet on") or "two on." In the first (and favored) approach, a single thread was used to sew each signature all along – that is, through the fold, from top to bottom. In contrast, when a book was sewn two on, two signatures shared a single thread that alternately ran through one and into the other. Clearly, signatures sewn two on had half as many stitches as signatures stitched all along.[20] The all-along technique was more expensive but resulted in stronger sewing.[21] A book that was sewn all along and whose stitching was still sound when its spine or cover wore out could simply be rebacked or recased, saving the library the costs of taking the book apart and resewing it.[22] In rebacking, the material covering the spine was removed and replaced, but the covers themselves were retained. Recasing, or recovering, called for removing the text block from the old, worn case and placing it in a new one. While sewing all along was the norm in quality binding, some librarians advocated sewing very small or slender volumes two on in order to reduce the swell that sewing all along created at the spines of such books.[23] The ALA Committee on Bookbinding recommended that every book be sewn all along.[24]

In addition to sewing through the fold, it was fairly common to overcast the first and last signatures of a book to strengthen them against the volume's opening and closing. Sometimes a muslin guard was also applied.[25] Overcasting or oversewing[26] was sometimes employed throughout an entire volume if the paper was so poor, or the signatures' backs so worn, that they could not withstand sewing through the folds.[27] The backs of the injured signatures were sliced off; small groups of leaves were then seamed (sometimes using a sewing machine) or overcast together before being sewn as "signatures" onto cords or tapes.[28]

Even so, any oversewn book was somewhat inflexible and difficult to open. Binder Cedric Chivers recommended this technique for books in which the paper's grain "runs up and down the page, making the book weak in its fold for sewing," but this view is the opposite of modern thinking, which holds that a book whose paper grain is vertical has the potential for maximum flexibility and least strain on the binding, making it an inappropriate candidate for oversewing. In any case, once a book was oversewn, seldom did enough inner margin remain to permit another rebinding.[29] This made oversewing appropriate only when the book was dispensable or unlikely to receive much wear. An exception was Chivers' method of oversewing, which left the book in signatures rather than slicing it into sheets. Each signature was then sewn through holes punched diagonally near its inner edge; the spacing of the holes varied from signature to adjoining signature. Popular opinion held that Chivers' technique resulted in flexible and unusually strong bindings.[30]

The signatures of books bound by hand were sewn onto either cords or tapes. The ends of these sewing supports then became the means of affixing the text block to the boards that formed the book's front and back covers. The number of cords or tapes varied, depending on the volume's height, thickness, and weight (the larger or heavier the volume, the greater the number).[31] There was not perfect agreement on the proper ratio of supports to book size, but in general, 16mo and smaller volumes required two; 12mo, three; octavos, four; and quartos and folios, four to six.[32] The Royal Society of Arts Committee on Leather for Bookbinding and the ALA Committee on Bookbinding prescribed no fewer than four cords or tapes, regardless of the book's size; five were recommended for very large volumes.[33]

Sewing onto raised cords (which formed little horizontal ridges, called bands, across the book's back) was favored for fine leather bindings. Binders and bookmen like Joseph W. Zaehnsdorf, Douglas Cockerell, F. J. Soldan, and William Matthews cited this style for maximum strength and flexibility, although it cost three to four times as much as sewing onto recessed cords or tapes. Using this technique, it was not necessary to damage the backs of the signatures with sawcuts, as when sewing on recessed cords. In general, sewing on cords was considered by some to give a book greater strength than did sewing on tapes.[34]

Recessed-cord (sawn-in, sunken) sewing was a popular method of the time. Three, four, or five furrows, or kerfs, were sawn into the backs of the sections; then the cord and some glue were sunk into these slots. It was important to make the cuts no deeper than the thickness of the cords themselves, lest they damage the folds or appear obvious when the book was opened, or lest the glue seep through them into the text block. Sewing on sunken cords sacrificed a certain amount of the binding's over-all flexibility.[35]

Many librarians achieved flexibility while avoiding the high cost of raised cords and the injury associated with sunken cords by sewing the signatures onto linen tapes about five-eighths of an inch wide. Rather than being either raised or sunken, these tapes lay flat across the signatures' backs. Since the thread simply passed across the tapes rather than actually encircling them (it wrapped around the supports in raised-cord sewing), it was not considered quite as strong as either of the cord methods.[36]

Flexible sewing ended with lacing the ends of the supports into the front and back boards that formed the book's covers. In its report on leather for bookbinding, the Royal Society of Arts cautioned that if the cords or tapes were not properly laced into the boards, "the attachment of the boards to the book [would be] almost entirely dependent on the strength of the leather."[37] Slits were cut in the boards; then the ends of the supports were laced into the grooves, frayed out, and hammered flat so that they would not show once the boards were covered.[38] Another approach was to use split boards and glue the ends of the cords or tapes into the slotted area along each board's inner edge.[39]

There was enormous discussion, but no clear agreement, about the superiority of either loose (hollow) or tight backs, or spine coverings. Cedric Chivers counseled that "tight or loose backs depend wholly on the paper, thick spongy paper being best in a loose back, which should also be used for large books. Thin volumes [are] best in tight backs." American bookbinder Gilbert Emerson, however, recommended the tight back for large, thick books. "In smaller books," he continued, "the tight back tends to break down the centre of the back, with frequent opening."[40]

In tight-back binding, the material (leather, cloth) covering the spine of the volume was glued directly onto it. In loose-back binding, a space existed between the spine and the covering material, which was attached to the text block at the joints. Tight backs provided greater support to the text block and were good for "hard-worked reference books, and for permanent bindings on books in use"; they were generally found on books that were sewn on raised cords. Volumes with tight backs opened easily, but the additional labor required made tight-back binding considerably more expensive than loose-back. In addition, extended use could cause a glued back to crack prematurely.[41] Loose-back binding provided flexibility for books sewn on recessed cords or tapes. As cloth bindings grew in popularity, so did loose backs.[42] The Jersey City (New Jersey) Public Library appears to have used a hybrid style that reportedly combined the strength of tight backs with the flexibility of loose backs. First a piece of thin leather was pasted onto the back of the text block for strength; then the cover was applied in loose-back fashion, ensuring that its back and the lettering thereon would not crack.[43]

The cost of library binding (of which labor was the largest part) was of considerable general interest. During the late 1800s, librarians asked to name their profession probably followed Melvil Dewey's example and called it "library economy"; certainly, there was considerable information exchange about the cost of everything from paste to encyclopedias to shelving. Almost every public librarian recorded in his or her annual report the number of volumes bound that year and either the total cost of the work or the cost per volume[44]:

Library	Year	Cost per Volume
Brooklyn Public Library	1905	$ .435
Brooklyn Public Library	1906	$ .50
Brooklyn Public Library	1909	$ .64

Library	Year	Cost per Volume
Cleveland Public Library	1878	$ .50 (approx.)
Cleveland Public Library	1887	$ .58
Detroit Public Library	1887	$ .57
Jacksonville (Florida) Public Library	1908	$ .42
New Haven (Connecticut) Free Public Library	1901	$ .25
New Haven Free Public Library	1904	$ .30
Queens Borough (New York) Public Library	1910	$ .57
St. Joseph (Missouri) Free Public Library	1910	$ .505
St. Louis Public Library	1891	$ .37
Seattle Public Library	1908	$ .69

It is probably fair to say that the cost of binding the "average" library book around the turn of the century was fifty cents. In some cases, variables that explained higher or lower costs per volume were supplied (Brooklyn's average cost in 1909 included periodical volumes; New Haven's 1901 cost was for binding inexpensively in imperial morocco cloth). It is not difficult, however, to add to the factors of volume size and materials cost certain other details that contributed to cost differentials.

Rebinding cost more than the initial binding of a book issued in paper covers, largely because of the labor involved in taking the book apart. The price of labor in a given locale, or of labor in an in-house bindery versus that in a commercial one, was an important item; transportation costs may or may not have been included in a library's per-volume cost. Larger libraries with higher volumes often negotiated better prices, and binding techniques (flexible cords, recessed cords, tapes, oversewing) were differently priced.[45] D. V. R. Johnston of the New York State Library obtained binding in duck at twenty-five to ninety cents per volume, in buckram at forty to sixty-five cents per volume, and in half levant morocco at seventy-five cents to $2.50 per volume.[46]

The Jacksonville (Florida) Public Library, in a single year, experimented with three different binders. Their costs for novels ranged from thirty-five to forty-five to fifty cents per volume. The New Haven Free Public Library could bind in leather (which type is not specified) for fifty cents per volume or in cloth for twenty-two cents. The Seattle Public Library bound fiction in-house for sixty-nine cents a volume. While Cedric Chivers in New York City and the New York Public Library would have bound fiction for Seattle at fifty cents and fifty-three cents, respectively, the transportation charges and the additional time required ruled out these options. In 1898 the bindery staff at the University of Michigan Library bound in leather for about $1.04 per volume and in cloth for thirty-five cents per volume; they appear to have used these two treatments equally.[47]

When books were purchased abroad in paper covers, it was quite common to have them bound there before being shipped to the United States, largely because of the cost savings. Among the libraries following this practice were the Chicago and Boston Public Libraries and those at the Johns Hopkins University and the University of Pennsylvania.[48] Some libraries went so far as to ship domestically purchased books abroad for binding.[49] The rule of thumb was that high-caliber binding (generally in half morocco) done abroad cost substantially less than similar American work – often about half as much.[50]

Perhaps European binders recognized the value of their American market and increased their charges as time passed. In 1902 the University of Pennsylvania reported that the expense of binding done abroad was similar to that of domestic binding, but a savings continued to lie in the preparation time the library's staff was spared. A year later, both the Newark (New Jersey) Free Public Library and the Salem (Massachusetts) Public Library reported paying more for British binding, which they nonetheless found a good buy because of the higher quality of the work. "Special attention," wrote the Salem librarian, "is given to the sewing and while the first cost is somewhat more than for copies bought in this country in cloth binding, yet the greater strength of the binding gives the book so much longer a life that it is a real economy in the end." The Newark library staff believed that their books, bound in half pig by Cedric Chivers, would last twice as long as books bound domestically.[51]

American libraries relied on domestic commercial binders for most of their work. Because of the quantity of books to be handled, even large libraries with in-house binderies often sent out a portion of their business.[52] In some cases, the binderies chosen were located in the same geographic areas as the libraries using their services; in others, libraries shipped their books a goodly distance in the name of securing better work or better prices. There was also significant concern about the danger of fire at commercial binderies. The New York Yacht Club Library carried $10,000 worth of insurance "as part of the risk attaching to material at the binders." In 1901 the John Crerar Library (Chicago) had cause to file a claim against a similar policy it held; $803.71 worth of books, periodical volumes, and pamphlets were lost in a fire at the bindery, Ringer and Hertzberg. Although the claim was honored, there was no compensation for the staff costs associated with reordering the lost materials, and many books could not be replaced. At the Woburn (Massachusetts) Public Library, the binder nightly placed any unfinished valuable books in a nearby fireproof safe.[53]

In 1906 the ALA Committee on Bookbinding conducted a study of libraries' experiences with in-house binding. Forty-one of the forty-four questionnaires sent out were returned; ten of the respondents operated library binderies.[54] Among the institutions running their own binding operations were the public libraries of Boston, New York, Cleveland, Milwaukee, Seattle, Pittsburgh, Philadelphia, Newark, Washington, D.C., Kansas City (Missouri), Minneapolis, Peoria, Detroit, and Easton and Braddock, Pennsylvania;[55] the New York Mercantile Library; the New York State Library; the Library of Congress; the Astor Library (New York City); and the libraries of Bowdoin College and the University of Michigan.[56]

The histories of the binderies at the Boston Public Library, the Newark Free Public Library, and the Seattle Public Library provide interesting examples of activity in large, medium, and small libraries. During the twenty-five year period between 1876 and 1901, the Boston Public Library's bindery changed size and focus several times. In 1876 it was a small in-house operation, binding perhaps $5,000 worth of work in a given year. In 1878 the library's binding won a gold medal at the Paris Universal Exhibition; there were fourteen employees binding almost fifteen thousand volumes that year. In 1887, with little explanation, the bindery's staff was reduced to two men, two women, and an apprentice; all but the most valuable books were sent out to a contract binder, who reportedly performed quality work more efficiently for less money. Gradually, however, the bindery staff grew again; in 1902 there were twenty-seven employees, and the intent was to bind everything in the library's shop. A few years later, even more staff (supposedly temporary) were added to eliminate large binding backlogs.[57]

In 1891 the Newark Free Public Library had an in-house bindery that was considered capable of binding more cheaply than a commercial shop. By 1902 some of the library's work was done in-house and some was sent out; there was too much binding for the library's plant to handle. In 1904 the library turned over the management of its bindery to contract binder Gilbert Emerson, who sent William Rademaekers, "a skilled binder," to serve as foreman. Two years later, when Emerson sold out to Rademaekers, the library contracted with him to continue operating its bindery.[58]

The Seattle Public Library opened its bindery in August 1896; at that time, the library owned about eleven thousand volumes. By 1899 the bindery had assumed other preservation work, including mounting pictures, binding pamphlets, and mounting maps. All book signatures were sewn onto tapes, and the tapes laced into the boards. Seattle was so confident in the superior quality of its work that it determined to go even further with its operation in the coming year by purchasing popular titles in sheets and binding them in-house.[59]

Some people believed that in-house binderies were cost-effective only for large libraries, or if a number of libraries joined together to form a cooperative. In some cases, an institution justified operating its own bindery by taking in additional work from other libraries. D. V. R. Johnston of the New York State Library felt that any organization with less than $2,500 worth of work per year would certainly lose money on an in-house bindery; even business of $2,500 to $3,000 per year might be questionable. Later, however, Johnston revised his thinking: if a library used inexpensive methods and materials, it might operate profitably with annual costs of just above $1,000. The University of Michigan Library, despite warnings that institutions generating less than $3,000 in binding a year were better served by contract binders, opened a library bindery in 1896 in anticipation of about $1,800 worth of work.[60]

Several libraries recorded the costs associated with setting up their binderies. The Easton Public Library spent $177.30 on equipment and training; clearly, this small library ran a less elaborate shop than did many larger institutions. The Minneapolis Public Library, in purchasing largely second-hand equipment, spent $626.64; similarly, the University of Michigan Library bought $725.00 worth of equipment. The Virginia State Library estimated that about $1,100.00 would be needed to outfit its bindery; the most expensive piece of hardware was a Seybold Monarch Cutter, priced at $790.00.[61]

Melvil Dewey argued that a library's best possible arrangement was a commercially operated in-house bindery, similar to the one at the Newark Free Public Library, run first by Emerson and then by Rademaekers. Dewey believed that a contract binder could run a bindery more cheaply and more efficiently than could the library. Additionally, the librarian would be spared the details of staffing and management. Charles Cutter employed a binder to whom he leased space in the Boston Athenaeum and who bound for the Athenaeum and other libraries as well. The binder owned his own machinery, and Cutter found him efficient. In a slightly different arrangement, the New York Circulating Library paid a binder and an assistant $1,000 a year and also furnished them with space, tools, and materials. In turn, the binder contracted to bind at least one hundred volumes a week, or an average of 425 a month. The Pittsburgh Carnegie Library also provided space on its premises for a contract binder. Eighteen workmen bound for both the main library and the six branches, which in 1908 had 179,506 and 100,582 volumes, respectively, and generated 13,844 and 12,371 binds and rebinds.[62]

One of the many perceived benefits of an in-house library bindery was cost savings. Justin Winsor, while director of the Boston Public Library, estimated a savings of twenty-five percent. William T. Peoples, librarian of the Mercantile Library of New York, doubled that to fifty percent. Other libraries were more conservative. The Braddock Carnegie Free Library found its own work a little cheaper than commercial binding, as did the Cleveland, Minneapolis, Newark, and Washington, D.C., public libraries, and the library of the University of Michigan. The most dramatic savings were reported by the Easton Public Library, which found it could bind in cloth with paper sides for four cents a volume, versus the thirty-five cents a commercial binder charged.[63]

Local library binderies held many attractions other than economy. Often, higher-quality binding was obtained through better control of materials, methods, and workmen (Justin Winsor noted how easy it was for commercial binders to produce handsome exterior work whose poor construction was well concealed.[64]) Books spent less time off the shelf, because they were sent to the bindery only when the binders were ready to perform the work and returned immediately thereafter.[65] Further, books never left the premises; thus, even while in the bindery, they were available to readers for emergency consultation.[66] The library saved freight costs, and the books were spared the wear and tear of transportation. At home, librarians could safeguard their materials against fire and other disasters; at commercial binderies, they lacked this important control.[67]

For many years the Newark Free Public Library used its bindery to experiment with binding techniques and to test different materials. As early as 1903, John Cotton Dana and his colleagues began collecting materials for a comprehensive exhibit of binding styles, materials, and tools – an exhibit whose authority would reach far beyond Newark. Samples were solicited from manufacturers and sellers of leather, imitation leather, boards, thread, glue, endpapers, and so forth. In the library bindery, dummies designed to show the many steps involved in bookbinding were produced, and libraries throughout the country sent samples of their own work for inclusion. A few examples of art binding from New York dealers and collectors were added, and binding tools were gathered. Publishers' edition bindings were to be contrasted with hand construction, and Newark wished to show, from its own years of work, "our partial successes and complete failures." Among the institutions contributing to the exhibit were the public libraries of Binghamton (New York), Boston, Cincinnati, Cleveland, Detroit, New Haven, New York, Springfield (Massachusetts), and St. Louis, the Columbia College Library, and the Library of Congress. Manufacturers included Joseph Bancroft & Sons, Holliston Mills, and the Keratol Company (book cloths); Weis Manufacturing Company (magazine binders); and the publishers Houghton Mifflin and Charles Scribner's Sons.[68]

The exhibit opened on 4 February 1905, in the library itself. The room offered 3,000 square feet of space and housed several tables, ten flat-top glass cases (three feet by six feet), and 150 linear feet of seven-foot tall screens for hanging photos. Invitations and advertisements placed in the local newspapers drew binders, binding collectors, staff from neighboring libraries, library journalists, newspaper people, and the general public. Ernest Dressel North presented an address on binding. The library prepared both a leaflet describing the exhibit and a binding bibliography. During the two weeks the exhibit was on view, it was visited by 2,580 persons. But perhaps its influence in Newark was small as compared with its impact during the next two years, as it toured the libraries of America.[69]

After the Newark show, the exhibit was packed up and sent to other libraries wishing to display it; included were the public libraries of Boston, Lansing (Michigan), Madison (Wisconsin), North Adams, Northampton, Springfield, and Worcester (Massachusetts), Queens, Washington, D.C., and Westerly (Rhode Island). The exhibit traveled as far west as Wisconsin and as far south as Virginia, "returning twice in that time to be refreshed and brought up to date." All in all, it visited thirty-four different cities whose libraries had only to pay associated transportation costs and a small fee of $2.50, which was used to keep the exhibit in good condition. On at least one occasion, when the show was on display in the Educational Museum of Teachers College of Columbia University, Dana himself lectured in conjunction with the exhibit.[70]

Often, libraries displaying the exhibit combined it with other special events designed to promote an interest in binding. At the annual meeting of the Western Massachusetts Library Club in 1905, the exhibit was coupled with papers and addresses on the theme "bookbinding in its various forms"; a staff member from a local library presented "a practical demonstration in book repairing." In Lansing, Michigan, the exhibit was "studied with much interest and profit by local binders, book-lovers, and others. Two evenings were given up to informal talks and explanations by some of our leading binders."[71]

Nineteenth-century binders, in addition to practicing their craft, often developed manuals. There were about a half-dozen such books in use during this period, chiefly authored by British binders. In addition, there were several guides that contained some useful advice about materials and techniques, but unlike the manuals, they covered little of the mechanics of binding. W. J. Eden Crane's *Book-Binding for Amateurs* was recommended by D. V. R. Johnston of the New York State Library, as was Joseph Zaehnsdorf's *The Art of Bookbinding*. Both were true textbooks; well-illustrated, they described tools and materials and covered every step in the binding process, from folding to finishing. Some librarians used James B. Nicholson's *A Manual of the Art of Bookbinding*, published mid-century; Nicholson had copied heavily from a manual by British binder and printer John Hannett, *Bibliopegia; or, the Art of Bookbinding*.[72]

Douglas Cockerell's *Bookbinding and the Care of Books: A Text-Book for Bookbinders and Librarians*, also quite popular, was given an excellent review in *Library Journal* the year it was published. The author's "Note on Bookbinding," while much briefer, was also excellent and was widely disseminated in this country, largely through the efforts of the ALA's Committee on Bookbinding.[73] Finally, George Stephen and Henry T. Coutts' *Manual of Library Bookbinding* was another staple, especially useful in that it described hand and machine bookbinding in equal detail.[74]

Binding for Small Libraries, from the ALA's Committee on Bookbinding, was one of several shorter guides to binding that lacked the specificity of the manuals but nonetheless contained useful information for the librarian wishing to better acquaint himself or herself with binding issues and methods. Dana's *Notes on Bookbinding for Libraries* also fell into this category (it briefly summarized much of Cockerell's and Zaehnsdorf's work, omitting much detail; this is not surprising, since Dana was a library administrator, not a binder). Similarly, there were Matthews' *Modern Bookbinding Practically Considered* and the efforts of two binders, Gilbert Emerson (*Bookbinding for Libraries*) and Louis H. Kinder (*Formulas for Bookbinders*). The latter is an interesting conglomeration of recipes for paste, glue, glair, shellac, oils of all kinds, petroleum jelly, varnishes, and grease removers.[75]

Turn-of-the-century binders and binding experts were not entirely faceless. Henry Evelyn Bliss wrote, "It is in the best interests of librarianship that a higher class of bookbinders should be trained in approved methods of library binding, that they should find it profitable to make a specialty of this branch of the business, and that in this higher grade of work the spirit of the true craftsman and artisan should be fostered apart from the meaner forms of competition." There were several binders, and at least one library administrator, whose work showed that they cared for quality; the frequency with which they are mentioned in the journals and reports of contemporary librarians is further evidence of the confidence their work inspired.

While himself not a binder, John Cotton Dana was one of the most influential figures of the time in this area. At one time the director of the Denver Public Library and the Springfield (Massachusetts) City Library Association, Dana did his most noteworthy work while the librarian at the Newark Free Public Library. Under his direction, the library's bindery experimented with a variety of materials and techniques, employed two of America's best contract binders (Emerson and Rademaekers), and prepared a superb binding exhibit that traveled throughout the country, educating librarians and the public alike. It was Dana who in 1904 requested that the ALA Council appoint "a committee of five members, to investigate the subjects of publishers' bindings, book papers, leathers and binding methods and processes, and to report thereon to members of the Association by means of bulletins, etc."; this was, of course, the Committee on Bookbinding. When the committee was appointed in 1906, Dana was asked to chair it, but he declined; he was writing a book on the topic. Still, the committee relied heavily upon his research and conclusions, and indeed determined that it would conduct research in separate but complementary areas, as "no good purpose would be served by duplicating his work." Several years later, the committee's booklet *Binding for Small Libraries* simply referred readers to Dana's book in some instances.[76]

In 1905 Dana began collecting data on the "qualities and characteristics of library bookbinding" in order to write a book. He used a questionnaire and sought samples of bindings, both good and poor. Dana's book was published in 1906, to generally favorable reviews. Bliss characterized it as "concise and so correct," noting that it contained "many briefer restatements from the Society's report." He criticized only its brevity, the appropriateness of a chapter on the poor quality of paper, and some data about the lifespan of cloth bindings. Conversely, George Stosskopf, an Illinois binder, praised the chapter on paper. In his opinion, Dana had done what Zaehnsdorf, Cockerell, the Royal Society of Arts, and the LAUK's Sound Leather Committee had failed to do–that is, acknowledge the major role that poor-quality paper played in the deterioration of library materials.[77]

American colleague Margaret Wright Brown also liked Dana's book, which went into a second edition in 1910 that added chapters on magazine binders, lettering and numbering the backs of books, covering books, and binding equipment. Writing in *Library World*, a British reviewer described *Notes on Bookbinding for Libraries* as "an admirable summary of the work done by the Society of Arts Committee, Mr. Douglas Cockerell, Mr. Cedric Chivers, and the Sound Leather Committee of the Library Association," and noted that Dana had also added "some special American experience." He criticized Dana for recommending bindings too good for books typically printed on very poor paper; "a librarian's business is to see that the expenditure on the shell is kept within reasonable bounds, and that money is not thrown away upon husks which simply have to shield for a brief period a kernel devoid of vitality or interest."[78]

Dana advanced the theory that the true cost of a binding must be figured as a ratio between cost and the number of times the book circulated before it was so worn it had to be discarded. This idea was widely accepted, and it promoted an interest in stronger bindings. The work done in the Newark library's bindery was also broadly emulated as a result of *Notes*, Dana's lectures and writings, the binding lessons provided by Rademaekers, and the traveling exhibit. Many libraries reported that they were binding in the Newark styles.

His traveling exhibit completed and his book published, Dana joined the ALA's Committee on Bookbuying and worked on such issues as publishers' reinforced library bindings.[79] He wrote and lectured on binding and developed a series of binding lessons offered by Rademaekers of the Newark bindery; the techniques taught were those described in *Notes on Bookbinding for Libraries*.[80] Dana was one of Cedric Chivers' champions during the latter's disputes with a New York City binders' union.[81]

Cedric Chivers, a British binder, operated a plant in Bath; he was the first English employer to adopt an eight-hour work day. Chivers pioneered research into the causes of the deterioration of book materials (leather, paper); he also developed some exceptional binding techniques for library volumes.[82] In 1905 Chivers opened a branch of his Bath bindery in the United States – on Fulton Street in Brooklyn. Before that, librarians had shipped their books to him for binding in England; with the Brooklyn plant in operation, even more availed themselves of the unique patented oversewing technique he used in rebinding. Chivers's method was praised by contemporary librarians as flexible and "uncommonly strong."[83] His manner of inserting hinges (either linen or leather) into split boards rather than simply sewing them to the first and last signatures of the book added further strength to his bindings, as did his use of tight backs (half pigskin was a favorite material).[84]

One of Chivers's most popular services was binding from the sheets. Rather than buying books in publishers' edition bindings, librarians instead ordered them from Chivers in his patented, strong duro-flexile binding. In 1908 when the ALA's Committee on Bookbuying began to promote the sale of "good books" by preparing reports on them and mailing the reports "to the publishers, to Mr. Cedric Chivers, and to the following journals: *ALA Booklist*, *Library Journal*, *Public Libraries*, *Publishers' Weekly*," it seems clear that the number of libraries ordering their books bound from the sheets by Chivers was great enough to warrant alerting him to new titles he might consider stocking.[85] Chivers also promoted his technique of vellucent binding (applying thin, transparent sheets of vellum over existing covers) as an approach to preserving and sealing crumbling leather volumes, but with little success.[86]

Bliss commended Chivers on his efforts to bring better binding methods, more durable binding materials, and better-skilled workmanship to American shores. Chivers was one of a dozen binders recommended by Indiana librarians, and Rademaekers was reportedly attempting "to make his work a close second to Chivers." Among the public libraries for which

Chivers bound were those of Brooklyn, East Orange (New Jersey), Haverhill (Massachusetts), Newark, Queens, and St. Louis.[87] Chivers was also an avid speaker and writer. In 1905 he addressed the Western Massachusetts Library Club on "The Principles of Technical Binding"; later that year he crossed the Atlantic and delivered a speech on "the exceedingly varied qualities of paper, or the material that went under such name" before the twenty-eighth conference of the Library Association. He spoke before the New York Library Club (the topic was relations between librarians and binders), and at the ALA's Bretton Woods conference in 1909, again on the topic of book papers. His booklet *The Paper of Lending Library Books* was published in New York by Baker and Taylor around 1910, and he himself published a catalog of Chivers bookbindings shown at the St. Louis Exhibition in 1904. The catalog included decorative bindings, vellucent bindings, and suggestions for shelving and preserving heavy books.[88]

It is not surprising that a businessman as expansive, successful, and self-aggrandizing as Cedric Chivers might provoke controversy. Perhaps one of the most interesting events surrounding him was the labor dispute in which the International Brotherhood of Bookbinders embroiled him in 1908. At this time, Chivers held many New York City binding contracts. A local "bookbinders' organization" reported to the city's board of aldermen that Chivers was shipping books to Bath for rebinding and thus violating New York State law, which required that the work be done by U.S. citizens. In response, the board issued a resolution: "'Resolved, That [th]is be an instruction from this Board that no further moneys be paid for the libraries appropriate for bookbinding, except such work as has been performed in accordance with the statute above quoted.'" One witness gave a deposition that he had asked Chivers to have the binding done in New York City to provide work for American citizens, but Chivers had declined, as work done in Bath was more profitable for him, owing to the cheaper wages.[89]

In the very next issue of *Library Journal*, an editorial described these recent events as "the onslaught of the unions upon Mr. Chivers," commended Chivers's work, and found him within the law. At that time, Chivers's Brooklyn business employed eighty persons and claimed five hundred libraries across America as customers. His volume of business was so great that the New York plant could not handle it all, and one quarter was sent to Bath for completion. The editor continued, "The statement of Mr. Chivers in the present number tells the other side of the story and corrects a number of misstatements."[90]

In his piece "The Other Side of the Bookbinding Controversy," Chivers expressed a fair amount of justified indignation. He pointed out that all but four of the "eighty hands" on Fulton Street were American citizens. The shop was an open one, and some employees belonged to the International Brotherhood of Bookbinders. Chivers continued, "The conditions under which my workshops are conducted, with regard to hours and wages, are second to none in advantages to the workers. . . . My improved methods of work and better materials are the basis of practically a new business in this city, and I repeat, there is today more bookbinding being done here because of my establishment, and not less, as is alleged."[91]

American librarians had asked him to establish a U.S. bindery, Chivers wrote; as business grew, he had added staff, and he had plans to enlarge the Brooklyn facility. Until those plans could be realized, he would have to "temporarily avail [him]self of [his] English workshops" in order to meet his many commitments. He ended by enumerating his many contributions to bookbinding (particularly to binding library materials and adapting bindings to the types and qualities of modern book papers) and listed the prizes his bindings had won (Gold Medal, St. Louis, 1904; Diplôme d' honneur, Liege, 1905; Grand prix, Milan, 1906, and so on).[92] In a letter to the editor of *Library Journal*, John Cotton Dana congratulated Chivers on his November piece, stating that "he has rendered public libraries a most valuable service by extending his bookbinding field to America."[93] It appears that Chivers suffered no harm from this upset with the International Brotherhood of Bookbinders.

There were also important American binders, although the information that survives about their various techniques is far less specific than that about Chivers's. One such craftsman was Gilbert D. Emerson of Philadelphia. As early as 1901, Emerson was running the Philadelphia Free Library's bindery; at various times, he also operated Emerson binderies in the Pittsburgh Carnegie Library, the Washington, D.C., Public Library, the Newark Free Public Library, the New York Public Library, the Pennsylvania State Library, and at 209 North 11th Street, Philadelphia, "where binding is done for many libraries in all parts of the country." In his 1909 gift and promotional booklet *Bookbinding for Libraries*, Emerson modestly recorded, "It may be a mere coincidence that we are doing the binding for the libraries presided over by the members of the Committee on Bookbinding of the American Library Association."[94]

Emerson, like Chivers, was one of the binders recommended in 1908 by Indiana librarians. His work was among that included by Dana in Newark's bookbinding exhibit, and a note in a 1907 issue of *Public Libraries* announced that Emerson was planning "to teach bookbinding through correspondence."[95] While the East Orange Free Public Library rated Chivers as best, "Gilbert D. Emerson, the Philadelphia binder, who rebinds books for the Philadelphia Free Library, the Pittsburgh Carnegie Library and the Newark Free Public Library, is somewhat less expensive and his binding is standing the test of hard wear." The staff of the East Orange (New Jersey) Free Public Library sorted books to be rebound according to their anticipated future use; those to receive hard wear went to Chivers, those to receive medium wear to Emerson. The Washington, D.C., Public Library reported that its Emerson bindery was doing considerable experimentation with binding technique and had developed one stronger than lacing in for fastening the text block to the cover, as well as a patented oversewing method.[96]

The first mention of William Rademaekers, who "learned his trade on the other side" (that is, in Europe) has him working as the foreman in Emerson's bindery at the Newark Free Public Library. In 1906 Emerson sold out the Newark bindery to Rademaekers, and the library contracted with him to continue operating it. It appears that some time after this Rademaekers began to compete with his former employer by taking in work from other libraries. Both the East Orange Free Public Library and the Jacksonville Public Library sent books to Rademaekers and found his work very satisfactory. In the spring of 1909 Rademaekers was invited to address the librarians of the Queens Borough (New York) Public Library, who found his words "most instructive and interesting." In 1907 Rademaekers began offering a course in bookbinding from the Newark Free Public Library's bindery. The series of twenty-five lessons cost twenty-five dollars, including materials, and was designed for librarians and other persons not wishing to become professional binders. Other libraries sent staff members to Rademaekers to take these lessons or to learn mending techniques. Rademaekers also analyzed books that had worn poorly and offered his advice as to the cause. Reportedly, his bindings wore well.[97]

A handful of other American contract binders should be mentioned. J. Rufus Wales of Marlborough, Massachusetts, advertised extensively in the library press. He claimed the "strongest system" of binding available and offered to bind a book free of charge, providing the library paid the postage. Wales bound for the New Haven Free Public Library, the Gloversville (New York) Free Library, and the Worcester County (Massachusetts) Law Library.[98] Another binder, George Stosskopf of Evanston, Illinois, described his methods in *American Libraries* and bound for the St. Louis Public Library, among others.[99]

Finally, there are the Los Angeles Public Library binders. In 1906, in an attempt to secure better work and to reduce a large annual mending expense, the librarian ceased the practice of awarding the library's binding contract to the lowest bidder. Three binders were selected (Davenport and Robison, the Southern California Printing Company, and B. F. Welker); the firm of Griesinger and Mundeviler was investigated and subsequently received some of the library's business. Welker owned the patent on a "cinchback" method of binding with recessed cords and linen tapes; Griesinger offered a special cloth-hinge process, especially useful when the backs of signatures were badly damaged. The Oakland

(California) Free Library sent some of its books to the Los Angeles Public Library, for binding by the Griesinger technique.[100]

The accomplishments of three British binders should also be mentioned; the books they wrote were studied by American librarians and binders, and their counsel followed. Douglas Cockerell, unlike Chivers, never ventured across the Atlantic to do business in America. Although a fellow Englishman recommended Cockerell's "'library binding'" as "good and cheap" (he sewed on tapes, fastened the tapes to the boards, and formed a flexible joint), and although Cockerell was a member of the Royal Society of Art's Committee on Leather for Bookbinding, it was through his writings that he influenced American librarians. *Bookbinding and the Care of Books* was one of a handful of binding manuals "describing . . . every process and tool connected with bookbinding, and containing much sensible advice on the care and preservation of books"; it was characterized by one reviewer as "one that the librarian should not do without." The ALA Committee on Bookbinding recommended it as a "systematic treatise on bookbinding," and Bliss found that it had "done much to instruct us in proper methods."[101]

Cockerell's booklet *Note on Bookbinding* was also widely read in U.S. libraries. A notice in a 1906 issue of *Library Journal* announced that he was revising this publication and that copies could be had by writing to Arthur L. Bailey, Chair of the ALA's Committee on Bookbinding and librarian of the Wilmington (Delaware) Institute. By 1907 Bailey had obtained 250 copies of this pamphlet, and he sent them to requesters as long as his supply lasted.[102]

Joseph Zaehnsdorf and George Stephen both did work important to American librarians, but at rather opposite ends of a scale. Zaehnsdorf's *The Art of Bookbinding* was counted as one of the period's best sources for binding and preservation information. As a skilled craftsman, he was also a member of the Royal Society of Arts' Committee on Leather for Bookbinding.[103] George Stephen, on the other hand, was an expert on publishers' edition bindings and reinforced library bindings. Stephen wrote extensively on a range of binding issues, but machine book sewing and commercial binding were his favorite topics. He was published and reviewed in the American library press, and in its 1909 report the ALA's Committee on Bookbinding reported, "The Committee has been in correspondence during the year with Mr. George A. Stephen, member of the Book Production Committee of the Library Association in England, and is especially indebted to him for his helpful suggestions concerning commercial binding."[104] He further influenced American librarians through the book *Manual of Library Bookbinding*, which he coauthored with Coutts.

Library binding (as opposed to publishers' work) was largely done by hand. Most books received by libraries either had to be bound immediately because they were still in paper covers, or rebound within a short period of time because they had begun life as poorly made publishers' editions. A book's physical survival was largely dependent on proper library binding, exemplified by strong sewing and sound joints.

Chapter 9

Cleaning and Repair

Cleaning the bindings and pages of books was a time-consuming and therefore costly activity, infrequently exercised in libraries whose collections were chiefly circulating. "Comparatively few libraries avail themselves of the practice of washing their soiled volumes," wrote Spofford, "as the practice is too expensive for most of them."[1] While cleaning might range from simple erasures to disbinding and immersing, most libraries found it was all they could do to keep their collections in good repair; volumes with dirty covers and pages were typically rebound or discarded rather than cleaned. This practice was hardly extravagant, because the dirty bindings were often also worn, and the stained book papers were often of such poor quality that cleaning was not good library economy. Nonetheless, some libraries did have cleaning projects or programs, and well-bound materials printed on good paper (which made up some portion of their collections) were cleaned as necessary.

In 1901 the Washington, D.C., Public Library reported that in preparation for its move to the new Carnegie building, every book in its collection would be cleaned and repaired; this included cleaning margins (presumably, removing readers' notations). The Pittsburgh Carnegie Library washed books returned from the public schools, and the library in Fairhaven, Massachusetts, also washed its cloth-covered volumes. The Wisconsin and Vermont library commissions gave advice on how to wash bindings, and the Queens Borough (New York) Public Library did some cleaning of the covers of its books. The Newark (New Jersey) Free Public Library and the public library of Oconto, Wisconsin, experimented with methods for cleaning cloth bindings, and the Philadelphia Mercantile Library, after its fire, tried various ways of removing water stains.[2]

While librarians were correctly cautioned to know their stains before attempting any particular remedy to remove them, to practice on inconsequential volumes before working on valuable ones, and to remove all traces of acids and bleaches thoroughly following any treatment,[3] such advice was largely useful only to the few librarians cleaning rare materials or the exceptional circulating volume.

William F. Poole criticized William Blades for his vague descriptions of how books ought to be cleaned; with a dose of irony, he asked whether Blades intended that librarians use "soap, Bristol-brick, and scrubbing brush." In fact, the cleaning of leather bindings to remove plain surface soil consisted of simply washing them with mild soap and water (though "old books" were not to be cleaned with water). If soap and water were not enough, a mild mixture of vinegar and water, citric acid, or alcohol was recommended, or perhaps a little turpentine. One could also apply "a coat of thin starch paste (cooked) over the book, avoiding the gold tooling," then wipe it off and oil the cover.[4]

Specific stains on leather bindings required a different approach. To remove grease or oil spots, one might sprinkle chalk, pipe clay, or magnesia on the stain, then touch it with a hot iron, causing the powdery substance to absorb the grease or oil. Alternately, either benzine or ether was applied to the spot.[5] Ink stains required sterner stuff, such as oxalic or hydrochloric acid (the latter often called spirit of salts). After the stain was removed, it was necessary to rinse the treated area thoroughly with water to wash out any residue of these potent acids.[6]

Cloth bindings (at least, those whose dyes did not run) could be washed with plain water, water and ammonia, vinegar and water, or soap and water. Different institutions appear to have developed their own ingredient ratios. While the Pittsburgh Carnegie Library added only a few drops of ammonia to its wash water, other libraries mixed one part of ammonia to two of water.[7]

The Millicent Library in Fairhaven, Massachusetts, had a thorough cleaning program for its linen and buckram bindings: "Another problem which we have had to meet was how to keep our books from becoming soiled and repulsive in a very short time after going into circulation as we do not, of course, cover our books. We have developed a regular library laundry practice of which someone may be glad to learn. . . . Using a common dishmop, the book is subjected to a thorough scrubbing in water in which is put a small quantity of ammonia, perhaps one-half teaspoonful to a quart or more of water."[8] The staff washed the lighter-colored books first and the darker last, as the darks faded a bit. The books were then dried on a sunny windowsill or near a heating register, and their covers varnished with shellac diluted with alcohol. The result, according to the librarian, was a "clean, fresh-looking volume that will not offend the most fastidious borrower."[9]

Some libraries preferred dry-cleaning cloth covers to washing them. The Providence Public Library used gasoline to clean its bindings, as well as the "leaf edge" of the book; the work was carefully performed with clean cloths, away from fires and lit lamps. The Newark library tried this same method but reported, "We have not found this a very good plan." In Oconto, Wisconsin, the children's librarian involved young readers in cleaning books with gasoline. In some cases, rubber erasers and pumice stones were used to dry clean cloth covers.[10]

Under one circumstance or another, many libraries used simple dry-cleaning methods on the pages of their books. Some readers found it difficult to resist adding their comments in the margins of library books, and staff sometimes found it desirable to remove dirt and smudges. Rubber sponges or erasers were used, as were pumice stones and bread (rolled into a ball) or bread crumbs.[11] When working with any of these implements, one held the page flat with one hand and rubbed gently but firmly from the inside of the page toward the outer edge with the other. This technique prevented the tearing or crumpling of the paper.[12]

Removing more resistant stains (ink, oil, or grease) was another matter. Potent solutions such as oxalic acid, hydrochloric acid, or the somewhat milder chlorine or Javelle water[13] were required for ink spots; certain commercially available products, such as Collins' ink eradicator, could also be used.[14] When soap and water or a hot iron applied over chalk failed to remove grease and oil, ether, benzine, carbolic acid, hydrochloric acid, or chloride of lime were recommended.[15] Some of these preparations were highly flammable and suitable only for laboratory use; further, their application required considerable knowledge and skill, lest the print disappear along with the stain. Since the use of any strong acid or chemical called for subsequent washing in a considerable amount of water, these processes typically required the disbinding of the book and individual treatment of the stained page. For such reasons, few circulating libraries applied these methods; instead, they confined themselves to simple methods of erasure. Similarly, washing pages in order to generally whiten or clean them required removing the binding, using chemicals, and resizing the paper; it was a practice for workers skilled in cleaning valuable materials.[16]

Though they may have cleaned sparingly, nineteenth-century librarians mended much. Library literature was filled with advice on proper repair technique, and librarians such as Spofford and Margaret Wright Brown published books on the topic. Almost every institution, however small or large, had a mending program, and by all appearances there were few American libraries who fit this description given by Ainsworth Spofford: "I have seen, in country libraries, the librarian and his lady assistant absorbed in reading newspapers, with no other readers in the room. This is a use of valuable time never to be indulged in during library hours. If they had given these moments to proper care of the books under their charge, their shelves would not have been found filled with neglected volumes, many of which had been plainly badly treated and injured, but not beyond reclamation by timely and provident care."[17]

In 1901 the Public Library of the City of Bangor (Maine) repaired 5,737 volumes. The librarian noted that the work was very time-consuming; up to one hour might be spent on a single volume. During a single year the Portland (Maine) Public Library, with a collection of 35,400 volumes, repaired 6,723. In 1908 Yale had a full-time employee who mended, rebacked, cleaned, and varnished library books. For a time, the Pratt Institute in Brooklyn appears to have repaired almost compulsively. In 1897-1898 the library owned 67,016 volumes and mended 77,059; clearly, some books were repaired more than once. "At one time, in November," wrote the librarian, "there were 1,300 volumes in various stages of repair, on the mending table, the weight causing the table to break through the glass floor on which it was standing."[18]

Some libraries kept detailed accounts of their repair costs. Pratt noted that its abundant repairs were funded from fines, payments for lost volumes, and the sale of old books and journals. In 1891 the St. Louis Public Library paid a trained binder's assistant a salary of $175; he or she repaired 1,336 volumes at a cost per volume (exclusive of materials) of thirteen cents. The Boston Athenaeum spent an average of thirty-five cents on each of the 1,282 volumes it repaired in 1905 ($431.95 in wages, $18.81 for materials). In 1907 the Oakland (California) Free Library's repairs averaged ten cents a volume, and a new mender handled 505 books in a month. By 1910 mending costs had been reduced to five cents a volume. For work of a slightly different type (applying petroleum jelly to book covers, or "vaselining" them), the Worcester County (Massachusetts) Law Library paid fifteen cents per hour for labor, sixteen cents per pound for Lucelline (petroleum jelly), $1.75 a quart for binder's varnish, and twenty cents a quart for the denatured alcohol used to dilute the varnish; unfortunately, there is no record of the speed with which this work was accomplished.[19]

In the quest for genuine library economy, the question of repair versus rebinding was an interesting one. The experts advised a policy of "'mend little; rebind early.'" Books were to be repaired only when they were of too little significance to replace, or so cheap that a replacement would cost about the same as rebinding. "Good books, that is to say, books which will not lose in value as time goes by, because of the intrinsic worth of their contents, and which are also of sufficient value from the mere money standpoint, should be but little mended, except for a tear or a loose leaf, but should be immediately rebound when showing signs of weakness and wear." If the stitching broke, or if signatures or leaves became loose, a title "of permanent value to the library" should be rebound at once. On the other hand, if the stitching and joints were sound, one might make minor repairs, such as pasting a torn page.[20]

Sending a book to the bindery at the first signs of weakness saved money in the long run, because too much repair shortened a book's life. Librarians urged their fellows to forsake "makeshift and temporary methods of repairing for more thorough and professional methods" of binding. In the pages of *Library Journal*, one librarian described how a previous practice of frequent repair and the unsparing application of paste created volume upon volume "formless and so swollen in bulk as to have outgrown its case." Further, "the paste used combined with the glue and the paper to form a brittle compound. This caused the back[s] of the signatures to crumble away when the book was taken apart for rebinding, leaving a collection of loose leaves which had to be whipstitched." Of course, once leaves were whipstitched, the book would never again "open as readily as one sewed on tapes."[21]

Thus, a book too often repaired could well become unfit for rebinding. Further, loose leaves, plates, and signatures might well be lost, rendering the volume incomplete. The Detroit and Dubuque (Iowa) public libraries both followed the "'mend little; rebind early'" policy, as the "experience of many libraries ha[d] proved that a book much mended cannot be rebound, thus shortening its life of usefulness." The Seattle Public Library rued the years during which low funding led to wholesale repairs with mucilage; the substance crystallized and actually cut the book papers. As a result of this misguided mending, the library withdrew twenty-five to fifty percent of its fiction and other popular materials in the course of a single year, replacing what little it could afford to.[22]

Nevertheless, for every library that mended little and rebound early, there existed at least one institution forced by economic necessity to take the less costly path and repair liberally. The Cincinnati Public Library saved the cost of an entire position, plus thirty to forty percent of its binding budget, by adopting the use of "flexible" glue to reattach book covers. The Fletcher Free Library in Burlington, Vermont, reported that "books are not sent to the bindery until they are hopelessly out of repair. Sewing, gluing, and mending form a part of our daily labors." The Providence Public Library attempted to lessen its rebinding costs by increasing the level of repair, as did the public libraries of Rockford (Illinois), Springfield, and Troy (New York).[23]

Training for book repairers occurred chiefly on the job. Often, one institution hired another's skilled mender to come instruct its assistants. The services of Rose Palmer of the Osterhout Library in Wilkes-Barre, Pennsylvania, were lent to both the Hartford and Wilmington (Delaware) public libraries, to train their staffs in preservation and repair methods, and the Rockford (Illinois) Public Library hired a temporary mender to train its assistants in repairing and recasing.[24] The Somerville (Massachusetts) Public Library arranged for a staff member to train herself in mending techniques through extended visits to both commercial binderies and the bindery of the Boston Public Library; the East Orange (New Jersey) Free Public Library sent two assistants to William Rademaekers of the Newark library's bindery. East Orange's librarian was of the opinion that the work of a trained mender could pay her salary in less than two years in a library of about 20,000 volumes, and more quickly in a larger library; in addition, the mender could train pages and apprentices to do repairs. Justin Winsor, during his tenure at the Boston Public Library, had one of the most interesting yet regrettable methods of identifying staff to be trained as menders: rather than firing poorly performing pages bored with their work, he apprenticed them in the library bindery.[25]

While some libraries set circulation assistants, the staff of the children's room, or any momentarily unoccupied personnel to mending books, many institutions dedicated trained personnel to repair work.[26] They held that repairs should be performed not by amateurs, but rather "by a professional or by someone on the staff who has greater experience"; further, every library should have staff whose only task is mending. At the St. Louis Public Library, repairs were done by a woman trained in a bindery. In the Oakland Free Library, "an experienced book mender" was hired from the Hicks-Judd bindery in San Francisco; a year later, a second mender was hired to handle the books of the branch libraries. The librarian was pleased with the results: "the department justifies our policy of putting professional bindery women to work mending Library books, rather than trying to get Library assistants to do it in an amateurish way," he wrote. Similarly, the Washington, D.C., Public Library planned to have its repair work performed by a contract binder present in the building rather than by library staff; the repairs would be "scientifically made under the direction of a skilled foreman."[27]

Some libraries repaired books on a project basis, hiring temporary specialists to perform the work. In 1879 the Boston Public Library hired a binder to go through its alcoves, dust the books and shelves, and make repairs to the bindings. The binder was considered to possess "experience and good judgment"; it was estimated that the work would require seven months. The 1905 annual report of the New York Yacht Club Library recorded that "a very extensive repairing, labeling, and binding of the books has been contracted for; work will be commenced upon this at once." For the month of December 1905, the Grand Rapids Public Library employed a full-time person to mend and repair its collections. The Woburn (Massachusetts) Public Library once temporarily hired an expert mender to repair its entire collection of oversize illustrated books, which were too valuable to be removed from the building.[28]

In 1904 the Worcester County Law Library established a repair unit where, among other things, books were recased when their covers were shabby but their sewing still good. At the Braddock (Pennsylvania) Carnegie Free Library, mending routines included strengthening covers, renewing cloth backs, and securing broken sewing. Assistants in the Dayton and Scranton public libraries added fresh endpapers and pasted in loose leaves and plates, while at the Boston Public Library missing pages were "written" (that is, hand-copied or typed from intact books) at the rate of several hundred per year. Some libraries strengthened new books before allowing them to circulate by reinforcing their spines or joints. Other routine activities included reinserting loose signatures, rebacking, resewing, regluing loose covers, replacing sides with fresh paper, and patching torn pages.[29] To do this work, an assortment of implements and materials was necessary. Among the tools found near the mender's glass-topped repair table might be a glue pot, knives, scissors, shears, a hammer, bone folders, presses, tins, brushes, needles, a ruler, and an eraser. Supply cabinets contained thread, paste, glue, mucilage, mending tissue, book cloth, leather, endpapers, tapes, pumice, cambric, and waxed paper.[30]

Glue and mucilage were not suitable for the repair of book papers or the backs of signatures; they caused pages to crack and made books difficult or impossible to rebind.[31] Instead, paste was the appropriate adhesive for most mending work. While quality commercial pastes (such as Charles M. Higgins' library and drawing-board paste) were available, a number of libraries used their own preparations, and many a personal recipe was published in the library press. There appear to have been three basic paste formulas (minor variations occurring within each), as well as assorted oddities. The simplest library pastes were made of little more than flour boiled with water; a few drops of oil of cloves, lavender, wintergreen, or peppermint might be added as a preservative.[32] Only slightly more complicated were recipes that included flour, water, powdered alum, and pulverized rosin. The latter two ingredients helped prevent the mixture from souring, and some scented oil might be added as well.[33]

The third generic paste recipe called for boiling together wheat flour, water, brown sugar, and corrosive sublimate; oil of peppermint or lavender acted as a further preservative.[34] Among the more unusual paste formulas were ones consisting of potato starch, water, and pure nitric acid; lump starch, water, and pulverized glue; and flour, water, alum, and "as much powdered borax as will lay on a ten-cent piece." The Pomona (California) Public Library used Jellitac, a commercial preparation manufactured for the purpose of hanging wallpaper and pasting labels on orange crates.[35] Recipes for mucilage were also published, but at a ratio to paste formulas of about one to nine. Typically, mucilage was made by combining gum tragacanth or gum arabic with water.[36]

Contemporary librarians used the terms *tissue paper, transparent paper, typing paper*, and *onion paper* to describe a variety of lightweight, fairly transparent papers with which torn book pages were mended.[37] In the most delicate repairs, a thin coat of paste was applied to the "fringe of the tear"; the edges were then joined, and tissue paper was placed beneath and atop the pasted area. The book was closed until the paste dried; later when the tissue was removed, a bit of it adhered to the repaired page, strengthening the joint of the mend.[38] Sometimes paste was generously applied to a piece of tissue, and the tissue was permanently pressed into place over the tear and the surrounding text; presumably, the tissue was fairly transparent when dry, and the print beneath it could be read.[39] The ALA Supply Department sold transparent adhesive paper for repairing torn leaves (it was available in sheets measuring fifty by seventy-five centimeters, at a cost of thirty cents each), as did A. I. Woodbury and Company, Boston, and the Library Bureau. However, Margaret Wright Brown cautioned against its use; it is likely that the gum or adhesive was not stable.[40]

As part of their general cleaning and repair activities, many libraries applied dressings to their leather bindings. These preparations included petroleum jelly, lard, various oils, and simple paste and egg washes. Such treatments were intended to prevent or slow deterioration, as well as to restore flexibility to desiccated bindings. They were thought to block the penetration of environmental pollutants but, while somewhat successful in consolidating powdery, crumbling surfaces, they did nothing to prevent continuing decay.[41]

Petroleum jelly was the most popular of these treatments; this was unfortunate, because with time it often caused leather to harden and crack. The Washington, D.C., Public Library applied this substance to old leather volumes, finding that it initially softened and cleaned them. Between 1907 and 1911 the Worcester County Law Library experimented with many approaches to "vaselining" leather, including treating both the leather's outer surface and underside, wetting the leather before applying the dressing, and varnishing over petroleum jelly; careful records of the procedures performed on each book were kept for future reference. The method on which the library settled involved first washing the binding with mild soap. After the leather dried, the dressing was applied with a cotton pad, and the book was allowed to dry overnight. The following day, any excess dressing was removed and the volume received a coat of varnish. Not only were the lives of cheaper leather bindings extended by this treatment, but less dust appeared on the library's floors, and the books' surfaces resisted water, dirt, and mud.[42]

Sperm oil, castor oil, neat's foot oil, "sweet oil," and olive oil were also used to dress leather bindings, as was lard.[43] Certain commercial products, including both shoe and furniture polish, were recommended.[44] There was no consensus about the frequency with which bindings should be treated; recommendations ranged from every three or four months to once a year. The Worcester County Law Library's practice of adding a coat of varnish was not an uncommon one.[45] Varnish kept books cleaner, made them washable, and (some thought) kept the salubrious effects of the leather dressing from evaporating.[46] Recipes for varnish included such substances as shellac, benzoin, and spirits of wine (alcohol); mastic varnish, corrosive sublimate, and spirits of wine; or shellac and denatured alcohol.[47] A few librarians were uneasy about shellacking leather volumes, believing that varnish eventually caused the covers to crack and discolor; further, readers often disliked the sticky surfaces of books treated in this manner. The Royal Society of Arts found that some varnishes would "interfere with the pliability of the leather at the joints, and at the portion of the leather which bends when the books is opened." Because of this, it recommended that librarians apply varnish so that it penetrated no deeper than the leather's surface.[48]

Paste and egg washes represented simpler methods of dressing leather bindings, with more modest goals. While some believed that paste washes and egg glairs would arrest decay, others expected largely cosmetic results from these treatments. The books simply looked better and fresher, as the dressing masked scuffs and at least temporarily consolidated crumbling areas.[49] Few (if any) paste washes actually contained paste. Typical concoctions consisted of kid glue, water, and small amounts of oxalic acid and ammonia, or simply wet starch with a little alum added. The technique involved sponging the mixture over the binding and polishing the book with a soft cloth the next day.[50] Egg glairs were also applied with a sponge and consisted of nothing more than the beaten white (or, in a few recipes, the yolk) of an egg. A little thymol, camphor, or oil might be added as an antiseptic. In some cases a hot iron was applied to the binding after the egg wash dried; this added lustre.[51] Rather than apply a wash to the entire binding, librarians sometimes treated only the decayed or broken areas (often, the corners). Paste, glue and paste, or glue alone was used as a filler; then the damaged area was hammered into shape and perhaps given a coat of egg glair and touched with an iron.[52]

In the first decade of this century, Cedric Chivers revived a technique of applying very thin, transparent sheets of vellum over colorful, elaborately decorated bindings as a means of sealing and protecting their ornamentation–a technique that had originated with the Edwards binders in

115

Halifax. Chivers called his method vellucent (vellum made translucent) binding, and many examples appear in the catalog of his bindings exhibited at the St. Louis Exhibition of 1904. Subsequently, Chivers promoted vellucent binding as a preservative for old leather volumes. The damaged binding, with its broken joints and rubbed corners, was covered with vellum, supposedly preventing further deterioration. One justification for this unorthodox method was modern binders' lack of skill in the art of restoration. Vellum, Chivers noted, possessed "perennial youth," and leathers protected by it would, he predicted, be "safe from the destroying hand of time." Vellucent binding made a crumbling book easy to handle again; further, the "familiar appearance" of the old binding was retained. Nevertheless, the vellucent technique for preserving bindings never gained popularity, and there is no evidence of its use in American libraries.[53]

Fire and water often provided patients upon which librarians could test their preservation theories. The best description of a library's response to fire and its aftermath is that reported by the librarian of Trinity College, Hartford, where a fire broke out on 22 May 1907. Water and smoke poured in through the library's ceiling. Outside the building, about two hundred students and a "score of professors" formed lines to the windows, "and the books were tumbled, tossed, thrown, and heaped upon the campus at a safe distance from the building." Forty thousand volumes and as many unbound pamphlets were scattered on the lawn, but work did not begin on the books (which were carried back in and randomly placed on shelves) until the librarian, who was absent, returned three days later.[54]

A dozen students examined every book, pamphlet, and magazine, setting aside any that had been damaged by water, cinders, or mishandling. This work was done piecemeal, as the students also had to attend classes and study. The librarian reviewed about a thousand damaged books, which were subsequently repaired in the library.

The chief cause of damage was the quick, rough handling of the books as they were removed from the building during the fire. Less than a hundred volumes were hurt by water; many of these were books with modern cloth and buckram bindings, whose colors ran and soiled the edges and the pages badly. This did not appear to happen with morocco-bound volumes that got wet. Volumes bound in morocco and cloth stood the rough handling splendidly, but the covers of older books bound in calf or sheep fell away with the ease and grace of autumn leaves at the first touch.[55]

The Trinity College librarian pointed out how much the unbound materials suffered, particularly periodical issues, and asked for an increase in the binding budget as protection against future emergencies.[56] The backs were sliced off burned but salvageable books; their threads were cut and their covers removed. The text block was soaked in clean water, causing the leaves to separate. Then the leaves were dried rapidly in a current of warm air and rebound.[57]

Counsel on treating water-damaged books came also from the Milwaukee Public Library and the Philadelphia Mercantile Library after their respective fires. In Milwaukee, following the fire of 14 October 1894, "many books which were seriously wet were dried, pressed, and of necessity kept in use in order not to withdraw certain classes entirely from public use"; later, the books were rebound in phases.[58] At Philadelphia, more experimentation occurred.

In the Philadelphia fire of 25 February 1877, very few books burned, but almost all those on the south side of the building were soaked with water. This collection was condemned, with a few exceptions. Valuable water-stained books were taken apart, washed, pressed, dried, and rebound. Other books were rebound because water had dissolved the glue and paste of their bindings. In a few cases, if only the binding was wet, the text block was simply rebound. Two methods of drying water-soaked books without disbinding them were also employed. First, fast drying was tested – tying books with string and baking them in an oven – but the bindings dried too rapidly, swelled, warped, and burst. Next, staff tried the slower method of fanning out books over wires strung in a warm room; this was more successful.[59]

This chapter concludes the group of four devoted to binding and repair. Because cleaning books was costly and time-consuming, most libraries simply rebound or discarded dirty volumes. Mending programs were common, however, and the economic question of repair versus rebinding was a controversial one whose answer greatly affected the lives of a library's books. The leather dressings, shellac, or paste washes so often a part of an institution's cleaning and repair program probably had little impact on the permanence of the high-use circulating volumes to which they were applied in the hope of somewhat extending their inescapably short lives.

Chapter 10

Publishers' Bindings

As the size of the American reading public and the emphasis on popular education created more book buyers, publishers began what was to be a gradual transition from hand binding to mechanized binding. Initially, binding was done entirely by hand. Machinery was gradually introduced in an attempt to meet the pressures exerted by the swiftness of the printing press. Eventually, publishers' binding was completely mechanized.[1] In a 1908 address before a monthly meeting of the LAUK, binder George Stephen spoke these words: "To meet the ever-increasing demand for cheap literature, the mechanical talent of both hemispheres was occupied during the greater part of last century before the elaborate machinery employed to-day in book production was perfected. . . . The result is that hand labour in what is known as 'edition work' has been almost, if not entirely superseded, and the cost of books has been reduced nearly to the price of a daily paper. 'Not as ours the books of old– / Things that steam can stamp and fold; / Not as ours the books of yore– / Rows of type and nothing more.'"[2] (No attribution was given for the verse.)

All books with publishers' bindings (also called case-made books or edition bindings) were made more or less the same way. First, a folding machine transformed the sheets into leaves. Another machine gathered them into sections at the incredible rate of two thousand to ten thousand signatures per hour. Illustrations were pasted to the appropriate signatures, endpapers were attached to the first and last signatures, and all the signatures were gathered together. The back of the text block was either sawed to accommodate cords or left intact for sewing on muslin or tapes. Equipment such as the Brehmer or Smyth sewing machines did the sewing, whether all along or two on, at half or less the cost of hand sewing. A smasher compacted the book, and the edges were trimmed by a machine called a cutter. After the text block was glued up, a rounding and backing machine shaped the text block's convex back and concave fore edge. The boards were cut by machine, and case-making equipment covered the boards with cloth. The cover was then stamped and lettered, and a casing-in machine glued it to the book's endpapers; there was no lacing in of cords or tapes. A fully automated bindery could produce ten thousand such volumes in a single day. As late as 1900 some of these processes (perhaps folding or gathering) might still have been performed by hand, but before the end of the twentieth century's first decade, the edition binding done by the major publishing houses that emerged between 1860 and 1900 was completely mechanized.[3]

Librarians had a litany of criticisms of publishers' bindings. As with hand binding, the two most important aspects of machine binding were sewing together the individual signatures and fastening them (the text block) to the boards. Unfortunately, casebound books were deficient in both areas. Their covers loosened or tore off easily; the sewing broke and unraveled, and signatures fell out. In addition, cheap boards warped, so that books slumped on the shelves; inexpensive book cloths quickly rubbed and wore; and pasted-on plates and illustrations became detached; "extravagant margins" caused books to be unnecessarily large and expensive.[4] While paper quality was somewhat unrelated to the binding techniques employed, librarians also railed against cheap, heavy paper "almost like cardboard in thickness and stiffness, and lead in weight."[5] Librarians entreated publishers to concentrate less on delivering low-cost, attractive volumes and more on producing sound bindings.[6]

For libraries, the results of this shoddy workmanship were quite clear. In the short term, "the present mania for cheap books" caused rebinding bills and replacement costs to escalate. Libraries from Rhode Island to San Francisco, from Brooklyn to Louisville, let their displeasure be known.[7] In the long term, the problem created by large numbers of casemade books was somewhat different. As one librarian wrote, "In an era of machinery, when books are multiplied as the sands of the sea, and their cheapness lessens our ideas of their value, and makes us also oblivious to an extent that we owe anything to posterity, it is well for us, as librarians, to consider whether some authors on our shelves are not entitled to special care, that they may be preserved [for] our successors."[8] The librarian hoping to retain edition bindings as part of his or her permanent collections had to take additional steps in order to ensure their survival.

Librarians were not shy about expressing their sense of injury. Ellen Biscoe of the Eau Claire (Wisconsin) Public Library called for "a crusade of librarians of this country against the wretched bindings with which they are at present afflicted." A librarian from the Milwaukee Public Library reported that although she mended the quickly worn casemade books in her collection, she did not do so "in a meek, submissive frame of mind. The time has passed when librarians submit to poor binding without protest."[9] Another librarian, while lambasting edition bindings, refused to identify the offending publishers; "I should as soon think of entering the sacred precincts on the banks of old Nile," he wrote with bitterness, "and throwing a brick at the awful image of the great god Phthah." A public librarian deplored the publishing industry's "prevailing spirit of greed and 'commercialism,'" while a colleague characterized inferior paper and mechanized binding as "almost fatal obstacles to a book's salvation."[10] In 1901 the director of the Washington, D.C., Public Library summarized the feelings of his peers in this way: "The new books bought for the library are from regular book dealers' stock, and neither paper nor cloth covers are suited to the constant handling they receive in a public library. The plates loosen, the stitches break, corners wear rough, and soon a popular book must be rebound or else it is unfit to circulate. The poor paper and bindings used in modern books is a matter frequently discussed at the meetings of the Library Association, and the experience of our own library is repeated in every large circulating library in the country."[11]

In their own domains, librarians took various steps that may have helped lessen their frustrations. Frederick Crunden of the St. Louis Public Library pasted a slip with this information into copies of current fiction: "Notice: Owing to the inferior paper, poor type, and excessive price of this author's works no more copies will be added to the Library until a better edition is issued." Henry J. Carr of the Scranton Public Library (at the time, president of the American Library Association) placed the following notice in his catalogs and library bulletins: "Because of the needless use of inferior paper, poor or worn-out type, and flimsy binding, publishers have in a degree made it impracticable for public libraries to continue the supply of certain books ordinarily in popular demand. Therefore, until the future issue of editions suitable and satisfactory for library purposes, works of the following named authors must be omitted from the stock and lists of this library."[12] A list followed.

The ALA's Committee on Bookbuying received a number of responses to its request for titles "poorly made and unfitted to stand library wear" and forwarded the names to the appropriate publishers. At its 1899 conference, the Wisconsin State Library Association resolved to cooperate with the State Department of Public Instruction in attempts to secure better bindings on books purchased for Wisconsin libraries. The librarians were asked to send lists of poorly bound popular titles to Ellen Biscoe of the Eau Claire Public Library, who made a composite list of the offenders.[13]

The sewing machinery responsible for these affronts to good bookmaking had begun to appear at mid-century. In 1856 David M. Smyth of Hartford invented the first thread booksewing machine. As time passed, Smyth made improvements in his initial model and introduced several variations. By 1879 a machine that could sew books all along, either with or without tapes or cords, was available. Another model that sewed two sheets on was considerably faster. In 1884 Brehmer joined those making booksewing machines, and by 1904 Martini was marketing his first models. Some equipment sewed with a double thread, some with a single thread. Because of their speed and flexibility, these new machines "found an immediate and world-wide market."[14]

Mechanized binding processes were fast, reduced costs, and saved bindery floor space. Books sewn with strong thread onto tapes could withstand hard use, "but, alas, it is to be regretted that keen competition has tempted the publishers and bookbinders to cut down their expenses in every conceivable way, and to lower the excellence of their work to increase trade profits."[15] In truth, even though their machines were capable, few publishers sewed on supports after about 1882. Rather, they simply sewed the signatures together, one to the other, then fastened them to the covers and endpapers with cheap cloth hinges; there was no lacing in of cords or tapes. If the single continuous thread that ran from first signature to last broke at any point, the entire volume began to unravel.[16]

The machines described above were all "through-the-fold" models; in this, they emulated hand-binding techniques. There were other machines, however, that employed different sewing methods. Sometimes signatures were stacked one atop the other, then run through a machine that punched holes at regular intervals near their inner folds; next, thread or wire was forced through these holes, through the entire thickness of the publication. Known as stab sewing, this method was appropriate only for unimportant periodicals, books, and pamphlets. Even though books sewn in this fashion were strong and cheap, they had narrow inner margins and were difficult to open; also, the inferior paper used tended to crack along the stitching.[17]

The wire stitcher was a sewing machine used largely for pamphlets. From the inside, two or three wire staples pierced the folds of the gathered sheets in each signature, penetrating and fastening into a wide tape placed against the signatures' backs. A single machine could bind two thousand pamphlets or signatures per hour. The wire sewing machine worked differently from the wire stitcher, using wire to sew signatures through their folds, one to the other; Brehmer manufactured a wire sewing machine, often used for pattern books, postcard albums, and guard books.[18]

Wire stitching and wire sewing had little to recommend them. Wire lacked thread's flexibility; supporting tapes were not used, although the wire might be laced in and out of a strip of webbing placed against the signatures' backs. Wire (usually aluminoid, tinned, or galvanized) rusted and corroded book papers, leaving signature backs so badly damaged that the book could not be rebound. Wire cut into pages, causing them to fall out, and wirebound books did not open easily.[19] Writing of wire stitching in its 1905 report, the LAUK's Sound Leather Committee reported that "these little clips are abominations." George Stephen opined that "however suitable wire sewing may be for stationery work, it is a most reprehensible method for library books, or indeed for any books that are intended for preservation and frequent handling, and is to be avoided as much as possible." "Well, well," exclaimed another librarian; "we live in a shoddy and a wire-stapling world, my brothers, and it's useless to blink the fact."[20] Although some American binders offered wire stitching, wire stitching and sewing were more popular in Germany and England than they were in this country.[21]

Not all edition binding involved sewing to fasten together a book's pages. The adhesive binding machine, in use from the last quarter of the nineteenth century but most popular after the second World War, applied an adhesive to the edges of a stack of single sheets, causing the pages to adhere to one another and preparing them to be attached to the case. "There is another kind of binding," wrote Spofford, "which dispenses entirely with sewing the sheets of a book. The backs are soaked with a solution of india-rubber, and each sheet must be thoroughly agglutinated to the backs, so as to adhere firmly to its fellows." Adhesive binding was often used with volumes of plates, music, or books trimmed to single sheets before binding.[22]

Another feature of the edition-bound volume was its machine-made case. Cases were made by hand in this country until the last decade of the nineteenth century, when the case-making machine was introduced. When a book was machine-sewn onto tapes, the tapes' ends were simply glued to the inside of the covers and pasted over with endpapers. Only the endpapers and glue held the book in its case, and even this frail bond was eliminated, as cords and tapes disappeared in machine booksewing. The Sheridan covering machine, introduced in 1893, performed every step in constructing the case except cutting the cloth and boards. In 1903 the Smyth casing-in machine represented the complete automation of case making; it accepted the unclothed text block at one end and presented it cased at the other.[23] Spofford described the case-made volume in this way: "The most vital distinction between a machine-made and a hand-made binding is that the cloth or casemade book is not fastened into its cover in a firm and permanent way, as in leather-backed books. It is simply pasted or glued to its boards – not interlaced by the cords or bands on which it is sewed. Hence one can easily tear off the whole cover of a cloth-bound book, by a slight effort, and such volumes tend to come to pieces early, under constant wear and tear of library service."[24]

Occasionally, a cloth or paper guard was hooked around the fold of the endpapers, one side attached to the cover board and the other tipped to the first signature. This gave greater strength to the binding, but not as much as the use of laced-in cords: "The handling of the book a few times is sufficient to break the hinge of weak paper and mull, the latter being made quite brittle by the common glue used."[25]

While the sewing and casing machines were the most important ones used in mechanized binding, many other pieces of equipment were also employed. The rolling press was among the earliest of the binder's machines; introduced in 1823, it compressed the book once it had been sewn. Folding machines followed, and in 1892 the Crawley rounder and backer was developed. Between 1900 and 1903, America continued her leadership in the production of bookbinding equipment with the invention of power-driven gathering machines.[26]

Librarians did more than murmur against casemade books. As the century was turning, they made some attempts to rank the quality of popular publishers' bindings. Ellen Biscoe of the Eau Claire Public Library collected information from librarians throughout Wisconsin and gathered examples from her own institution. Houghton Mifflin, Macmillan, Dodd, Mead & Company, Appleton, and the American Book Company received the highest ratings; Harper's was severely condemned, and Scribner's fell close behind. In 1906 the ALA's Committee on Bookbinding attempted to compare the "relative wearing qualities of books of different publishers"; however, only nineteen libraries provided statistics, and the committee felt that those received did not "indicate anything of great value." A better test, the committee thought, would be to keep statistics on five hundred titles per publisher, but most libraries owned fewer than one hundred fifty titles from any given house. Since several publishers had indicated interest in issuing their books in "bindings suitable for library use," the committee felt it inappropriate to move ahead with the ranking.[27]

Ellen Biscoe wrote to Harper's, Scribner's, and Houghton Mifflin, asking their attitudes about binding (as she stated in her letter, too many new books "fall to pieces at the third reading"). Harper and Brothers reported that it was working on the problem and would be in touch when a remedy was found. Scribner's replied that it was trying to bind better every year but that it was nearly impossible to bind books on coated paper well. The company asked for more specific criticism, particularly the names of any books that were especially poorly made. Houghton Mifflin (whose bindings, unlike those of Harper's and Scribner's, were judged by Miss Biscoe to be among the most durable) was asked to explain its technique. The publisher replied that when book papers were heavy or stiff, fewer pages were assigned to each section. Further, sewing was done on "flexible thread sewing-machines, using the highest quality of thread, and a flexible glue when lining up the backs before the books are put in their covers."[28]

The ALA's Committee on Bookbinding, appointed in 1905 at the suggestion of John Cotton Dana and on the basis of a motion by Melvil Dewey, was charged with investigating "the subject of publishers' bindings, book papers, leathers, and binding methods and processes." Its original members were George F. Bowerman of the Washington, D.C., Public Library, William Cutter of the Forbes Library (Northampton, Massachusetts), and Arthur L. Bailey of the Wilmington (Delaware) Institute. Bowerman and Bailey were logical appointees: both their institutions were actively experimenting with a variety of binding techniques. The committee purposely had no "practical binder" as a member; its investigations were to be pursued "purely from the point of view of economical administration." Librarians were urged to communicate their binding experiences to the committee, and even to send "samples of bindings . . . that may be out of the ordinary, and that have proved satisfactory and economical." Again, library economy was the issue.[29]

It seems likely that a combination of Dana's interest in library binding, the activity (from 1901 to 1905) of the Royal Society of Arts and the LAUK's Sound Leather Committee, and the generally inferior quality of publishers' bindings and modern book papers led to the formation of the Committee on Bookbinding. The committee reported regularly in *Library Journal* until 1907, when the *American Library Association Bulletin* began to publish the reports of the organization's committees. It recommended binding manuals, described foreign research in paper and leather testing, and conducted countless surveys whose topics ranged from the wearing qualities of various publishers' titles to the value of in-house binderies. In 1906 George E. Wire of the Worcester County (Massachusetts) Law Library (another institution with a serious interest in library binding) replaced Bowerman on the committee.[30]

In 1907 the committee described its mission a bit differently; now it would study "rebinding, book-papers, pamphlet and magazine binders, and publishers' bindings." Further, it declared its intent to secure from publishers specially bound library editions and urged librarians to view the cost of rebinding in terms of cost per circulation rather than the flat cost of binding. Later that same year, the committee published the titles of books available in library editions, described the work of the U.S. Leather and Paper Laboratory, and publicized the availability of Cockerell's *Note on Bookbinding*. At the Asheville (North Carolina) conference of the association, librarians responded favorably to the committee's work by asking that time be scheduled for a discussion of its report at the 1908 ALA conference. Tessa L. Kelso of Baker and Taylor requested that the committee report more fully in the future. A difference of opinion arose about the questions that most merited the committee's consideration, and the group suggested that librarians send statements about which issues should be "settled first."[31]

The following year, the committee announced its intent to "continue the campaign" for reinforced library bindings, criticized library schools for devoting so little time to the study of binding, discussed binding problems of libraries in the south and west, invited libraries to identify poorly bound books (whose names would be sent to their publishers), and described the book cloth selected for the binding of federal documents. In 1909 an open letter to publishers, suggesting binding standards for library editions, was published; librarians were encouraged to protest poorly made books to their publishers, and a letter requesting information on methods of binding illustrative matter was sent to thirty publishers.

The committee expressed disappointment in the slender support that reinforced publishers' bindings had received and published the results of a study of the number of circulations an ordinary casemade book could withstand before requiring rebinding. It reported on its correspondence with British binder George A. Stephen, a member of the LAUK's corresponding Book Production Committee. In turn, Stephen used the pages of the *Library Association Record*, as well as his own books, to encourage the LAUK to follow the example of the ALA and induce publishers to offer "special library editions bound according to a standard specification." He thought that the work already done by the American Library Association would give the LAUK needed leverage with British publishers regarding similarly bound books.[32]

It was the call for quantities of cheap reading material that led to the mechanization of edition binding and the consequent decline in the quality of book construction. As machine-sewn, cased-in books began to predominate on library shelves and as bindery bills escalated, librarians organized to challenge major publishing houses to produce a better book. The publishers' response (to provide special library editions on a sort of subscription basis), and other solutions to the problem of poorly bound books are the topics covered in the next chapter.

Chapter 11

Library Editions
and Binding Specifications

There were two ways for American librarians dissatisfied with the modern case-made book to obtain stronger bindings for their collections. One was to purchase the reinforced library editions offered by several of the major publishing houses. Another was to order new titles securely bound from the printed sheets by one of several concerns specializing in this work. While Cedric Chivers, with plants in Bath (England), Brooklyn, and New York City, was the best-known firm that bound from sheets, other binders also offered this service. One of these was Frederich Schleuning of New York City, whose books were available through Baker and Taylor.[1] The Seattle Public Library bound from the sheets in its own bindery; its 1899 *Report* stated, "We have determined to try to buy at least the most popular books in the sheets and bind them ourselves before they have run the gauntlet of the gang-saw, cotton thread sewing machine and cheap glue of sixpenny case work."[2]

Publishers offered no discount on books bought in sheets; the price was the same whether the title was purchased bound or unbound. Thus, volumes bound from the sheets were not inexpensive, as the cost of binding was added to the price of the book. Binders such as Chivers and Schleuning may have received quantity discounts from publishers and passed the savings on to the librarians who ordered their books, so that a copy bound from the sheets sometimes cost as little as ten to forty cents more than a case-made book.[3] Binding from the sheets offered libraries many benefits and was recommended by the ALA's Committee on Book-binding, George Stephen, Douglas Cockerell, Henry Evelyn Bliss, and other binders and bookmen. One librarian suggested that for new libraries, "complete sets of standard authors should be procured in strong special bindings."[4]

Books bound from the sheets may have cost more initially, "but the prolonged life of the book much more than compensate[d] for the extra

127

cost," according to the ALA's Committee on Bookbinding which recommended that "when possible all worn-out fiction and juveniles should be replaced with such books." Not only was the hand sewing stronger than the sewing of a case-made book, but binders further strengthened the volumes by guarding the first and last sections with cloth, guarding illustrations in the same way, and using linen joints with the endpapers. Better-quality boards, thread, glue, and covering materials (often quarter morocco or pig) were also used.[5] Some librarians, however, suggested that binding from the sheets did not always represent good library economy: why pay more for a special binding that would certainly last longer than the paper it sheltered? Further, librarians might find themselves discarding expensive, still-strong bindings because the book's pages were too dirty for continued use. Binding from the sheets also delayed getting books onto the shelves; patrons complained that the books were available in stores, while the library was "behind the times." As a compromise, some libraries initially purchased publishers' bindings, then replaced those in which interest was still high with books bound from the sheets.[6]

Although several American binders bound from the sheets, Chivers's duro-flexile bindings, as the strongest and most popular, deserve further discussion. The ALA's Committee on Book Prices recommended Chivers's method, citing its "very exceptional strength." The Committee on Bookbinding's study of contract binding showed that most libraries were reasonably pleased with the work they received from commercial binders, but those who purchased Chivers's books bound from the sheets "reported their entire satisfaction." A California librarian advised her colleagues to have "books which are both popular and which are well worth having always in your collection" bound from the sheets by Chivers.[7]

Chivers patented his duro-flexile technique in 1885. This binding style was intended to give a book additional strength in two critical areas – the hinges and the first and last signatures. Chivers achieved this by lining his special three-jointed endpapers with a lightweight but strong cloth. Each volume was sewn all along on linen tapes, and its spine was lined with flexible leather. The ends of the tapes, as well as the spine lining, were fixed between split boards. Chivers generally used a vegetable-tanned pigskin back and linen sides.[8]

Some libraries reported that a Chivers volume bound from the sheets cost about one-third more than a publisher's binding. Others paid almost half again as much for duro-flexile binding ($2.00 versus $1.35) but deemed the money well spent, "considering the fact that there is to be no further expense put into the book in time or money, and that readers are to have the use of it from the time it comes to the library." The Silas Bronson Library in Waterbury, Connecticut, bought juveniles bound from the sheets by Chivers for $1.50 per volume, about 80 percent higher than the average cost of eighty-two cents for a publishers' cloth binding. "The extra 68 cents required by the Chivers process is partly justified by the saving of the cost of rebinding (about 44 cents per volume, including freight and other expenses), and the fact that the public is not inconvenienced by the breaking down and withdrawal from circulation of the most popular books at the busiest season of the year."[9]

Duro-flexile bindings were indeed durable and flexible. Their presence in numbers reduced library repair work and rebinding costs. A Chivers-bound book was continuously available to the public, attractive in appearance, and pleasant to handle. The Brooklyn Public Library compared the strength of Chivers's books bound from the sheets to that of publishers' bindings by comparing the binding records of two new branches, one stocked primarily with case-made books, the other with Chivers's duro-flexile bindings. Within the first six months of operation, the branch furnished chiefly with case-made books rebound 920 volumes at a cost of $522. During the same period, the branch equipped with numbers of Chivers's duro-flexile bindings rebound only 187 volumes at a cost of $95. At the Hartford (Connecticut) Public Library, "the enthusiastic verdict of the librarian is that they [books with duro-flexile bindings] will outwear five ordinary books."[10]

Chivers guaranteed to supply "any recently published book" in a duro-flexile binding; further, he warranted that he would rebind free of charge any book whose binding failed, unless its pages were "too dirty for further use."[11] Among his customers were the public libraries of New Haven (Connecticut), Dayton, Dubuque (Iowa), East Orange (New Jersey), Rockford (Illinois), Galveston (Texas), St. Louis, Washington D.C., Wilmington (Delaware), and Springfield, Brockton, Haverhill, and Quincy (Massachusetts).[12]

In 1893 Melvil Dewey forwarded to the *Library Journal* a letter written by R. W. Woodbury, chairman of the managing body of the Denver Mercantile Library. Woodbury, who was also president of the Denver Chamber of Commerce and Board of Trade, complained of the shoddiness of modern books: "I have frequently had occasion to note the utter worthlessness, in many respects, of the majority of books for popular use that we have been obliged to buy. The paper is worthless for durability, the covers shabbily put on, and the whole job utterly unworthy of purchase for continuous use. Sections pull out from the sewing, the covers frequently become loose, the leaves tear, and rebinding necessarily follows in a few weeks, unless the book has been thrown away altogether."[13]

Woodbury thought that the American Library Association ought to attempt some reform: "Librarians are too influential in the purchase of books, and in making them popular with readers, for it to be presumed that their unanimous request should not receive serious consideration, and if possible adoption." In Woodbury's opinion, librarians should guarantee publishers that they would purchase a given quantity of books printed on durable paper and strongly bound in plain, undecorated covers of duck or canvas. They should also promise to buy no more of the "cheap, worthless, and flimsy productions now flooding the country." Dewey asked that anyone interested in this idea, or anyone who had done research in the area, come to the annual ALA conference in Chicago to discuss it, or send the information to him in Albany.[14]

That same year, Francis D. Tandy, assistant librarian in the Denver Public Library, wrote to Dewey to propose the establishment of a library "publishing concern" that would produce books in "good, clear type on a specially prepared linen texture paper. They [would] be strongly sewed on parchment or tape, and bound in a smooth-surface linen cover." On the flyleaf would appear full cataloging records "made in accordance with Cutter's rules." "I have nearly completed the arrangements necessary to carry out this plan," wrote Tandy, whose letter was published in *Library Journal*. He asked librarians for assurances that they would purchase books so produced, saying he would await their responses.[15]

For reasons unknown, nothing more was heard of Tandy's plan. In the 1899 annual report of the Silas Bronson Library, its director called for special library editions: "Books are cheap as compared with their cost in earlier times, but when the question of durability is considered, libraries could well afford to pay a much higher price for the better material and workmanship of the old days. Librarians ought to demand of many publishers special editions for public libraries."[16] However, the year was 1906 before any real activity was observable. In 1905 Bliss announced that a number of American publishers had communicated to him their willingness to place stronger library bindings on copies of certain titles "provided this demand of the libraries should be well defined." They also agreed to "print on more durable paper at a slight additional cost two or three hundred copies, say, for a well defined demand chiefly from libraries, and to supply these in sheets for permanent binding." While printing special library editions on durable paper for "the more important libraries" was not a perfect solution to the contemporary problem of inferior book production, it could secure the future of "books which it is desirable to preserve."[17]

In 1906, perhaps in response to this idea, the ALA's new Committee on Bookbinding asked twenty-five publishers to consider issuing novels and children's books in special library bindings. Of the twenty-five, six failed to respond, three answered negatively, and sixteen said they were willing to discuss the proposal further. To its surprise, the committee noted: "we learned that several years ago Doubleday, Page & Co. issued all their fiction in a special binding for library use, but they found the demand from libraries so very small that they were obliged to abandon the plan. . . . The failure of librarians to take any interest in this effort of Doubleday, Page & Co. to provide specially for their needs shows great neglect of a very important part of library economy. No attempt to get better bindings from the publishers will meet with success unless librarians all over the country give it systematic support."[18]

Not unexpectedly, those publishers showing interest agreed that they would require advance "assurance . . . of the number of copies libraries would order" and a guarantee of five hundred or more subscriptions per title. "At [the time] only one plan for learning the number of copies wanted by libraries occurred to the Committee"; each institution would send a note about the number it required to ALA headquarters, where the numbers would be tallied and each publisher notified on a monthly basis. The publishers would bind the proper number of copies, which libraries would then "order through their regular agents." The publishers agreed that the stronger bindings, which would be sewn on tapes with the first and last signatures guarded in muslin, would cost no more than an additional ten cents per volume. The committee felt that these books would last twice as long as ordinary publishers' bindings, or through seventy circulations instead of thirty-five. Among the interested houses were Appleton, Barnes, Doubleday, Dutton, Holt, Century, Scribner's, and Little, Brown. "The publishers are willing to meet us at least half way," the committee cautioned, "and permanent failure will be charged to librarians rather than to publishers."[19]

In February 1907 *Library Journal* printed an editorial urging publishers to issue "extra" bound library editions, and librarians to support the publishers who did so; special library bindings were preferable to binding from sheets, each book in the same monotonous style. The ALA's Bookbinding Committee announced that its "principal work" for the new year would be to determine the number of library-bound copies per title that libraries wanted and to persuade more publishers "to adopt the specifications of the Committee for the library trade" (i.e., to produce books that would withstand seventy-five circulations before needing rebinding). At the Asheville (North Carolina) conference, the committee reported the results of a questionnaire designed to determine the demand for *ALA Booklist* fiction in special editions. Although 1,500 circulars were mailed, the committee received only 430 responses. Most respondents answered that they would order such volumes, providing the additional cost was no more than ten cents per volume. An almost insurmountable problem of the proposal, however, was that *Booklist* reviewed fiction about two months after it had been published; most libraries purchased their copies long before the *Booklist* reviews appeared. Following the committee's report, Miss Kelso of Baker and Taylor invited any and all members of the committee to tour her company's New York City binderies in order to "hear their side of the story."[20]

The committee published a brief list of the novels several publishers had agreed, "with some reluctance," to issue in a reinforced library binding, and announced Doubleday's plans to issue large-print editions of standard fiction in library bindings. The publishers' reluctance was well founded. It was not particularly good business to implement new production routines to sell only five hundred to two thousand copies of a book. Further, it was difficult to know how many copies of the more expensive editions would be purchased, and publishers lost money on copies left unordered. Library editions also meant more work in the warehouse – another edition to inventory and monitor.[21]

Early in 1908 the members of the Committee on Bookbinding asked their colleagues whether they should continue the "campaign to get special library editions of popular fiction and juvenile books"; librarians had now had eighteen months' experience with such bindings. The opinions sent in response "were almost unanimously in favor of continuing" to press for more such work.[22] That same year, two other ALA groups showed an interest in library editions. The Committee on Library Administration received 185 replies to a questionnaire, sent to 246 libraries that raised various questions related to "economy in service." Among those responding, 133 libraries bought books in special library bindings; 93 found them satisfactory; six, unsatisfactory; nine, fair; and nineteen reported they had had insufficient experience to make a judgment. Although many found the books unattractive, the collective feeling was so positive that the committee recommended them, with the suggestion that either individual libraries or the ALA's Committee on Bookbinding advise publishers on how to make the bindings more handsome.[23]

The Committee on Bookbuying (John Cotton Dana, Bernard C. Steiner, and William Cutter) engaged in some interesting correspondence with publishers. In a letter to the American Publishers' Association, the committee cited its pleasure with "publishers' reinforced bindings for libraries" and elaborated on the value represented by the extra ten cents per volume. In his response, F. C. J. Tessaro, Manager of the Association, noted that his group's board of directors had appointed a committee consisting of F. N. Doubleday and F. A. Stokes to confer with the Committee on Bookbuying "regarding the various interesting questions submitted. I might add that copies of this letter will be mailed to the members of our Association."[24]

Perhaps in response to his copy of Tessaro's letter, Roger L. Scaife, a representative of Houghton Mifflin, sent the Committee on Bookbuying a rambling and rather unpleasant letter that read, in part: "We looked into the reinforced binding question. After much study and correspondence we hit upon a reinforcement satisfactory to your Book Binding Committee, and then found that the only books libraries cared to buy in such form were either poorly edited editions or editions with banged up plates which we could not recommend a library to purchase. Moreover, your Book Binding Committee could not tell how many copies libraries would take. Manufacturing difficulties arose, and we had to let the matter drop."[25]

Mr. Scaife went on to complain that librarians did not buy enough books in general, and even failed to purchase titles authored by their fellow librarians. When Houghton Mifflin reprinted a particularly significant title, "an acknowledged classic in its field," practically no copies were sold to libraries, even though it was publicized with many flyers. Scaife's single constructive suggestion, "that librarians and publishers get together and understand one another," seemed to lack sincerity.[26]

In its report for 1909, the ALA's Committee on Bookbinding gave a dispirited account of the campaign for reinforced library bindings. For three years the committee had attempted to persuade publishers to issue popular and standard works in special library editions and to convince librarians to buy them; "both efforts ha[d] met with but indifferent success." During the previous year, the committee asked librarians for "tentative orders" for 112 titles that were "standard and on the shelves of nearly all libraries, both large and small." In only a single case were over 300 copies of a book ordered from a publisher; in all other instances, the numbers were much lower. Despite this disappointing level of commitment, fourteen publishers brought out 70 books bound to ALA specifications. "In view of all these facts," the ALA reported, "the Committee has not been so aggressive this year as formerly in demanding reinforced bindings, although it still believes in them."[27]

If the committee was discouraged in 1909, by 1910 it was positively morose. Although Everyman's Library, a series of literary classics published by E. P. Dutton, had been brought out in special library bindings at thirty-five cents a volume for cloth or sixty for leather ("narrow margins of the books make it impossible to rebind them, but their small cost renders it possible to purchase a second copy"), the gap between the number of books published in reinforced bindings and the number that libraries bought continued to grow. Publishers sent flyers giving advance notice of new titles, notices appeared in the *Book Buyer*, and advertisements were printed in many other places, yet libraries did not respond.[28] One person strongly questioned the real need for specially bound library editions: "There can be no reason librarians should not know of the special library edition and what titles are so bound. With all this publicity, the demand grows smaller and smaller. . . . From this brief summary of conditions, one naturally asks: 'Is the special library edition a real need, or a repetition of a request as persistently urged – the reprinting of out of print titles, which was an absolute failure?' Are the requests from sixteen of the three thousand libraries sufficient evidence that the libraries want the special library binding and that it should therefore be continued?"[29]

By the time Scribner's issued its first novel bound according to the new ALA specifications – sewn on tapes, reinforced with muslin, and covered in plain buckram (after 142 circulations in one library, the book was "still sound but shabby") – many other companies had ceased publishing library editions because of insufficient support from those who had promised to buy them. "Charles Scribner's Sons are now practically alone in the manufacture of special library bindings and the interest shown by libraries hardly warrants its continuance."[30]

Even though the drive to obtain special library editions was unsuccessful, some libraries (generally, the leaders in binding experimentation) did purchase these books. The public libraries of East Orange (New Jersey), Rockford, Salem (Massachusetts), Wilmington (Delaware), Buffalo, Dubuque (Iowa), Jacksonville (Florida), Lynn (Massachusetts), Queens (New York), Sedalia (Missouri), Woburn (Massachusetts), and Atlantic City (New Jersey) found that the purchase of fiction and children's books in reinforced bindings enabled them to avoid subsequent rebinding and to keep those books in continuous circulation.[31]

Reinforced library bindings probably failed for several reasons. Some libraries hesitated to pay even ten cents extra for a book. The inconvenience of "double ordering" – first notifying the ALA of one's intent to order, then actually ordering – was time-consuming and unappealing. Because so few books were available in library editions, many libraries may have felt that any impact such books might have on their collections would be inconsequential. Some librarians questioned the wisdom of spending extra money for a reinforced binding that might stand up under considerable wear yet became dirty and unattractive before long. Binder Gilbert Emerson advised that "by buying the book in the publisher's binding, and later, should it be deemed advisable, having it rebound, you have the advantage of two clean bindings on the book for about the same cost as the original reinforced binding."[32] Of course, this approach generated business for binders like Emerson.

The delays associated with getting library editions into readers' hands represented a significant drawback for most libraries. In 1909 the public library in Redlands, California, noted that "as the special editions are evidently not published simultaneously with the trade editions, we have the annoyance of seeing the latter in the stores several weeks in advance of receiving our own. In that case it is not surprising that we do not order again." The public library in Ogdensburg, New York, reported the same experience. Since they rented novels to patrons for a fee of two cents a day, "we must have them damp from the press or they will not pay."[33]

A great deal was written comparing the longevity of publisher's bindings, extra-bound library editions, and books bound from the sheets; after all, this was the age of library economy. One method of measuring thrift in binding was the analysis of circulation statistics; librarians examined volumes in terms of the number of circulations they could withstand before being rebound or discarded. The standard of the ALA's Committee on Bookbinding called for a minimum of seventy-five circulations for special library editions. The committee urged librarians to view the cost of a book not in terms of the simple price of the volume but instead in terms of its cost per circulation; the lower the per-circulation cost, the better the value.[34] A one-dollar title that circulated fifty times cost two cents per circulation, whereas a two-dollar volume that circulated four hundred times cost a half cent per circulation and thus represented superior economy.

Not surprisingly, books in publisher's bindings did not wear as well as did books bound from the sheets and those in reinforced library bindings. Nonetheless, the circulation statistics librarians collected for case-made volumes varied. Certain publishers enjoyed better reputations than others, and some communities' readers may have been gentler than others, but this does not explain why some institutions' books survived an average of sixty-six circulations, while other library's books endured only a half dozen.[35] Despite reports of library editions that circulated 100 to 150 times,[36] most libraries could circulate such volumes only 20 to 30 times before they had to rebind or discard them; the degree to which a given library mended was probably a major variable.[37]

In 1909 a study of "the relative wearing quality of books of different publishers" also indicated an average of twenty to thirty circulations for case-made volumes. The ALA's Committee on Bookbinding collected statistics from twenty-five libraries, covering the circulation of new books in their original publishers' bindings. Included were titles from twenty-two publishers of fiction and twenty-eight publishers of juveniles. Books from Doubleday, Stokes, Holt, Century, Bobbs-Merrill, and Little, Brown enjoyed an average of twenty-eight to twenty-nine circulations each. The median number of circulations was about twenty-six, and the lowest about twenty-one. Children's books endured eleven to twenty-one circulations, with a median of around sixteen. The committee stated its intent to encourage those publishers with poorer records to strive toward "the standard of the leaders in the above table."[38]

Reinforced library bindings received high marks for durability. In 1909 the Committee on Bookbinding mounted an exhibit of special library bindings at ALA headquarters in Boston. A volume from the Jacksonville Public Library had circulated ninety-six times and was "still in passable condition." Volumes from the Washington, D.C., and Newark (New Jersey) public libraries had circulated sixty times, and records showed that some volumes had circulated seventy times and were still in use. The committee concluded that the reinforced binding represented a great value, owing to its superior circulation record and modest additional cost.[39] The Brooklyn and East Orange (New Jersey) public libraries reported equally impressive service from their library bindings. At Brooklyn, books in Scribner's reinforced bindings circulated an average of sixty-six times before rebinding, versus twenty-seven times for books bought in ordinary publisher's bindings; some reinforced volumes circulated over one hundred times. East Orange reported a book that had circulated fifty times and was still in good condition.[40]

The Committee on Bookbinding and local libraries conducted several interesting comparisons of publisher's bindings with library editions. The committee followed three copies of F. Hopkinson Smith's *The Tides of Barnegat* into circulation. At the time of its report, a copy bound from the sheets had circulated thirty-seven times and showed "no signs of coming to pieces." The second copy, one bought in a reinforced library binding for $1.10, had circulated thirty-one times; its cover was a bit warped, but it had no loose leaves and was generally in good condition. The third copy, in an ordinary publisher's binding that had cost one dollar, had circulated twenty times and, in the committee's estimation, had no more than five to six circulations left in it before it would require rebinding.[41]

In February and March 1909, when the Brooklyn Public Library discarded about seven hundred books, it took the opportunity to compare their circulation figures, with the following results:

Binding	Fiction	Juveniles
Bound from the sheets by Chivers	77	63
Publishers' bindings	11	13
Rebound by Chivers	65	50

The Philadelphia Free Library, whose binder was Gilbert Emerson, collected similar figures when it compared circulation figures for case-made books and those rebound in-house. Books in their original publishers' bindings enjoyed an average of twenty to twenty-five circulations, "while after being rebound in our own establishment it is not an unusual thing to find the same volume go out ninety to one hundred and ten times and yet be in good, serviceable condition for home use."[42]

At the Wilmington Institute, over a three-year period, Arthur L. Bailey (a member of the ALA's Committee on Bookbinding) conducted rather elaborate evaluations of the cost per circulation of books bound from the sheets by Chivers, as well as volumes rebound by a local binder and a Philadelphia binder (perhaps Emerson). In the end, Chivers's books triumphed at a cost per circulation of .0155 cents, versus .0184 and .019 cents for books bought initially in publishers' bindings and then rebound in Wilmington or Philadelphia, respectively.[43]

By 1905 there were a variety of binding standards from which libraries might choose, among them those of the ALA's Committee on Bookbinding, the Royal Society of Arts, and various public libraries. None was terribly long or detailed, and all were quite similar. It seems fair to call this period the infancy of library binding specifications – a time when librarians were struggling to find a way to hold both publishers and binders accountable for their workmanship, and no one standard predominated. Perhaps there is an analogy to the development and standardization of cataloging codes, which also occurred in the late nineteenth and early twentieth centuries: there were a number of somewhat similar alternatives, and while some were more popular than others, no single standard prevailed.

In 1906, speaking before the New York Library Club on the topic of publishers' bindings, John Cotton Dana reminded his audience that "one great difficulty at present is that we are almost without standards."[44] Perhaps he was reflecting on the brevity and the general nature of the several specifications available at the time. An early attempt to develop a binding standard to which publishers would adhere was made in 1877 by the ALA's Cooperation Committee. It contained the three major elements of any binding specification: materials, manufacturing, and workmanship. Sections were to be sewn all along, and volumes larger than 12mo were to have at least three cords; covers' backs and corners should be goat or vellum, with paper sides; the binding style should be tight-back rather than spring-back; the text block was to be laced into the boards; all edges should be burnished.[45] There is no evidence that publishers embraced these specifications.

A number of libraries, binders, and organizations developed their own standards. The binding specifications devised by F. J. Soldan for use in the Peoria (Illinois) Public Library bindery were frequently mentioned. Soldan called for collating the volume, mending all torn pages with onion paper, and sewing all along with quality thread on linen tapes five-eighths of an inch wide. Two tapes should be used for 12mo volumes (three if the book was over half an inch thick), and four for octavos and larger books. The volume was to be sewn all along with quality thread, and the first and last sections guarded with muslin; the boards were to be laced on, and the text block trimmed only moderately. Tar millboard, spring backs, and half-morocco covers with cloth sides were also specified.[46]

The San Francisco Public Library and the New York State Library developed their own "binding rules," and the "specifications for library bookbinding" of the Monastery Hill Bindery in Chicago were published in *Library Occurrent* in 1910. These were almost identical to Soldan's, with the added stipulations that plates should be guarded around their adjoining sections, and sawing should be "no deeper than the thickness of the cords around which the thread for sewing passes." A 1907 issue of the *Wisconsin Library Bulletin* offered "Specifications for Binding." "It does not purport to be a 'model' contract, but may be found useful," wrote the anonymous author. Again, the content was reflective of Soldan, but an interesting touch was the addition of some fill-in-the-blank worksheets for use by librarians wishing to develop their own specifications.[47]

The two most publicized binding specifications were those of the ALA's Committee on Bookbinding and the Royal Society of Arts' Committee on Leather for Bookbinding. Following its simple "seventy-five circulations" standard for reinforced library bindings, the Committee on Bookbinding offered slightly more detailed specifications "which would add but little to the cost of any book, but which would add greatly to its serviceability." Thick, spongy papers were to be avoided, and each section should contain no more than sixteen pages. Machine sewing was acceptable, but stitches should be no more than one inch apart and must come within three-fourths of an inch of the head and tail of the book. Sewing should be all along, and good glue, thinly applied, was required. "It will be noted," wrote the committee in its 1909 report, "that these specifications are in the main general rather than specific, and aim to call the attention of publishers and binders to important items." Apparently, a longer version of the specifications was sent out to publishers, with a request for their comments. Publishers such as E. P. Dutton reported binding according to these specifications, and the Oakland (California) Free Library followed them for its rebinding work.[48]

British binder George A. Stephen published and promoted these American standards in England, where he enriched them with his own additions. Signatures should be sewn with linen thread onto unbleached linen tapes. The first and last signatures were to be guarded with muslin or cambric, and single illustrations and plates guarded around adjoining sections. Endpapers with cloth joints were to be sewn as if they were a separate section, and elastic glue was to be used on the volume's back. Quality millboards and buckram or other good cloth (versus "common cloth") were also specified.[49]

The Royal Society of Arts' standard emerged from the work of its Committee on Leather for Bookbinding. Actually, there were two separate standards, one an enhancement of the other. Valuable or heavy library books were to be sewn all along on at least five raised hemp cords, using unbleached linen thread. Leaves whose backs were injured were to be guarded, and single sheets and plates guarded around the adjoining signatures; no tipping in was permitted. The endpapers were to be sewn on as a separate section, and the cords laced into the boards. The best black millboard was specified, as were worked headbands, leather- or linen-lined backs, and tight-back construction. On the other hand, some economy might safely be observed in binding ordinary library books, which could be sewn onto tapes whose ends would be secured between split boards; for ease in opening, a French joint was recommended. Cockerell, a member of the Committee on Leather for Bookbinding, further refined these two standards into four, covering reference works or other fine books, large or heavy books, books in current use, and little-used materials.[50]

The Royal Society of Arts' standard for binding leathers also had some influence in this country. The U.S. Leather and Paper Laboratory urged librarians, until there were standards for binding documents printed by the U.S. government, to include a clause in all binding contracts that leathers must meet the standard of the Royal Society of Arts. In 1907 the Pratt Institute reported that its periodicals binder had succeeded in importing leathers that met the society's specifications.[51]

The impact on libraries of volumes that could circulate only as many as twenty times before having to be rebound was stunning: a staple on which they had come to depend, the well-bound newly published volume, was no more. When librarians chose titles bound either from the sheets or in special library editions, they paid higher prices, hoping to realize an eventual economy by saving the cost of rebinding. The poor quality of the typical publishers' edition was one factor that led librarians to promulgate binding standards to be followed by publishers and library binders. While the specifications developed were neither long nor detailed, these early models were significant in that they represented attempts by librarians to regulate those who either provided or preserved their stock.

Chapter 12

Paper and Ink

Although archivists aired their concerns about the writing inks of the past and the present, librarians expressed almost no interest in printing inks. This was probably because modern printing inks were largely permanent, and contemporary book papers were so short-lived that the ink on them had only brief opportunity to do harm. There was some thought that the oily binding material in certain inks acted as a nutrient for mold, and that acidic inks would eventually cause paper to yellow, crack, or rot around the printed lines. If for any reason ink failed to penetrate the page's surface adequately, washing the paper could erase the print.[1] Since many library materials wore out before inks could effect any injury, and since there was little cleaning of their pages, it is understandable that librarians concerned themselves more with paper than with ink.

American research into the quality of book papers originated not in the library community but in the federal government. In 1908, in one of several Bureau of Chemistry circulars published in the interest of promoting more permanent federal documents, Fletcher Veitch, Chief of the U.S. Leather and Paper Laboratory, gave this simple explanation of the factors contributing to permanence and durability in book papers:

> Practically all fibrous vegetable materials will make paper, the quality being governed by the percentage of fiber sufficiently resistant to stand the action of the chemicals necessary to reduce to a working condition the most resistant fibers, while the quality of the paper which these materials will make is determined by the length, strength, and felting qualities of the fibers and the chemical nature of the cellulose which they contain; the longer and stronger the fibers and the purer the cellulose (the more closely it corresponds to normal cellulose), the better the paper, the longer it will last, the more wear it will stand, and the less it will discolor with time or use.[2]

Librarians tended to write and speak more vibrantly about the external features of a book (its sewing and binding) than about its paper;

Paper and Ink

nonetheless, there were librarians and binders who understood the fundamental importance of the book's most fundamental component. A 1909 editorial in *Library Journal* urged its readers to give greater consideration to paper quality when making book purchases, losing no opportunity to influence publishers to use better paper. Another librarian suggested the development of "library quality papers," watermarked for ease of recognition.[3] Walter Powell, Deputy Librarian of the Birmingham (England) Free Public Library, spoke to American librarians on the topic of the British publishing industry at their 1904 St. Louis conference. "In the production of a book the quality of the paper used is perhaps the most important consideration," Powell said. Even if the binding were bad, a book could always be rebound if the paper were good enough.[4]

Writing in *Public Libraries* a few years later, Indiana binder George Stosskopf pointed out that while all binding authorities agreed that good sewing was critical, one read "very little about the poor stock used by the publisher of today." "If we mean to improve upon the binding," Stosskopf continued, "we must begin with the paper and demand of the printer as well as the binder better material and up-to-date methods. I hold it a fallacy to claim that any particular method of sewing will eliminate or even reduce to a material extent the trouble brought on by the using of a poor grade of paper." Other librarians, including Henry Evelyn Bliss, also labeled poor paper as one of the "chief infirmities of modern bookmaking"; if a book was available in a number of editions, one should choose the edition printed on the best paper.[5]

Thanks to the research of scientists within the federal government and the private sector, American librarians were familiar with the twin concepts of paper permanence (resistance to the effects of aging) and durability (retention of strength during use). The 1908 U.S. Department of Agriculture *Yearbook* reported that permanence and durability in paper almost precluded a pleasing appearance: "The operations which make clean, white paper make it weak and subject to slow changes which lead ultimately to its destruction. Those which make a strong paper do not give as clean a sheet and at the same time increase its transparency greatly." It seemed that the papermaking technology of the time often produced an attractive product which, while good for presswork, also had qualities that contributed to its ruin.[6]

Writing in *Printing Art* in 1903, scientist Arthur D. Little expressed these concerns about the permanence of modern book papers: "Speaking generally, however, it cannot be denied that the product of the modern paper mill is incomparably more perishable than that which the vatman formed slowly, sheet by sheet, a hundred years ago. This is especially true of the papers used for printing; and the growing apprehension of librarians that many of the books upon their shelves will not outlast their authors is wholly justified. The rapid deterioration of newspaper is a matter of everyday observation, but the transactions of many learned societies are printed upon paper which can scarcely prove more permanent."[7]

Others also doubted the permanence of contemporary paper. Although Cedric Chivers was optimistic about a skilled binder's ability to compensate for inferior book papers when a volume was required to last no more than a dozen years and a few hundred circulations, "it is another question to determine the value and life for the reference library of books made of these papers. Here the mischief is greater and the ingenuity of the bookbinder is less effective." Librarians were assured of more than enough space on their shelves for new books in the future, "in consequence of those of the past day having crumbled to dust. This is no freak of imagination, or result of hysterical fears, but is sadly confirmed by the chemical analysis of distinguished analysts." Many volumes, even if left untouched, would not outlast that generation's readers.[8]

One librarian, while half glad that "the utilitarian cheapness of the last two decades of the nineteenth century" would eventually rid society of common contemporary fiction, regretted deeply that "the same fate [would] overtake the bound volumes of periodicals and newspapers which contain matter, historical and scientific, of priceless worth." A prescient John Russell Young, Librarian of Congress in 1898, used a section in his annual report entitled "The Durability of Paper" to draw Congress' attention to the impermanence of the paper on which much of the library's collection was printed. "Under modern conditions of paper manufacture," Young wrote, "the press sending forth from day to day so much that is perishable, newspapers crumbling in the readers' hands, the question may well arise as affecting, not only our own, but all modern libraries, as to how much of our collections will become useless because of the deterioration and disintegration of the paper used in the cheapest forms of literature."[9]

There was some thought that publishers should bring out a few copies of every title "supposed to have permanent value" on linen or cotton paper for purchase by libraries. In a somewhat eccentric article in *Scientific American*, William J. Manning described his proposal to the Joint Committee on Printing that it print two copies each of the "more important government publications" on linen. The fabric for two copies of the *Congressional Record* would cost $65. Manning's recommendations were based on his study of mummy wrappings from the collections of New York's Metropolitan Museum of Art.[10]

Bliss suggested that special library editions of "books which it is desirable to preserve" be printed for "the important public libraries." Another librarian sent letters to several publishers, asking about their willingness to publish "small editions of your more important future works on special paper for the use of libraries." The responses were predictable. One publisher indicated that any title of continuing interest should be reprinted, and that libraries could simply purchase a new copy. Others felt that there were no permanent modern book papers, that it would be difficult to gauge the demand for such volumes, and that the associated expenses would be great. Both American and British librarians proposed that copyright law be used to effect the publication of library editions on permanent papers.[11]

Librarians regretted the impermanence of modern book paper, but its lack of durability was a bigger complaint: ". . . within the last few years some of our publishers have issued their books (especially the cheaper standard novels) printed upon a paper which is certainly thick and nice to handle, but which will scarcely bend without cracking. To a person buying such a book for his own use, this is not of much moment; but when the same book is handled by a few ordinary library borrowers, the result is simply disastrous. The leaves . . . drop off in autumnal showers, although the binding may be perfect and the stitching beyond reproach."[12]

Librarians who purchased popular titles printed on "wood-pulp feather-weight paper" were soon faced with shelves full of worn-out books–books represented in their card and printed catalogs and, in many cases, not easily replaced. Papers used in fiction and juvenile books were soft, light, and spongy–often not strong enough to hold their stitching. Because the thick paper on which these titles were printed gave many volumes the appearance of great length, one librarian suggested that "the literary shortage was made good by the help of more wood pulp." The clay-coated paper on which many art books and illustrations were printed was stiff and brittle; with a minimum of use, the pages broke from their bindings. "The large number of withdrawals is caused by the poor quality of paper . . . used for the books of the present day," wrote the director of the Salem (Massachusetts) Public Library in 1908.[13]

The general lack of durability in book papers was exacerbated by many publishers' practice of printing so that the grain of the paper ran across, rather than parallel to, the fold, reducing the ability of the paper to flex and increasing the likelihood that the book's pages would break and fall out. An innovator like Cedric Chivers might bind books printed on poor paper in a compensating manner, but publishers and most standard binders gave them no special attention.[14]

One librarian termed weak papers "a question of reform which librarians and others interested should agitate for until we obtain books which will stand usage." Since contemporary papers were "worthless for durability," a library trustee suggested that librarians ask publishers to print a sufficient quantity of books "on paper of cheap quality, but great durability," for purchase by libraries. Cedric Chivers encouraged librarians to approach publishers with the idea of printing popular works on better paper for use in public libraries.[15]

Material and method were the two partners necessary for the manufacture of good papers. Papers properly processed from quality rags were both more durable and more permanent than most made from wood pulp; consisting of "a very pure form of cellulose, which is extremely resistant to all changes," they also cost two to six times as much.[16] As society's increasing demand for paper brought about the change from pure rags to a mixture of rags and wood to wood alone, or even straw, librarians looked on with dismay. They observed that the newer papers lacked the "strength and wearing qualities of the cotton or rag fibre" of the past.[17]

In discussions at an 1893 meeting of the New York Library Club, one member commented, "There is so much wood-pulp paper used in making books that there is more danger of a book of this kind going to pieces than of its binding wearing out. . . . The paper disintegrates and the glue and paper soon separate, the paper leaving off in thin flakes with the glue." Another librarian urged, "Don't buy any books issued by those publishers who resort to the cheap, nasty, spongy, and altogether objectionable quality of paper now so frequently used in this country since the days of wood-pulp prevail." Wood-pulp paper "wears but little handling, and falls apart simply standing upon the shelves unused."[18]

Of the two types of wood-pulp paper, "chemical wood" was superior to groundwood; processed so that the strong chemicals used to break down the wood were removed, it produced a fairly durable and permanent paper. On the other hand, groundwood papers, with their heavy lignin content, were doomed by simple exposure to air and light. In defense of chemical-wood pulp, scientist Arthur D. Little noted that "papers made from properly purified wood fibres, as bleached sulphite [*sic*] and soda fibre, have shown no sign of change in twenty years at least," and George A. Stephen pointed out that paper made of chemical-wood pulp was not necessarily bad if it were not produced by a cheap, hurried process.[19]

While it was possible to manufacture both an inferior rag paper and a quality wood paper, most librarians remained doubtful about the permanence of chemical-wood papers. "Many of the books of the present," wrote the Pennsylvania State Librarian in 1898, "especially cheap literature, are printed upon 'wood pulp' paper, some of it looking so well as probably to 'deceive the very elect,' that it compels the State Librarian to be very cautious as to the purchase of such published works. Fifty years hence books printed upon wood-pulp paper will be almost wholly destroyed, because of the ephemeral character of the paper used." Papers made of mechanical wood, or groundwood, were held to be still worse. Their fibers were shorter, having been ground, cut, and beaten in various stages of mechanically processing the pulp; further, they contained complex cellulose compounds and associated chemicals such as lignin, which proved particularly vulnerable to decay. Groundwood paper (such as newsprint and the paper used in "dime novels") was considered suitable only for items of "transient value."[20]

One of the specific complaints librarians had about modern book papers was their excessive weight. Publishers liked thick, heavy papers on which they could achieve better presswork. But as a result of the over-beating of the pulp and the addition of fillers, papers were becoming so heavy that librarians objected to the unnecessary "inconvenience and expense of handling and shelving useless material."[21]

Papers to which fillers (chiefly china clay) had been added were said to be "loaded," while those to whose surfaces clay or other substances were applied (to enhance their appearance or printability) were called coated, clay-coated, glazed, or art papers. Though coated and loaded pages were lovely to look at, librarians characterized them as tender, brittle, and stiff. Their own weight often caused them to tear from the stitching; they were liable to crack, buckle, and break with much use. Coated surfaces would sometimes flake, and in a damp atmosphere, they often stuck together.[22] The loading process consisted of "adding china clay, sulphate [*sic*] of lime, or other white insoluble mineral matter" to paper during its manufacture, making it more opaque and giving it the finer printing surface needed to reproduce halftone illustrations.[23] Loading substantially reduced a paper's elasticity and durability; the addition of 15 percent clay decreased paper strength by 30 percent. Because clay and other fillers lacked fiber, their addition also weakened paper and made it heavier. "This seems to us quite a serious matter in itself," wrote Fletcher Veitch, "particularly in large collections where the total weight on the shelves and building may be fifteen to twenty per cent greater than it should be."[24]

Scientists recognized the danger in any process or ingredient that allowed certain chemicals or acids to remain in the book paper. If the bleaching agent were not completely removed, it continued its work after the papermaking process was finished. "To prevent this," the U.S. Department of Agriculture advised, "the chemicals used should be thoroughly washed out of the pulp before it is made into paper, as even very small quantities of . . . bleaching materials . . . slowly act on paper and gradually make it weak and brittle."[25]

Acids were also destructive. "We cannot, therefore, expect a paper to be durable if it contains acids or acid salts," one authority wrote. Veitch learned in his research that free acids negatively affected paper strength. Over time they promoted the disintegration of fiber, and the paper became weak and brittle.[26] Unhappily, the size added to most book papers had highly acidic components. Typical sizing products were alum rosin, starch, and glue. While sizes gave book papers needed body and made them fit for presswork, they were subject to chemical change over time and could bring about decay. Rosin size was particularly targeted as a threat to paper permanence. The U.S. Department of Agriculture advised librarians, "Excess of rosin size is another cause for the deterioration of paper, as the rosin gradually oxidizes, forming free acids." Since alkaline paper seemed somewhat susceptible to bacterial attacks, a neutral paper, neither acidic or alkaline, was recommended.[27]

Paper testing and the development of specifications for book papers was almost an international pastime; related activity taking place in many European nations was brought to the attention of American librarians by their professional press. In Italy in 1898, the Societa Bibliographica Italiana recommended that the government regulate by law the character of paper to be used for printing legislation, documents to be preserved in archives, and books that publishers were required to distribute to government libraries. That same year, Librarian of Congress John Russell Young acquired a copy of the Prussian government's specifications for paper on which official records were to be printed. Ten years later, in 1908, "elaborate physical and chemical tests of paper" performed by the "imperial government in Germany" were reported in *Library Journal*.[28]

Meanwhile, Cedric Chivers was busy with his own paper research. In 1909 the editor of *Library Journal* wrote, "Much that is called paper in these days is scarcely entitled to the name. It is a mere aggregation of pulp or other cheap material which will stand no wear and tear, and may go to pieces even sooner than the flimsy binding." Chivers, the editor went on, had been studying book papers, "testing the paper in books bought both from American and English publishers with results sadly surprising"; he was to read a paper on these studies before the annual ALA conference. At the Bretton Woods meeting, Chivers described his work of testing papers from twenty different books published by eleven different publishers. He found that the ratio of chemical-wood pulp to rag to mechanical-wood pulp made little difference in a paper's durability. "It is clear then," he told his audience, "that something happens to paper, apart from its fibrous composition, which seriously affects it from the librarian's and bookbinder's point of view."[29] While older book papers could withstand strains of thirty, forty, or fifty pounds per inch, modern ones could withstand strains of no more than one to four pounds per inch. Chivers believed that this lack of strength resulted from overheating the pulp, which produced weak, short-fibered papers.[30]

Both the Royal Society of Arts and the U.S. Leather and Paper Laboratory conducted research into the permanence and durability of book papers. The society's Committee on the Deterioration of Paper was appointed in 1897. "'It has been brought to the attention of the Council of the Royal Society of Arts,'" read a letter published in *Library Journal*, "'that many books of an important character are now printed on paper of a very perishable nature, so that there is considerable risk of the deterioration and even destruction of such books within a limited period of time.'" Librarians were asked to write to the committee, giving "'any instances of books, published within the last thirty years, which already show signs of perishing.'"[31]

The committee submitted its forty-two-page report in 1898. Consisting of three pages of text prepared by its members and thirty-six pages of abstracts from the official research of Berlin's Imperial Testing Institution, the report did not represent much new thinking about the composition of book papers or paper specifications, though its very creation was an important event in preservation history. The committee classed paper-making fibers into four categories, designated A (cotton, flax, hemp) through D (mechanical-wood pulp). The standard recommended for "book papers required for publications of permanent value" required that at least 70 percent of the fibers come from class A materials and that no more than 10 percent loading matter and 2 percent rosin size be added. An interesting appendix contained responses to the committee's 1897 circular letter. Two publishers simply stated that their book papers did not deteriorate, while another declared that "owing to the use of wood pulp and vegetable substances, ninety-nine out of a hundred books will not be legible thirty or more years hence." One chemist forwarded information on his "patent for preserving paper," and a Dr. Garnett submitted a "printed memorandum respecting chemical preparation for the preservation of printed matter."[32]

Between 1904 and 1909 the U.S. Leather and Paper Laboratory conducted prodigious inquiries into the causes Lof paper deterioration. During this period Fletcher Veitch, chief of the laboratory, reported much of its research, sometimes in documents of the Bureau of Chemistry (the laboratory's parent body) and sometimes under the banner of the Department of Agriculture (the bureau's parent body). It was Veitch who kept American librarians abreast of the laboratory's work through his close contact with the ALA's Committee on Bookbinding.

Through the pages of *Library Journal*, the laboratory kept librarians informed of its work and invited them to send "samples of papers . . . which have long withstood wear and tear and also those which have deteriorated rapidly." Among the topics the laboratory explored were sizing, the effect of chemical residues, and the "strength, durability, and value of paper under the conditions of use."[33] The laboratory maintained that "the papers used for . . . all Federal, State, and county records which are preserved for many years and subject to much handling, should be strong and uniform" and that book papers for publications of permanent value should be of the same general character.[34]

In 1907 *Examinations of Paper*, a description of the laboratory's testing abilities, was published as a Bureau of Chemistry circular. The laboratory could test a paper for fiber type, length of fiber, thickness, mean breaking weight, loss of strength on folding, transparency, moisture and ash content, type of sizing and loading, presence of bleaching agents, and presence of chlorides and sulfates. While "examinations can not be made for individuals, manufacturers, or dealers," instructions were given for the use of the testing service by any branch of the federal government.[35]

The laboratory's work culminated with in its 1909 report *Durability and Economy in Papers for Permanent Records*, by H. W. Wiley, chief of the Bureau of Chemistry, and C. Hart Merriam, chief of the Bureau of Biological Survey's Committee on Paper for Departmental Use. According to these authors, "In view of the great value to mankind of the results of scientific research and discovery achieved and published in the various bureaus of the Government; and in view of the fact that the paper on which these results are now published is highly perishable, its life in many instances being only a few years, we urgently recommend that the necessary steps be taken to secure the printing on durable paper of at least part of the edition of each publication of lasting value, so that copies may be permanently preserved in the Library of Congress and other great libraries in this country and abroad."[36]

In 1904 the secretary of agriculture asked the Bureau of Chemistry to investigate suitable papers for government use. This investigation, based on the analysis of about five thousand paper samples sent to the bureau for testing, resulted in three reports: Veitch's *Paper-Making Materials and Their Conservation* (1908), "Suitable Paper for Permanent Records" (1908), and "Paper Specifications" (an appendix to Wiley and Merriam's 1909 report). Wiley and Merriam summarized data from all three sources and recommended "certain broad, general specifications for various kinds of paper." They concluded that government publications distributed to the public could be printed on "fourth grade printing paper" but that "a small edition of each publication, or certainly of those of scientific value, should be printed on high-grade paper for distribution as permanent records to public and institution libraries."[37]

Veitch's "Paper Specifications" then provided detailed standards for a variety of paper types. In testing papers and developing its regulations, the laboratory had used "chemical, physical, and microscopical examinations." "While this work is well-developed in Europe," Veitch wrote, "but few systematic tests of paper were made in this country until the work was taken up by the Bureau of Chemistry five years ago, where it has been conducted in constantly increasing quantities since."[38] Referring to his research, he concluded: "From the foregoing it is evident that the best and most durable papers, made from given materials, are those which have been properly cooked and bleached, contain no free bleaching agents, have been well washed to remove soluble salts, do not contain free acids, have been sized with a minimum quantity of sizing material, have been beaten to give the greatest strength consistent with the maximum flexibility, have been made on the machine at not too great speed, and have been dried at low temperature."[39]

The second-grade machine-finish paper recommended for libraries' copies contained 75 percent rag fiber, 25 percent chemical wood, and maximums of 5 percent ash and 1 percent rosin. It displayed strength and folding factors of 0.40 and 0.25, respectively.[40]

If the degree to which a topic is addressed in the professional press may be taken as a fair measure of interest, we may infer that despite progress in research and thinking about paper, turn-of-the-century librarians remained largely concerned with the book's binding rather than the pages that binding sheltered. Indeed, members of the library community were followers, not leaders, in paper research, and seemed more troubled by modern book papers' lack of durability than by their impermanence. For many, a certain degree of mystery and misconception still surrounded the deterioration of papers, and few understood that processing shortcuts and remnants of injurious chemicals were chiefly responsible for their weakness.

Chapter 13

Pamphlets, Periodicals, Newspapers, and Maps

In addition to books, American libraries also collected pamphlets, periodicals, newspapers, and maps. In some instances, the preservation problems and solutions associated with these materials were similar to those associated with monographs. These formats were generally more slender and more delicate, however, lacking the fundamental protection of a book cover; often, they were also printed on poorer paper. Consequently, they were more costly to care for and required a thoughtful and somewhat different preservation approach.

It was Charles A. Cutter who pointed out in the new *American Library Journal* that pamphlets could not go onto library shelves unprotected; they were "thin, limp," would not stand up, tended to curl, and became "dog's-eared and dirty." Staff at the Boston Public Library concurred; pamphlets were indeed problematic, and their flimsiness made them difficult to use.[1]

Nonetheless, there was agreement that pamphlets were an important element in any library collection and ought to be preserved. Cutter counseled libraries to retain only those pamphlets of specific interest to their readers, lest the costs of organizing and preserving them become unjustifiably large; "the pamphlets themselves are much more likely to be preserved where a business is made of sorting and cataloguing them than where they are likely to be regarded as a nuisance, thrust away in corners, covered with dust, and nibbled by literary mice." Other librarians took a more liberal view of pamphlets. Speaking at the first ALA conference, Joseph Walter of the Wilmington (Delaware) Institute said that "all libraries should be encouraged to preserve, if not arrange [pamphlets] in view of the fact that the community at large is already prone to destroy these fugitive scraps of history, or allow them to perish." Similarly, from the Brookline (Massachusetts) Public Library's 1876 report: "The Trustees would urge upon the citizens the importance of preserving for the benefit of the

Library the multitude of pamphlets now used for lighting fires or condemned to the waste basket."[2]

Librarians employed a variety of preservation approaches with pamphlets. Because their numbers were so great, a library did not always treat every pamphlet the same way. In 1901 the Boston Athenaeum reported, "Thousands of our pamphlets lie in what may be termed the attic, covered with the dust of at least a quarter of a century, thousands more are in boxes, catalogued by authors, and many more are fully catalogued, but unbound." At Harvard University, a pamphlet might begin its shelf life in a manila envelope, graduate to a thin pamphlet box, go from there (as more pamphlets accumulated on the same topic) to a larger pamphlet box, and eventually be bound with a group of its topical fellows.[3]

The Bowdoin College librarian favored binding pamphlets; "it seems absurd as well as inexpedient to determine the treatment of small books from the circumstance of their having a paper instead of a cloth cover, rather than by the character of their contents." A Midwestern library administrator took exactly the opposite view. The very fact of a pamphlet's having been issued with soft covers made it questionable for a librarian to bind it. The pamphlet's insubstantial format was a comment on the slightness of its content; in binding a pamphlet, the librarian revised the publisher's initial assessment.[4]

In truth, most libraries' preservation practices for pamphlets lay somewhere between binding all and binding none. Harvard's convention of "graduating" a pamphlet from one manner of protective covering to another was fairly common. Although Cutter thought that "bundling" pamphlets (that is, tying them in bundles, often braced between two pieces of millboard) was inefficient and placed too many demands on the time of both staff and readers, institutions such as the Boston Public Library, the Boston Athenaeum, and the Brooklyn Mercantile Library sometimes bundled pamphlets in subject groupings, often as a preliminary step to binding them or placing them in boxes.[5]

Many libraries placed loose pamphlets in boxes. Sometimes a pamphlet box was the permanent home for items "of such transient value or such vague import as not to warrant binding." For more valuable titles, the box was an intermediate protective device, useful for accumulating a group of subject-related pamphlets that would later be bound. Often, these boxes were arranged on library shelves by subject, with brief contents lists either pasted on the spine or placed inside. Sometimes each box was labeled with a classification number and placed at the end of the appropriate shelf of books. While at Columbia College, Melvil Dewey wrote, "We have also avoided the inconvenience of having to consult a separate pamphlet and serial collection, by devising a cheap but most satisfactory pamphlet-case, which, without wasting room on the shelves, enables us to keep side by side with the books on each minute topic all the pamphlets, clippings, and manuscripts which we may have bearing on that topic."[6]

Cutter pointed out that the ideal box must not be open on the top; such boxes rapidly became "dust bins" whose contents would first "bulge out" and then "come to pieces."[7] The two most popular pamphlet boxes or cases were the "institute case" and the "Woodruff file-holder." The institute case was faced with a door on which the title of each pamphlet was printed; it contained a separate brown paper wrapper for each title. The door attached to the box with "elastic hinges," of which Cutter was quite critical – they frequently broke or wore out and required replacement. In their report for 1876, the trustees of the Brookline Public Library provided this description of the institute case: "A large number of pamphlet-boxes have been ordered from the manufacturer. These are cases made of wood and covered in the semblance of a large volume. The back is made to open and disclose the contents in place, with an index showing the position of each enclosed document; thus once arranged in their proper order every pamphlet will be easily accessible without disturbing the remainder."[8]

The Woodruff file-holder appears to have been adapted for library use from a business product, the "Woodruff bill-file." In 1880 over 100,000 of the latter were reportedly in use in the offices of the federal government. The file-holder, said to be a specially made version of this successful office device, consisted of a wooden box in which pamphlets were arranged like cards in a catalog drawer and held in place by a movable block with a "patent spring." The pamphlets were kept smooth and clean as a result of being tightly pressed together while in the file. Among the libraries using the Woodruff file-holder were the National Library of Medicine, the Johns Hopkins University Library, and the Boston Athenaeum. At Johns Hopkins, pamphlets were afforded extra protection by being individually placed in a "Koch patent spring back binder" before being lent to readers. The librarian felt that the combined use of the file-holder and the spring-back binder enabled the library to economize on storage space and at the same time to present the pamphlet to the reader as "a bound volume to all intents and purposes."[9]

At least one library reported keeping pamphlets in a special chest that was fifty-two inches high, fourteen inches deep, and twenty-seven inches wide. Each drawer represented a particular subject and was labeled accordingly. The librarian reported that "the pamphlets are perfectly safe from dust."[10] Some institutions protected pamphlets with purchased or homemade binders. The Koch spring-back binder, used by the Johns Hopkins Library and recommended by the American Library Association, was quite expensive at ninety cents; it offered the advantage of not piercing or otherwise defacing the pamphlet, as did most other binders.

Another commercially available product, the Common-sense binder, pierced and then clamped the pamphlet with a pair of metal stubs covered by a protective slide. The Common-sense binder was manufactured in seventy-two styles and sizes and could also be custom-made. The Gaylord company also offered its pamphlet binder in a variety of sizes; pamphlets were pasted into it with a gummed strip, and the use of "an Acme wire stapler" was also recommended.[11] Other products were the Harvard and Holliston binders (similar to the Gaylord) and the Reform self-binder. The latter expanded to accommodate increasing numbers of titles and had stubs with eyelets, by which the pamphlet was both pasted and laced into the binder.[12]

Often, library staff made their own pamphlet binders, using techniques ranging from the simple to the ingenious. Perhaps the cheapest approach was a plain "manila cover, which can be put on with klips [*sic*] or patent novelty paper-fasteners. The manila cover with cloth back is more durable, and costs only three cents." Some libraries punched holes along the backs of their pamphlets and laced them into manila covers; others attached a stub to which the pamphlet could be pasted or an envelope into which the pamphlet could be placed. Some institutions substituted the sturdier, more flexible red-rope paper for manila.[13] At one time the Boston Public Library fastened pamphlets, via guards, into their own prefabricated, standard-size board-and-leather binders. Other libraries laced or tied pamphlets into empty book covers, either pulled off of volumes to be sent to the bindery or purchased new or secondhand from binders.[14]

Those institutions that bound pamphlets used a variety of techniques and materials. Otis H. Robinson, librarian at the University of Rochester, explained to colleagues at the 1876 ALA conference that his library bound every pamphlet, usually in a "cheap binding, either by itself or with a few others of its class," at about thirty cents per volume. Similarly, the Bowdoin College Library bound every pamphlet "deemed worthy of preservation," as did the University of Michigan Library.[15] At the Boston Public Library, all pamphlets that were bound were covered in goatskin. In contrast, most libraries followed the practice of the University of Rochester, where pamphlets were bound in book cloth over millboard, as were lesser-used books.[16] Some institutions that bound pamphlets (including Harvard University, the Boston Public Library, the Pennsylvania State Library, the Boston Athenaeum, and Columbia College) did so by subject, in groups of ten or twelve titles per volume. A very few, including the Library of Congress, bound pamphlets individually.[17] Perhaps the pamphlets were protected equally whichever approach a library selected.

Many of the protective measures employed with pamphlets were also used for periodical issues. This is not surprising, since both formats were thin and issued in soft covers. At the Redwood Library in Newport, Rhode Island, where binding funds would not stretch to cover periodicals, completed volumes were tied together in bundles, then shelved. This practice was both unsatisfactory and uneconomical, as individual issues quickly became warped, dirty, and ragged. A 1908 issue of *News Notes of California Libraries* described a somewhat superior version of this approach, which included bracing each bundle by cutting manila paper to fit the width and height of the periodicals' spines. This provided some support (enough to shelve the bundle as if it were a book), and the paper brace could be labeled.[18]

Unable to preserve many of its periodical runs, the Queens Borough (New York) Public Library disposed of them. In 1904, the ninth year of its existence, the library possessed $1,000 worth of periodicals it could not afford to bind. The public was not permitted to use these journals because of their worth and fragile condition. "The storage of these magazines is becoming a burden and it is hoped that this valuable material may be made available this year," wrote the trustees. In 1909, finding itself with fifteen hundred volumes of unbound titles and still no binding funds, the library chose to dispose of most of the collection "by exchange, sale, gift to institutions, . . . reserving only those most needed for our reference files."[19] Alternatively, the library might have continued to store the unbound volumes in the hope that binding funds would become available, or permitted the public to use the loose issues. But disposing of the journals seemed preferable to seeing them perish unprotected on the shelf or in the hands of the public.

Most libraries bound complete volumes of periodicals, and many placed current individual numbers in protective binders as an interim measure. Some binders did not require puncturing the item along its back; these included Von Laer's perfect binder (which held the issue in place with flat steel wires) and the Emerson binder. In choosing a binder, the most important issue was "how best to preserve without diminishing the usefulness" of the item; thus, rod and spring-back binders were recommended over those requiring that the periodical have holes punched in it.[20] Some libraries manufactured their own periodical covers, using everything from red-rope paper to cloth-covered boards with morocco backs.[21] This was probably an economical use of morocco, as these reusable binders were doubtless opened and closed frequently and thus needed strong spines.

Although some libraries bound volumes of periodicals in rather mean ways (lacing them into cheap pasteboard-and-muslin covers through holes drilled along each issue's spine; sewing them onto a fabric hinge attached to two bare pieces of millboard), most libraries treated their journals with considerable respect.[22] The Hartford (Connecticut) Public Library bound each periodical volume in two parts; "the result has been to prevent the premature breaking of backs from overweight and the poor quality of paper now used, which has of late been the cause of the short life of books of this class."[23] While some institutions bound periodicals in canvas or some other sturdy cloth, many used leather.[24] Since most libraries considered periodical volumes to be items of permanent value to their collections, the use of half-morocco was not uncommon. The Pratt Institute in Brooklyn succeeded in obtaining leather that met the standards of the Royal Society of Arts.[25]

In 1909 the ALA Committee on Bookbinding published general specifications for binding periodicals. They included the use of Irish linen thread, either four or five tapes, quality millboard, and half-morocco with cloth or paper sides (American cowhide or India goat "sold exclusively by Benjamin Moore and Sons" might be substituted). Volumes were to be sewn all along and trimmed as little as possible; plates were to be guarded.[26] This standard, however, failed to address perhaps the biggest controversy in periodical binding: whether to bind or discard covers and advertisements.

Many librarians advocated including both; they thought serial issues should be bound into volumes "intack [*sic*] . . . simply for protection and preservation, without being dismembered by the binder's hand or knife." Not only did "the unconsidered trifles of to-day become the history of tomorrow," but also covers often possessed valuable information that was lost forever if they were removed. Dewey cautioned, "When librarians who take several hundred serials assume in a moment or two that such and such parts are valueless and throw others away, we are going into the 'weeding' process in a way to seriously embarrass us later"; his students were taught that covers and advertisements should always be retained. Spofford also recommended that covers and advertisements be bound; to neglect them was to fail to preserve "valuable contemporary records respecting prices, bibliographical information, etc., which should never be destroyed, as it is illustrative of the life and history of the period." This was also the approach favored by members of the ALA's 1893 Chicago conference.[27]

There were a few variations on this "save everything" theme. Some librarians felt that only large research libraries could afford the cost and storage space required to bind covers and commercial messages. A member of the Boston Public Library staff supported the preservation of advertisements but suggested that they might be bound separately from the periodicals in which they appeared. "Even the advertisements of medical magazines are carefully bound apart," he wrote, "and, if the merits of Lamplough's Pyretic Saline or Pears' Soap are not appreciated in the next century, it will not be the fault of that institution."[28] Similar sentiments were expressed in an 1889 letter to *Library Journal*; if librarians thought posterity would want to examine "silly advertisements," these should be bound into separate volumes. The writer continued:

> I confess that I am barbarian enough to object to handing down to posterity, as part of a magazine, the monthly paid advertisements of the virtues of "Ball's corsets" or the alluring promises – repeated ad nauseam in a half-dozen magazines every month – "how any lady or gentleman can easily make from forty to fifty dollars a day." A large proportion of these advertisements are simply barefaced swindles, and whatever archaeological interest they may have a hundred years hence, it is surely no business of the librarian to bind them up with magazines, with whose contents these have no more to do than the paper wrapper in which these magazines are sent through the mails. . . . For the sane librarian no rule can be clearer than this one: nothing should go into a bound book, issued in parts, that is not consecutively paged.[29]

Even more delicate than pamphlets and periodicals were newspapers. Librarians were almost frightened by the speed with which these valuable historic records deteriorated. In one American library, labels cautioning readers to handle newspapers with care were placed in each bound volume. "Too much care," the director wrote, "cannot be taken to preserve from rough handling and neglect these volumes, which, in most cases, are irreplaceable, and increase in value and in importance to the student as the years go by."[30] While librarians took special care in binding and shelving newspapers, efforts to compensate for the weak, delicate nature of the paper on which they were printed were unsuccessful.

In 1893 the Trustees of the Minnesota Historical Society called attention to the problems associated with newsprint. "The flimsy nature of the paper used by newspapers nowadays has been referred to in our previous reports," they wrote in their 1893 annual report; "its quality is steadily deteriorating, and a considerable proportion of the newspapers which we take reach us in a very dilapidated state, being torn and some very badly so." Librarian of Congress John Russell Young described "newspapers crumbling in the readers' hands," and the Pennsylvania state librarian declared that contemporary newsprint was so poor that it could last no more than fifty years. Another librarian, condemning the "cheap wood pulp paper" on which newspapers were printed, summed up the problem in this way: "It means that the material for history contained in the newspapers will not be available after the period mentioned, and that all such historical records will eventually disappear unless provision is made for reprinting or preserving the volumes as they exist at present."[31]

Some libraries attempted to offset the inferior nature of newsprint by binding two sets of every title, one as a service copy, the other "for the permanent file." The director of the Lawrence (Massachusetts) Free Public

Library suggested that publishers might provide libraries with free second copies of local papers, "if it were known that they would be carefully preserved." The Montana Historical Society Library retained a duplicate unbound set of every title, carefully wrapped to shut out damaging dust and light. However, attempts to convince publishers to employ "a better quality of paper for such files of newspapers as are to be preserved" failed.[32]

Frank Hill, director of the Brooklyn Public Library in 1910, became aware of the brittle condition of many of the bound newspaper volumes on the shelves of his institution. He wrote to several publishers, asking whether they experienced similar problems with their backfile issues, whether these issues were printed on better paper than those sold to the public, and whether they took any particular steps to preserve older issues. No publisher reported the use of special paper or preservation methods of any type. Newspaper publishers raised two major objections to printing certain copies on superior paper. First, there was no better paper that would fit their presses. Second, the profits from sales of their newspapers certainly would not compensate them for the cost of the better paper or of the labor required to change the paper in the machines. Hill recommended that the American Library Association appoint a committee to talk with publishers about the inferior quality of newsprint, and suggested the alternatives of reprinting older issues or using "some chemical process as a preservative."[33] Unfortunately, these ideas were not taken up.

Because they were so fragile, and because no better preservation method existed, newspapers were bound. In an address before the Conference of Librarians (London, 1877), John Winter Jones, Librarian of the British Museum and president of the meeting, advised that newspapers be bound at the earliest possible moment; "no class of papers are more liable to injury from use without the protection of binding." In 1889 the Cincinnati Public Library reported that its entire newspaper collection was being gradually rebound "and is now in condition to insure better preservation than heretofore." At the Lenox Library of the New York Public Library, each newspaper leaf was guarded before it was bound; additionally, a stiff sheet of paper that extended an inch beyond all three edges of the bound sheet was used to separate the individual issues in each volume.[34]

Because newspapers were large formats, librarians typically bound them in duck or canvas. First, a number of sections might be created by whipstitching or machine sewing a half-dozen individual issues together. These sections would then be sewn all along to make a strong volume. In his 1880 report, the Provost of Baltimore's Peabody Institute wrote, "Finding that leather bindings on heavy newspaper volumes are easily defaced and broken as well as very expensive, we have had a large number of the volumes of the *American* bound in canvas, which proves to be very satisfactory. It is cheaper, stronger, and much less easily injured than leather." The Pratt Institute bound newspapers in canvas with paper sides (roan proved too expensive), the Providence Public Library switched from sheep to canvas (which was more durable and less costly), and the Massachusetts State Library also traded leather for canvas.[35] The ALA's Committee on Bookbinding recommended half-duck with paper sides for newspaper binding, and the public libraries of the District of Columbia, St. Louis, and Boston followed this advice.[36]

Bound newspaper volumes were frequently housed under substandard conditions. In crowded libraries where space was at a premium, low-use materials were often shelved in remote, inconvenient locations. Unfortunately, this sometimes meant basements or other environmentally unsound spaces. In 1876 Justin Winsor described the basement in which the Boston Public Library's newspapers were kept as "out-of-the-way, half-lighted, damp and dingy. . . . The situation is discreditable." At Harvard University, newspapers were housed "in a cave opening from the basement where there is no direct ventilation and no light, and where dampness cannot be avoided in summer."[37] The combination of a damp, dirty atmosphere and newspapers' inherent physical weakness was a perilous one. Along the same lines, the Cincinnati Public Library reported one of the more curious housing arrangements for newspapers: "On account of the inconvenience arising from the storing of the bound volumes of the city in the top story of the building, which was a source of great delay in getting them for consultation, one of the toilet rooms on the first floor has been fitted up for the purpose of holding a portion of them, with marked good effect. . . . These files of newspapers are valuable property, always in danger of destruction, and not easy to replace. I have therefore thrown additional safeguards around them."[38]

Newspapers also presented special shelving problems. Like large monographs, they were typically stored flat rather than upright. In 1897 the librarian of the Boston Athenaeum noted that "the chief improvement made in the Library building during the year has been the construction of new shelves for the newspapers, so that now almost all the volumes of our valuable collection are kept flat on their sides instead of standing on end." A year later, the Brookline Public Library reported that "the volumes [of newspapers] now lie flat on the shelves and will be better preserved in the future."[39] Some libraries shelved their newspaper collections on sliding shelving. At the Massachusetts State Library, roller shelves were installed; the upright divisions of the stacks also rolled, so that every part of the shelving that the volume touched, turned. The St. Joseph (Missouri) Free Public Library and the Indiana State Library also employed roller shelving, and in 1896 the Boston Public Library installed sliding newspaper shelves "to save wear on the volumes in constant use."[40]

While newspapers (along with periodicals and pamphlets) were generally preserved as bound volumes, few libraries attempted to bind maps, which were so unlike other materials they collected in format.[41] It was agreed that maps should be handled gently and as infrequently as possible. One librarian stamped his every map "'Please handle with care,'" and reported, "I find the above little stamp to be very preservativ [sic] of maps, charts, etc." While atlases were typically treated as books, other sorts of maps were issued and preserved in a variety of attitudes, including flat, folded, and rolled. They were variously stored in drawers or on shelves, loose or in portfolios. The Brooklyn Mercantile Library occasionally folded maps and tied them into bundles, but this was an exceptional treatment.[42]

Many libraries, including Harvard University's, the Boston Athenaeum, and the Boston Public Library, routinely mounted maps. Occasionally, paper was used, but more often muslin, cotton, cambric, linen, or cheesecloth was selected. A thin coat of paste affixed the map to its backing. "All librarians agree that maps should be mounted if it can be afforded," wrote the librarian of the University of Illinois.[43] Some libraries may have stiffened maps with size. A recipe for a "white hard varnish" for maps appeared in an 1891 issue of *Library Journal*, but there is no evidence of its widespread use, except perhaps for schoolroom maps.[44]

When preparing sheet maps for use, library staff sometimes folded them so that they would fit standard-size portfolios or drawers. In such cases, rather than mount the map, staff would strengthen and reinforce each fold by pasting a wide strip of cloth over it.[45] Many libraries cut sheet maps into conveniently sized sections. Then the several pieces were either mounted on a single sheet of muslin or hinged together with cloth so that they could be folded into a suitable size. The Buffalo Public Library, the Library of Congress, the Indiana State Library, and the library of the University of Illinois all treated some maps in this way.[46]

Once maps had been mounted or otherwise reinforced, many libraries placed them in protective folders or portfolios. Sometimes each container held a single map and sometimes it housed several. The Boston Athenaeum made map folders from manila paper, "turning over the edges to keep out the dust"; the public libraries of New York and Newark, New Jersey, also used manila paper, while the Harvard University Library employed "stout paper," simply folded. At the District of Columbia Public Library, red-rope paper was bought in rolls of five hundred square feet and used to make map folders.[47] Other institutions devised sturdier, more elaborate containers. The Boston Public Library's map portfolio consisted of two boards joined by a back of leather or cloth. Cloth flaps that folded over the case's contents were attached to three sides of the bottom board, and tapes were added so that the portfolio could be tied when closed. The Buffalo Public Library used portfolios made of millboard covered in heavy cotton, and the University of Illinois also made its own board portfolios.[48]

Folders or portfolios of maps were often kept on special shelves. The New York Public Library advised laying portfolios "upon loose boards sliding in grooves or rods, with no stops at the back, as all such tend to shake the sheets up at the back and fold and crease and tear them." If the library could afford to do so, a "falling flap" should be placed over each sliding board to keep out dust. Horizontal sliding shelves were also recommended for map folders.[49]

Some libraries placed maps, either loose or in portfolios, in map cases. In 1891 Harvard used cabinets thirty-three inches wide, fifty-two inches deep, and thirty-six inches high; each had nine shelves, and each shelf housed five to ten portfolios. The U.S. Geological Survey employed custom-built map cases forty inches wide, sixty-one inches deep, and thirty inches high. The Boston Public Library also placed maps in cabinets with open, sliding shelves.[50]

Another type of map case was equipped with drawers rather than shelves. Sometimes maps were first placed in folders or envelopes, but often they went into drawers loose, since the front edges of the drawers protected their contents from dust. These edges often dropped down to facilitate perusal. Shallow drawers (about 1.5 inches high) were recommended; when the reader had fewer maps to sort through, there was less chance he or she would damage their edges and corners in the process. The librarian of the University of Illinois described an interesting new steel map cabinet, installed around 1910. It was fifty-seven inches wide, eighty-four inches deep, and fifty inches high. "In appearance it resembles a large box with a slanting, roof-like top." The case was double-faced, with five large extension drawers on each side. "For consultation the roof-like top is provided upon which maps up to fifty-seven inches by ninety-two inches can be spread." All told, the case held six thousand maps.[51]

Often, libraries rolled large wall maps to store them, although it was acknowledged that as a result, they seldom lay flat when subsequently opened for use. At the Boston Athenaeum, rolled maps were suspended from individual hooks. The Brooklyn Mercantile Library placed them in protective pasteboard cylinders. Some libraries tied rolled maps and placed them in a case with pigeonholes, "similar to an umbrella rack"; others lay rolled maps in long, narrow drawers. At the Newark Free Public Library, each rolled map was tied with tapes and kept in storage until requested by an interested reader; "when brought to the reference room, it [was] thrown over a large screen and consulted in that position."[52]

Rolled maps are not to be confused with roller maps. While both were typically large, single-sheet maps, the top edge of a roller map was affixed to a roller (often, the map was issued this way by its publisher). When the map was in use it was unfurled, suspended from the roller; at other times it was stored wrapped around this bar. Sometimes, a roller contained several maps, sometimes only one. At least two companies (Hartshorn of East Newark, New Jersey, and Charles S. Jenkins of Lansdale, Pennsylvania) manufactured spring rollers to which libraries could attach their own maps; Hartshorn also sold a matching case. In 1908 the Jenkins map roller cost fifty dollars and held between 30 and 150 maps, depending on their sizes. It looked and worked like a roller for a continuous linen hand towel: only one map was before the reader's eyes at a time, and as he or she cranked it into the machine and out of sight, another one appeared.[53]

Other devices were simpler. At the Buffalo Public Library, wooden dowels were split lengthwise, then pulled together by screws, with the maps' edges held tightly between the two halves. When not in use, these rollers, each of which held six to eight maps, were kept in pasteboard tubes and stored in a rack seven feet long, three feet deep, and five feet tall. This rack could hold 198 tubes and 1,188 maps. Other libraries kept roller maps in "bags resembling those used for fishing-rods, with a flap at the top to exclude the dust." At the Business Men's Branch of the Newark Free Public Library, maps were placed on rollers attached to the underside of a shelf positioned eight feet above the floor; the reader simply pulled the map down when he or she wished to see it. By 1900 the Library of Congress purchased few maps issued on rollers, finding that older such maps in its collections had become "stiff and hardened with age" (it is likely that a manufacturer's coating contributed to this condition). When the Library of Congress did acquire roller maps, its storage approach was little better than the publishers': staff separated map and roller, flattened the map under heavy weights until it was smooth, and then cut it into squares and hinged it.[54]

Maps, newspapers, periodicals, pamphlets – the more fragile materials in a library – lacked protective covers and consequently required somewhat different preservation techniques than those applied to books. The paper on which these materials were printed was even more tenuous than that used for monographs, and the preservation approaches of the time (binding and the use of various protective enclosures) had only limited effects. Deterioration was inevitable and usually swift, heightening librarians' frustration as these culturally significant materials progressed toward dust.

Chapter 14

The Influence of Rare Books, Documents, Manuscripts, and Works of Art on Paper

Indications that techniques for preserving special library materials may have influenced the treatment of library materials in general are seldom clear-cut. Near the turn of the century, many American librarians were aware of certain work relating to rare books, documents, or manuscripts, and we may perceive some similarities between such activity and librarians' approaches to preserving circulating monographs, periodicals, and maps. It is risky, however, to conclude that a common origin is shared by treatments for several types of materials during approximately the same period. At best, we can identify cases in which the transference of a practice from special materials to general library materials seems likely.

Many of the preservation techniques employed with mainstream library materials were borrowed from practices employed with rare books. Most of the instruction on removing dirt and stains from paper and bindings, mending torn pages, and lubricating leather derived from procedures associated with such volumes. It also seems safe to say that what preservation ethic existed (chiefly, a sense of the importance of retaining the integrity of the book as an artifact and using unproven techniques with caution) derived from contemporary thinking about rare materials.[1] In a lantern lecture delivered before the 1898 conference of the Library Association of the United Kingdom, Cyril Davenport of the British Museum revealed a growing awareness that clues about a book's provenance and chronology were contained in its more anonymous physical components and that it was thus necessary to protect these features from insensitive restoration or rebinding. Similarly, Ainsworth Spofford urged caution in the application of new preservation approaches, particularly when treating valuable or unique materials.[2]

Key among the material types librarians felt a responsibility to preserve were documents, whether local, state, or federal. These items were considered critical, irreplaceable parts of American history, and this perception may have promoted the development of a broader preservation mission. The first large-scale American attempt to restore printed or written government records on paper occurred in the Department of State's Bureau of Rolls and Library in the 1880s. The methods employed, such as hinging documents with linen and binding them, were not innovative. Francis W. R. Emery, a binder in Taunton, Massachusetts, patented his document restoration technique in 1896. It involved piecing together damaged sheets, pasting silk or tissue paper on both sides, and applying a coat of paraffin to seal the tissue or silk against air and insects.[3]

Emery used his method on many priceless documents from New England and New York. In his report for 1900, Harvard librarian William Coolidge Lane described Emery's restoration of early records of the college, which had "suffered from a long sojourn in John Hancock's carriage house where they were eaten by insects and discolored and rotted by damp." The Library of Congress investigated the Emery method for use with its collections but rejected it. There is no mention of Emery's rather elaborate technique having been used with books.[4]

In 1888 the Massachusetts Commission of Public Records began to publish its *Report on the Custody and Condition of the Public Records of Parishes, Towns, and Counties*, which discussed the conditions of various types of state records (church, town, birth, marriage, and death) and often offered preservation advice. The first report included two special chapters, "Record Inks" and "Record Paper." Robert T. Swan, the commissioner during the early years of the *Report*, addressed the Massachusetts Library Club on 1 March 1895. His presentation, later published in *Library Journal*, apprised American librarians of the commission's studies of writing inks and papers. This research was not directly applicable to general library materials, and there is no indication that it had any bearing on that undertaken a few years later by the U.S. Leather and Paper Laboratory. Letters from Herbert Friedenwald, chief of the Library of Congress' Manuscript Division, indicate that the commission engaged in some restoration of documents by silking. However, there is no clear relationship between preserving documents with pasted sheets of silk or tissue and making tissue repairs to the pages of general library materials.[5]

Perhaps the greatest impact of document-related research on general library materials was the standard for book cloths developed by the U.S. Bureau of Standards. Through the work of the ALA's Committee on Bookbinding, American librarians were kept informed about the bureau's efforts to develop a standard for the cloth used in binding government publications, and they participated in the selection of a suitable cloth. Subsequently, many libraries asked binders hired to do general binding to provide cloths that met the bureau's standards.[6]

The work of another federal unit, the U.S. Leather and Paper Laboratory, was closely followed by American librarians through the pages of *Library Journal*.[7] A unit of the Department of Agriculture's Bureau of Chemistry, the laboratory had the following objectives: to investigate papers and leathers with a view toward identifying the factors that affected their permanence and durability, and to develop standards against which materials to be used in federal publications would be measured. Perceiving that librarians shared its interest in the quality of paper and leather, the laboratory sent frequent updates on its work to *Library Journal* and invited readers to submit "samples of papers and leather bindings which have long withstood wear and tear and also those which have deteriorated rapidly" for use in the laboratory's experiments.[8]

While the Leather and Paper Laboratory published several reports, *Durability and Economy in Papers for Permanent Records* (1909) summarized their most important findings and recommendations. Paper should be suited to the nature and purpose of the publication, and "a small edition of each publication, or certainly of those of scientific value, should be printed on high-grade paper for distribution as permanent records to public and institution libraries." The government was advised to purchase all papers on the basis of specifications and to develop two sets of specifications: one for permanent records and another for those intended only for temporary use. The laboratory conducted "chemical, physical, and microscopical examinations" of many papers. "While this work is well-developed in Europe," it reported, "but few systematic tests of paper were made in this country until the work was taken up by the Bureau of Chemistry five years ago, where it has been conducted in constantly increasing quantities since."[9] Librarians considered the laboratory's research important enough to abstract and summarize it in *Library Journal*, their major organ.

American librarians were also aware of Italian and German efforts to develop paper specifications for government records. An 1899 issue of *Library Journal* described the recommendation made by the Societa Bibliographica Italiana that the Italian government regulate the character of the paper used in public documents to be preserved in archives, as well as that used for the books every printer was required to contribute to government libraries.[10] The Prussian Regulations for Supply and Examination of Paper ("Vorschriften für die Lieferung und Prüfung von Papier in Kraft"), developed in 1886 and subsequently revised, were mentioned in *Library Journal*, summarized in English in the Royal Society of Arts' 1898 *Report of the Committee on the Deterioration of Paper* (itself cited in *Library Journal*), and studied by Librarian of Congress John Russell Young.[11] Preceding the work of the U.S. Leather and Paper Laboratory, this German research (which also established four classes of paper appropriate for printing various classes of government documents) may have influenced American efforts.

With regard to manuscript preservation techniques, it is important to acknowledge that the turn of the century was a time of considerable experimentation. Archivists were undecided about which methods were best, as the investigations of Herbert Friedenwald, chief of the Library of Congress Manuscript Division, show. Some of the cleaning and repair techniques used with book papers may have derived from similar treatments for manuscripts, perhaps via rare books.[12] Certainly it was the desire to preserve and share manuscripts that inspired initial attempts to use photography as a preservation procedure. It is almost impossible to say whether manuscript silking techniques (like those employed with documents during the same period) or the use of various preservative baths influenced preservation methods used with general library materials; there is no evidence of any direct transference.

"A manuscript, unlike a rare imprint, is the only one of its kind existent and any defacement is irreparable," wrote J. C. Fitzpatrick in his book *Notes on the Care, Cataloging, Calendaring and Arranging of Manuscripts*. Similarly, speaking before the 1897 Philadelphia conference of the American Library Association, Herbert Friedenwald remarked, "No treasures that come to a library are so precious as its manuscript collections. They are usually unique, and in but few instances have seen the light of the printer's day." It was the quality of uniqueness that both restrained and spurred activity in manuscript preservation and lay at the heart of its influence on preservation thinking (perhaps more than technique) for other types of materials. Repairs, which required "a wide knowledge of paper, the kinds, the qualities, the effects of age and of accident, and its behavior under every condition," were not the province of the inexperienced.[13] Father Franz Ehrle, the Vatican librarian, described the archival community's fear of the danger and responsibility associated with manuscript restoration, as well as "'a series of sad experiences'" in which treatments had destroyed the very items they were intended to preserve. "'In the greater part of the cases one cannot judge of the success of this attempt to save except after an experience of a decade of years,'" he continued.[14]

Because manuscripts were both ancient and unique, leaving them "ragged and dirty" was often favored over attempting to clean, size, or bind them. Such treatments were too risky, as little was known of their effects on inks or paper. When repairs or restorative treatments were attempted, "only material which [was] entirely sound and good" was to be employed. Dr. Otto Posse of the Royal Archive in Saxony, Germany, thought it unlikely that librarians would espouse any of the new methods of manuscript preservation until experience had proved them harmless over time.[15]

The first conference devoted to the preservation of library and archival materials was held at St. Gall, Switzerland, in 1898. Eighteen delegates, as well as official government representatives from eleven countries, responded to Father Ehrle's call for an international meeting of librarians to examine manuscripts in various stages of decay, to demonstrate and discuss different methods of treatment, and to consider how further deterioration might be prevented. Otto Posse, one of those invited, asked Ehrle to extend the conference's discussions to include materials found in archives. He believed that there was a relatively small number of disintegrating manuscripts and that these could be satisfactorily preserved by photography. Of greater concern to Posse were the large numbers of documents moldering in archives everywhere. Because of their sheer numbers, they required methods of preservation different from those suited to manuscripts. Ehrle agreed, and what was announced as a meeting devoted to manuscript preservation became one aimed at both manuscripts and documents.[16]

While no American librarian was invited to the conference, it was described in the pages of *Library Journal*. Following the meeting, Herbert Friedenwald of the Library of Congress' Manuscript Division corresponded with Ehrle and Edward W. B. Nicholson, who represented the Bodleian.[17] It was Friedenwald who, after examining a number of preservation procedures for manuscript materials, committed the Library of Congress to silking and tissuing with pure, unimpregnated materials. The information he gathered from Ehrle and Nicholson greatly influenced his decision.

Preservation measures described at the St. Gall conference included silking and tissuing, photoreproduction, and treating manuscripts with gelatin-formol, ammonia-collodion, and nitrocellulose (Zapon).[18] Among the meeting's unresolved questions were how long the process of deterioration lasted ("Does the power of a corroding agent never exhaust itself so long as it has anything to feed upon?") and whether it was advisable to attempt to neutralize corrosive forces before applying preservation techniques. Pondering the possibility that decomposition continued even after an item had been treated, Ehrle concluded, "In spite of that, I warmly hope that, even putting things at the worst, our process will diminish and will retard corrosion by offering the acids, if they continue to eat, another nourishment, and in thus turning them aside, at least partially. . . ."[19] A positive feature of any treatment was its ability to be removed quickly and easily, "should anything go wrong"; the concept of reversibility had begun to develop.[20]

The resolutions passed at the conference's close showed a certain prudence but encouraged the continued investigation and application of preservation techniques. A list of the world's oldest, most valuable manuscripts was to be made, and photographs of these taken. All relevant preservation methods were to be studied, and those applicable carried out. Archivists were encouraged to begin practical examinations of possible preservation methods and to collect and share their own experiences. They should not confine themselves to ancient, handmade papers and parchments but should also consider modern papers made during the previous fifty years. Similar resolutions followed the German Archivists' Conference held in Dresden in 1899. Governments, noblemen, and city administrators who had sent representatives to the conference were urged to test the liquid preservative Zapon in their own archives, publish specifications for papers for government use, and publish the results of research on writing inks.[21]

During the twelve years between the St. Gall conference and the International Congress of Archivists and Librarians (Brussels, 1910), librarians grew wiser and more cautious about new preservation techniques. They learned firsthand that impurities or incompatible properties in the materials and substances of preservation (tissue, silk, paste, and the various baths) could harm the very items they were intended to protect. Such injury might not manifest itself for some time, so that caution and thorough testing were imperative, lest precious manuscripts and documents eventually become "monuments to misplaced confidence."[22] "Strong, thin, and chemically pure" tissue paper or silk, while it might eventually deteriorate and require removal and replacement, proved superior to "the best French vegetal paper" used by Nicholson and to other papers impregnated with turpentine and other oily or resinous substances. The Library of Congress used rice-flour paste and applied silk to both sides of the paper being treated; other libraries followed its example.[23] None of the baths with which the Germans experimented proved satisfactory; in as little as ten years, the materials to which they were applied became stiff and brittle.

Perhaps the less-than-satisfactory nature of preservation techniques for manuscripts as physical objects increased interest in finding an effective way to use photography to preserve the intellectual content of these materials. A few large libraries offered reprographic services. As early as 1896, the Boston Public Library reported "a photograph-room where copies may be made of manuscripts, plates, or other material of which a photographic reproduction is desired." Waldo Leland of the Carnegie Institution in Washington, D.C., regretted that only a small number of American libraries offered such services. While a "photographic installation" could be found in "numerous European libraries . . . in America few libraries have gone further than to set apart a dark room." The cost of offering reproductions was low and could be recouped by charging a few cents a copy. Additionally, such copies were accurate (as manual transcriptions often were not), the service assisted scholars who were at a distance from the material they needed, and "wear on valuable documents [was] saved." "It is not too much to hope that before long some sort of photographic apparatus will be considered an indispensable part of the equipment of all archive depositories, as well as of all libraries, societies, or other institutions having the custody of historical manuscripts," Leland concluded.[24]

In a detailed description of the many photoreproduction methods available for use in libraries, a British librarian wrote, "There is another important matter which should not be omitted, namely, the regulations under which photography of rare, often fragile and easily injured, objects should be allowed." Others shared this concern. The creation of photographic facsimiles should occur "under the eyes of the library officials who can take due care to prevent damage to the treasures thus copied. There is unfortunately an utter want of conscience on the part of many professional photographers in this respect. The chief European libraries permit only experts on whose honor and efficiency they can rely to photograph their treasures." Among the libraries with "photographic workrooms" were the Bibliothèque Nationale, the Bodleian, the libraries of the British Museum and the Vatican, and the Royal Libraries at Göttingen, Copenhagen, and Berlin. Some libraries charged fees or asked for negatives in return. At the British Museum, the reader brought and paid his or her own photographer. Prior to the visit, the reader was required to file an application that included a statement of any intent "to introduce combustible chemicals into the Museum." The library extended permission to photograph "'subject to any copyright which may be claimed by authors or others, but as to which the Trustees . . . cannot undertake to give information or offer an opinion.'"[25]

In 1880 a blaze in the Vatican burned the library of Professor Theodor Mommsen; at the time, this noted scholar had in his possession many rare books borrowed from other European libraries, which also perished. Highlighting this event in *Library Journal*, an American librarian suggested the use of photography to produce "replicas of some of the unique works possessed by the chief libraries of Europe," to which libraries and scholars might then subscribe. Speaking in 1893 before the International Congress of Librarians in Chicago, Dr. O. Hartwig of the University Library in Halle, Germany, first suggested international cooperation in the photoreproduction of manuscripts. His idea was referred to the American Library Association, which took no action. At Hartwig's suggestion, Dr. W. Du Rieu of the

University of Leiden (Holland) Library attempted to get the project under-way but had no success.[26]

In 1896 Du Rieu died. A year later, Charles Mills Gayley, Chairman of the English Department at the University of California at Berkeley, proposed to the university's regents that they establish a bureau for systematically reproducing the manuscripts of Europe. His program was to include both "unique manuscripts and rare printed works." In 1898 the regents accepted Gayley's plan and appointed a committee (with Gayley as chair) to carry it out. The committee's first charge was to obtain an endowment of $30,000.[27]

That same year, at the preservation conference at St. Gall, a resolution calling for the photoreproduction of the oldest, most important European manuscripts was passed. A committee was appointed to accomplish this task, as well as to seek subsidies for the work from various governments. In 1899 A. W. Sijthoff of Leiden, Holland, wrote to ALA President William Coolidge Lane, describing a series of manuscript reproductions available for purchase from him. These had probably been prepared as a prospectus for Du Rieu before his death. At the 1900 Congress of Librarians in Paris, Leopold Delisle, director of the Bibliothèque Nationale, reintroduced the issue of manuscript photoreproduction, but again no action occurred.[28]

In January 1904 the National Library of Turin burned. Taking heed of this tragedy, France proposed to set aside 100,000 francs to reproduce the "principal manuscripts" of France. Later that year, speaking before the Library Section of the International Congress of Arts and Science, St. Louis, Guido Biagi (director of the Biblioteca Mediceo-Laurenziana in Florence, Italy) linked the fire with the need to preserve the intellectual content of manuscripts: ". . . These reproductions render less disastrous the effects of a fire such as that which lately destroyed the library of Turin." Every country should identify its own list of materials to be preserved photographically and calculate the total cost. The following year, Belgium planned an international conference on the photoreproduction of manuscripts.[29]

In 1905 Charles M. Gayley's project at the University of California, Berkeley, caught the attention of the *New York Evening Post*, which gave it some publicity. A number of librarians wrote to the *Post* endorsing Gayley's plan, and their letters were published. The Belgian government's International Congress for the Reproduction of Manuscripts began on 21 August in Liège. Its two purposes were the "preservation of historical, philological, scientific, and artistic monuments against the perils of decay, mutilation, theft, and fires, by reproducing them and manifolding them in facsimile" and to "facilitate the pursuit of original research for countries and students far removed from the few great depositories of these sources of human knowledge." Gayley was appointed to the international congress, along with four other American delegates, including Librarian of Congress Herbert Putnam and New York Public Library Director John Shaw Billings. Apparently, however, only Gayley actually attended.[30]

The question of "the propriety of appealing to national governments for direct financial assistance" was hotly debated, but the international congress passed a resolution endorsing the Berkeley plan (which had as yet produced no facsimiles). As part of the American project, major European libraries (including the Bibliothèque Nationale, the Bodleian, and the libraries at the British Museum and the Vatican) offered to permit "the reproduction of manuscripts without restriction and on the most liberal terms." Another committee to explore the idea of reproducing manuscripts cooperatively was appointed. Gayley planned to submit a proposal for the creation of a "bureau for reproductions of rare manuscripts" at the 1906 meeting of the Association of American Universities.[31]

The Berkeley project never materialized. In 1908 the ALA's Publishing Board announced that it would publish catalog cards for "photographic fac-similes [*sic*] of rare books and manuscripts in the Bodleian library at Oxford," which were made for American libraries. Information on all facsimiles made would be sent to Professor John William Cunliffe of the University of Wisconsin, who would provide the cataloging copy. By 1909 the committee appointed at the close of the St. Gall conference seems to have had some success in identifying deteriorating manuscripts and raising money to photograph them. Then, after 1909, nothing more was heard from that group.[32]

Although these international schemes for the photoreproduction of manuscripts and other rare materials failed, they are strong examples of early cooperative attempts and demonstrate the effect disasters could have on preservation thinking and activity. They represent an important, practical recognition of the possibility of separating the preservation of an item's intellectual content from the preservation of the artifact itself.

While manuscripts, documents, and monographs share many characteristics in terms of appearance and use, the distinctions between works of art on paper and library books are arguably greater than the similarities. Produced for different purposes, the two types of materials consequently receive very different treatment. Prints, which are created to be exhibited and admired, are not required to withstand the constant handling to which books are subjected. Books enjoy the solid security of their covers; prints, fragile and more vulnerable to a variety of dangers, often require the added protection of mounts or portfolios. Whereas nineteenth- and twentieth-century printing inks typically remain stable when immersed in water or cleaning preparations, drawing inks, pastels, watercolors, and other print media are far from uniform in their responses to such treatments and demand an extremely cautious preservation approach.[33] Further, the posttreatment appearance of the item is of much greater concern to one preserving prints or drawings than it is to one working with books.

Many works of art on paper (drawings, watercolors) are unique, while others (prints, engravings) are produced in limited series. Conversely, library books are published and collected in great quantities and therefore demand preservation approaches that are swifter and less painstaking than those suited to works of art on paper. The element common to books and works of art on paper is paper. Despite important differences in the papers used (including the distinctions between machine-made and handmade papers), this shared base has led to some exchange of techniques for cleaning, repair, and other aspects of preservation.[34]

In the late nineteenth and early twentieth centuries, works of art on paper were subject to many of the same deteriorating influences (fire, flood, light, dampness, mold, dust, heat, insects) that affected books and other library materials. The same high-intensity lighting, atmospheric pollution, and central heating that the industrial revolution brought to the shelves of libraries affected the walls and cases of museums. Norman Brommelle has pointed out the very poor environmental conditions present in the National Gallery (London) in the mid-nineteenth century; these were probably very similar to those in urban libraries. The museum staff noticed that some "mysterious agency" left a greasy deposit on the pictures' surfaces and was causing their deterioration. "This agency was variously stated to be the human exhalations from the enormous crowds, the sulphurous smoke from the outside atmosphere, curious black stains emitted . . . by ventilator pipes, . . . and the dirt from muddy boots." The museum was very crowded; the number of visitors in 1851 exceeded that a hundred years later, when the floor space was six times as great. "When the atmosphere grew heavy the windows were opened and the smoke from the chimneys of the nearby municipal wash-house, which was described as 'very opaque' came in through the windows, which were not protected with gauze."[35]

Some treatises on preservation techniques linked methods for manuscripts, rare books, drawings, and prints.[36] This is not surprising, since materials in special collections and archives, like drawings and prints, were often rare or unique. Like old and valuable library materials, works of art on paper were best served by a conservative preservation approach. "Unless a print is very dirty or is pasted or laid down on paper or card, it is better let alone," wrote one authority. Prints were to be "laid down" (pasted to supporting material) "only when they are very badly torn"; in general, they were better placed in portfolios. Another art historian counseled, "When the question rises whether to disturb a valuable drawing whose condition causes alarm, we must balance the risk of damage through restoration against the risk incurred by neglect: can we afford not to try to improve its condition? Damage has been wrought by skillful restorers who did not know enough about the history of art, as well as by people who were well-informed but manually incompetent."[37]

Works of art on paper were routinely cleaned and mended, although the instability of their pigments and inks required more caution than might be necessary when working with books. Nevertheless, methods and materials were similar. Prints and drawings were dry-cleaned, washed, bleached, rinsed, and dried, much like pages of valuable books and sheets of manuscripts, although one author noted the need to exercise greater care for the surface and appearance of works of art on paper.[38] Tears were repaired by joining their dampened edges, applying a little paste, and tapping the surface with a spoon to push the fibers together (clearly, the tissue repairs suited for books were too unsightly for drawings and prints). Holes were filled with macerated paper similar to that of the print, or with patches whose edges were shaved and beveled to fit the space in question perfectly.[39] A thymol chamber was sometimes used to sterilize prints and drawings by killing mold and mildew.[40]

Art conservation is a profession of the mid-twentieth century.[41] Many of the world's largest museums opened their doors during the nineteenth century, but "not until the twentieth century did museums clearly realize that one of their chief functions as well as an all-important duty was to pass on their collections in pristine condition to succeeding generations."[42] Although there are indications that some people working on prints and drawings were concerned with developing proper preservation procedures, the art conservator's precursor, the restorer or "cleaner," generally "had a background of artistic training . . . and ordinarily knew no chemistry except of a practical nature." The intent of his work was largely cosmetic – to clean the artwork, thus improving its appearance. In general, he took no steps to protect the painting, print, or drawing against harmful influences, to analyze the causes of its deterioration, or to perfect better repair techniques.[43]

Because neither library nor museum conservation was a well-developed discipline at the turn of the century, it is difficult (and perhaps not too important) to determine whether those attempting to preserve library materials borrowed from the techniques of persons treating works of art on paper, or vice versa. While there were common methods of cleaning and repair, it cannot be demonstrated that librarians took their preservation approaches from the methodology for prints and drawings, and there is no evidence that librarians studied, or were aware of, preservation procedures associated with works of art. Vatican librarian Franz Ehrle (in a position paper he wrote before the St. Gall Conference was held) spoke of techniques for manuscripts as deriving from those for works of art on paper:

> The restoration of manuscripts on paper presents incomparably fewer difficulties than that of manuscripts on parchment. On this ground the workman can move in paths already firm and tried. One thing which has contributed not a little to this state of things is the extraordinary value of extremely numerous deteriorated pieces which form part of collections of engravings on wood and on copper, such as cartoons and studies of celebrated masters; but another is the greater facility with which one restores and renews paper. For the working of paper, the elementary methods, thanks to manuals of binding, and the methods rarely employed and more delicate, thanks to the well-known book of Bonnardot, have long ago fallen within the public domain. It is true that in practice these sure results and processes have not yet, even in the workrooms of celebrated collections of manuscripts and of archives, obtained all the extension which would be desirable in the interest of knowledge.[44]

On the other hand, paper conservator Marilyn Kemp Weidner, commenting on the paucity of research and investigation devoted to works of art on paper, wrote:

> What we are able to learn comes mainly from those working on library and archival materials. But solutions for the treatment of this type of material, which is usually printed in fairly insoluble ink, must be adapted by the fine arts conservator because of the possibility of the solubility of the artists' media and the need for concern to preserve the surface appearance of the work of art. Also, in handling the large masses of library material, the need for speed is often a major consideration, whereas, with works of art, a slow, more tedious method is sometimes considered a safer solution.[45]

Weidner's observations were made in 1967, almost a hundred years after the beginning of the period examined in this book. Perhaps her ideas were affected by the work of that group of British book binders and conservators who influenced librarians and art conservators alike during the 1960s and 1970s. People such as Peter Waters, Christopher Clarkson, Don Etherington, Roger Powell, and Sydney Cockerell–book binders and conservators with common experiences at London's Royal College of Art and other British schools, as well as in Florence after the flood–visited this country during that period, speaking, teaching bookbinding, and sharing their expertise. Waters, Clarkson, and Etherington took up American residence and assumed positions in the Preservation Office of the Library of Congress, where they helped develop and improve its preservation program. The writings and research of the others (Powell was the conservator of the Book of Kells) influenced conservators of books and works of art on paper alike. It is likely that these men, in turn, learned much of their craft and technique from persons working in the field of art. If the conservators of library and archival materials appear to be in a position of leadership at the present, perhaps the work of those caring for works of art on paper was instructive to librarians in the past. Ascendancy has probably see-sawed between the two groups over a long period, with each borrowing from the techniques or research of the other.

The value and uniqueness of works of art on paper, manuscripts, and rare books, along with the historic significance of government documents, contributed to the development of a preservation mission that carried over to more general library materials. At the same time, the singular nature of these special types of materials also inspired an ethic of caution in the application of new techniques and a consciousness of the value of these items as artifacts. The turn of the century was a time of experimentation in preservation methods for all type of materials. Over time, many of the substances that were used, such as Nicholson's French vegetal papers, caused further deterioration in the materials to which they were applied; nonetheless, some modern conservators argue that they served an important purpose because they held together valuable, deteriorating manuscripts and books until contemporary preservation technology permitted the removal of those substances and the application of more stable techniques. While some of the cleaning and repair methods used with book papers may have derived from similar treatments for other materials, it cannot be demonstrated that librarians took their preservation approaches from techniques used with other paper formats. The use of photography as a method for manuscript preservation is probably the clearest example of a borrowed preservation approach that would eventually have a major influence on mainstream monographs and periodicals.

Chapter 15

Looking Forward, Looking Back: 1910

From 1876 forward, preservation practice in American libraries can be clearly documented. In fact, the degree of concern and level of activity may be surprising to librarians of the late twentieth century who find the reports of earlier library administrators and the contents of the professional press charged with expressions of alarm about poorly made, deteriorating collections, dismay over buildings vulnerable to fire, and counsel on cleaning, mending, and binding materials. A simple survey of the transition in interests that occurred during the years surrounding the turn of the century underscores a consistency in preservation activity but also identifies several shifts in emphasis.

Certainly, many preservation concerns persisted throughout the period between 1876 and 1910 (and still exist today) – yet at various times, some were more prominent than others. During the last quarter of the nineteenth century, librarians' interests, as expressed in their reports and library literature, were largely confined to sound custodial and fire-prevention measures, the qualities of various binding materials, binding techniques, and various library appliances (shelving, book supports, book jackets, and pamphlet binders and boxes). Andrew Carnegie's gifts (which, as R. Kathleen Molz points out, were occurring at the rate of two or three libraries a day during "the wholesale period of his benefaction") and the planning for the new Library of Congress gave importance to library architecture: the relationship of building design to preservation was another popular topic throughout the 1880s.[1]

Between 1876 and 1890 there was also considerable concern about the decay of leather, popularly attributed to gas lighting. However, electric lighting (introduced in American libraries in the early 1880s) and the increased use of book cloths (first manufactured in the United States in 1883) made the issue less pressing. By the time the Royal Society of Arts completed its report on leathers for bookbinding (1901), American interest in the topic had diminished. It seems fair to say that the transitions from gas to electrical lighting, and from leather to book cloths, permitted the shift of interest from the potential damage done by illuminating gas to the inferior publishers' bindings that were to characterize the 1890s and the first decade of the new century.

In the 1890s librarians began openly protesting the poor construction and flimsiness of publishers' bindings. Their complaints were the result of a steady increase in the mechanization of edition binding. Early in the twentieth century, the idea of special, sturdier library editions emerged. The first examples were published in 1907, but their level of acceptance never corresponded to the degree of publicity they were given. During the same decade, American librarians became interested in the quality of book papers. Although the Prussian Regulations had been acquired for study by the Librarian of Congress in 1896 and the Royal Society of Arts' Committee on Paper Deterioration had published its report in 1898, not until 1904 to 1909, when the U.S. Leather and Paper Laboratory began its work on book papers (well-publicized in *Library Journal*), did this issue capture the attention of American librarians.

Despite the nascent interest in the preservation of paper – the very marrow of the book – the greater part of the period's research and activity focused on external preservation approaches rather than the problems inherent in the materials of which books were made. This is not to say that librarians were unconcerned about deteriorating bindings and book papers, but that they devoted less energy to these topics; when they did address them, they only infrequently did so in terms of "inherent vice." The Royal Society of Arts' 1901 report blamed tanning and dyeing residues for subsequent leather decay, and the U.S. Leather and Paper Laboratory wrote about the destructiveness of chemical remnants in book papers. Many librarians, however, continued (incorrectly) to ascribe the decay they decried to external factors such as gas lighting. More typical, however, were articles like Rossiter Johnson's "Inferior Paper a Menace to the Permanency of Literature" and Frank Hill's "The Deterioration of Newspaper Paper," which simply did not address cause. Johnson worried about the disintegration of modern book papers but displayed no understanding of the origins of deterioration. Hill deplored the loss of newspapers as valuable historical records but expressed no sense of the determinants of their disintegration. Perhaps librarians chose to concentrate on external matters (library buildings, book stacks and book supports, book construction) because these were easily grasped and fully understood. While paper deterioration was a problem whose solution was basic to the success of all other preservation techniques, its enormity and mystery may have combined to confound librarians, leading them to address topics whose dimensions they could more easily control.

Like specifications for paper, standards for book cloths and publishers' edition bindings were also largely products of the first decade of the new century. John Cotton Dana's binding exhibit and the appointment of the ALA's Committee on Bookbinding (1905) exemplified librarians' early-twentieth-century interest in the qualities of publishers' bindings, book papers, and standards for binding and binding materials. Thus, as the decades passed, American preservation interests became both more sophisticated and more cooperative. Changes in technology and materials (gas to electric lighting; leather to book cloths) addressed the major problem perceived in the first part of the period. In the second part, librarians organized themselves to seek better-quality publishers' bindings and book papers and, if not to conduct relevant research themselves, then at least to follow and publicize the research conducted by others. The St. Gall Conference, initiated to address conservation problems associated with manuscripts and documents, was organized by a librarian; its membership was largely librarians, and it represented the first instance of collective, international concern for deteriorating materials.[2] The stage was set for the considerable research and cooperation to come in the next decades.

What factors engendered or heightened turn-of-the-century librarians' preservation concerns? Changes in nineteenth-century paper and binding technology were arguably more instrumental in creating and sustaining preservation interest and activity than anything else. Initially, librarians responded most strongly to the deterioration of leather bindings; by 1890, however, book cloths and electric lighting had all but eliminated this concern. As the public's demand for reasonably priced reading material grew, publishers moved rapidly from partial to complete mechanization of the binding process. In a period also characterized by great growth of collections, librarians found their shelves filling with cheaply made volumes printed on poor-quality paper.

It was not necessary that machine-made books be poorly made books; sewing machines were capable of sewing all along and onto tapes, and quality threads and book cloths were available. But most publishing houses aimed at producing volumes acceptable to the private citizen, not to libraries, which demanded books of much more permanence and durability. Likewise, there were alternative methods of paper production that, while making use of cheaper, more readily available materials, did not produce papers that shortly became brittle and broke from their bindings. But again, then as today, manufacturers targeted the individual consumer, who was perceived to want a book for a finite period of time, rather than libraries, which wanted many volumes to last indefinitely.

The anger engendered by the inferior products of new binding and paper technologies produced the ALA's first subgroup charged with a preservation-related mission, the Committee on Bookbinding and Book Papers. This committee focused its work on obtaining better standards for publishers' bindings, securing special library editions of certain titles, and publicizing and promoting the work of the U.S. Leather and Paper Laboratory. Even though librarians were not in agreement on precisely what they wanted from publishers (some wanted special library editions; others wanted better publishers' editions at little or no additional cost), they were unanimous in their unhappiness with the contemporary publisher's product and looked for the first time to their professional organization for help with a preservation matter. No library-related issue dominated the first decade of the twentieth century as did the inferior nature of contemporary book construction.

While the condition of the materials on their shelves was the primary basis of librarians' preservation concerns, other factors also influenced their interest in conservation matters; disaster was one of these. Between 1876 and 1910 there were no recorded floods which affected libraries, but fires were frequent. Certainly the frame buildings occupied by many libraries, coupled with a fair amount of open-flame lighting and heating, made such disasters more common then than now. While those that resulted in the destruction of large, significant collections were widely publicized and heightened the preservation consciousness, none of these events sparked international or even national work in the way the flood in Florence, Italy, would three-quarters of a century later, when such calamities were less expected and more electrifying. Nonetheless, each blaze – whether at home or abroad, whether publicized in the professional press or simply recorded in an internal library document – prompted some sort of preservation-related activity, even if it was only the publicizing of the necessity for precaution and fireproof architecture. As might be expected, many fires were followed by experimentation with various drying and mending techniques.

A library's size and sense of mission also bore a relationship to its degree of interest in preservation. Clearly, most large libraries (particularly those of sizable universities and cities) perceived themselves as having an archival or research function. Their inability to judge which materials future scholars might need created a responsibility to preserve the complete collections. Among the libraries that underscored this obligation to safeguard their materials for the use of generations to come were those of Yale, Cornell, and Harvard universities, those of the cities of Boston, Buffalo, Cincinnati, Cleveland, Detroit, and St. Louis, and the Library of Congress. Nevertheless, many much smaller institutions also described their responsibility to keep their materials safe for the scholars of the future. Such libraries included those of Bangor (Maine), Brookline (Massachusetts), New Bedford (Massachusetts), Paterson (New Jersey),

Wilmington (Delaware), Amherst College, and the state of Iowa, as well as the Boston Athenaeum.

Dozens of other libraries, both large (the Brooklyn and Milwaukee public libraries and those of Columbia College and New York State) and small (the Bowdoin College Library and the public libraries of East Orange [New Jersey], Burlington [Vermont], and Lawrence [Massachusetts]), exhibited a strong interest in preservation, whether through mending, binding, shelf maintenance, or other areas of activity. It seems fair to say that while most large university and public libraries perceived that they had a distinct preservation mission and displayed a corresponding interest in preservation work, this sense of mission and show of interest was not confined to large libraries. Many smaller institutions also involved themselves in a variety of preservation concerns and activities.

In several instances there appears to have been a direct relationship between the level of preservation activity in a given library and the specific professional interests of the librarian. For example, the Wilmington Institute, the Worcester County (Massachusetts) Law Library, and the Washington, D.C., Public Library – managed by Arthur L. Bailey, George E. Wire, and George F. Bowerman of ALA's Committee on Bookbinding, respectively – were leaders in research and experimentation with binding materials and techniques. Similarly, F. J. Soldan, director of the Peoria (Illinois) Public Library, had a special professional interest in binding, which was reflected in his institution's development of binding standards.

More common, perhaps, was the institution managed by one (or a succession) of the period's major library figures, under whose leadership it engaged in considerable preservation thinking and activity. Such leaders included John Cotton Dana, director of the Springfield (Massachusetts) and Newark (New Jersey) public libraries; Melvil Dewey of Columbia College and the New York State Library; Justin Winsor of the Boston Public Library and Harvard University; Charles A. Cutter of the Boston Athenaeum; Frederick Crunden of the St. Louis Public Library; William I. Fletcher of the Silas Bronson Library (Waterbury, Connecticut) and Amherst College; Frank Hill of the Paterson (New Jersey) Free Library, Salem (Massachusetts) Public Library, Newark Free Public Library, and Brooklyn Public Library; Henry J. Carr of the Grand Rapids Public Library, St. Joseph (Missouri) Free Public Library, and Scranton Public Library; Herbert J. Putnam of the Minneapolis Public Library, Boston Public Library, and Library of Congress; and H. M. Utley of the public libraries of Detroit and Jacksonville (Florida).

It would be risky – except in the case of the members of the bookbinding committee and perhaps Dana and Dewey – to assume that these librarians' individual professional interests led directly to the preservation concern and action observable in the institutions they managed. But this was probably true for such leaders as Dana, Fletcher, Hill, and Carr each of whom administered several small collections successively. In considering larger university and city libraries, it may well be that the size and mission of the libraries themselves, rather than the personal interests of their chief administrators, were responsible for these organizations' preservation efforts.

The availability of funding had enormous influence on a library's level of preservation activity. While any library could keep its facility clean and encourage its staff and readers to handle materials with care, almost all other preservation measures cost money. Even the largest libraries cut corners when dollars were short. Economies ranged from the gross (conserving fuel by not heating stack areas, as did the Redwood Library in Newport, Rhode Island) to those less immediately obvious (buying a cheaper grade of binding cloth). There appears to have been no library with resources adequate to its every preservation need.

Areas of economy could be roughly categorized as affecting either the library facility, labor, or collection maintenance. Those involving the building included the use of gas rather than electricity for lighting, the use of unsuitably prepared shelving space (e.g., basements), and the absence of adequate fire precautions. While most new buildings were built along fireproof principles, many libraries lacked the funding necessary to take adequate preventive measures in older, existing structures. In some cases, such as that of the Public Library of Bangor, the result was complete destruction.

Some libraries were unable to employ enough janitors, dusters, or menders to maintain their collections properly. Many institutions lacked an adequate binding fund; this was particularly detrimental to the preservation mission. Often, such libraries mended extensively, ultimately ruining many of their volumes. The use of cheaper, less durable materials and poorer-quality sewing also contributed to the deterioration of collections. Some libraries with insufficient binding funds allowed materials to continue to circulate until they fell apart. Others withdrew such titles and held them aside until binding money became available. Still others rebound injured volumes by diverting money earmarked for the purchase of new books for the collections. Libraries often attempted to stretch their book budgets further by purchasing books in publishers' bindings rather than paying the extra few cents per title for a copy bound from the sheets or a special library edition.

It would be incorrect to say that large libraries, such as the Boston Public Library, were better able to fund their preservation activities than were smaller ones. The Boston library's annual reports show years of shortages of binding revenue. Indeed, the Newark Free Public Library and the libraries of Wilmington, Delaware, and Washington, D.C. – administered by managers with great interests in preservation issues – were arguably better-budgeted for binding, the period's chief preservation activity.

Another significant preservation influence for American librarians was the work done by their colleagues across the Atlantic. Among the vehicles that made possible the international exchange of preservation research and technique were library organizations, journals, monographs, and conferences. A country with a library association and a library press had the means to share its thinking with other nations; at conferences with multinational memberships, librarians met and talked. A common language and culture (such as that shared by the United States and Great Britain) facilitated the communication necessary for influence to occur. It is clear that preservation research and activity in Great Britain had considerable impact on American practice. Less certain is the effect that work in Germany, Belgium, the Vatican, and Italy may have had.

The Library Association of the United Kingdom was organized in 1877, one year after the ALA. By 1900 a German library association, Verein deutscher Bibliothekare, and an Italian one, Società Bibliographica Italiana, were both established and holding regular conferences.[3] British librarians quickly developed a lively press, including such journals as *Library World*, *Library*, *Library Assistant*, *Library Chronicle*, and several titles published by the Library Association, including *Monthly Notes*, *Transactions*, and the *Library Association Record*. Articles about preservation from these publications were often abstracted, summarized, or republished in American library periodicals, and the presence in modern American libraries of early backruns indicates that they were read by U.S. librarians. British figures active in library preservation, such as Cedric Chivers and Edward W. B. Nicholson, published in *Library Journal* and other American journals.[4] Any number of British monographs were studied by American librarians, including those written by Blades, Cockerell, Coutts, Stephen, and Zaehnsdorf, and the several publications of the Royal Society of Arts and the LAUK.

German preservation news appeared from time to time in *Library Journal* (sometimes abstracted from *Zentralblatt für Bibliothekswesen* and other German periodicals). Included were articles about German-led attempts to produce manuscript facsimiles and about the cellulose bath Zapon, first employed in the preservation of library materials by the Saxon government. A paper by Dr. O. Hartwig of the University Library at Halle was published in translation in *Library Journal*; it was Hartwig who first proposed the photographic reproduction of manuscripts.[5]

Two papers by Guido Biagi, director of the Biblioteca Mediceo-Laurenziana in Florence, appeared in *Library Journal* in 1904; one described the fire in the National Library of Turin on 26 January of that year, and the other addressed the reproduction of manuscripts by photography. A few months later, *Library Journal* provided references to two Italian periodicals that described document-restoration measures applied to materials that survived the Turin fire.[6]

Conferences were another forum for sharing ideas. In 1877 representatives from seventeen American libraries in eight states attended the Conference of Librarians in London. Among the attendees were Dewey, Cutter, Poole, and Winsor, who had the opportunity to hear Edward W. B. Nicholson lecture on book cloths, including the new fabric buckram, and to hear other British librarians describe damage to their collections that they attributed to illuminating gas. At the International Congress for the Reproduction of Manuscripts, held in Liège, Belgium, in 1905, Charles Mills Gayley of the University of California improved his understanding of photographic techniques for preserving and sharing archival materials. The Chief of the Manuscript Division of the Library of Congress attended the August 1910 International Congress of Archivists and Librarians in Brussels, where preservation was a topic.[7]

How did access to the preservation literature and experience of foreign countries affect American thought and activity? While the archivists and librarians of Germany, Belgium, Italy, and the Vatican were influential in shaping American practices in the preservation of a variety of special materials, it was England that shared research and work related to the preservation of mainstream library materials. It is not surprising that older European nations, possessing large collections of unique and deteriorating manuscripts and documents, concentrated their preservation efforts on those types of materials. Work done in Germany and the Vatican in the preservation of manuscripts and documents was significant; Belgian librarians were an important force in the photoreproduction of manuscripts; and Italy's fire at Turin in 1904 led to the development of document-repair techniques that were communicated to American librarians.

British contributions to American preservation practice for general library materials were significant and deserve to be summarized. During the period addressed by this study, well-developed public library systems and substantial academic and research libraries existed in both the United States and England. It is logical that the two countries were concerned with preserving contemporary materials. Rich cultural correspondences and well-developed professional library organizations and publications made sharing research and ideas simple. It may be that some of the most basic tenets and techniques of American library preservation have British roots (e.g., the importance of preserving local materials; fundamental repair and binding techniques), but there are many clearer examples of the transfer of knowledge from one country to the other.

Books like Blades's *The Enemies of Books* may have contributed to the general American preservation consciousness, and the binding manuals of Cockerell, Stephen and Coutts, and Zaehnsdorf prescribed American hand-binding techniques.[8] English book cloths covered American volumes for many years before New England factories began to manufacture such products.[9] Cedric Chivers was an undisputed genius in library binding; his services were used by many American librarians, and American binders attempted to match the strength of his bindings. The work of every U.S. binder was inevitably compared, either favorably or unfavorably, to Chivers's.[10]

The fire at the Birmingham, England, public library produced a rash of writings in American library journals, urging fireproof construction and various fire-prevention techniques.[11] The British pioneered research in protective colored window glass, although no immediate American response is evident. The Library of Congress did, however, respond to the Royal Society of Arts' conclusions about the injurious nature of sunlight by installing a mechanical window-blind system.[12] British libraries also led the way with electric lighting.[13]

The Royal Society of Arts' report on the causes of deterioration in binding leathers (that concluded that modern tanning methods were responsible for most of the faults in modern leathers) was covered completely in the American library press, and some librarians began to ask their binders to supply them with leathers that met the society's standards. The research conducted by the IAUK's Sound Leather Committee (which underscored the damaging nature of contemporary tanning techniques) was also available to American librarians and predated the major work of the U.S. Leather and Paper Laboratory.[14]

The British also introduced research into the causes of paper deterioration. While the Royal Society of Arts' 1898 report was slender and largely summarized certain German findings in translation, it identified the qualities in mechanical-wood papers that led to their rapid deterioration and recommended against the addition of too many minerals or too much size. It preceded any American work on the subject and was anticipated in the pages of *Library Journal*. Cedric Chivers's research on paper was also followed by American librarians, although it is difficult to compare it with that of the U.S. Leather and Paper Laboratory, which was underway at about the same time.[15]

The British also led in the development of binding specifications. Those set forth by the Royal Society of Arts in the report of its Committee on Leather for Bookbinding preceded the standards of the ALA's Committee on Bookbinding (and Stephen's enhancement thereof). Included in

Cockerell's popular binding manual *Bookbinding and the Care of Books*, they were certain to be employed in American libraries.[16]

American librarians were also conscious of the technologic gifts the new century might bring, and they had a number of intriguing ideas about the preservation possibilities the future could hold. Perhaps a method of fireproofing book papers would be discovered.[17] The use of yet-to-be-developed photoreproduction processes seemed the only hope for preserving badly deteriorated materials. In effect, they would create images of unique items that would freeze them forever in time:

> The application of photography and of photogravure to the reproduction of texts ... makes it possible for us not only to have several examples of a precious codex or manuscript, but to fix the invisible deterioration which began in it at a certain date so that, as regards its state of preservation, the facsimile represents an anterior stage to the future state of the original. By thus wonderfully forecasting the future these reproductions render less disastrous the effects of a fire such as that which lately destroyed the library of Turin. . . . This, I think, would, nay, should, be the most serious principal duty assumed by the library of the future: to preserve these treasures of the past while hoping that the present and the future may add to them new ones worthy of public veneration.[18]

"The twentieth century has the task of evoking method and order among rather than within libraries," predicted another librarian, whose "phantasy" included a nationwide system of regional "reservoir" libraries, each of which would collect and preserve in certain assigned areas.[19] More fascinating forecasts, however, came from the visionary Charles A. Cutter, in an address he delivered on the occasion of the dedication of the new Buffalo Public Library building in 1883. Entitled "The Buffalo Public Library in 1983," Cutter's piece contemplated what library facilities and systems might be like one hundred years in the future. He described a library building surrounded on three sides by "wide avenues" that "gave it air and light, and protected it against fire." The neighboring streets were kept clean "to prevent, as far as might be, the evil of dust." "With electric illumination," Cutter continued, "we are both light and cool." The reading room was not heated above seventy degrees, and the stacks were kept at sixty.[20]

Cutter, too, anticipated cooperative collecting and conservation. He believed that in 1983 the library would keep only the newspapers of Buffalo and neighboring towns, since "half a century before the preservation of newspapers had become one of the most perplexing problems of library economy." With regard to the library facility, "the passages [would be] covered with a noiseless and dustless covering," and the rooms would be low-ceilinged to avoid the accumulation of "bad air." The old idea "of dipping books in the solution they use for actresses' dresses and scenery" would have been abandoned in favor of constructing walls, floors, and shelving of incombustible materials.[21] Finally, instead of photographic images that preserved the intellectual content of library materials, Cutter predicted that libraries would stock "fonografic [*sic*] editions prepared by the best readers."[22] Twenty years later, Italian librarian Guido Biagi, speaking before the International Congress of Arts and Sciences in St. Louis, echoed Cutter's prediction of the audible book: "There will be," he proclaimed, ". . . an infinite number of hearers, who will listen from their own homes to the spoken paper, to the spoken book." Biagi went even further than Cutter with his conjecture that "the electric post or . . . the telephone will make it possible to hear at Melbourne a graphophone [*sic*] disc asked for, a few minutes earlier, from the British Museum."[23]

To what extent were these visions of new, more effective preservation techniques and cooperation realized? Following World War I, preservation-related research began to increase. At the New York Public Library, interested since its beginnings in preservation matters, Harry Lydenberg established a laboratory where he conducted experiments in manual and mechanical methods of paper treatment. The results were published in 1931 in *The Care and Repair of Books*. In 1934 the National Bureau of Standards sponsored widely discussed studies of book papers, which attributed the deterioration of library materials chiefly to air pollution, inherently poor paper, ruinous humidity and heat, and overexposure to light. A year later, the *Minimum Standard Specifications for Class A Library Binding* was published, and the founding of the Library Binding Institute enhanced cooperation between librarians and library binders.[24]

While articles on specific aspects of preservation (binding, repair, care and cleaning) were common to library literature from its inception, more comprehensive pieces appeared for the first time as the idea of a preservation element in a total library program began to emerge.[25] Perhaps the most significant contribution of the 1930s was the development of film as a preservation technique. Among the pioneers in reprography was Herman Fussler, whose *Photographic Reproduction in Libraries* became a classic. During the same period, Carolyn Horton joined the American Philosophical Society as the nation's first library conservator. As the decade ended, William Barrow began the research in various aspects of paper permanence and durability that would flower in the 1950s.[26]

World War II heightened preservation concerns. The index entry "War and the Library," under which were listed numerous articles recommending disaster measures and methods for treating burned books, appeared in *Library Literature*.[27] In the first year following the war, Pelham Barr published one of the most-quoted articles in the collective literature of library preservation, "Book Conservation and University Library Administration."

In it, he presented basic problems (deterioration, binding, wear and tear) and outlined a program for combating them; thus the concept of preservation as a distinct function of the library was further developed.[28]

Conservator Paul Banks has termed the period between the end of the second World War and the early 1960s "the silent years" because it offers so little evidence of preservation work and research. A quick examination of the pages of *Library Literature* confirms this impression. Nonetheless, there was some activity. The 1950s marked the beginning of foundation interest in library conservation. Shortly after its founding, the Council on Library Resources (CLR) funded Barrow's research on the physical strength of paper (1957), then the Barrow Laboratory (1961) and the Library Technology Program (1960).

The Association of Research Libraries appointed its Committee on Preservation of Research Library Materials in 1960. The severity of the problem of paper deterioration and the threat it posed to the nation's library collections was documented when Gordon Williams's report *The Preservation of Deteriorating Books: An Examination of the Problem with Recommendations for a Solution* was published by the association in 1964. Williams's research supported and further publicized Barrow's finding that 90 percent of all books printed in the United States between 1900 and 1949 would be virtually unusable by the year 2000. He proposed that a federally funded agency be formed to address the problem.[29]

Over the next twenty years, research and other conservation activity continued apace. In 1965 the *National Register of Microform Masters* appeared, aiding the preservation effort by listing the titles and locations of microform master films from which service copies could be made.[30] Of the fires and floods at home and abroad covered in the library and general press,[31] the 1966 Florence flood was the most sensational. In addition to generating considerable publicity for conservation issues, these disasters also provided many opportunities to test and develop new conservation techniques.[32]

In the year that followed the Florence flood, the Library of Congress began its CLR-funded Pilot Preservation Project. The Library of Congress soon identified a list of deteriorating titles within its collections and located copies in better condition in other American libraries. In accordance with Williams's recommendations, it planned to establish a central register of best copies. By 1972 Warren J. Haas, chair of the Association of Research Libraries' Preservation Committee, had prepared a report rethinking those recommendations. While advocating the same roles for a national preservation program as Williams had, Haas proposed that these could be fulfilled more pragmatically by a "preservation consortium" than by a central national agency.[33]

In the sixties and seventies several important research libraries began formal preservation programs; among these were the Newberry Library (Chicago), the Yale University Library, and the New York Public Library. Peter Waters, Christopher Clarkson, and Don Etherington, British designer/binders and book conservators, came to the Library of Congress to help develop its preservation program. The work of other English conservation experts such as Roger Powell and Sidney Cockerell also influenced American preservation technique and thinking. The New England Document Conservation Center, the first cooperative workshop established primarily to preserve and restore library materials, opened its doors in 1973. Since that time, other cooperative centers or regional programs have been established, such as the Book Preservation Center at the New York Botanical Garden and the Research Libraries Group's preservation program. In 1979, to promote a different type of cooperation and standardization, the National Endowment for the Humanities awarded the Association of Research Libraries a grant for a project to design a self-study preservation-planning procedure for use by individual libraries.[34]

While preservation publishing had begun in other countries, the 1970s saw the development of an American preservation press, including such publications as the *Abbey Newsletter* (1975) and *Conservation Administration News* (1979). Conferences with titles such as "Deterioration and Preservation of Library Materials" (University of Chicago Graduate Library School) were held. Library schools like those at Columbia University, and the universities of Chicago, Maryland, and California (Berkeley), began to offer preservation seminars and courses. Research, particularly in deacidification, progressed on several fronts as the Barrow Research Laboratory, Richard Smith, and the Library of Congress all worked on nonaqueous processes.[35]

In 1981 Columbia University's School of Library Service became the nation's first degree-granting conservation education program and admitted its initial class of students. With this, library conservation moved an important step further in establishing itself as a "distinct professional discipline" with the fully developed and recognized methods, standards, ethics, and educational programs to which Paul Banks refers in his article "Preservation of Library Materials" in the *Encyclopaedia of Library and Information Science.*[36] The eighties also saw the Library of Congress pioneer the use of optical-disk technology for preservation purposes and, despite accidents and political setbacks, continue its research on diethyl zinc as a deacidification agent. This work was of enormous importance, as few publishers other than university presses used neutral paper, and new books seemed as doomed as those already crumbling on library shelves.[37]

The national preservation program envisioned by Williams and Haas seemed somewhat nearer in 1984, as the Council on Library Resources

189

(under the leadership of Haas, now its president) convened a study group of librarians, scholars, and university administrators to consider this possibility again. The group recommended the creation of the Commission on Preservation and Access, whose work would be to support, coordinate, and develop funding for a decentralized national program. In 1987, as American library leaders testified before the U.S. Congress about the acute nature of "the brittle books problem," Patricia Battin (who had succeeded Haas as Columbia University's vice-president for university libraries when he assumed the presidency of the CLR and whose career reflects a serious interest in preservation matters) was appointed the commission's first chair.[38]

While a hundred years had passed since turn-of-the-century librarians began discussing the still unsolved "brittle books problem," American librarians seemed better positioned than at any other time in their history to address this issue, called by the Librarian of Congress "'one of our most pressing national problems.'"[39] Many volumes had perished, and most contemporary books seemed fated to follow their example. Although earlier librarians' hopes for library editions printed on sound paper had not been fulfilled, the technologies of film and optical disk promised that intellectual content of books, if not the books themselves, could survive to be studied by future generations.

Clearly, the preservation activity that began in turn-of-the-century American libraries increased as the twentieth century progressed, with the most notable advances occurring after 1960. Several reasons for this suggest themselves. Of course, the world wars interrupted most aspects of American culture, research, and scholarship; little progress (except for work related to disaster preparedness) occurred during these periods or the years of recovery that followed. But the third quarter of the twentieth century brought remarkable scientific achievements, resulting in preservation possibilities that librarians presiding over enormous deteriorating collections were eager to explore.

Nevertheless, the simple existence of large, decaying collections and potential scientific solutions may not be enough to explain why preservation interest and activity burgeoned after 1960–why preservation of library materials, like that of architectural landmarks, became a virtual cultural crusade during this period. In fact, the library community's concern with the conservation of library materials may be related to the nation's growth of interest in preserving other parts of its cultural heritage. Like library preservation, architectural conservation began as a grass-roots movement in America. From 1850 until the post-World War II establishment of the National Trust for Historic Preservation (1949), landmark preservationists worked diligently, but without a national organization or a clearly defined leadership. Much was accomplished during this early period, as historic sites such as Mount Vernon, the Old South Meeting House, and Williamsburg were claimed, preserved, or restored. But it was the 1960s that witnessed the major flurry of activity, including the passage of the Historic Preservation Act of 1966.[40]

Like the work of library conservation, that of architectural preservation has continued to grow at the local, regional, and national levels. There may be a single explanation for this heightening of preservation interest in the parallel areas of intellectual and physical history. The 1960s saw a considerable stirring of interest in the things of the past. Perhaps our young nation was beginning to come of age; another possibility is that the prosperity of the 1960s provided Americans more free time to consider and pursue their cultural heritage. "Whatever the case may be," wrote one architectural historian, "the fact is that historical sites, old buildings, forts, covered bridges, and other visible manifestations of our past way of life are enjoying an unprecedented degree of attention from the public at large."[41] One might easily add "old books, documents, and manuscripts" to this list and argue that the nation's bicentennial year, which followed in the next decade, served to maintain the American fascination with the past and its monuments, whether paper or stone. Thus, the "cultural crusade" for library preservation that began in the 1960s and continues today may have grown from more than the presence of a problem of considerable national magnitude and the availability of potential solutions. Perhaps the strong interest of the American public in its past was the stimulus needed to launch an organized, systematic effort.

Library preservation has advanced from a state of simple activity at the turn of the century to status as a modern twentieth-century movement characterized by concern, organization, and funding. Thus, it is not surprising that the major preservation interests of the late nineteenth century (book construction, binding materials, and mending practices) are quite different from those of the present (the impermanence of book papers, the need to preserve massive numbers of embrittled materials, and the distribution of responsibility for preserving materials). These shifts in emphasis are the outgrowth of the intensification and systematization of the American preservation concern, as well as of modern science.

At the turn of the century, preservation was one of many issues competing for librarians' attention as their relatively young profession developed its ethics, methods, and collections. While there was clear interest in preservation issues, that interest was perhaps not as intense as it is today, with the mission and systems of librarianship much more settled and the sizes of deteriorating collections considerably larger. Additionally, nineteenth-century librarians were a pragmatic lot, interested in housekeeping, book supports, and library economy; their twentieth-century counterparts are better able to theorize and to avail themselves of the outcomes of research.

In the late nineteenth century, preservation lacked the organization that characterizes it at present. Today, the American Library Association, the Council on Library Resources, the Association of Research Libraries, and the federal government are working together in developing a decentralized national preservation program. Finally, faced with cheap publishers' bindings and having no solutions for the problems of inherent vice, turn-of-the-century librarians had little choice but to make their intellectual and financial commitment to the external book, concentrating on the preservation of its protective shell, the binding. Today, sophisticated deacidification research, coupled with film and digital reproduction techniques, has led librarians to focus on the heart of the preservation problem: permanent book papers and the preservation of intellectual content.

Between 1876 and 1910–in response to the aging and growth of American library collections, urban environmental problems, and changes in manufacturing methods for books and book papers–preservation interests expanded. Once concerned mainly with simple custodial and mending routines, librarians became increasingly interested in the qualities of the materials used in the manufacture of books, the construction of modern volumes, and the need for a method of preserving at least the content of badly deteriorated yet valuable materials. By the close of the period, a fair amount of cooperative activity in lobbying for better-made books, quality binding materials, and binding standards is observable. It would be difficult to overestimate the role that *Library Journal* and the American Library Association played in spreading the word about preservation practices, concerns, and research efforts, thereby furthering interest in such matters across the nation.

Some might argue that much of what passed for preservation work in general collections of this period was actually simple library economy–that librarians, responding to Dewey's philosophy, concerned themselves with mending, binding, standards, and sturdier publishers' editions more out of a sense of fiscal prudence than out of a wish to preserve their collections for future generations. In other words, some might say, the prevailing attitude was that the better a book was made, mended, or bound, the longer it would serve the contemporary public. It is probably true that not every circulating collection perceived or could afford to adopt a preservation mission; perhaps smaller society or public libraries were especially vulnerable. Books purchased by such libraries may have chiefly served the interest of popular reading; discarded when they wore out, they were replaced by newer titles. There is broad evidence in the literature and internal library documents of the period, however, that a large number of libraries considered at least portions of their collections to be of permanent value and wished them to last indefinitely.

While there existed no functional area of library work called preservation, it would be a mistake to suppose that the subject held little interest. Preservation may not have been viewed as the same group of activities performed by librarians in the late twentieth century, but with the exception of photoreproduction and atmospheric controls, almost all contemporary measures were practiced in libraries a hundred years ago. One could contend that local preservation procedures have changed very little, that the similarity between modern and Victorian techniques is striking, and that the librarians of today might have much to gain by closely examining the methods of their forebears. Of course, modern preservation issues are quite different from those of 1910, largely because of late-twentieth-century systematization and the possibilities offered by modern science. This book, a representation of preservation thought and activity during the early years of American librarianship, provides a basis for the examination and analysis of the work to be done in the decades to follow; it sets the stage for the cultural crusade of the late twentieth century.

Appendix

A Preservation Timeline—1842-1910

1842   Faraday studies the effects of illuminating gas on the leather bindings in London's Athenaeum Club Library.

1851   Calvert, a chemist in Manchester, England, concludes that the sulfuric acid used in tanning is the chief cause of decay in bookbinding leathers.

               Charles Jewett publishes his *Notices of Public Libraries in the United States of America*.

1853   The Librarians' Convention is held in New York City.

1854   A report to the Commissioners of Sewers of the City of London suggests that poor ventilation, overheated buildings, and the poor quality of modern materials are the chief causes of decay in binding leathers.

1856   Smyth invents the first thread booksewing machine.

1876   *Library Journal* begins to publish.

               The American Library Association (ALA) is founded.

               The U.S. Bureau of Education publishes a special report, *Public Libraries in the United States of America: Their History, Condition, and Management*.

1877	The Library Association of the United Kingdom (LAUK) is founded.
	The Conference of Librarians is held in London, and a study of the causes of leather deterioration is suggested.
	The Philadelphia Mercantile Library burns.
	The ALA's Cooperation Committee develops a binding standard for publishers' editions.
1879	Electric lighting is introduced at the British Museum.
	The Free Public Library of Birmingham (England) burns.
	Smyth invents a thread machine that sews all along.
1880	Fire in the Vatican destroys Mommsen's library.
1882-83	Poole and Spofford debate styles of library architecture.
1883	Interlaken Mills (Providence, Rhode Island) is the first U.S. company to manufacture book cloth.
1884	Brehmer markets his first booksewing machine.
1885	Chivers patents his duro-flexile binding technique.
1886	The Prussian Regulations for Supply and Examination of Paper (Vorschriften für die Lieferung und Prüfung von Papier in Kraft) are developed.
1887	Woodward concludes from his experiments that the acidic residues of illuminating gas are the chief cause of leather decay.
1888	The Massachusetts Commission of Public Records begins to publish its *Report on the Custody and Condition of the Public Records of Parishes, Towns, and Counties*.
1891	Rossiter Johnson publishes his article "Inferior Paper a Menace to the Permanency of Literature."

1893   Tandy proposes the establishment of a library publishing company that will market well-bound books printed on quality papers.

         Hartwig calls for international cooperation in the photoreproduction of manuscripts.

1896   Emery patents his technique for document repair.

         Young, Librarian of Congress, acquires a copy of the Prussian Regulations for Supply and Examination of Paper.

         Società Bibliographica Italiana recommends government regulation of papers used in printing documents and books to be preserved in archives.

1898   Linda Eastman starts the Children's Library League at the Cleveland Public Library.

         The Royal Society of Arts' Committee on the Deterioration of Paper submits its report.

         A conference on the preservation of manuscripts and archival materials is held in St. Gall, Switzerland.

1899   Biscoe evaluates the quality of the bindings of several large publishing houses.

         An informal meeting of persons concerned about the deterioration of binding leathers is held in London.

         A conference on the preservation of manuscript and archival materials is held in Dresden.

1900   The Royal Society of Arts appoints its Committee on Leather for Bookbinding.

1901   The Royal Society of Arts' Committee on Leather for Bookbinding submits its report.

1903	Smyth invents the casing-in machine.
	Dana begins collecting material for his binding exhibit.
1904	The National Library of Turin burns.
	Dana requests that the ALA appoint a committee on bookbinding.
1905	The LAUK's Sound Leather Committee submits its report *Leather for Libraries*.
	Dana distributes his questionnaire requesting information on binding practices.
	The second edition of the report of the Royal Society of Arts' Committee on Leather for Bookbinding is published.
	Dana's binding exhibit opens at the Newark (New Jersey) Free Public Library.
	Chivers opens a bindery on Fulton Street in Brooklyn.
	The first ALA Committee on Bookbinding is appointed.
	The International Congress for the Reproduction of Manuscripts is held in Liége, Belgium.
1906	Libraries in San Francisco area burn after an earthquake.
	The ALA's Committee on Bookbinding surveys libraries on the topics of in-house binderies and the qualities of publishers' bindings.
	The ALA's Committee on Bookbinding asks publishers to bring out specially bound library editions.
	The U.S. Leather and Paper Laboratory asks librarians for samples of good and bad paper.
	Dana's *Notes on Bookbinding for Libraries* appears.
	A fire occurs in the Trinity College Library.

1907   Emerson announces he will teach bookbinding by correspondence.

Rademaekers offers a binding course from the Newark Free Public Library.

The first specially bound publishers' library editions are available.

1908   Bancroft cloth no. 666 is chosen for binding government publications.

Chivers is involved in a dispute with the International Brotherhood of Bookbinders.

1909   Hill proposes the establishment of "storage libraries."

The ALA's Committee on Bookbinding sends an open letter to publishers suggesting standards for binding library editions.

The ALA's Committee on Bookbinding surveys the wearing qualities of various publishers' bindings.

The ALA's Committee on Bookbinding publishes its standards for publishers' bindings.

The U.S. Department of Agriculture publishes *Durability and Economy in Papers for Permanent Records*.

1910   The second edition of Dana's *Notes on Bookbinding for Libraries* appears.

Hill inquires of newspaper publishers how they preserve their backfiles.

The International Congress of Archivists and Librarians is held in Brussels.

Notes

Introduction

1. Works that include some treatment of preservation history include George M. Cunha and Dorothy G. Cunha, *Conservation of Library Materials: A Manual and Bibliography on the Care, Repair, and Restoration of Library Materials*, 2d ed., 2 vols. (Metuchen, N.J.: Scarecrow Press, 1971), 1:1-17; Ludovico Santucci, "The Application of Chemical and Physical Methods to Conservation of Archival Materials," *Bolletino dell'Istituto di Patologia del Libro* 20 (January 1961): 85-111; James W. Henderson and Robert G. Krupp, "The Librarian as Conservator," in *Deterioration and Preservation of Library Materials: The Thirty-fourth Annual Conference of the Graduate Library School, August 4-6, 1969*, ed. Howard W. Winger and Richard D. Smith (Chicago: University of Chicago Press, 1970), 176-92; Edwin Williams, "Deterioration of Library Collections Today," in *Deterioration and Preservation of Library Materials: The Thirty-fourth Annual Conference of the Graduate Library School, August 4-6, 1969*, ed. Howard W. Winger and Richard D. Smith (Chicago: University of Chicago Press, 1970), 3-17; Richard Smith, "Non-Aqueous Deacidification of Paper and Books" (Ph.D. thesis, University of Chicago, 1971); Nancy Gwinn, "CLR and Preservation," *College and Research Libraries* 42 (March 1981): 105-107; Sherelyn Ogden, "A Study of the Impact of the Florence Flood on the Development of Library Conservation in the United States: 1966-1976" (M.A. thesis, University of Chicago, 1978); Claire S. Marwick, "An Historical Study of Paper Document Restoration Methods" (M.A. thesis, American University, 1964); Keith A. Manley, "E. W. B. Nicholson (1849-1912) and His Importance to Librarianship" (D.Phil. thesis, Trinity College, Oxford, 1977); William J. Crowe, "Verner W. Clapp as Opinion Leader and Change Agent in the Preservation of Library Materials" (Ph.D. thesis, Indiana University, 1986).

2. Pamela W. Darling and Sherelyn Ogden, "From Problems Perceived to Programs in Practice: The Preservation of Library Resources in the U.S.A., 1956-1980," *Library Resources and Technical Services* 25 (January-March 1981): 9-29.

3. Council on Library Resources, *The Commission on Preservation and Access* (Washington, D.C.: Council on Library Resources, 1987); U.S. Congress, House Committee on Education and Labor, *Oversight Hearing on the Problem of "Brittle Books" in Our Nation's Libraries, Hearing before the Subcommittee on Postsecondary Education*. 100th Cong., 1st sess., 1987; "An Appeal to Preserve Old Books," *New York Times*, 5 March 1987, sec. C, 28; Eric Stange, "Millions of Books Are Turning to Dust–Can They Be Saved?" *New York Times Book Review*, 29 March 1987, 3, 38.

4. Douglas Cockerell, *Bookbinding and the Care of Books: A Text-Book for Bookbinders and Librarians* (New York: Appleton, 1902); George A. Stephen and Henry T. Coutts, *Manual of Library Bookbinding* (London: Libraco Ltd., 1911); George A. Stephen, *Commercial Bookbinding* (London: Stonhill & Co., 1910); Joseph W. Zaehnsdorf, *The Art of Bookbinding: A Practical Treatise*, 2d ed., rev. and enl. (London: Bell & Sons, 1890).

5. Matt T. Roberts and Don Etherington, *Bookbinding and the Conservation of Books: A Dictionary of Descriptive Terminology* (Washington, D.C.: Library of Congress, 1982).

6. Wayne A. Wiegand presents an excellent overview of the issues in which the American Library Association interested itself in his *The Politics of an Emerging Profession: The American Library Association, 1876-1917* (New York: Greenwood Press, 1986).

7. Reuben G. Thwaites, "Ten Years of American Library Progress," *Library Journal* 25 (August 1900): 1-7; Isabel E. Lord, "Open Shelves and Public Morals," *Library Journal* 26 (February 1901): 65-70.

8. Boston Public Library, *Annual Report of the Trustees, 1881*, 19.

9. Jesse H. Shera, *Foundations of the Public Library Movement in New England, 1629-1855* (Hamden, Conn.: Shoestring Press, 1965), 163.

10. Edward P. Alexander, *Museums in Motion: An Introduction to the History and Functions of Museums* (Nashville: American Association for State and Local History, 1979), 9-10.

11. *Library Journal* began to publish in 1876.

12. Ainsworth R. Spofford, "Binding and Preservation of Books," in *Public Libraries in the United States of America: Their History, Condition, and Management: Special Report* (Washington, D.C.: U.S. Bureau of Education, 1876), 673-78; Justin Winsor, "Library Buildings," in *Public Libraries in the United States of America: Their History, Condition, and Management: Special Report* (Washington, D.C.: U.S. Bureau of Education, 1876), 465-75.

13. Henderson and Krupp, "The Librarian as Conservator," 178; Herman H. Fussler, *Photographic Reproduction for Libraries: A Study of Administrative Problems* (Chicago: University of Chicago Press, 1942); R. W. Church, ed., *Deterioration of Book Stock: Causes and Remedies, Two Studies on the Permanence of Book Paper Conducted by W. J. Barrow* (Richmond: Virginia State Library, 1959); R. W. Church, ed., *The Manufacture and Testing of Durable Book Papers, Based on the Investigations of W. J. Barrow* (Richmond: Virginia State Library, 1960); W. J. Barrow Research Laboratory, *Permanence/Durability of the Book*, 5 vols. (Richmond, Va.: W. J. Barrow Research Laboratory, 1963-1976); William J. Barrow, *The Barrow Method of Restoring Deteriorated Documents* (Richmond, Va.: Barrow, 1965).

14. Charles B. Hosmer, Jr., *Presence of the Past: A History of the Preservation Movement in the United States before Williamsburg* (New York: Putnam, 1965), 25.

Chapter 1. In the Beginning

1. *Proceedings of the Librarians' Convention Held in New York City, September 15, 16, and 17, 1853* (Cedar Rapids, Iowa: Torch Press, 1915), 5, 40, 62-63.

2. Charles C. Jewett, *Notices of Public Libraries in the United States of America* (Washington, D.C.: Printed for the House of Representatives, 1851), 4, 192.

3. Ibid., 4-6, 71.

4. Ibid., 154. The belief that binding in russia leather deterred insects was false. For a discussion, see chapter 3.

5. Ibid., 155.

6. S. R. Warren and S. N. Clark, "Library Reports and Statistics," in *Public Libraries in the United States of America: Their History, Condition, and Management: Special Report* (Washington, D.C.: U. S. Bureau of Education, 1876), 762-73.

7. Spofford, "Binding and Preservation of Books," 673-78.

8. Justin Winsor, "Library Memoranda," in *Public Libraries in the United States of America: Their History, Condition, and Management: Special Report* (Washington, D.C.: U.S. Bureau of Education, 1876), 712-13.

9. Winsor, "Library Buildings," 467, 471-72.

10. William F. Poole, "The Organization and Management of Public Libraries," in *Public Libraries in the United States of America: Their History, Condition, and Management: Special Report* (Washington, D.C.: U.S. Bureau of Education, 1876), 490-91, 504; Otis H. Robinson, "College Library Administration," in *Public Libraries in the United States of Amer-*

ica: Their History, Condition, and Management: Special Report (Washington, D.C.: U.S. Bureau of Education, 1876), 511.

11. Spofford, "Binding and Preservation of Books," 673-78.

12. Astor Library (New York City), *Annual Report of the Trustees, 1878*, 10.

13. Advertisement for the Holden System for Preserving Books, *Library Journal* 32 (April 1907): lxxi.

14. New York State Library, *Annual Report of the Trustees, 1891*, 26-31.

15. Ainsworth R. Spofford, *A Book for All Readers: Designed as an Aid to the Collection, Use, and Preservation of Books and the Formation of Public and Private Libraries*, 2d ed. (New York: Putnam, 1900), 101; Boston Public Library, *Annual Report of the Trustees*, 1894, 23; U.S. Department of Agriculture, *Durability and Economy in Papers for Permanent Records: A Report Submitted by H. W. Wiley, Chief of Bureau of Chemistry, and C. Hart Merriam, Chief of Bureau of Biological Survey, Committee on Paper for Departmental Use. Including "Paper Specifications," by F. Veitch, Chief, Leather and Paper Laboratory, Bureau of Chemistry* (Washington, D.C.: Government Printing Office, 1909), 3-4; Detroit Public Library, *Annual Report, 1882*, 40; Wilmington (Del.) Institute, *Annual Report, 1894-1895*, 32-33.

16. William F. Poole, "Progress of Library Architecture," *Library Journal* 7 (July-August 1882): 134; Yale University, *Report of the Librarian, 1908-1909*, 27; Cornell University Library, *Report of the Librarian, 1902-1903*, 6-9; Lindsay Swift, "Pamphlets and Continuations of Serials," *Library Journal* 12 (September-October 1887): 353; "Preservation of Bound Newspapers," *Library Journal* 22 (March 1897): 161.

17. Harvard University, *Third Report of William Coolidge Lane, Librarian, 1900*, 214.

18. Norman C. Perkins, "How to Bind Periodicals," *Library Journal* 12 (September-October 1887): 356; Public Library of the City of Bangor (Maine), *Annual Reports, 1892*, 10.

19. Cincinnati Public Library, *Annual Report of the Librarian and Treasurer, 1889-1890*, 8; Buffalo Public Library, *Annual Report, 1900*, 9.

20. Frank Hill, "Storage Libraries," *ALA Bulletin* 3 (September 1909): 141-42; Charles A. Cutter, "The Preservation of Pamphlets," *American Library Journal* 1 (30 November 1876): 52; William I. Fletcher, "Some Library Superstitions," *Library Journal* 14 (May-June 1889): 157; Charles W. Eliot, "The Division of a Library into Books in Use, and Books Not in Use, With Different Storage Methods for the Two Classes of Books," *Library Journal* 27 (July 1902): 56.

21. Hill, "Storage Libraries," 142; Public Library of the City of Bangor (Maine), *Annual Reports, 1891*, 9; Council Bluffs (Iowa) Free Public

Library, *Annual Report, 1895*, 16; Lawrence (Mass.) Free Public Library, *Annual Report of the Board of Trustees and Librarian, 1876*, 28.

22. Malden (Mass.) Public Library, *Annual Report, 1879*, 11-12; Poughkeepsie (N.Y.) City Library, *Report, 1896*, 12-13; Paterson (N.J.) Free Public Library, *Report, 1890-1891*, 9.

23. Boston Public Library, *Annual Report of the Trustees, 1875*, 19-20.

24. Harvard University, *First Report of Justin Winsor, Librarian, 1878*, 14.

25. Dover (N.H.) Public Library, *Annual Report of the Trustees, 1897*, 12-13; Cleveland Public Library, *Annual Report of the Library Board and Librarian, 1885*, 15.

26. "Appeal of a State Librarian," *Library Journal* 8 (May 1883): 72; William M. Hepburn, "Selection and Preservation of Agricultural Periodicals," *Library Journal* 35 (July 1910): 309-11.

27. Charles H. Gould, "Co-Ordination, or Method in Co-Operation," *ALA Bulletin* 3 (September 1909): 122, 126.

28. Brookline (Mass.) Public Library, *Annual Report of the Trustees, 1876*, 7; New Bedford (Mass.) Free Public Library, *Annual Report of the Trustees, 1902*, 10.

29. Boston Public Library, *Annual Report of the Trustees, 1875*, 15.

30. Fletcher Battershall, *Bookbinding for Bibliophiles: Being Notes on the Technical Features of the Well-Bound Book for the Aid of Connoisseurs; With a Sketch of Gold Tooling, Ancient and Modern* (Greenwich, Conn.: Library Collector Press, 1905), 6; William Blades, *The Enemies of Books* (London: E. Stock, 1896), 94-95; Herbert J. Slater, *The Library Manual: A Guide to the Formation of a Library, and the Valuation of Books*, 3d, enl. ed. (London: Gill, n.d.), 14; Walter Powell, "Library Bookbinding," *Library World* 5 (January 1903): 173; Cyril Davenport, "Bookbinding and Book-production," *Library Association Record* 7 (November 1905): 553-55.

31. Spofford, *A Book for All Readers*, 130.

32. These baths (the best-known trade name was Zapon) were never popular in America. Although the Library of Congress considered Zapon as a method of manuscript preservation, it chose instead overlaying with silk or tissue.

33. "Preservation of Manuscripts," *Library Journal* 35 (February 1910): 64.

34. Alice B. Kroeger, "The Care of Books," *Public Libraries* 8 (July 1903): 319; Arthur L. Bailey, "Report of the Committee on Bookbinding," *ALA Bulletin* 2 (September 1908): 174-75.

35. Melvil Dewey, "School of Library Economy at Columbia College," *Library Journal* 9 (July 1884): 120; "Library Handicraft at Colorado State

Normal School," *Library Journal* 25 (July 1900): 335; Lovina Knowlton, "Library Mending Kit," *Library Occurrent* 1 (December 1907): 4.

36. "Binding Kit," *Public Libraries* 12 (June 1907): 237; Sarah J. Freeman, *Syllabus of a Course on Elementary Bookmaking and Book-binding* (New York: Teachers College of Columbia University, 1910); Wisconsin Free Library Commission, *Biennial Report, 1895-1896*, 58-66.

Chapter 2. The Environment as Enemy

1. Spofford, *A Book for All Readers*, 101.

2. Ibid., 56; F. Chance, "Preservation of Bookbindings," *Notes and Queries*, 7th ser., 2 (4 December 1886): 444; Henry Marsden, "Decay of Leather Bindings," *Public Libraries* 11 (June 1906): 312.

3. Gardner M. Jones and H. E. Green, "Linen Bindings," *Library Journal* 17 (July-August 1892): 29.

4. W. W. Keen, "Library Book-Stacks without Daylight," *Science*, n.s., 29 (18 June 1909): 974; "Michigan Library Association," *Library Journal* 27 (November 1902): 955.

5. W. L. Ropes, "'Evaporation,'" *Library Journal* 10 (May 1885): 105.

6. Robert D. MacLeod, "The Preservation of Books in Libraries," *Library World*, n.s., 11 (January 1909): 256; Bernard R. Green, "The New Building for the Library of Congress," *Library Journal* 21 (December 1896): 16.

7. Royal Society of Arts, Committee on Leather for Bookbinding, *Report of the Committee on Leather for Bookbinding*, ed. Viscount Cobham and Sir Henry Trueman Wood (London: Bell & Sons, 1905), 73.

8. "How We Protect Rare and Illustrated Books II," *Library Journal* 15 (May 1890): 133.

9. William F. Poole, review of *The Enemies of Books*, by William Blades, *Dial* 9 (July 1888): 64.

10. Spofford, *A Book for All Readers*, 102.

11. Boston Public Library, *Annual Report of the Trustees, 1903*, 7; Harvard University Library, *Annual Report, 1908*, 23.

12. Normand S. Patton, "Light, Heat, and Ventilation," *Library Journal* 18 (September 1893): 29.

13. H. B. Wheatley, "Leather for Bookbinding," *Library*, n.s., 2 (1 July 1901): 312.

14. "The Newberry Library: Dr. Poole's Plans for the New Structure Examined," *Chicago Tribune*, 29 December 1889, 6; William F. Poole, "The Construction of Library Buildings," *Library Journal* 6 (April 1881): 70.

15. Bernard R. Green, "Library Buildings and Book Stacks," *Library Journal* 31 (August 1906): 54; Library Association of the United Kingdom, Sound Leather Committee, *Leather for Libraries*, by E. Wyndham Hulme,

J. Gordon Parker, A. Seymour-Jones, Cyril Davenport, and F. J. Williamson (London: Library Supply Co., 1905), 27; Spofford, *A Book for All Readers*, 105; Patton, "Light, Heat, and Ventilation," 29.

16. "Library Buildings," *Library Journal* 6 (April 1881): 124; Wilberforce Eames, "The Care of Special Collections," *Library Journal* 22 (October 1897): 50; Eliot, "The Division of a Library into Books in Use, and Books Not in Use," 53; Minneapolis Public Library, *Annual Report, 1895*, 16.

17. Worcester County (Mass.) Law Library, *Annual Report, 1909*, 6; MacLeod, "The Preservation of Books in Libraries," 258.

18. Douglas Cockerell, "Leather for Bookbinding," *Journal of the Society of Arts* 48 (30 March 1900): 402; "On Buckram as a Binding Material," *American Library Journal* 2 (January-February 1878): 271-72; Bernard R. Green, "Planning and Construction of Library Buildings," *Library Journal* 25 (November 1900): 680; Fletcher Free Library (Burlington, Vt.), *Annual Report of the Trustees, 1898*, 4; Washington, D.C., Public Library, *Annual Report, 1901*, 31.

19. New York State Library, *Annual Report of the Trustees, 1898*, 45; "Library Buildings," 124; Minneapolis Public Library, *Annual Report, 1898*, 21; "The Newberry Library: Dr. Poole's Plans," 6.

20. Peabody Institute (Baltimore), *Annual Report of the Provost to the Trustees, 1879*, 32-33.

21. Poole, review of *The Enemies of Books*, 64; San Francisco Public Library, *Report of the Board of Trustees, 1890*, 5.

22. "On Buckram as a Binding Material," 271-72; Cyril Davenport, "Library Bookbinding," *Library Association Report* 5 (January 1903): 13; Philadelphia Mercantile Library Company, *Annual Report of the Board of Directors, 1881*, 8; Iowa State Library, *Report of the Librarian, 1886-1887*, iii.

23. Cornelius Walford, "On Binding of Books for Public and Private Libraries; and On Shelf-Arrangement as Associated Therewith," *American Library Journal* 2 (November-December 1877): 201-2.

24. "Library Buildings," 124.

25. Eames, "The Care of Special Collections," 50; Salem (Mass.) Public Library, *Report of the Trustees, 1900*, 11-12; Wheatley, "Leather for Bookbinding," 311.

26. Redwood Library and Athenaeum (Newport, R.I.), *Annual Report of the Directors, 1898*, 16, and *1899*, 8.

27. Mercantile Library Association of the City of New York, *Annual Report of the Board of Direction, 1882-1883*, 10-11; St. Louis Mercantile Library Association, *Annual Report of the Board of Directors, 1892*, 23; Providence Public Library, *Annual Report, 1889*, 12; Buffalo Public Library, *Annual Report, 1907*, 20; Manchester (N.H.) City Library, *Annual*

Report of the Trustees, 1885, 18; Brookline (Mass.) Public Library, *Annual Report of the Trustees, 1887*, 7; Gloversville (N.Y.) Free Library, *Annual Report of the Librarian, 1899*, 8.

28. Winsor, "Library Memoranda," 713; Fletcher Veitch, "Suitable Paper for Permanent Records," in *U.S. Department of Agriculture Yearbook, 1908* (Washington, D.C.: Government Printing Office, 1909), 266; U.S. Department of Agriculture, *Durability and Economy in Papers for Permanent Records*, 16.

29. Edward W. B. Nicholson, "On Buckram as a Binding Material," *American Library Journal* 2 (November-December 1877): 208; "Mercantile L., N.Y.," *Library Journal* 8 (July 1883): 129-30; "Gas and Bindings Again," *Library Journal* 12 (November 1887): 522; William H. Greenhough, "On the Ventilation, Heating, and Lighting, Especially Electric Lighting, of Public Libraries and Reading Rooms," *Library* 2 (1890): 426; "On Library Buildings," in *Transactions and Proceedings of the Conference of Librarians Held in London October, 1877*, ed. Edward B. Nicholson and Henry R. Tedder (London: Printed at Chiswick Press by Charles Whittingham, 1878), 147.

30. A. H. Church, "Destruction of Leather by Gas," *Chemical News* 36 (19 October 1877): 179; Poole, "The Construction of Library Buildings," 70; Marsden, "Decay of Leather Bindings," 312; Blades, *The Enemies of Books*, 29-30; Spofford, *A Book for All Readers*, 105.

31. "Injuries from Gas and Heat," *American Library Journal* 1 (30 November 1876): 124-25; "The Deterioration of Bindings," *Library Journal* 3 (August 1878): 229; William H. Browne, "Bindings Deteriorated without Gas," *Library Journal* 5 (February 1880): 50; Cockerell, "Leather for Bookbinding," 403.

32. "The Library of the Athenaeum Club," in *Transactions and Proceedings of the Conference of Librarians Held in London October, 1877*, ed. Edward B. Nicholson and Henry R. Tedder (London: Printed at Chiswick Press by Charles Whittingham, 1878), 231-32; Wheatley, "Leather for Bookbinding," 313-14; Royal Society of Arts, Committee on Leather for Bookbinding, *Report*, 1; Library Association of the United Kingdom, Sound Leather Committee, *Leather for Libraries*, 11.

33. J. B. Bailey, "The Library of the Royal College of Surgeons of England," *Library* 1 (1889): 259; William R. Nichols, "On the Deterioration of Library Bindings," *Library Journal* 4 (December 1879): 435.

34. Church, "Destruction of Leather by Gas," 179; Nichols, "On the Deterioration of Library Bindings," 435-38.

35. "On Library Buildings," *American Library Journal* 2 (January-February 1878): 252; Library Association of the United Kingdom, Sound Leather Committee, *Leather for Libraries*, 11.

36. C. J. Woodward, "A Preliminary Experimental Inquiry as to the Action of Burning-Gas on Leather Used for Book-Binding," *Library Journal* 12 (September-October 1887): 321-22; C. J. Woodward, "The Action of Gas on Leather Bookbindings: A Preliminary Experimental Enquiry," *Library Chronicle* 5 (1888): 25-29.

37. Royal Society of Arts, Committee on Leather for Bookbinding, *Report*, 42, 89; Wheatley, "Leather for Bookbinding," 315-16, 319; J. Gordon Parker, "Leather for Bookbinding," *Journal of the Society of Arts* 50 (November 29, 1901): 27.

38. Society for the Encouragement of Arts, Manufactures, and Commerce, Committee on the Deterioration of Paper, *Report of the Committee on the Deterioration of Paper. With Two Appendixes: 1. Abstracts of Papers on German Official Tests, 1885-96. 2. Précis of Correspondence* (London: Society, 1898), 3.

39. Library Association of the United Kingdom, Sound Leather Committee, *Leather for Libraries*, 27.

40. "The Effect of Illuminating Gas on Leather," *Scientific American Supplement* 67 (1 May 1909): 287.

41. Davenport, "Library Bookbinding," 13; Library Association of the United Kingdom, Sound Leather Committee, *Leather for Libraries*, 27.

42. Poole, review of *The Enemies of Books*, 64; Blades, *The Enemies of Books*, 22-23; Arthur L. Humphreys, *The Private Library: What We Do Know, What We Don't Know, What We Ought to Know about Our Books* (New York: J. W. Bouton, 1897), 17-18; Veitch, "Suitable Paper for Permanent Records," 266; Spofford, *A Book for All Readers*, 104; Cockerell, "Leather for Bookbinding," 402; "On Buckram as a Binding Material," 271-72.

43. Dover (N.H.) Public Library, *Annual Report of the Trustees, 1891*, 5.

44. Nebraska State Library, *Report, 1905-1906*, 4.

45. Harvard University, *Third Report of William Coolidge Lane, Librarian, 1900*, 237.

46. Redwood Library and Athenaeum (Newport, R.I.), *Annual Report of the Directors, 1896*, 20, and *1899*, 17-18.

47. Providence Athenaeum, *Annual Report of the Directors, 1886*, 33.

48. Boston Public Library, *Annual Report of the Trustees, 1876*, 10.

49. Forbes Library (Northampton, Mass.), *Annual Report of the Trustees, 1910*, 7.

50. Library of Congress, *Report, 1905-1906*, 75.

51. Dedham (Mass.) Public Library, *Annual Report of the Trustees, 1888*, 19; Detroit Public Library, *Annual Report, 1886*, 78; Rhode Island State Library, *Annual Report, 1902*, 7.

52. Frank Browne, "The Preservation of Books in Hot Climates," *Scientific American Supplement* 56 (15 August 1903): 23095; Green, "Library Buildings and Book Stacks," 55; John McFarlane, *Library Administration* (London: G. Harper; New York: F. Harper, 1898), 234.

53. Eames, "The Care of Special Collections," 50; Edith D. Fuller, "United States, State, and Town Documents in Small Libraries," *Library Journal* 23 (October 1898): 566.

54. "Quicklime," *Library Journal* 13 (February 1888): 56; W. Haslam, *Book of Trade Secrets: Receipts and Instructions for Renovating, Repairing, Improving and Preserving Old Books and Prints* (New York: Scribner, 1909), 27-28; Slater, *The Library Manual*, 12.

55. "On Library Buildings," *American Library Journal*, 254; "On Library Buildings," in *Transactions and Proceedings of the Conference of Librarians Held in London October 1877*, 150; Humphreys, *The Private Library*, 18; Spofford, *A Book for All Readers*, 104.

56. "On Library Buildings," *American Library Journal*, 254; William F. Poole, "Small Library Buildings," *Library Journal* 10 (September-October 1885): 252.

57. Browne, "The Preservation of Books in Hot Climates," 23095; Humphreys, *The Private Library*, 18.

58. Keen, "Library Book-Stacks without Daylight," 974; Bernard R. Green, "Library Book Stacks without Daylight," *Science*, n.s., 29 (9 April 1909): 592; Veitch, "Suitable Paper for Permanent Records," 266; Fletcher, "Some Library Superstitions," 156; William Fletcher, "The Proper Lighting of Library Rooms," *Library Journal* 15 (December 1890): 10-11; Walter Powell, "Book Production in Great Britain," *Library Journal* 29 (December 1904): 52; "Book Surgery in Libraries," *Public Libraries* 11 (June 1906): 311; Wheatley, "Leather for Bookbinding," 311; Davenport, "Library Bookbinding," 13; Library Association of the United Kingdom, Sound Leather Committee, *Leather for Libraries*, 27; "Rapid Discoloration of Paper," *Library Journal* 11 (November 1886): 442; "Electric Lighting," *Library Journal* 12 (July 1887): 270.

59. Arthur D. Little, "The Durability of Paper," *Printing Art* 1 (June 1903): 115.

60. A. Seymour-Jones, "On the Glazing of Libraries, with Reference to the Chemical Action of Light on Leather," *Library Association Record* 8 (December 1906): 644; Parker, "Leather for Bookbinding," 28; "Michigan Library Association," 955.

61. Green, "Library Buildings and Book Stacks," 55; Library of Congress, *Report, 1901-1902*, 31-32; Kroeger, "The Care of Books," 321.

62. Spofford, *A Book for All Readers*, 110; "Library Architecture," *Library Journal* 8 (September-October 1883): 274.

Notes

63. Willard Austen, "Bookworms in Fact and Fancy," *Popular Science Monthly* 55 (June 1899): 244-45; "Insects Which Injure Books," *Zoölogist* 3 (October 1879): 430; "The Enemies of Books," *Scientific American,* suppl. 6 (24 August 1878): 2201; "Report of Committee on Bookbinding," *ALA Bulletin* 1 (July 1907): 114; U.S. Department of Agriculture, *Durability and Economy in Papers for Permanent Records,* 16; E. Wyndham Hulme, "Insect Book-Pests: A Review of the Recent Literature," *Library Association Record* 1 (June 1899): 372.

64. J. F. X. O'Conor, *Facts about Bookworms: Their History in Literature and Work in Libraries* (New York: F. Harper, 1898), 10; Jacques Boyer, "The Insect Enemies of Books," *Scientific American* 98 (6 June 1908): 413.

65. Anna C. Tyler, "A Live Bookworm–A Nature Study," *Library Journal* 33 (August 1908): 312.

66. Both Poole and Spofford maintained that bookworms were not a serious problem in American libraries; Poole chastened Blades for making more of this pest than was warranted. See Poole, review of *The Enemies of Books,* 64-65; Spofford, *A Book for All Readers,* 108.

67. William R. Reinick, "Insects Destructive to Books," *Scientific American Supplement* 70 (24 December 1910): 408; Hulme, "Insect Book-Pests," 371-72; Blades, *The Enemies of Books,* 68, 70; O'Conor, *Facts about Bookworms,* 51, 57.

68. Austen, "Bookworms in Fact and Fancy," 240-43.

69. "The Ravages of Bookworms," *Library Journal* 19 (July 1894): 230-31; Tyler, "A Live Bookworm," 311-12; O'Conor, *Facts about Bookworms,* 70-71; Austen, "Bookworms in Fact and Fancy," 246.

70. "The Ravages of Bookworms," 230-31; O'Conor, *Facts about Bookworms,* 74; Tyler, "A Live Bookworm," 311-12; Blades, *The Enemies of Books,* 76-77.

71. "The Ravages of Bookworms," 230-31.

72. Tyler, "A Live Bookworm," 311-312.

73. Blades, *The Enemies of Books,* 71-72; "A Book Worm," *Library Journal* 10 (June 1885): 131.

74. O'Conor, *Facts about Bookworms,* 15-18, 51, 53.

75. Spofford, *A Book for All Readers,* 109; Blades, *The Enemies of Books,* 83.

76. "The Croton Bug as a Library Pest," *Library Journal* 4 (September-October 1879): 376; Blades, *The Enemies of Books,* 83-84.

77. Austen, "Bookworms in Fact and Fancy," 244; Walford, "On Binding of Books for Public and Private Libraries," 201-2; "The Croton Bug as a Library Pest," 376; Blades, *The Enemies of Books,* 83; Spofford, *A Book for All Readers,* 109.

78. H. A. Hagen, "On a New Library Pest," *Boston Weekly Transcript*, 16 March 1886, 6; Austen, "Bookworms in Fact and Fancy," 244; "The Enemies of Books," 2201; "The Ravages of Bookworms," 230-31; Blades, *The Enemies of Books*, 84; Redwood Library and Athenaeum (Newport, R.I.), *Annual Report of the Directors, 1898*, 14-15.

79. Austen, "Bookworms in Fact and Fancy," 244; "The Enemies of Books," 2201.

80. Hagen, "On a New Library Pest," 186.

81. Manchester (N.H.) City Library, *Annual Report of the Trustees, 1908*, 6-8.

82. It seems that most of these methods were intended to be multi-purpose rather than to be used with particular types of insects. One scientist, however, advised that most poisons also attract certain insects and that one must target a pest with the proper toxin. See Reinick, "Insects Destructive to Books," 410.

83. "Insects Which Injure Books," 430; "Insects," *Library Journal* 11 (April 1886): 123; Robert D. MacLeod, "The Preservation of Books in Libraries III," *Library World*, n.s., 11 (April 1909): 368-71; Boyer, "Insect Enemies of Books," 413; "The Ravages of Bookworms," 231; "On Binding Books for Public Libraries," *American Library Journal* 2 (January-February 1878): 271; "Preserving Bindings," *Library Journal* 17 (February 1892): 72; O'Conor, *Facts about Bookworms*, 77.

84. Boyer, "The Insect Enemies of Books," 414; "Insects," 123; "The Ravages of Bookworms," 231; "Study of the Hygiene of Libraries: Methods of Preserving Books against Their Enemies Suggested by the International Congress of Librarians – Suffocation the Best," *Public Opinion* 36 (18 February 1904): 213.

85. Browne, "The Preservation of Books in Hot Climates," 23095; "Preserving Bindings," 72.

86. Boyer, "The Insect Enemies of Books," 414.

87. Ibid.

88. St. Joseph (Mo.) Free Public Library, *Annual Report, 1901-1902*, 30.

89. "The Croton Bug as a Library Pest," 377.

90. Ibid.; O'Conor, *Facts about Bookworms*, 77; "The Croton Bug as a Library Pest," 376; "The Ravages of Bookworms," 231; Walford, "On Binding of Books for Public and Private Libraries," 201-202; H. A. Hagen, "Insect Pests in Libraries," *Library Journal* 4 (July-August 1879): 251; Katharine L. Sharp, "Library Recipes," *Library Notes* 4 (July 1895): 205; "Bookworms," *Library Journal* 11 (July 1886): 191; "Bookworms," *Library Journal* 12 (April 1887): 174; Slater, *The Library Manual*, 6.

91. Hagen, "Insect Pests in Libraries," 254.

92. Boyer, "The Insect Enemies of Books," 414; "International Congress of Librarians, Paris, August 20-23, 1900," *Library Journal* 25 (September 1900): 581; "The Insect Enemies of Books," *Library Journal* 11 (December 1886): 484; O'Conor, *Facts about Bookworms*, 78; "On Buckram as a Binding Material," 272.

93. Browne, "The Preservation of Books in Hot Climates," 23095; Walford, "On Binding of Books for Public and Private Libraries," 201-202; "The Insect Enemies of Books," 484; "Preserving Bindings," 72.

94. Chance, "Preservation of Bookbindings," 444; Hagen, "Insect Pests in Libraries," 251; O'Conor, *Facts about Bookworms*, 78.

95. D. V. R. Johnston, "Binding and Binderies," *Library Journal* 16 (December 1891): 12; "Preserving Bindings," 72; George A. Stephen, "Notes on Materials for Library Bookbinding," *Library Assistant* 5 (September 1906): 162.

96. Boyer, "The Insect Enemies of Books," 414; "The Insect Enemies of Books," 484; Zaehnsdorf, *The Art of Bookbinding*, 169; O'Conor, *Facts about Bookworms*, 78.

97. Zaehnsdorf, *The Art of Bookbinding*, 167.

98. Boyer, "The Insect Enemies of Books," 414.

99. Hagen, "Insect Pests in Libraries," 252.

100. O'Conor, *Facts about Bookworms*, 87.

101. "Study of the Hygiene of Libraries," 213; "International Congress of Librarians, Paris, August 20-23, 1900," 582; "French Prizes for Monographs on Bookworms," *Library Journal* 26 (July 1901): 388-89; "French Prizes for Essays on Insects Destructive to Books," *Library Journal* 27 (December 1902): 1026.

Chapter 3. The Library Building

1. Boston Public Library, *Annual Report of the Trustees, 1876*, 9-11; *1877*, 24-26, 36; *1878*, 1, 3-4, 14, 19.

2. Boston Public Library, *Annual Report of the Trustees, 1879*, 2-3, 18, 19; *1880*, 10-11; *1881*, 2; *1882*, 5-6; *1883*, 6-9; *1885*, 11-13; *1886*, 3; *1887*, 3-4; *1888*, 6; *1891*, 21-22; *1894*, 23.

3. Henry J. Carr, "Fixtures, Furniture, and Fittings," in U.S. Office of Education, *Annual Report, 1892-1893*, 735, 737; "Injuries from Gas and Heat," 124-25.

4. "On Library Buildings," in *Transactions and Proceedings of the Conference of Librarians Held in London, October 1877*, 148.

5. "The Newberry Library," 6.

6. Poole, "The Construction of Library Buildings," 72; H. Woodbine, "Essay on Modern Methods of Book Storage," *Library Association Record* 12 (September 1910): 452-53.

7. "Library Buildings," 123; "On Library Buildings," in *Transactions and Proceedings of the Conference of Librarians Held in London, October 1877*, 148.

8. Poole, "Progress of Library Architecture," 133; "Library Architecture," *Library Journal* 7 (July-August 1882): 197; "Resolutions," *Library Journal* 7 (July-August 1882): 203.

9. "Library Architecture," *Library Journal* 8, 270, 272-73.

10. Ibid., 273-74.

11. Spofford, *A Book for All Readers*, 101-102.

12. Public Library of the City of Bangor (Maine), *Annual Reports, 1890*, 13; Paterson (N.J.) Free Public Library, *Report, 1901-1902*, 15-17.

13. Spofford, *A Book for All Readers*, 108; Public Library of the City of Bangor (Maine), *Annual Reports, 1890*, 13.

14. Newberry Library (Chicago), *Report of the Trustees, 1889*, 3.

15. Fletcher Free Library (Burlington, Vt.), *Annual Report of the Trustees, 1878*, 8.

16. H. A. Homes, "Deterioration of Bindings," *Library Journal* 5 (July-August 1880): 214; "Library Buildings," 124.

17. Melvil Dewey, "Heating Libraries," *Library Journal* 6 (April 1881): 94-95.

18. Redwood Library and Athenaeum (Newport, R.I.), *Annual Report of the Directors, 1899*, 7.

19. Brookline (Mass.) Public Library, *Annual Report of the Trustees, 1899*, 4.

20. John Emands, "Report on Library Architecture," *Library Journal* 8 (September-October 1883): 201.

21. Nebraska State Library, *Report, 1905-1906*, 4; Rhode Island State Library, *Annual Report, 1902*, 7; "Injuries from Gas and Heat," 124; Green, "Library Buildings and Book Stacks," 56.

22. Greenhough, "On Ventilation, Heating, and Lighting," 427; E. R. Norris Mathews, "Library Binderies," *Library Association Record* 8 (15 March 1906): 76; Royal Society of Arts, Committee on Leather for Bookbinding, *Report*, 20-21; Library Association of the United Kingdom, Sound Leather Committee, *Leather for Libraries*, 11.

23. "Injuries from Gas and Heat," 125; Harvard University, *Twelfth Report of Justin Winsor, Librarian, 1889*, 11.

24. Fletcher, "The Proper Lighting of Library Rooms," 10-11.

25. Library of Congress, *Report, 1901-1902*, 31-32; Green, "Library Buildings and Book Stacks," 55.

26. Seymour-Jones, "On the Glazing of Libraries," 642-46; Wheatley, "Leather for Bookbinding," 318; Royal Society of Arts, Committee on Leather for Bookbinding, *Report*, 69-70.

27. There exists at least one instance of the use of tinted glass in a museum environment; this example predates the Society of Arts' research. As an experiment, in 1894 the skylight in the Raphael Cartoon Gallery of the South Kensington Museum (now Room 94 of the Victoria and Albert Museum) was replaced with alternating strips of green and orange glass. While "favourable to preservation," the light that entered the room had a decidedly yellow cast that proved irritating to museumgoers. The glass remained until it was damaged in a World War II air raid. See Norman S. Brommelle, "The Russell and Abney Report on the Action of Light on Water Colours," *Studies in Conservation* 9 (1984): 148-49.

28. "Notes," *Library Journal* 10 (December 1885): 406; Providence Athenaeum, *Annual Report of the Directors, 1899*, 6-7.

29. Brooklyn Mercantile Library Association, *Annual Report of the Board of Directors, 1883*, 16.

30. Columbia College Library, *Annual Report of the Chief Librarian, 1887*, 3.

31. Around 1882 electric lighting began making inroads into American libraries, and by 1910 most libraries were illuminated with electricity. In the intervening years, some libraries – among them the Providence Athenaeum, the Salem (Mass.) Public Library, and the Somerville (Mass.) Public Library – used a combination of gas and electricity. See Providence Athenaeum, *Annual Report of the Directors, 1899*, 6-7; Salem (Mass.) Public Library, *Report of the Trustees, 1889*, 55; Somerville (Mass.) Public Library, *Annual Report, 1895*, 14.

32. Frank C. Caldwell, *Modern Lighting* (New York: Macmillan, 1930), 31; Greenhough, "On Ventilation, Heating, and Lighting," 426-28.

33. Blades, *The Enemies of Books*, 29; Bailey, "The Library of the Royal College of Surgeons," 259.

34. "The Electric Light in the British Museum Reading-Room," *Chemical News* 39 (7 March 1879): 101-102; "The Siemens Light at the British Museum," *Chemical News* 40 (31 October 1897): 212-13; "British Museum: Further Reforms," *Library Journal* 4 (31 March 1879): 101-102; "Dangers From Electric Light," *Library Journal* 5 (May 1880): 153; "The Electric Light at the British Museum," *Library Journal* 5 (June 1880): 171; Blades, *The Enemies of Books*, 31-32.

35. Normand S. Patton, "Heating, Ventilation, and Lighting of Libraries," in U.S. Office of Education, *Annual Report, 1892-1893*, 723; Greenhough, "On Ventilation, Heating, and Lighting," 428; Royal Society of Arts, Committee on Leather for Bookbinding, *Report*, 42.

36. Editorial, *Library Journal* 7 (March 1882): 43; Greenhough, "On Ventilation, Heating, and Lighting," 428; Royal Society of Arts, Committee on Leather for Bookbinding, *Report*, 42.

37. "Best Light for Libraries," *Library Journal* 17 (December 1892): 501. Note that Julius Wiesner's research ("Rapid Discoloration of Paper," 442; "Electric Lighting," 270) contradicts this.

38. Reuben B. Poole, "Fires, Protection, Insurance," *Library Journal* 18 (July 1893): 224; Cecil T. Davis, "Insurance of Public Libraries," *Library World* 2 (November 1899): 122; Greenhough, "On Ventilation, Heating, and Lighting," 431.

39. Providence Athenaeum, *Annual Report of the Directors, 1897*, 8; Redwood Library and Athenaeum (Newport, R.I.), *Annual Report of the Directors, 1909*, 16; Columbia College Library, *Annual Report of the Chief Librarian, 1884*, 32; Yale University, *Report of the Librarian, 1902-1903*, 7; Brookline (Mass.) Public Library, *Annual Report of the Trustees, 1889*, 9; Chicago Public Library, *Annual Report of the Board of Directors, 1886*, 27; Cincinnati Public Library, *Annual Report of the Librarian and Treasurer, 1888-1889*, 11; Detroit Public Library, *Annual Report, 1887*, 15; Lawrence (Mass.) Free Public Library, *Annual Report of the Board of Trustees and Librarian, 1893*, 17-18; Manchester (N.H.) City Library, *Annual Report of the Trustees, 1885*, 18; Paterson (N.J.) Free Public Library, *Report, 1888-1889*, 5; Providence Public Library, *Annual Report, 1891*, 15; Woburn (Mass.) Public Library, *Annual Report, 1889*, 22.

40. Trinity College Library, *Report of the Librarian, 1900*, 16-17; Cleveland Public Library, *Annual Report, 1891*, 5-6; Minneapolis Public Library, *Annual Report, 1898*, 21; San Francisco Public Library, *Report of the Board of Trustees, 1890*, 5; Springfield (Mass.) City Library Association, *Annual Report, 1888*, 10; Watertown (Mass.) Free Public Library, *Annual Report, 1892*, 5.

41. San Francisco Public Library, *Report of the Board of Trustees, 1890*, 5.

42. Springfield (Mass.) City Library Association, *Annual Report, 1888*, 10.

43. New Bedford (Mass.) Free Public Library, *Annual Report of the Trustees, 1892*, 5.

44. Queens Borough (N.Y.) Public Library, *Annual Report of the Board of Trustees, 1910*, 12-13; Silas Bronson Library (Waterbury, Conn.), *Annual Report of the Board of Agents, 1909-1910*, 15.

45. Omaha Public Library, *Annual Report of the Board of Directors, 1896-1897*, 12; New Haven (Conn.) Free Public Library, *Annual Report of the Board of Directors, 1901*, 18; Springfield (Mass.) City Library Association, *Annual Report, 1889*, 13-14, and *1892*, 18.

46. "Electric Lights," *Library Journal* 10 (September-October 1885): 334-35; "Action of Electric Lights on Paper," *Library Journal* 12 (September-October 1887): 428-29.

47. St. Joseph (Mo.) Free Public Library, *Annual Report, 1901-1902*, 30.

48. Newark (N.J.) Free Public Library, *Annual Report of the Board of Trustees, 1895*, 11; Omaha Public Library, *Annual Report of the Board of Directors, 1896-1897*, 12; St. Louis Public Library, *Annual Report, 1895-1896*, 8.

49. R. D., "Dirt in the City Library," *Indianapolis Journal*, 12 December 1886, 6.

50. W. D. Hooper, "Dirt in the City Library," *Indianapolis Journal*, 14 December 1886, 3.

51. Brookline (Mass.) Public Library, *Annual Report of the Trustees, 1878*, 13.

52. Boston Public Library, *Annual Report of the Trustees, 1903*, 7.

53. "A Library in Ruins," *Library Journal* 8 (December 1883): 337.

54. Providence Athenaeum, *Annual Report of the Directors, 1895*, 6-7; Andover (Mass.) Memorial Hall Library, *Annual Report, 1907*, 2; Bowdoin College Library, *Annual Report of the Librarian, 1903*, 31.

55. W. E. Gladstone, "On Books and the Housing of Them," *Nineteenth Century* 27 (March 1890): 393; Carr, "Fixtures, Furniture, and Fittings," 741; "Dust," *Library Journal* 4 (April 1893): 122; Lutie E. Stearns, *Essentials in Library Administration* (Boston: ALA Publishing Board, 1905), 80; Providence Athenaeum, *Annual Report of the Directors, 1876*, 6.

56. "Association Bindings," *American Library Journal* 2 (31 August 1877): 432; Redwood Library and Athenaeum (Newport, R.I.), *Annual Report of the Directors, 1882*, 21; Worcester County (Mass.) Law Library, *Annual Report, 1902*, 7; New York Yacht Club Library, *Report of Library Committee, 1905*, 1; Boston Public Library, *Annual Report of the Trustees, 1898*, 30; Manchester (N.H.) City Library, *Annual Report of the Trustees, 1882*, 15.

57. Silas Bronson Library (Waterbury, Conn.), *Annual Report of the Board of Agents, 1878-1879*, 10.

58. Melvil Dewey, "Doors on Bookcases," *Library Notes* 2 (September 1887): 112-13; Providence Athenaeum, *Annual Report of the Directors, 1894*, 7; Cleveland Public Library, *Annual Report, 1900*, 45.

59. University of Michigan Library, *Annual Report of the Director, 1890*, 3; *1891*, 3; *1892*, 3; Atlantic City (N.J.) Free Public Library, *Annual Report, 1907*, 12.

60. Cincinnati Public Library, *Annual Report of the Librarian and Treasurer, 1907-1908*, 18, 68; Lawrence (Mass.) Free Public Library, *Annual Report of the Board of Trustees and Librarian, 1886*, 17, and *1900*, 18; New York State Library, *Annual Report of the Trustees, 1891*, 31.

61. Ohio State Library, *Annual Report, 1876,* 5; Harvard University Library, *Annual Report, 1908,* 23.

62. McFarlane, *Library Administration,* 233.

63. Harold Klett, "Don't," *Library Journal* 11 (April 1886): 117; Blades, *The Enemies of Books,* 119; O'Conor, *Facts about Bookworms,* 78; Harvard University Library, *Annual Report, 1908,* 23.

64. Sharp, "Library Recipes," 207; MacLeod, "The Preservation of Books in Libraries," 257; Spofford, *A Book for All Readers,* 103; "The Dust Problem in Libraries," *Library World,* n.s., 9 (January 1907): 242.

65. Sharp, "Library Recipes," 207; Spofford, *A Book for All Readers,* 103.

66. Grand Rapids Public Library, *Annual Report, 1904-1905,* 23.

67. Cleveland Public Library, *Annual Report, 1905,* 61; "A Book-Dusting Machine," *Library Journal* 29 (February 1904): 99.

68. Harvard University Library, *Annual Report, 1908,* 23-24.

69. "American Libraries: Chicago, Ill. John Crerar L.," *Library Journal* 34 (April 1909): 184; MacLeod, "The Preservation of Books in Libraries," 257; Francis K. W. Drury, "Labor Savers in Library Service," *Library Journal* 35 (December 1910): 539.

70. Boston Athenaeum, *Reports of the Library Committee and of the Librarian, 1908,* 2-3; Brooklyn Public Library, *Annual Report of the Board of Directors, 1910,* 28; Chicago Public Library, *Annual Report of the Board of Directors, 1908-1909,* 12.

71. Fitchburg (Mass.) Public Library, *Annual Report, 1910,* 13; Wilmington (Del.) Institute, *Annual Report, 1909-1910,* 22.

72. Grand Rapids Public Library, *Annual Report, 1909-1910,* 84.

73. Boston Public Library, *Annual Report of the Trustees, 1905,* 7, and *1907,* 12; Cincinnati Public Library, *Annual Report of the Librarian and Treasurer, 1905-1906,* 22; Providence Public Library, *Annual Report, 1900,* 21; St. Joseph (Mo.) Free Public Library, *Annual Report, 1901-1902,* 30; St. Louis Public Library, *Annual Report, 1908-1909,* 51-52.

74. Cincinnati Public Library, *Annual Report of the Librarian and Treasurer, 1905-1906,* 22; St. Louis Public Library, *Annual Report, 1908-1909,* 51-52; New Hampshire State Library, *Report, 1908-1910,* 8.

75. Providence Athenaeum, *Annual Report of the Directors, 1876,* 6-8.

76. Redwood Library and Athenaeum (Newport, R.I.), *Annual Report of the Directors, 1903,* 14; Fletcher Free Library (Burlington, Vt.), *Annual Report of the Trustees, 1879,* 7; *1880,* 8; *1885,* 6.

77. Maine State Library, *Annual Report of the Librarian, 1885-1886,* 9-10.

78. Poole, "Fires, Protection, Insurance," 224.

79. Poole, "The Construction of Library Buildings," 72; "Notes," 406; Johns Hopkins University Library, *Report of the Librarian, 1908-1909*, 1; Trinity College Library, *Report of the Librarian, 1908*, 5-8; William F. Poole, "Three Libraries More Destroyed by Fire," *Library Journal* 6 (May 1881): 163-64; Chicago Public Library, *Annual Report of the Board of Directors, 1873*, 17; Milwaukee Public Library, *Annual Report of the Board of Trustees, 1894-1895*, 11, 13-14; Paterson (N.J.) Free Public Library, *Report, 1901-1902*, 5, 7-8; Lowell (Mass.) City Library, *Annual Report of the Directors, 1891*, 6; Marlborough (Mass.) Public Library, *Annual Report of the Library Committee, 1902*, 3.

80. Public Library of the City of Bangor (Maine), *Annual Reports, 1893*, 9-11, and *1896*, 13.

81. Public Library of the City of Bangor (Maine), *Annual Reports, 1910*, 21; Ibid., 1.

82. "The Birmingham Library," *Athenaeum*, 18 January 1879, 89; "The Birmingham Fire," *Library Journal* 4 (January 1879): 19-20; "The Prevention of Fires in Libraries," *Library Journal* 4 (28 February 1879): 52-54; Cornelius Walford, "The Destruction of Libraries by Fire Considered Practically and Historically," *Library Association Transactions* 2 (1879): 65; Spofford, *A Book for All Readers*, 107; Boston Public Library, *Annual Report of the Trustees, 1879*, 19.

83. Guido Biagi, "A Note on Italian Library Affairs," *Library Journal* 29 (December 1904): 58; Guido Biagi, "The Library: Its Past and Future," *Library Journal* 29 (December 1904): 13; "Turin, Italy. National L.," *Library Journal* (May 1905): 308.

84. "Philadelphia Mercantile Library," *American Library Journal* 1 · (31 March 1877): 269; Philadelphia Mercantile Library Company, *Annual Report of the Board of Directors, 1877*, 5-6; "Fires – The Repair of Books," *American Library Journal* 2 (September 1877): 22-23; Spofford, *A Book for All Readers*, 131-32; Poole, "Fires, Protection, Insurance," 223.

85. "Destruction of San Francisco and Other California Libraries," *Library Journal* 31 (May 1906): 213-14; San Francisco Public Library, *Report of the Board of Trustees, 1906*, 7-8; George T. Clark, "Lessons as to Construction from the San Francisco Fire," *Public Libraries* 12 (July 1907): 255-57; California State Library, *Biennial Report of the Trustees, 1904-1906*, 18.

86. Brookline (Mass.) Public Library, *Annual Report of the Trustees, 1905*, 5; Council Bluffs (Iowa) Free Public Library, *Annual Report, 1892*, 14; Providence Public Library, *Annual Report, 1891*, 14-15; Thomas Crane Public Library (Quincy, Mass.), *Annual Report, 1878*, 5; Nebraska State Library, *Report, 1905-1906*, 4, 6; North Carolina State Library, *Biennial Report, 1903-1904*, 10; Library of Congress, *Report, 1881*, 3; Washington State Library, *Biennial Report of the State Librarian, 1906*, 7.

87. New Bedford (Mass.) Free Public Library, *Annual Report of the Trustees, 1906*,4.

88. Watertown (Mass.) Free Public Library, *Annual Report, 1880*, 22.

89. Reynolds Library (Rochester, N.Y.), *Annual Report, 1890-1891*, 5.

90. Bowdoin College Library, *Annual Report of the Librarian, 1904*, 7; Peoria (Ill.) Public Library, *Annual Report, 1893-1894*, 4; Poughkeepsie (N.Y.) City Library, *Report, 1896*, 13; Syracuse Public Library, *Yearbook, 1893-1894 and 1894-1895*, 9.

91. Philadelphia Free Library, *Annual Report, 1900*, 6; St. Louis Public Library, *Annual Report, 1887-1888*, 21.

92. "Fire Protection of Public Libraries," *American Architect* 30 (11 October 1890): 26; Poole, "The Construction of Library Buildings," 72; Poole, "Three Libraries More Destroyed by Fire," 163-64; Columbia College Library, *Annual Report of the Chief Librarian, 1886*, 17.

93. Poole, "Fires, Protection, Insurance," 223-24.

94. Yale University Library, *Report of the Librarian, 1907-1908*, 26; Detroit Public Library, *Annual Report, 1895*, 14; Syracuse Public Library, *Yearbook, 1899*, 11; Columbia College Library, *Annual Report of the Chief Librarian, 1886*, 17.

95. Reuben B. Poole, "Fires, Protection, Insurance," in U.S. Office of Education, *Annual Report, 1892-1893*, 729-30; Clark, "Lessons as to Construction from the San Francisco Fire," 255-56.

96. Spofford, *A Book for All Readers*, 106; Clark, "Lessons as to Construction from the San Francisco Fire," 256.

97. Clark, "Lessons as to Construction from the San Francisco Fire," 256-57; St. Louis Mercantile Library Association, *Annual Report of the Board of Directors, 1876*, 20; Boston Public Library, *Annual Report of the Trustees, 1879*, 18, and *1907*, 13-15; Boston Athenaeum, *Reports of the Library Committee and the Librarian, 1904*, 1; Bowdoin College Library, *Annual Report of the Librarian, 1895*, 248.

98. Boston Athenaeum, *Reports of the Library Committee and the Librarian, 1904*, 1; Boston Public Library, *Annual Report of the Trustees, 1907*, 13-15; Poole, "Fires, Protection, Insurance," in U.S. Office of Education, *Annual Report, 1892-1893*, 730-31; Clark, "Lessons as to Construction from the San Francisco Fire," 256-57; Boston Public Library, *Annual Report of the Trustees, 1879*, 18.

99. Boston Athenaeum, *Reports of the Library Committee and the Librarian, 1904*, 1; Providence Athenaeum, *Annual Report of the Directors, 1906*, 6; St. Louis Mercantile Library, *Annual Report of the Board of Directors, 1876*, 20; Boston Public Library, *Annual Report of the Trustees, 1879*, 18; Boston Public Library, *Annual Report of the Trustees, 1907*, 13-15; Bowdoin College Library, *Annual Report of the Librarian, 1895*, 248;

Chicago Public Library, *Annual Report of the Board of Directors, 1873*, 17-18.

100. University of Michigan Library, *Annual Report of the Director, 1896-1897*, 6; Massachusetts Commission of Public Records, *Third Report on the Custody and Condition of the Public Records of Parishes, Towns, and Counties, 1891*, 95; Emands, "Report on Library Architecture," 202; "Local Records," *Library World* 2 (June 1900): 314-15; Providence Athenaeum, *Annual Report of the Directors, 1897*, 8-9; Providence Athenaeum, *Annual Report of the Directors, 1906*, 13; Detroit Public Library, *Annual Report, 1886*, 78.

101. Indiana State Library, *Report, 1905-1906*, 24; New York State Library, *Annual Report of the Trustees, 1899*, 62.

102. "The Birmingham Library," 89.

103. "The Prevention of Fires in Libraries," 52; Poole, "Fires, Protection, Insurance," *Library Journal*, 224.

104. Emands, "Report on Library Architecture," 201; Boston Public Library, *Annual Report of the Trustees, 1905*, 9; Boston Athenaeum, *Reports of the Library Committee and of the Librarian, 1908*, 2.

105. Boston Public Library, *Annual Report of the Trustees, 1907*, 13-15; Samuel S. Green, "The Elevator in the Worcester Public Library – Precautions against Fire," *Library Journal* 4 (30 June 1879): 202; Astor Library (New York City), *Annual Report of the Trustees, 1882*, 8; Poole, "Fires, Protection, Insurance," *Library Journal*, 224.

106. Providence Athenaeum, *Annual Report of the Directors, 1904*, 5-6.

107. "Fire Protection of Public Libraries," 26; Davis, "Insurance of Public Libraries," 122; Green, "The Elevator in the Worcester Public Library," 202; Astor Library (New York City), *Annual Report of the Trustees, 1882*, 8.

108. Poole, "Fires, Protection, Insurance," *Library Journal*, 224; Boston Public Library, *Annual Report of the Trustees, 1905*, 9, and *1907*, 14; "The Prevention of Fires in Libraries," 52.

Chapter 4. Precautions for Readers

1. McFarlane, *Library Administration*, 182-83.

2. "Proposed Charging System," *Library Journal* 25 (July 1900): 350.

3. "Notes and Queries," *Library Journal* 8 (June 1883): 111; MacLeod, "The Preservation of Books in Libraries," 258; Spofford, *A Book for All Readers*, 113; Bradford (Pa.) Carnegie Public Library, *Annual Report, 1904*, 5; Lansing (Mich.) Public Library, *Annual Report, 1905-1906*, 9.

4. "Preservation of Bound Newspapers," 161; Boston Athenaeum, *Reports of the Library Committee and of the Librarian, 1897*, 3.

5. W. S. Rae, "A Conference of Books," *Library World* 2 (January 1900): 188; Kroeger, "The Care of Books," 320; Lawrence (Mass.) Free Public Library, *Annual Report of the Board of Trustees and Librarian, 1880*, 20.

6. Lansing (Mich.) Public Library, *Annual Report, 1880*, 20; "How We Protect Rare and Illustrated Books II," 133.

7. "Ragged Books," *New York Libraries* 1 (January 1909): 185; "A. L. A. Library Primer (Under Revision)," *Public Libraries* 1 (June 1896): 44; Clara Field, "Book Repairing," *News Notes of California Libraries* 2 (February 1907): 105; Otis Library (Norwich, Conn.), *Annual Report, 1897-1898*, 11-12; "Suggestions to Readers on the Care of Books," *Monthly Bulletin of the Providence Public Library* 4 (February 1898): 44.

8. Annie Carroll, "Library Membership as a Civic Force," *Library Journal* 7 (July 1908): 271.

9. Chance, "Preservation of Bookbindings," 444; Field, "Book Repairing," 105; Humphreys, *The Private Library*, 24.

10. Manchester (N.H.) City Library, *Annual Report of the Trustees, 1884*, 18.

11. Brookline (Mass.) Public Library, *Annual Report of the Trustees, 1876*, 10; *1877*, 6; *1879*, 3-4; Boston Public Library, *Annual Report of the Trustees, 1875*, 15.

12. "Proposed Charging System," 350; "Suggestions to Readers on the Care of Books," 43-44; Kroeger, "The Care of Books," 320; Spofford, *A Book for All Readers*, 113, 117; Peabody Institute (Baltimore), *Annual Report of the Provost to the Trustees, 1882*, 25; Blades, *The Enemies of Books*, 120-21.

13. Kroeger, "The Care of Books," 320-21; Spofford, *A Book for All Readers*, 113-17; "Suggestions to Readers on the Care of Books," 44.

14. Klett, "Don't," 117; "Proposed Charging System," 350; Kroeger, "The Care of Books," 320; "Suggestions to Readers on the Care of Books," 43-44; Spofford, *A Book for All Readers*, 114, 116.

15. MacLeod, "The Preservation of Books in Libraries III," 368; Providence Athenaeum, *Annual Report of the Directors, 1883*, 9; Spofford, "Binding and Preservation of Books," 678; Boston Athenaeum, *Annual Report of the Directors, 1882*, 9-10; Brookline (Mass.) Public Library, *Annual Report of the Trustees, 1878*, 5.

16. Lawrence (Mass.) Free Public Library, *Annual Report of the Board of Trustees and Librarian, 1876*, 26; Brookline (Mass.) Public Library, *Annual Report of the Trustees, 1889*, 3.

17. "Proposed Charging System," 350; Kroeger, "The Care of Books," 320; "Suggestions to Readers on the Care of Books," 43; Spofford, *A Book*

for All Readers, 116; Watertown (Mass.) Free Public Library, *Annual Report, 1882*, 16.

18. "Defacing of Books," *American Library Journal* 1 (31 January 1877): 194; "Proposed Charging System," 350; Spofford, *A Book For All Readers*, 114; Iowa Library Commission, *Report, 1900-1903*, 48; Boston Public Library, *Annual Report of the Trustees, 1889*, 4.

19. Boston Public Library, *Annual Report of the Trustees, 1889*, 4.

20. Kroeger, "The Care of Books," 320; "Suggestions to Readers on the Care of Books," 44; Spofford, *A Book for All Readers*, 115.

21. Klett, "Don't," 117; "Suggestions to Readers on the Care of Books," 43; Humphreys, *The Private Library*, 16; McFarlane, *Library Administration*, 195-96.

22. Marsden, "Decay of Leather Bindings," 312; Wheatley, "Leather for Bookbinding," 316; Davenport, "Library Bookbinding," 13; Royal Society of Arts, Committee on Leather for Bookbinding, *Report*, 21; Humphreys, *The Private Library*, 16; Astor Library (New York City), *Annual Report of the Trustees, 1890*, 12; Adriance Memorial Library of the City of Poughkeepsie, *Annual Report, 1903*, 15; Columbia College Library, *Annual Report of the Chief Librarian, 1886*, 43.

23. Kroeger, "The Care of Books," 320; Astor Library (New York City), *Annual Report of the Trustees, 1890*, 12; McFarlane, *Library Administration*, 196; Spofford, *A Book for All Readers*, 113; "How We Protect Rare and Illustrated Books II," 133.

24. Blades, *The Enemies of Books*, 122-23.

25. Cleveland Public Library, *Annual Report, 1899*, 57-59.

26. Ibid., 59.

27. Linda Eastman, "The Library and the Children; An Account of the Children's Work in the Cleveland Public Library," *Library Journal* 23 (April 1898): 142.

28. William E. Foster, "Methods of Inducing Care of Books–II," *Library Journal* 25 (August 1900): 63-64; Mary E. Dousman, "Methods of Inducing Care of Books–I," *Library Journal* 25 (August 1900): 62; Evanston (Ill.) Public Library, *Annual Report, 1899*, 9; Braddock (Pa.) Carnegie Free Library, *Annual Report, 1903*, 39-40; Minneapolis Public Library, *Annual Report, 1897*, 17; "Michigan Library Association," *Library Journal* 25 (December 1900): 748-49.

29. Dousman, "Methods of Inducing Care of Books–I," 62.

30. Ibid.; Cornelia Marvin, "The Care of Books," *Wisconsin Library Bulletin* 1 (May 1905): 36; "Menasha," *Wisconsin Library Bulletin* 1 (June 1905): 67; Duluth Public Library, *Annual Report of the Public Library Board, 1903*, 7.

31. Katharine D. Cramer, "Methods for Keeping Books Clean," *Wisconsin Library Bulletin* 1 (June 1905): 66; Medford (Mass.) Public Library, *Report of the Trustees, 1899*, 12.

32. Helen Dodd, "The Care of Books in a Children's Room," *Public Libraries* 12 (March 1907): 83; Pratt Institute, *Report of the Pratt Institute Free Library and School of Library Science, 1897-1898*, 10; Marvin, "The Care of Books," 36.

33. "Miss Hewins' 'Goop' Verse," *Wisconsin Library Bulletin* 1 (September 1905): 79; Dodd, "The Care of Books in a Children's Room," 84; North Adams (Mass.) Public Library, *Annual Report, 1905*, 9.

34. "Book Mark," *Public Libraries* 11 (January 1906): 21.

35. "The Children's 'Story' Bookmark," *Library Journal* 22 (May 1897): 257; "A Children's Book Mark," *Library Journal* 22 (April 1897): 199; Eastman, "The Library and the Children," 142; Dodd, "The Care of Books in a Children's Room," 488.

36. Dousman, "Methods of Inducing Care of Books – I," 62; Marvin, "The Care of Books," 35.

37. "Enforcing Cleanliness in Public Libraries," *Library Journal* 15 (September 1890): 260; Mary E. Dousman, "Children's Departments," *Library Journal* 21 (September 1896): 408; Dousman, "Methods of Inducing Care of Books – I," 62; Field, "Book Repairing," 105; Marvin, "The Care of Books," 36.

38. "Menasha," 67; Dodd, "The Care of Books in a Children's Room," 83.

Chapter 5. The Preparation and Maintenance of Library Materials

1. Spofford, "Binding and Preservation of Books," 673; "How We Treat New Books," *Library Journal* 14 (April 1889): 110; Stearns, *Essentials in Library Administration*, 42; Bradford (Pa.) Carnegie Public Library, *Annual Report, 1904*, 1.

2. "A. L. A. Library Primer (Under Revision)," 44; H. W. Reid, "Hints on Bookbinding," *Public Libraries* 12 (February 1907): 64; Bradford (Pa.) Carnegie Public Library, *Annual Report, 1905*, 42; Harriet Sawyer, "How to Care for Books in a Library," *Wisconsin Library Bulletin* 5 (January-February 1909): 6; Kroeger, "The Care of Books," 44; Cedric Chivers, "How to Open a New Book," *Library*, 2d ser., 1 (1 June 1900): 326.

3. A. M. Pendleton, "How to Start Libraries in Small Towns, V," *American Library Journal* 1 (30 June 1877): 357; MacLeod, "The Preservation of Books in Libraries," 259; Kroeger, "The Care of Books," 319; "In Cutting a Book with a Paper-Knife," *Public Libraries* 1 (May 1896): 10.

4. "In Cutting a Book with a Paper-Knife," 10; "Practical Notes," *Library Journal* 16 (July 1891): 223; Sharp, "Library Recipes," 221.

5. "Perforating Punch," *Library Journal* 19 (February 1894): 66-67; Stearns, *Essentials in Library Administration*, 42; Bradford (Pa.) Carnegie Public Library, *Annual Report, 1904*, 5; McFarlane, *Library Administration*, 181; Howard Memorial Library (New Orleans), *Annual Report of the Librarian, 1889-1890*, 3.

6. Kroeger, "The Care of Books," 320.

7. "Paper Covers," *American Library Journal* 1 (30 November 1876): 132-33; Mary W. Plummer, *Hints to Small Libraries*, 2d ed., rev. and enl. (New York: Truslove & Comba, 1898), 30-31; John W. Jones, "Inaugural Address," *American Library Journal* 2 (November-December 1877): 115; Cambridge (Mass.) Public Library, *Annual Report of the Trustees, 1889*, 8; Spofford, *A Book for All Readers*, 97; Minneapolis Public Library, *Annual Report, 1895*, 15-16.

8. Pendleton, "How to Start Libraries in Small Towns, V," 356-57; Spofford, *A Book for All Readers*, 97; Brookline (Mass.) Public Library, *Annual Report of the Trustees, 1909*, 16.

9. Dousman, "Methods of Inducing Care of Books – I," 62; Cambridge (Mass.) Public Library, *Annual Report of the Trustees, 1889*, 8; Lawrence (Mass.) Free Public Library, *Annual Report of the Board of Trustees and Librarian, 1877*, 21, and *1878*, 17-18; Boston Public Library, *Annual Report of the Trustees, 1880*, 10-11; East Orange (N.J.) Free Public Library, *Annual Report of the Board of Directors, 1910*, 19; University of Michigan Library, *Annual Report of the Director, 1897-1898*, 10.

10. Marvin, "The Care of Books," 36; Brooklyn Mercantile Library Association, *Annual Report of the Board of Directors, 1885*, 27; Silas Bronson Library (Waterbury, Conn.), *Annual Report of the Board of Agents, 1879-1880*, 12; Southbridge (Mass.) Public Library, *Annual Report, 1878-1879*, 76; Watertown (Mass.) Free Public Library, *Annual Report, 1883*, 9; Cooper Union, *Annual Report of the Trustees, 1896*, 30.

11. "Covering Paper," *Library Journal* 4 (January 1879): 14.

12. "How We Treat New Books," 110; "Repairing Books," *Public Libraries* 12 (April 1907): 126.

13. Louisville (Ky.) Free Public Library, *Annual Report of the Board of Trustees, 1905-1906*, 43.

14. Brookline (Mass.) Public Library, *Annual Report of the Trustees, 1909*, 16; Queens Borough (N.Y.) Public Library, *Annual Report of the Board of Trustees, 1905*, 19; Haverhill (Mass.) Public Library, *Annual Report, 1906*, 27.

15. Advertisement for the Holden System for Preserving Books, *Library Journal* 20 (April 1895): 144; Advertisement for the Holden System for Preserving Books, April 1907, lxxi; Advertisement for Adjustable

Book Covers, *Library Journal* 20 (April 1895): 152; "Practical Notes," *Library Journal* 28 (June 1903): 319.

16. "Covering Paper," 14; Marvin, "The Care of Books," 36; Watertown (Mass.) Free Public Library, *Annual Report, 1882*, 16; Fletcher Free Library (Burlington, Vt.), *Annual Report of the Trustees, 1886*, 9.

17. Kroeger, "The Care of Books," 321; Peabody Institute (Danvers, Mass.), *Annual Report of the Trustees, 1887*, 16; Field, "Book Repairing," 105; Adriance Memorial Library of the City of Poughkeepsie (N.Y.), *Annual Report, 1903*, 15.

18. Eastman, "The Library and the Children," 142; Dodd, "The Care of Books in a Children's Room," 86; "Suggestions to Readers on the Care of Books," 44; Marvin, "The Care of Books," 35; Pratt Institute, *Report of the Pratt Institute Free Library and School of Library Science, 1897-1898*, 10; Fitchburg (Mass.) Public Library, *Annual Report, 1907*, 11.

19. "The Preservation of Books From Fire," *Academy* 26 (26 July 1884): 61.

20. Gladstone, "On Books and the Housing of Them," 393; Kroeger, "The Care of Books," 321; Humphreys, *The Private Library*, 97; Royal Society of Arts, Committee on Leather for Bookbinding, *Report*, 73; A. M. Pendleton, "How to Start Libraries in Small Towns, IV," *American Library Journal* 1 (31 May 1877): 313.

21. Pendleton, "How to Start Libraries in Small Towns, IV," 314; Royal Society of Arts, Committee on Leather for Bookbinding, *Report*, 75; Humphreys, *The Private Library*, 95-96.

22. Advertisement for the Boston Stack, *Library Journal* 21 (April 1896): 199; Green, "The New Building for the Library of Congress," 16.

23. Jones, "Inaugural Address," 104; Redmond Barry, "On Binding," *American Library Journal* 2 (November-December 1877): 206; MacLeod, "The Preservation of Books in Libraries," 257; Humphreys, *The Private Library*, 97; "On Library Buildings," in *Transactions and Proceedings of the Conference of Librarians Held in London October 1877*, 150; "Dust," 122; "Action of Electric Lights on Paper," 429; Dewey, "Doors on Bookcases," 114.

24. "How We Protect Rare and Illustrated Books II," 133; Eames, "The Care of Special Collections," 49; Powell, "Book Production in Great Britain," 52; Boston Public Library, *Annual Report of the Trustees, 1880*, 11; Woburn (Mass.) Public Library, *Annual Report, 1894*, 23.

25. Dewey, "Doors on Bookcases," 112-13; Blades, *The Enemies of Books*, 25; Humphreys, *The Private Library*, 99; Green, "Planning and Construction of Library Buildings," 677; "On Library Buildings," in *Transactions and Proceedings of the Conference of Librarians Held in London October 1877*, 150; New York Yacht Club Library, *Report of Library Committee, 1905*, 1.

26. Eames, "The Care of Special Collections," 50; MacLeod, "The Preservation of Books in Libraries," 259.

27. Humphreys, *The Private Library*, 17; H. M. Utley, "Newspaper Volumes in a Library" (Discussion), *Library Journal* 12 (September-October 1887): 438; William I. Fletcher, "Economy of Shelf Room," *Library Journal* 15 (May 1890): 135; "How We Protect Rare and Illustrated Books," *Library Journal* 15 (April 1890): 104; Kroeger, "The Care of Books," 321; Woodbine, "Essay on Modern Methods of Book Storage," 451; Spofford, *A Book for All Readers*, 113.

28. "How We Protect Rare and Illustrated Books II," 133; Kroeger, "The Care of Books," 321; Humphreys, *The Private Library*, 100; "Shelves for Heavy Books," *Library Journal* (August-September 1886): 355.

29. "Roller Shelves for Large Volumes," *Library Journal* 11 (December 1886): 491-92; Woburn (Mass.) Public Library, *Annual Report, 1910*, 27-28; "Shelves for Heavy Books," 355; Frank Carney, "Some Problems of a Shelf Department," *Library Journal* 33 (November 1908): 436; Peabody Institute (Baltimore), *Annual Report of the Provost to the Trustees, 1891*, 22; Cedric Chivers, *Bookbindings at the St. Louis Exhibition, 1905, by Cedric Chivers, Bath, England* (New York: Chivers, 1904 or 1905), 28.

30. Eames, "The Care of Special Collections," 49; Harvard University, *Second Report of William Coolidge Lane, Librarian, 1899*, 208; Spofford, *A Book for All Readers*, 114; "How We Protect Rare and Illustrated Books II," 134.

31. E. Atkinson, "Fire-Proof Wood," *American Architect and Building News* 77 (6 September 1902): 75; "The Prevention of Fires in Libraries," 52; Spofford, *A Book for All Readers*, 106.

32. Springfield (Mass.) City Library Association, *Annual Report, 1899*, 30-31.

33. Carr, "Fixtures, Furniture, and Fittings," 738; William F. Poole, "Why Wood Shelving Is Better than Iron," *Library Notes* 2 (September 1887): 95; Fletcher, "Some Library Superstitions," 156.

34. Harvard University, *Seventh Report of William Coolidge Lane, Librarian, 1904*, 210; Redwood Library and Athenaeum (Newport, R.I.), *Annual Report of the Directors, 1898*, 14-15; Somerville (Mass.) Public Library, *Annual Report, 1895*, 14.

35. St. Joseph (Mo.) Free Public Library, *Annual Report, 1901-1902*, 30; Providence Public Library, *Annual Report, 1900*, 20.

36. "Green's Book-Stack and Shelving for Libraries," *Library Journal* 18 (May 1893): 155; Advertisement for Library Bureau Steel Stack, *Library Journal* 20 (April 1895): 146-47.

37. A wooden book or document box invented by Daniel Charles Solander at the British Museum (1773-1782); when properly constructed,

it is dustproof and nearly waterproof. See Roberts and Etherington, *Bookbinding and the Conservation of Books: A Dictionary of Descriptive Terminology*, 243.

38. "The Preservation of Books from Fire," 61.

39. Atkinson, "Fire-Proof Wood," 75.

40. Ibid., 75-76.

41. Spofford, "Binding and Preservation of Books," 673; Carroll, "Library Membership as a Civic Force," 271; MacLeod, "The Preservation of Books in Libraries," 257; Kroeger, "The Care of Books," 320; Sawyer, "How to Care for Books in a Library," 6; Spofford, *A Book for All Readers*, 95; Public Library of the City of Bangor (Maine), *Annual Reports, 1896*, 29; Dayton Public Library, *Annual Report of the Board of Managers and Librarian, 1898-1899*, 7; Fletcher Free Library (Burlington, Vt.), *Annual Report of the Trustees, 1894*, 6; Gloversville (N.Y.) Free Library, *Annual Report of the Librarian, 1898*, 37; Grand Rapids Public Library, *Annual Report, 1901-1902*, 16; Lawrence (Mass.) Free Public Library, *Annual Report of the Board of Trustees and Librarian, 1880*, 18-19; Manchester (N.H.) City Library, *Annual Report of the Trustees, 1885*, 18.

42. Providence Athenaeum, *Annual Report of the Directors, 1884*, 8.

43. Spofford, "Binding and Preservation of Books," 673; "Repairing Books," 124; Council Bluffs (Iowa) Free Public Library, *Annual Report, 1906*, 7; Dayton Public Library, *Annual Report of the Board of Managers and Librarian, 1898-1899*, 7; Queens Borough (N.Y.) Public Library, *Annual Report of the Board of Trustees, 1908*, 15-16; St. Louis Public Library, *Annual Report, 1880-1881*, 32, and *1888-1889*, 13, 15.

44. Cincinnati Public Library, *Annual Report of the Librarian and Treasurer, 1888-1889*, 11; "Binding," *Library Journal* 16 (December 1891): 84; Manchester (N.H.) City Library, *Annual Report of the Trustees, 1882*, 15; Washington, D.C., Public Library, *Annual Report, 1901*, 29.

45. MacLeod, "The Preservation of Books in Libraries," 259; Spofford, *A Book for All Readers*, 116; New York Yacht Club Library, *Report of Library Committee, 1906*, 3; Kroeger, "The Care of Books," 321; Royal Society of Arts, Committee on Leather for Bookbinding, *Report*, 74; Gladstone, "On Books and the Housing of Them," 393.

46. Cooper Union, *Annual Report of the Trustees, 1910*, 54; Harvard University Library, *Annual Report, 1905*, 227, and *1906*, 215; Cincinnati Public Library, *Annual Report of the Librarian and Treasurer, 1903-1904*, 26; Iowa State Library, *Report of the Librarian, 1880-1881*, 4.

47. Peabody Institute (Baltimore), *Annual Report of the Provost to the Trustees, 1876*, 11-12; Providence Public Library, *Annual Report, 1900*, 21.

48. "Shelving on the Fore-Edge" (Response), *American Library Journal* 2 (January-February 1878): 309.

49. Spofford, *A Book for All Readers*, 117; Harriet Sawyer, *How to Care for Books in a Library* (Madison: Wisconsin Free Library Commission, 1910), 4; Spofford, "Binding and Preservation of Books," 678; "Shelving on the Fore Edge," *American Library Journal* 1 (30 June 1877): 377.

50. "Book Supports," *Library Journal* 3 (July 1878): 192; Melvil Dewey, "Book Braces, Supports, or Props," *Library Notes* 1 (December 1886): 214; Spofford, *A Book for All Readers*, 96; Royal Society of Arts, Committee on Leather for Bookbinding, *Report*, 75; Kroeger, "The Care of Books," 321.

51. "Keeping Books Upright," *American Library Journal* 1 (30 September 1876): 24; "Book Supports," 192; Pendleton, "How to Start Libraries in Small Towns, V," 357; Dewey, "Book Braces, Supports, or Props," 214; "Keeping Books Upright," *American Library Journal* 1 (28 February 1877): 233; "Book Supports," *Library Journal* 10 (September-October 1885): 312; Carney, "Some Problems of a Shelf Department," 435; Sawyer, "How to Care for Books in a Library," 6; Sawyer, *How to Care for Books in a Library*, 4.

52. Dewey, "Book Braces, Supports, or Props," 214.

53. "Book Support," *Library Journal* 3 (March 1878): 35; Dewey, "Book Braces, Supports, or Props," 215, 217.

54. Dewey, "Book Braces, Supports, or Props," 215-19; "Crocker Book-Support," *Library Journal* 12 (January-February 1887): 85; "Book Supports," 1885, 312; Advertisement for Library Bureau book support, *Library Journal* 19 (February 1894): 40; Astor Library (New York City), *Annual Report of the Trustees, 1890*, 18.

55. Dewey, "Book Braces, Supports, or Props," 220-223; "Spring Book Supports," *Library Journal* 11 (April 1886): 122; "Crocker Book-Support," 85; Pratt Institute, *Report of the Pratt Institute Free Library and School of Library Science, 1903-1904*, 8.

56. "Book Supports," 1885, 312; Advertisement for the Yale Book Support, *Library Journal* 23 (October 1898): 595; "Mason's Book Support," *Library Journal* 11 (December 1886): 491; "The Lowell Book Support," *Library Journal* 9 (January 1884): 16; Dewey, "Book Braces, Supports, or Props," 219-20; "Keeping Books Upright," *American Library Journal* 1 (31 March 1877): 267.

57. Melvil Dewey, "Pamphlets Ruined by Rolling," *Library Journal* 16 (July 1891): 202.

58. Harvard University Library, *Annual Report, 1909*, 28.

59. Sharp, "Library Recipes," 217; Humphreys, *The Private Library*, 24-25.

60. Los Angeles Public Library, *Annual Report of the Board of Directors and the Librarian, 1907*, 31-32.

61. Iowa Library Commission, *Report, 1900-1903*, 48; "Corrugated Paper Boxes," *Library Journal* 21 (July 1896): 342.

Chapter 6. Binding: Its Importance and Economics

1. Spofford, "Binding and Preservation of Books," 673.

2. Reuben B. Poole, "Elements of Good Binding," *Library Journal* 17 (July-August 1892): 15.

3. Spofford, *A Book for All Readers*, 87.

4. "Cloth as a Book Binding Material," *Library Journal* 31 (January 1906): 43; Alameda (Calif.) Free Library and Reading Room, *Annual Report of the Board of Trustees, 1894*, 16; "A. L. A Library Primer (Under Revision)," 44.

5. Trinity College Library, *Report of the Librarian, 1906*, 14; Bowdoin College Library, *Annual Report of the Librarian, 1891*, 33-34; New Hampshire State Library, *Report, 1896-1898*, 50.

6. Pratt Institute, *Report of the Pratt Institute Free Library and School of Library Science, 1910-1911*, 20.

7. George F. Bowerman, "Committee on Bookbinding and Book Papers," *Library Journal* 30 (September 1905): 147; George F. Bowerman, William P. Cutter, and Arthur L. Bailey, "Report of the Committee on Bookbinding," *Library Journal* 31 (August 1906): 136; "Committee on Bookbinding," *Library Journal* 32 (February 1907): 76; "Bookbinding," *ALA Bulletin* 3 (January 1909): 9.

8. "Report of the A. L. A. Committee on Library Administration, 1908," *ALA Bulletin* 2 (September 1908): 225-26; "Bookbinding for Libraries," *Library Journal* 30 (August 1905): 499; Wilmington (Del.) Institute, *Annual Report, 1905-1906*, 19; "The Question of Publishers' Bindings," *Quarterly of the Iowa Library Commission*, 2 (April 1902): 34.

9. Wheatley, "Leather for Bookbinding," 315; Royal Society of Arts, Committee on Leather for Bookbinding, *Report*, 2-3; Society for the Encouragement of Arts, Manufactures, and Commerce, Committee on the Deterioration of Paper, *Report*, 40; "United Kingdom Association," *Library Journal* 6 (July 1881): 204; "Binding: Digest of Answers to a Circular," *Library Association Transactions* 4-5 (1881-1882): 243-44; George A. Stephen, "Book-Cloths," *Library Association Record* 11 (January 1909): 5.

10. Winsor, "Library Memoranda," 712; D. V. R. Johnston, "Elements in Library Binding," in U.S. Office of Education, *Annual Report, 1892-1893*, 907; James B. Nicholson, "What a Librarian Should Know about Binding," *Library Journal* 9 (June 1884): 102; Reuben B. Poole, "Book-Binding Memoranda," *Library Journal* 14 (May-June 1889): 262; Johnston, "Binding and Binderies," 9-10; Henry E. Bliss, "Better Bookbinding for Libraries," *Library Journal* 30 (November 1905): 849.

11. Bliss, "Better Bookbinding for Libraries," 849; Nicholson, "What a Librarian Should Know about Binding," 102.

12. Johnston, "Binding and Binderies," 9; East Orange (N.J.) Free Public Library, *Annual Report of the Board of Directors, 1906*, 20; John Crerar Library (Chicago), *Annual Report, 1896*, 12; Pratt Institute, *Report of the Pratt Institute Free Library and School of Library Science, 1910-1911*, 21.

13. Sarah B. Askew, "Problems of a Small Town Library," *Library Journal* 31 (October 1906): 707.

14. Alice Wilde, "New York Library Club," *Library Journal* 31 (April 1906): 183; John C. Dana, "Binding for a Public Library," *Public Libraries* 7 (April 1902): 147-48.

15. Wilde, "New York Library Club," 183; "Bookbuying," *ALA Bulletin* 4 (May 1910): 525; American Library Association, Committee on Bookbinding, *Binding for Small Libraries; Suggestions* (Chicago: American Library Association, 1909), 7; Margaret W. Brown, *Mending and Repair of Books* (Chicago: American Library Association, 1910), 7.

16. Frederick M. Crunden, "How Things Are Done in One American Library," *Library*, n.s., 2 (1 January 1901): 28; St. Louis Public Library, *Annual Report, 1894-1895*, 29.

17. Winsor, "Library Memoranda," 712; Spofford, "Binding and Preservation of Books," 674; Douglas Cockerell, "Note on Bookbinding," in his *Some Notes on Bookbinding*, 94-105 (Oxford: Oxford University Press, 1929), 96; Walter Pyle, "The Durability of Leather in Bookbinding," *Library Journal* 26 (July 1901): 387; J. Gordon Parker, "The Leather Question," *Library Association Record* 8 (October 1906): 490-91.

18. Grand Rapids Public Library, *Annual Report, 1904-1905*, 36; Melvil Dewey, "Buckram and Morocco," *Library Journal* 11 (June 1886): 162.

19. Pratt Institute, *Report of the Pratt Institute Free Library and School of Library Science, 1910-1911*, 21; Pyle, "The Durability of Leather in Bookbinding," 387; American Library Association, Committee on Bookbinding, *Binding for Small Libraries*, 7.

20. Cockerell, "Note on Bookbinding," 94-95.

21. Spofford, "Binding and Preservation of Books," 674; Johnston, "Elements in Library Binding," 907; William Matthews, *Modern Bookbinding Practically Considered* (New York: Grolier Club, 1889), 39.

22. Johnston, "Binding and Binderies," 9; Seattle Public Library, *Report, 1899*, 9.

23. Johnston, "Elements in Library Binding," 907; Pratt Institute, *Report of the Pratt Institute Free Library and School of Library Science, 1906-1907*, 16.

24. Winsor, "Library Memoranda," 713.

25. Charlotte Martins, "Intricacies of Binding," *Library Journal* 27 (June 1902): 312; Wilmington (Del.) Institute, *Annual Report, 1895-1896*, 14.

26. Gilbert D. Emerson, *Bookbinding for Libraries* (Philadelphia: Emerson, 1909), 10; Boston Athenaeum, *Reports of the Library Committee and of the Librarian, 1906*, 7.

27. Frances L. Rathbone, "A Trained Person in Charge of Condition of Books," *Public Libraries* 12 (June 1907): 236; Boston Athenaeum, *Reports of the Library Committee and of the Librarian, 1899*, 2; George A. Stephen, "Publishers' Binding," *Library Association Record* 12 (January 1910): 10; Silas Bronson Library (Waterbury, Conn.), *Annual Report of the Board of Agents, 1898-1899*, 3.

28. Boston Athenaeum, *Reports of the Library Committee and of the Librarian, 1906*, 6-7; Buffalo Public Library, *Annual Report, 1899*, 15; *1900*, 9; *1908*, 15; Louisville (Ky.) Free Public Library, *Annual Report of the Board of Trustees, 1909-1910*, 12, 19; Trinity College Library, *Report of the Librarian, 1906*, 14.

29. Springfield (Mass.) City Library Association, *Annual Report, 1904*, 20-21; New York Society Library, *Annual Report, 1899*, 4.

30. Queens Borough (N.Y.) Public Library, *Annual Report of the Board of Trustees, 1908*, 15; *1909*, 16; *1910*, 21-22.

31. Boston Public Library, *Annual Report of the Trustees, 1891*, 10; *1899*, 23; *1900*, 19; *1908*, 7.

32. Alameda (Calif.) Free Library and Reading Room, *Annual Report of the Board of Trustees, 1894*, 16; General Theological Library (New York City), *Annual Report of the Directors and Treasurer, 1875*, 27.

33. Bradford (Pa.) Carnegie Public Library, *Annual Report, 1901*, 9, and *1903*, 18.

34. Pennsylvania State Library, *Report of the State Librarian, 1888*, 3; Washington Territory Library, *Report of the Librarian, 1889*, 8.

35. Redwood Library and Athenaeum (Newport, R.I.), *Annual Report of the Directors, 1878*, 7; *1880*, 7; *1884*, 14; *1900*, 8-9.

36. Redwood Library and Athenaeum (Newport, R.I.), *Annual Report of the Directors*, 1879, 6, and *1882*, 9, 12.

37. Redwood Library and Athenaeum (Newport, R.I.), *Annual Report of the Directors, 1885*, 9, and *1902*, 15-16.

38. Redwood Library and Athenaeum (Newport, R.I.), *Annual Report of the Directors, 1886*, 9; *1887*, 8, 18; *1888*, 8; *1889*, 17; *1891*, 21; *1892*, 18; *1894*, 18-19; *1902*, 15-16.

Chapter 7. Binding Materials: Costs and Choices

1. Descriptions of the qualities of the many different binding leathers and cloths appear later in this chapter.

2. Newark (N.J.) Free Public Library, *Annual Report of the Board of Trustees, 1891*, 21; *1893*, 17; *1902*, 36; *1903*, 37.

3. "Western Massachusetts Library Club," *Library Journal* 26 (February 1901): 87-88.

4. The prices included in this section are representative of the middle part of the period, 1886-92.

5. Johnston, "Binding and Binderies," 10; "Binding," *Library Journal* 11 (August-September 1886): 374; Dewey, "Buckram and Morocco," 161; Spofford, *A Book for All Readers*, 59.

6. Johnston, "Binding and Binderies," 11; Dewey, "Buckram and Morocco," 161.

7. Johnston, "Binding and Binderies," 12.

8. Ibid., 12, 11.

9. D. V. R. Johnston, "Notes on Binding," *Library Journal* 17 (July-August 1892): 14.

10. Dewey, "Buckram and Morocco," 161; Poole, "Book-Binding Memoranda," 262; Johnston, "Binding and Binderies," 12.

11. Johnston, "Binding and Binderies," 12-13; "Cloth as a Book-Binding Material," 43; Poole, "Book-Binding Memoranda," 263; H. M. Utley, "Newspaper Volumes in a Library," *Library Journal* 12 (September-October 1887): 349.

12. Barry, "On Binding," 203-204; F. J. Soldan, "Specifications for Binding," *Library Journal* 8 (June 1883): 106; Henry F. Marx, "The Value of a Bindery in a Small Library," *Library Journal* 30 (October 1905): 796; Stearns, *Essentials in Library Administration*, 75.

13. "Association Bindings," 432; Johnston, "Binding and Binderies," 15; Spofford, *A Book for All Readers*, 58; Kansas City (Mo.) Public Library, *Annual Report, 1897-1898*, 30.

14. Wilde, "New York Library Club," 183; "Binding Materials," *Library Journal* 31 (May 1906): 246; Spofford, *A Book for All Readers*, 59.

15. "Library Buildings," 125; Poole, "Book-Binding Memoranda," 263; "Rebinding for General Circulation," *Library Journal* 18 (June 1893): 186-87; Martins, "Intricacies of Binding," 312; Edith Tobitt, "What a Librarian Should Know about Binding," *Iowa Library Quarterly* 5 (April 1905): 20; "December Meeting," *Library Assistant* 1 (January 1901): 173; Stearns, *Essentials in Library Administration*, 74; "Cloth as a Book-Binding Material," 43.

16. Spofford, *A Book for All Readers*, 56; Johnston, "Binding and Binderies," 10; Joanna Hagey, "Binding," *Public Libraries* 9 (June 1904):

269; "Book Surgery in Libraries," 311; George A. Stephen, "Notes on Materials for Library Bookbinding," *Library Assistant* 5 (August 1906): 144; Cockerell, "Note on Bookbinding," 99; Henry E. Bliss, "Better Bookbinding for Libraries," *Public Libraries* 11 (June 1906): 298; Emerson, *Bookbinding for Libraries*, 12; Cyril Davenport, "Leather as Used in Bookbinding," *Library* 10 (1898): 16.

17. Nicholson, "On Buckram as a Binding Material," 208; M. E. Sargent, "Binding for Library Use," *Library Journal* 19 (July 1894): 262; Blades, *The Enemies of Books*, 30; Mercantile Library Association of the City of New York, *Annual Report of the Board of Direction, 1882-1883*, 11; Johnston, "Binding and Binderies," 10; Hagey, "Binding," 269; Stephen, "Notes on Materials for Library Bookbinding," August 1906, 144; Spofford, *A Book for All Readers*, 58.

18. George E. Wire, "Book Selection, Buying, and Binding," *Library Journal* 24 (July 1899): 65.

19. Spofford, "Binding and Preservation of Books," 675; Johnston, "Binding and Binderies," 10; "Massachusetts Library Club," *Library Journal* 19 (May 1894): 172; Pyle, "The Durability of Leather in Bookbinding," 387; Willard O. Water, "District of Columbia Library Association," *Library Journal* 33 (December 1908): 512; Stephen, "Notes on Materials for Library Bookbinding," August 1906, 144; Mathews, "Library Binderies," 76; Alexander J. Philip, "Bookbinding for Lending Libraries," *Library Assistant* 4 (1903): 74; American Library Association, Committee on Bookbinding, *Binding for Small Libraries*, 5; Newark (N.J.) Free Public Library, *Annual Report of the Board of Trustees, 1903*, 37; Washington, D.C., Public Library, *Annual Report, 1907-1908*, 53.

20. Joseph Zaehnsdorf, "Practical Suggestions in Bookbinding," *Library Chronicle* 4 (September 1887): 110; Stephen and Coutts, *Manual of Library Bookbinding*, 25.

21. "Binding in the Building," *Library Journal* 10 (September-October 1885): 345; Jones, "Inaugural Address," 115; Spofford, *A Book for All Readers*, 51-52; Spofford, "Binding and Preservation of Books," 676; Wilde, "New York Library Club," 183; Cockerell, "Note on Bookbinding," 96; Humphreys, *The Private Library*, 54.

22. Johnston, "Notes on Binding," 13; "Binding," Library Journal 17 (July-August 1892): 62; John Crerar Library (Chicago), *Annual Report, 1896*, 12; Columbia College Library, *Annual Report of the Chief Librarian, 1886*, 40; Library of Congress, *Report, 1909-1910*, 57; Soldan, "Specifications for Binding," 106; Jones and Green, "Linen Bindings," 29; Wilde, "New York Library Club," 183; Crunden, "How Things Are Done in One American Library," 25-26; Cleveland Public Library, *Annual Report, 1887*, 9; Cleveland Public Library, *Annual Report, 1907*, 72; Silas Bronson

Library (Waterbury, Conn.), *Annual Report of the Board of Agents, 1898-1899*, 8.

23. Stephen, "Notes on Materials for Library Bookbinding," August 1906, 145; Fred N. Moore, "The Art of Leather Making," *Library Journal* 32 (August 1907): 368.

24. Bliss, "Better Bookbinding for Libraries," *Public Libraries*, 298; Philip, "Bookbinding for Lending Libraries," 72.

25. Stephen, "Notes on Materials for Library Bookbinding," August 1906, 145; Bliss, "Better Bookbinding for Libraries," *Library Journal*, 853; Johnston, "Binding and Binderies," 11; Parker, "The Leather Question," 490.

26. Stephen, "Notes on Materials for Library Bookbinding," August 1906, 144; Philip, "Bookbinding for Lending Libraries," 72.

27. East Orange (N.J.) Free Public Library, *Annual Report of the Board of Directors, 1906*, 24; Zaehnsdorf, "Practical Suggestions in Bookbinding," 110; Humphreys, *The Private Library*, 64; "Pig-Skins for Bookbinding," *Library Journal* 11 (June 1886): 166; Johnston, "Binding and Binderies," 12; Water, "District of Columbia Library Association," 512; Davenport, "Leather as Used in Bookbinding," 18.

28. Barry, "On Binding," 203-204; Bliss, "Better Bookbinding for Libraries," *Library Journal*, 854; "Book Surgery in Libraries," 311; Johnston, "Binding and Binderies," 12.

29. Johnston, "Binding and Binderies," 12; Bliss, "Better Bookbinding for Libraries," *Library Journal*, 854; Stephen, "Notes on Materials for Library Bookbinding," August 1906, 144; Parker, "The Leather Question," 489; Hiller C. Wellman, "Some Points about Library Bookbindings," *Bulletin of the New Hampshire Public Libraries*, n.s., 4 (n.d.): 24; Philip, "Bookbinding for Lending Libraries," 74; Cockerell, "Note on Bookbinding," 99; Royal Society of Arts, Committee on Leather for Bookbinding, *Report*, 24; Library Association of the United Kingdom, Sound Leather Committee, *Leather for Libraries*, 25-26; Wisconsin Free Library Commission, *Biennial Report, 1895-1896*, 59.

30. Bliss, "Better Bookbinding for Libraries," *Public Libraries*, 298.

31. Stephen, "Notes on Materials for Library Bookbinding," August 1906, 145; Parker, "The Leather Question," 491; Cockerell, *Bookbinding and the Care of Books*, 99; Cockerell, "Note on Bookbinding," 99; Royal Society of Arts, Committee on Leather for Bookbinding, *Report*, 54; Library Association of the United Kingdom, Sound Leather Committee, *Leather for Libraries*, 26.

32. "Library Buildings," 125; Moore, "The Art of Leather Making," 368; Blades, *The Enemies of Books*, 30; Humphreys, *The Private Library*, 64; Library Association of the United Kingdom, Sound Leather Committee, *Leather for Libraries*, 26; Edward W. B. Nicholson, "The Use of Buckram,

Linoleum, and Cretonne for Binding," *Library Journal* 5 (November-December 1880): 304-5.

33. Spofford, "Binding and Preservation of Books," 675; Spofford, *A Book for All Readers*, 55; Wisconsin Free Library Commission, *Biennial Report, 1895-1896*, 58-59; Worcester County (Mass.) Law Library, *Annual Report, 1902*, 9; Davenport, "Leather as Used in Bookbinding," 17.

34. Johnston, "Binding and Binderies," 11; Spofford, "Binding and Preservation of Books," 675; Mathews, "Library Binderies," 76; Stearns, *Essentials in Library Administration*, 75; Spofford, *A Book for All Readers*, 56; Stephen, "Notes on Materials for Library Bookbinding," September 1906, 162; Edward B. Nicholson, "On Buckram as a Binding Material," in *Transactions and Proceedings of the Conference of Librarians held in London October, 1877*, ed. Edward B. Nicholson and Henry R. Tedder (London: Printed at the Chiswick Press by Charles Whittingham, 1878), 124; Royal Society of Arts, Committee on Leather for Bookbinding, *Report*, 23; Worcester County (Mass.) Law Library, *Annual Report, 1902*, 9; Mercantile Library Association of the City of New York, *Annual Report of the Board of Direction, 1882-1883*, 11.

35. Bliss, "Better Bookbinding for Libraries," *Library Journal*, 854; Moore, "The Art of Leather Making," 368; Bliss, "Better Bookbinding for Libraries," *Public Libraries*, 298.

36. Pyle, "The Durability of Leather in Bookbinding," 387; "Binding Materials," 246; East Orange (N.J.) Free Public Library, *Annual Report of the Board of Directors, 1906*, 24; "Colors in Binding," *Library Journal* 10 (September-October 1885): 340; Stearns, *Essentials in Library Administration*, 75; Arthur L. Bailey, William P. Cutter, and George E. Wire, "Points Worth Remembering in Rebinding Fiction and Juvenile Books," *ALA Bulletin* 1 (March 1907): 11; American Library Association, Committee on Bookbinding, *Binding for Small Libraries*, 4.

37. Library of Congress, *Report, 1909-1910*, 57; New Hampshire State Library, *Report, 1896-1898*, 50; Water, "District of Columbia Library Association," 512; Washington, D.C., Public Library, *Annual Report, 1906-1907*, 52; Washington, D.C., Public Library, *Annual Report, 1907-1908*, 53; Marsden, "Decay of Leather Bindings," 312; Newark (N.J.) Free Public Library, *Annual Report of the Board of Trustees, 1902*, 36; Wilmington (Del.) Institute, *Annual Report, 1894-1895*, 32.

38. Roberts and Etherington, *Bookbinding and the Conservation of Books*, 224; Stephen, "Notes on Materials for Library Bookbinding," September 1906, 162; Spofford, *A Book for All Readers*, 56.

39. Barry, "On Binding," 203-204; "Bindery Notes," *Library Journal* 20 (August 1895): 280; Bliss, "Better Bookbinding for Libraries," *Public Libraries*, 298; Johnston, "Binding and Binderies," 12; Blades, *The Enemies of Books*, 30; Royal Society of Arts, Committee on Leather for

Bookbinding, *Report*, 24; Library Association of the United Kingdom, Sound Leather Committee, *Leather for Libraries*, 26; Spofford, *A Book for All Readers*, 56; Mercantile Library Association of the City of New York, *Annual Report of the Board of Direction, 1882-1883*, 11; Davenport, "Leather As Used in Bookbinding," 17.

40. Johnston, "Elements in Library Binding," 910; Johnston, "Notes on Binding," 14; Wellman, "Some Points about Library Bookbindings," 24; Emerson, *Bookbinding for Libraries*, 13; Newark (N.J.) Free Public Library, *Annual Report of the Board of Trustees, 1893*, 17; Washington, D.C., Public Library, *Annual Report, 1900*, 22; Wisconsin Free Library Commission, *Biennial Report, 1895-1896*, 59.

41. Bliss, "Better Bookbinding for Libraries," *Library Journal*, 854; Johnston, "Elements in Library Binding," 910; Sargent, "Binding for Library Use," 262; Tobitt, "What a Librarian Should Know about Binding," 20.

42. Poole, "Book-Binding Memoranda," 263; Moore, "The Art of Leather Making," 368; San Francisco Public Library, *Report of the Board of Trustees, 1909*, 16; "Rebinding for General Circulation," 186; American Library Association, Committee on Bookbinding, *Binding for Small Libraries*, 5.

43. "Rebinding for General Circulation," 186; Seattle Public Library, *Report, 1896*, 17; San Francisco Public Library, *Report of the Board of Trustees, 1909*, 16; Portland (Oreg.) Library Association, *Annual Report, 1900-1901*, 28; Newark (N.J.) Free Public Library, *Annual Report of the Board of Trustees, 1889-1890*, 21, and *1893*, 17.

44. Matthews, *Modern Bookbinding Practically Considered*, 37; Spofford, *A Book for All Readers*, 53; Poole, "Book-Binding Memoranda," 263; Stephen, "Notes on Materials for Library Bookbinding," September 1906, 162; Stearns, *Essentials in Library Administration*, 75; Davenport, "Leather As Used in Bookbinding," 17.

45. Stearns, *Essentials in Library Administration*, 75; Bliss, "Better Bookbinding for Libraries," *Library Journal*, 854; Wisconsin Free Library Commission, *Biennial Report, 1895-1896*, 59; Wire, "Book Selection, Buying, and Binding," 65; Bailey, Cutter, and Wire, "Points Worth Remembering in Rebinding Fiction and Juvenile Books," 11; Sawyer, "How to Care for Books in a Library," 8; Johnston, "Elements in Library Binding," 910; Johnston, "Binding and Binderies," 11; "Binding," *Library Journal* 17, 62.

46. "Library Buildings," 125; Johnston, "Elements in Library Binding," 910; William L. Post, "Report of the Committee on Public Documents: Address of Mr. Post," *ALA Bulletin* 1 (July 1907): 138; Royal Society of Arts, Committee on Leather for Bookbinding, *Report*, 24; Library of Congress, *Report, 1900-1901*, 22; Boston Public Library, *Annual Report of the Trustees, 1880*, 10-11.

47. Martins, "Intricacies of Binding," 312; Tobitt, "What a Librarian Should Know about Binding," 20; Wellman, "Some Points about Library Bookbindings," 23; Spofford, *A Book for All Readers*, 55; Wisconsin Free Library Commission, *Biennial Report, 1895-1896*, 59; Connecticut State Library, *Report of the State Librarian, 1905-1906*, 18-19; Utley, "Newspaper Volumes in a Library," 349; Poole, "Book-Binding Memoranda," 263; Bliss, "Better Bookbinding for Libraries," *Library Journal*, 853; Worcester County (Mass.) Law Library, *Annual Report, 1907*, 14.

48. Moore, "The Art of Leather Making," 367; Johnston, "Notes on Binding," 13.

49. Bailey, Cutter, and Wire, "Points Worth Remembering in Rebinding Fiction and Juvenile Books," 11; Post, "Report of the Committee on Public Documents," 138; Connecticut State Library, *Report of the State Librarian, 1907-1908*, 36.

50. Bliss, "Better Bookbinding for Libraries," *Library Journal*, 854; Stephen, "Notes on Materials for Library Bookbinding," September 1906, 162; Wellman, "Some Points about Library Bookbindings," 23; Matthews, *Modern Bookbinding Practically Considered*, 37; Library Association of the United Kingdom, Sound Leather Committee, *Leather for Libraries*, 26; Davenport, "Leather as Used in Bookbinding," 17.

51. Columbia College Library, *Annual Report of the Chief Librarian, 1886*, 40; San Francisco Public Library, *Report of the Board of Trustees, 1882-1883*, 12; Johnston, "Binding and Binderies," 11.

52. Roberts and Etherington, *Bookbinding and the Conservation of Books*, 277; Spofford, *A Book for All Readers*, 54.

53. Stephen, "Notes on Materials for Library Bookbinding," August 1906, 145; "On Binding of Books for Public and Private Libraries," 271; Spofford, *A Book for All Readers*, 54.

54. Emerson, *Bookbinding for Libraries*, 14.

55. Winsor, "Library Memoranda," 713.

56. F. P. Hathaway, "Bindings for a Public Library," *Library Journal* 4 (July-August 1879): 248; "Binding," *Library Journal* 11, 374; Edward C. J. Hertzberg, "Specifications for Library Bookbinding," *Library Occurrent* 2 (June 1910): 136; Wilmington (Del.) Institute, *Annual Report, 1885-1886*, 19.

57. Henry Marsden, "Bookbinders and Paper Rulers' Forum on the Premature Decay of Leather Used in Modern Bookbinding, Part II," *International Bookbinder* (October 1905): 358.

58. Dana, "Binding for a Public Library," 147.

59. Cockerell, "Leather for Bookbinding," 401-3; "The Deterioration of Bindings," 229; Browne, "Bindings Deteriorated without Gas," 50; Homes, "Deterioration of Bindings," 213.

60. Library Association, Sound Leather Committee, *Leather for Libraries*, 11.

61. Royal Society of Arts, Committee on Leather for Bookbinding, *Report*, 2-3.

62. "Libraries and Librarians," *Library World* 6 (June 1904): 330; Library Association, Sound Leather Committee, *Leather for Libraries*, 12.

63. Library Association, Sound Leather Committee, *Leather for Libraries*, 3-4, 20.

64. For more complete explanations of the various tanning processes discussed in this section, see Roberts and Etherington's *Bookbinding and the Conservation of Books: A Dictionary of Descriptive Terminology*. Among the useful entries are *Chrome Tanning, Over-tanned, Pickling, Retanning, Sulphuric* [*sic*] *acid*, and *Vegetable tannins*.

65. Marsden, "Bookbinders and Paper Rulers' Forum, Part II," 356.

66. "Library Bookbinding," *Library Association Record* 7 (November 1905): 560.

67. Library Association, Sound Leather Committee, *Leather for Libraries*, 8-9, 17; Pyle, "The Durability of Leather in Bookbinding," 387.

68. Cockerell, "Leather for Bookbinding," 404-5; Poole, "The Construction of Library Buildings," 70; Bliss, "Better Bookbinding for Libraries," *Public Libraries*, 297; Grand Rapids Public Library, *Annual Report, 1904-1905*, 36; Royal Society of Arts, Committee on Leather for Bookbinding, *Report*, 48, 61; Marsden, "Bookbinders and Paper Rulers' Forum, Part II," 358.

69. "The Effect of Illuminating Gas on Leather," 287; Worcester County (Mass.) Law Library, *Annual Report, 1902*, 9.

70. "Durability of Leather," 292; Royal Society of Arts, Committee on Leather for Bookbinding, *Report*, 25, 58; Library Association of the United Kingdom, Sound Leather Committee, *Leather for Libraries*, 19.

71. Library Association of the United Kingdom, Sound Leather Committee, *Leather for Libraries*, 19; Marsden, "Bookbinders and Paper Rulers' Forum, Part II," 358; Royal Society of Arts, Committee on Leather for Bookbinding, *Report*, 57-58.

72. Royal Society of Arts, Committee on Leather for Bookbinding, *Report*, 42-44; Stephen, "Notes on Materials for Library Bookbinding," August 1906, 145.

73. Stephen, "Notes on Materials for Library Bookbinding," August 1906, 145; Royal Society of Arts, Committee on Leather for Bookbinding, *Report*, 52, 60-61; Library Association of the United Kingdom, Sound Leather Committee, *Leather for Libraries*, 22-23.

74. "On Binding of Books for Public and Private Libraries; and on Shelf Arrangement as Associated Therewith [Discussion]," *American*

Library Journal 2 (January-February 1878): 271; F. Hathaway, "Bindings for a Public Library," *Library Journal* 4 (July-August 1879): 248.

75. "Library Buildings," 125; "Colors in Binding," 341; Johnston, "Binding and Binderies," 13.

76. Marsden, "Bookbinders and Paper Rulers' Forum, Part II," 358; Pyle, "The Durability of Leather in Bookbinding," 387; Henry E. Bliss, review of *Report of the Committee on Leather for Bookbinding*, by the Royal Society of Arts' Committee on Leather for Bookbinding, and *Notes on Bookbinding for Libraries*, by John C. Dana, in *Library Journal* 31 (October 1906): 737; Library Association, Sound Leather Committee, *Leather for Libraries*, 20-21; "Colors in Binding," 340.

77. Bliss, "Better Bookbinding for Libraries," *Public Libraries*, 297; Library Association of the United Kingdom, Sound Leather Committee, *Leather for Libraries*, 20-21; Royal Society of Arts, Committee on Leather for Bookbinding, *Report*, 45; Cyril Davenport, "Leathers Used in Bookbinding," *Transactions of the Bibliographical Society* 5 (1899): 162.

78. Nicholson, "The Use of Buckram, Linoleum, and Cretonne for Binding," 305; M. Charles Lamb, "Colors in Bookbinding Leathers," *Library World* 7 (March 1905): 256; Library Association of the United Kingdom, Sound Leather Committee, *Leather for Libraries*, 21.

79. "Library Bookbinding," 560; Cockerell, "Note on Bookbinding," 100; Royal Society of Arts, Committee on Leather for Bookbinding, *Report*, 64; Library Association of the United Kingdom, Sound Leather Committee, *Leather for Libraries*, 22; Spofford, *A Book for All Readers*, 53; Parker, "Leather for Bookbinding," 31; Nicholson, "What a Librarian Should Know about Binding," 102; Wire, "Book Selection, Buying, and Binding," 65; Martins, "Intricacies of Binding," 312; Bliss, "Better Bookbinding for Libraries," *Library Journal*, 853; Davenport, "Leathers Used in Bookbinding," 162.

80. Cockerell, "Leather for Bookbinding," 405; Bliss, "Better Bookbinding for Libraries," *Public Libraries*, 298; Cockerell, "Note on Bookbinding," 100; Royal Society of Arts, Committee on Leather for Bookbinding, *Report*, 64; Library Association of the United Kingdom, Sound Leather Committee, *Leather for Libraries*, 22; Parker, "The Leather Question," 489.

81. Homes, "Deterioration of Bindings," 213; Bliss, "Better Bookbinding for Libraries," *Public Libraries*, 298; Parker, "The Leather Question," 489; Royal Society of Arts, Committee on Leather for Bookbinding, *Report*, 62-63; Cockerell, "Note on Bookbinding," 100; Library Association of the United Kingdom, Sound Leather Committee, *Leather for Libraries*, 21; Worcester County (Mass.) Law Library, *Annual Report, 1902*, 9.

82. Pyle, "The Durability of Leather in Bookbinding," 387; Bailey, "Report of the Committee on Bookbinding," 173; New Orleans Public Library, *Annual Report, 1908*, 16-17.

83. "Bindery Notes," 280.

84. "Cloth as a Bookbinding Material," 43; Wilde, "New York Library Club," 183.

85. Bailey, "Report of the Committee on Bookbinding," 173; Library Association of the United Kingdom, Sound Leather Committee, *Leather for Libraries*, 25.

86. E. Wyndham Hulme, "Decay in Leather Bindings," *Library Association Record* 9 (April 1901): 231; Yale University, *Report of the Librarian, 1907-1908*, 32-33.

87. Hellmut Lehmann-Haupt, ed., *Bookbinding in America: Three Essays* (Portland, Maine: Southworth-Anthoensen Press, 1941), 135-36, 163-66.

88. Lehmann-Haupt, ed., *Bookbinding in America*, 166-68.

89. Wilmington (Del.) Institute, *Annual Report, 1896-1897*, 15. Interestingly, the Wilmington Institute and Joseph Bancroft were located in the same city. Further, the Newark (N.J.) Free Public Library, which used Keratol for rebinding, was located in the same city as the manufacturer of that product.

90. Barry, "On Binding," 206; Gertrude E. Woodard, "Notes on Bookbinding," *Library Journal* 23 (June 1898): 236; Nicholson, "On Buckram as a Binding Material," *Conference of Librarians*, 124; Spofford, *A Book for All Readers*, 54; Arthur L. Bailey, William P. Cutter, and George E. Wire, "Notes from A. L. A. Committee on Bookbinding," *Public Libraries* 12 (May 1907): 187.

91. Johnston, "Binding and Binderies," 13; Bliss, "Better Bookbinding for Libraries," *Library Journal*, 854; Bliss, "Better Bookbinding for Libraries," *Public Libraries*, 298; Spofford, *A Book for All Readers*, 54.

92. "Cloth as a Book-Binding Material," 43; Worcester County (Mass.) Law Library, *Annual Report, 1902*, 9; Seattle Public Library, *Report, 1908*, 9.

93. Johnston, "Elements in Library Binding," 911; Johnston, "Binding and Binderies," 13; Water, "District of Columbia Library Association," 512; Stephen, "Notes on Materials for Library Bookbinding," August 1906, 143; Stephen, "Notes on Materials for Library Bookbinding," September 1906, 163; Spofford, *A Book for All Readers*, 54; Cleveland Public Library, *Annual Report, 1907*, 72; Washington, D.C., Public Library, *Annual Report, 1907-1908*, 53; Columbia College Library, *Annual Report of the Chief Librarian, 1886*, 40.

94. Poole, "Bookbinding Memoranda," 263; American Library Association, Committee on Bookbinding, *Binding for Small Libraries*, 5; Emer-

son, *Bookbinding for Libraries*, 14; Library of Congress, *Report, 1900-1901*, 222.

95. Yale University, *Report of the Librarian, 1907-1908*, 32-33; Newark (N.J.) Free Public Library, *Annual Report of the Board of Trustees, 1902*, 36.

96. Martins, "Intricacies of Binding," 312; "Western Massachusetts Library Club," 88; Wellman, "Some Points about Library Bookbindings," 24; St. Louis Mercantile Library Association, *Annual Report of the Board of Directors, 1892*, 24.

97. St. Louis Mercantile Library Association, *Annual Report of the Board of Directors, 1892*, 24; Cleveland Public Library, *Annual Report, 1885*, 14; Grand Rapids Public Library, *Annual Report, 1904-1905*, 36; Providence Public Library, *Annual Report, 1900*, 21.

98. "Massachusetts Library Club," 172; "Cloth as a Book-Binding Material," 43; Wellman, "Some Points about Library Bookbindings," 24; Springfield (Mass.) City Library Association, *Annual Report, 1899*, 31.

99. Johnston, "Elements in Library Binding," 911; Johnston, "Binding and Binderies," 12-13; "Rebinding for General Circulation," 187; Woodard, "Notes on Bookbinding," 236; Bliss, "Better Bookbinding for Libraries," *Library Journal*, 854; Wilde, "New York Library Club," 183; Wellman, "Some Points about Library Bookbindings," 24; Emerson, *Bookbinding for Libraries*, 14; Worcester County (Mass.) Law Library, *Annual Report, 1907*, 14-15; Wisconsin Free Library Commission, *Biennial Report, 1895-1896*, 59.

100. Martins, "Intricacies of Binding," 312.

101. Jones and Green, "Linen Bindings," 29; "Binding," *Library Journal* 17, 62; W. K. Stetson, "Bookbinding from the Librarian's Standpoint," *Public Libraries* 11 (June 1906): 300; Crunden, "How Things Are Done in One American Library," 25; Connecticut State Library, *Report of the State Librarian, 1905-1906*, 18; Library of Congress, *Report, 1900-1901*, 222.

102. Philip, "Bookbinding for Lending Libraries," 73-74; Wilmington (Del.) Institute, *Annual Report, 1895-1896*, 14; Woodard, "Notes on Bookbinding," 237.

103. Jones and Green, "Linen Bindings," 29; Cockerell, *Bookbinding and the Care of Books*, 308; Newark (N.J.) Free Public Library, *Annual Report of the Board of Trustees, 1903*, 37.

104. "Bindery Notes," 280; Yale University, *Report of the Librarian, 1907-1908*, 33.

105. "Buckram for Bindings," *American Library Journal* 2 (September 1877): 34; "Buckram Bindings," *American Library Journal* 1 (31 July 1877): 410.

106. Nicholson, "On Buckram as a Binding Material," *American Library Journal*, 208-209; Nicholson, "On Buckram as a Binding Material,"

Conference of Librarians, 125-26; Boston Public Library, *Annual Report of the Trustees, 1877*, 61.

107. Dewey, "Buckram and Morocco," 161.

108. Nicholson, "The Use of Buckram, Linoleum, and Cretonne for Binding," 304.

109. Johnston, "Elements in Library Binding," 911; Bliss, "Better Bookbinding for Libraries," *Library Journal*, 854; Poole, "Book-Binding Memoranda," 262; Johnston, "Binding and Binderies," 12; Woodard, "Notes on Bookbinding," 236.

110. "On Buckram as a Binding Material," 272.

111. "Binding in Duck," *Library Journal* 10 (September-October 1885): 346; Spofford, *A Book for All Readers*, 59; Detroit Public Library, *Annual Report, 1887*, 13; New Orleans Public Library, *Annual Report, 1901*, 14.

112. Johns Hopkins University Library, *Report of the Librarian, 1909-1910*, 7; Cooper Union, *Annual Report of the Trustees, 1910*, 53; Worcester County (Mass.) Law Library, *Annual Report, 1903*, 7-8; and *1906*, 8; Iowa State Library, *Report of the Librarian, 1908-1910*, 7; Water, "District of Columbia Library Association," 511-512; Washington, D.C., Public Library, *Annual Report, 1907-1908*, and *1909-1910*, 51; Brockton (Mass.) Public Library, *Report of the Trustees, 1907*, 21; East Orange (N.J.) Free Public Library, *Annual Report of the Board of Directors, 1909*, 28; Grand Rapids Public Library, *Annual Report, 1904-1905*, 36; Providence Public Library, *Annual Report, 1900*, 21; St. Louis Public Library, *Annual Report, 1910-1911*, 54; Wisconsin Free Library Commission, *Biennial Report, 1895-1896*, 59.

113. American Library Association, Committee on Bookbinding, *Binding for Small Libraries*, 1909.

114. Martins, "Intricacies of Binding," 312.

115. Water, "District of Columbia Library Association," 512; "Binding Materials," 246; Seattle Public Library, *Report, 1896*, 17; Seattle Public Library, *Report, 1897*, 7; Seattle Public Library, *Report, 1899*, 9; "Cloth as a Book-Binding Material," 43.

116. "Western Massachusetts Library Club," 88; Springfield (Mass.) City Library Association, *Annual Report, 1899*, 31; Water, "District of Columbia Library Association," 512; Washington, D.C., Public Library, *Annual Report, 1907-1908*, 53.

117. Wilde, "New York Library Club," 183; Newark (N.J.) Free Public Library, *Annual Report of the Board of Trustees, 1903*, 37; Stetson, "Bookbinding from the Librarian's Standpoint," 300; New Haven (Conn.) Free Public Library, *Annual Report of the Board of Directors, 1901*, 17; *1903*, 17; *1904*, 17; East Orange (N.J.) Free Public Library, *Annual Report of the Board of Directors, 1906*, 24; Seattle Public Library, *Report, 1908*, 8-

9; Bailey, Cutter, and Wire, "Points Worth Remembering in Rebinding Fiction and Juvenile Books," 11; American Library Association, Committee on Bookbinding, *Binding for Small Libraries*, 5.

118. "Western Massachusetts Library Club," 88; John Crerar Library (Chicago), *Annual Report, 1896*, 12; "Binding Materials," 246; East Orange (N.J.) Free Public Library, *Annual Report of the Board of Directors, 1906*, 24; Newark (N.J.) Free Public Library, *Annual Report of the Board of Trustees, 1903*, 37.

119. Emerson, *Bookbinding for Libraries*, 14; Boston Public Library, *Annual Report of the Trustees, 1897*, 30.

120. Bailey, "Report of the Committee on Bookbinding," 175.

121. Ibid., 176.

122. "Specifications for Book Cloths," *Library Journal* 34 (March 1909): 120-21.

Chapter 8. Hand Binding

1. Poole, "Elements of Good Binding," 16; Matthews, *Modern Bookbinding Practically Considered*, 18.

2. Spofford, *A Book for All Readers*, 64-66; Peoria (Ill.) Public Library, *Annual Report, 1898-1899*, 12; Wisconsin Free Library Commission, *Biennial Report, 1895-1896*, 60.

3. F. J. Soldan, "Directions for Binding," *Public Libraries* 9 (June 1904): 259; Sargent, "Binding for Library Use," 262; "Specifications for Binding," *Wisconsin Library Bulletin* 3 (July-August 1907): 66; Tobitt, "What a Librarian Should Know about Binding," 19.

4. Soldan, "Specifications for Binding," 106; Wisconsin Free Library Commission, *Biennial Report, 1895-1896*, 61; Spofford, *A Book for All Readers*, 67-70.

5. Spofford, *A Book for All Readers*, 70; Woodard, "Notes on Bookbinding," 233; "Massachusetts Library Club," 172; A. W. Pollard, "Notes on Books and Work," *Library*, n.s., 2 (1 July 1901): 336; Royal Society of Arts, Committee on Leather for Bookbinding, *Report*, 36; Stearns, *Essentials in Library Administration*, 75; Poole, "Book-Binding Memoranda," 264; Adolf Growoll, *The Profession of Bookselling*, 3 vols. (New York: Publishers' Weekly, 1893-1913), 2:94.

6. American Library Association, Committee on Bookbinding, *Binding for Small Libraries*, 6; Cockerell, *Bookbinding and the Care of Books*, 310-11; Growoll, *The Profession of Bookselling* 2:94.

7. Growoll, *The Profession of Bookselling* 2:94; Johnston, "Binding and Binderies," 14; Spofford, *A Book for All Readers*, 68-69; John Crerar Library (Chicago), *Annual Report, 1896*, 12.

8. Spofford, *A Book for All Readers*, 71.

9. Bailey, Cutter, and Wire, "Points Worth Remembering in Rebinding Fiction and Juvenile Books," 11; American Library Association, Committee on Bookbinding, *Binding for Small Libraries*, 6.

10. Pollard, "Notes on Books and Work," 335; Philip, "Bookbinding for Lending Libraries," 72; Royal Society of Arts, Committee on Leather for Bookbinding, *Report*, 34.

11. Bailey, Cutter, and Wire, "Rebinding Fiction and Juvenile Books," 11; Pollard, "Notes on Books and Work," 335; American Library Association, Committee on Bookbinding, *Binding for Small Libraries*, 2, 6; Cockerell, *Book-Binding and the Care of Books*, 308; Matthews, *Modern Bookbinding Practically Considered*, 22.

12. Hertzberg, "Specifications for Library Bookbinding," 135; Bailey, Cutter, and Wire, "Notes from ALA Committee on Bookbinding," 187; "Specifications for Binding," 66; Royal Society of Arts, Committee on Leather for Bookbinding, *Report*, 34; Wisconsin Free Library Commission, *Biennial Report, 1895-1896*, 60.

13. Spofford, "Binding and Preservation," 677; Hathaway, "Bindings for a Public Library," 249; Johnston, "Binding and Binderies," 14; Woodard, "Notes on Bookbinding," 237; Spofford, *A Book for All Readers*, 60.

14. Astor Library (New York City), *Annual Report of the Trustees, 1880*, 8.

15. Spofford, *A Book for All Readers*, 66.

16. Davenport, "Leathers Used in Bookbinding," 161.

17. Matthews, *Modern Bookbinding Practically Considered*, 23-24.

18. Poole, "Book-Binding Memoranda," 263; Emerson, *Bookbinding for Libraries*, 14; Wellman, "Some Points about Library Bookbindings," 24; "Specifications for Binding," 66; Brown, *Mending and Repair of Books*, 9; "Materials for Mending Books," *Bulletin of the Vermont Library Commission* 5 (September 1909): 8.

19. Emerson, *Bookbinding for Libraries*, 10-11; Peoria (Ill.) Public Library, *Annual Report, 1898-1899*, 10.

20. Hagey, "Binding," 271; Bliss, "Better Bookbinding for Libraries," *Public Libraries*, 295.

21. Wire, "Book Selection, Buying, and Binding," 65; Hertzberg, "Specifications for Library Bookbinding," 136; Soldan, "Directions for Binding," 259; Bailey, Cutter, and Wire, "Notes from ALA Committee on Bookbinding," 187; George Stosskopf, "Library Bookbinding," *Public Libraries* 14 (March 1909): 88; Wellman, "Some Points about Library Bookbindings," 24; "Specifications for Binding," 66; Growoll, *The Profession of Bookselling* 2:94; Spofford, *A Book for All Readers*, 66.

22. Hathaway, "Bindings for a Public Library," 248; Johnston, "Binding and Binderies," 13.

23. Poole, "Elements of Good Binding," 16; Wellman, "Some Points about Library Bookbindings," 24.

24. Bailey, Cutter, and Wire, "Rebinding Fiction and Juvenile Books," 11; American Library Association, Committee on Bookbinding, *Binding for Small Libraries*, 2.

25. Soldan, "Specifications for Binding," 106; Stearns, *Essentials in Library Administration*, 75.

26. In the terminology of the time, *oversewing, whipstitching,* and *overcasting* were somewhat different methods of sewing together single sheets (versus folded leaves). In oversewing, a simple straight seam was sewn down the inner edge of a group of sheets; in overcasting, the thread passed through the paper and over the back or inner edges of the sheets. Whipstitching meant overcasting single sheets together into pseudosignatures, which would later be flexibly sewn. The term *oversewing,* as it applies to turn-of-the-century hand binding, should not be confused with the modern machine technique of the same name. See Roberts and Etherington, *Bookbinding and the Conservation of Books*, 182, 283.

27. "Committee on Binding," *Library Journal* 34 (May 1909): 224; Growoll, *The Profession of Bookselling* 2:94.

28. Bliss, "Better Bookbinding for Libraries," *Library Journal*, 851; Stosskopf, "Library Bookbinding," 88; Cockerell, *Bookbinding and the Care of Books*, 309; Seattle Public Library, *Report, 1899*, 9; Soldan, "Directions for Binding," 259.

29. Cedric Chivers, "The Paper and Binding of Lending Library Books," *ALA Bulletin* 3 (September 1909): 251; Cedric Chivers, *The Paper of Lending Library Books* (New York: Baker & Taylor, 1909 or 1910), 20; Bailey, Cutter, and Wire, "Rebinding Fiction and Juvenile Books," 11; Bliss, "Better Bookbinding for Libraries," *Public Libraries*, 295.

30. Stephen and Coutts, *Manual of Library Bookbinding*, 30; Brooklyn Public Library, *Annual Report of the Board of Directors, 1910*, 35.

31. Wire, "Book Selection, Buying, and Binding," 65; Emerson, *Bookbinding for Libraries*, 11; Growoll, *The Profession of Bookselling* 2:94.

32. Hathaway, "Bindings for a Public Library," 248; Soldan, "Specifications for Binding," 106; Soldan, "Directions for Binding," 259; Hertzberg, "Specifications for Library Bookbinding," 136; Stearns, *Essentials in Library Administration*, 75; Wellman, "Some Points about Library Book-Bindings," 24; "Specifications for Binding," 66.

33. Philip, "Bookbinding for Lending Libraries," 70; Royal Society of Arts, Committee on Leather for Bookbinding, *Report*, 36; Cockerell, *Bookbinding and the Care of Books*, 308-309; American Library Association, Committee on Bookbinding, *Binding for Small Libraries*, 1.

34. Soldan, "Specifications for Binding," 106; Zaehnsdorf, "Practical Suggestions in Bookbinding," 109; Cockerell, "Note on Bookbinding," 96; Matthews, *Modern Bookbinding Practically Considered*, 25, 27.

35. Matthews, *Modern Bookbinding Practically Considered*, 27-28; Poole, "Elements of Good Binding," 26; Hagey, "Binding," 271; "Specifications for Binding," 66; Hertzberg, "Specifications for Library Bookbinding," 136; Wisconsin Free Library Commission, *Biennial Report, 1895-1896*, 60.

36. Soldan, "Specifications for Binding," 106; Soldan, "Directions for Binding," 259; Bailey, Cutter, and Wire, "Notes from A.L.A. Committee on Bookbinding," 187; Francis T. Barrett, "Note on the Manner of Binding Adopted by the Mitchell Library," *Library Association Transactions* 4-5 (1881-82): 185; Johnston, "Binding and Binderies," 14.

37. Royal Society of Arts, Committee on Leather for Bookbinding, *Report*, 26.

38. Hathaway, "Bindings for a Public Library," 272; Soldan, "Specifications for Binding," 106; Soldan, "Directions for Binding," 259; Bailey, Cutter, and Wire, "Notes from A.L.A. Committee on Bookbinding," 187; Wellman, "Some Points about Library Bookbindings," 24; Growoll, *The Profession of Bookselling* 2:94.

39. Bliss, "Better Bookbinding for Libraries," *Library Journal*, 851.

40. "December Meeting," 173; Emerson, *Bookbinding for Libraries*, 17.

41. Bliss, "Better Bookbinding for Libraries," *Library Journal*, 850; Emerson, *Bookbinding for Libraries*, 17; Matthews, *Modern Bookbinding Practically Considered*, 48; "A.L.A. Library Primer (under revision)," 44; Zaehnsdorf, "Practical Suggestions in Bookbinding," 110; Johnston, "Binding and Binderies," 14.

42. Johnston, "Binding and Binderies," 14; "Specifications for Binding," 66; Stearns, *Essentials in Library Administration*, 75; Soldan, "Directions for Binding," 260.

43. Johnston, "Binding and Repair," *Library Journal* 18 (September 1893): 83.

44. Brooklyn Public Library, *Annual Report of the Board of Directors, 1905*, 39; *1906*, 35; *1909*, 34; Cleveland Public Library, *Annual Report, 1878*, 9, and *1887*, 9; Detroit Public Library, *Annual Report, 1887*, 13; Jacksonville (Fla.) Public Library, *Annual Report of the Board of Trustees, 1908*, 15; New Haven (Conn.) Free Public Library, *Annual Report of the Board of Directors, 1901*, 17; *1904*, 17; Queens Borough (N.Y.) Public Library, *Annual Report of the Board of Trustees, 1910*, 22; St. Joseph (Mo.) Free Public Library, *Annual Report, 1909-1910*, 15; St. Louis Public Library, *Annual Report, 1891-1892*, 12; Seattle Public Library, *Report, 1908*, 8-9.

45. Neumann Bros., Bookbinders, "Notes on Bookbinding: The Bookbinder's Side of the Question," *Library Journal* 23 (September 1898): 526; Askew, "Problems of a Small Town Library," 707.

46. Johnston, "Elements in Library Binding," 914.

47. Jacksonville (Fla.) Public Library, *Annual Report of the Board of Trustees, 1908*, 15; New Haven (Conn.) Free Public Library, *Annual Report of the Board of Directors, 1904*, 17; Seattle Public Library, *Report, 1908*, 8-9; University of Michigan Library, *Annual Report of the Director, 1897-1898*, 10.

48. "Paper Covers," 132-33; Boston Public Library, *Annual Report of the Trustees, 1877*, 45; Johns Hopkins University Library, *Report of the Librarian, 1909-1910*, 7; University of Pennsylvania Library, *Report, 1901-1902*, 135.

49. Winsor, "Library Memoranda," 713; "On Binding of Books for Public and Private Libraries," 271; Astor Library (New York City), *Annual Report of the Trustees, 1879*, 9.

50. Winsor, "Library Memoranda," 713; Poole, "Book-Binding Memoranda," 263; Johnston, "Binding and Binderies," 15; "Binding," *American Library Journal* 1 (30 November 1876): 124.

51. University of Pennsylvania Library, *Report, 1901-1902*, 135; Newark (N.J.) Free Public Library, *Annual Report of the Board of Trustees, 1903*, 37; Salem (Mass.) Public Library, *Report of the Trustees, 1903*, 8.

52. Bowerman, Cutter, and Bailey, "Report of the Committee on Bookbinding," 138.

53. New York Yacht Club, *Report of Library Committee, 1898*, 1; John Crerar Library (Chicago), *Annual Report, 1901*, 14; Woburn (Mass.) Public Library, *Annual Report, 1892*, 14-15.

54. Bowerman, Cutter, and Bailey, "Report of the Committee on Bookbinding," 136.

55. Ibid.; Cleveland Public Library, *Annual Report, 1894*, 6; Philadelphia Free Library, *Annual Report, 1901*, 10; Washington, D.C., Public Library, *Annual Report, 1901*, 31; Kansas City (Mo.) Public Library, *Annual Report, 1897-1898*, 30; Minneapolis Public Library, *Annual Report, 1909*, 28-29; Peoria (Ill.) Public Library, *Annual Report, 1892-1893*, 10; Detroit Public Library, *Annual Report, 1904*, 15; Braddock (Pa.) Carnegie Free Library, *Annual Report, 1909*, 14; "Paper Covers," 133.

56. New York State Library, *Annual Report of the Trustees, 1891*, 26; Library of Congress, *Report, 1899-1900*, 10; *1900-1901*, 222-23; Astor Library (New York City), *Annual Report of the Trustees, 1879*, 9; Bowdoin College Library, *Annual Report of the Librarian, 1891*, 34; University of Michigan Library, *Annual Report of the Director, 1896-1897*, 9.

57. Boston Public Library, *Annual Report of the Trustees, 1876*, 12; *1877*, 20, 45; *1879*, 9; *1887*, 34-35; *1888*, 5; *1902*, 16-17; *1909*, 4; *1910*, 4.

58. Newark (N.J.) Free Public Library, *Annual Report of the Board of Trustees, 1891*, 21-22; *1902*, 30; *1904*, 21-22; *1906*, 15.

59. Seattle Public Library, *Report, 1896*, 16-17; *1899*, 8-9.

60. "Binding in Building," *American Library Journal* 2 (January-February 1878): 308-9; Johnston, "Binding and Binderies," 15; Mathews, "Library Binderies," 73-74; Braddock (Pa.) Carnegie Free Library, *Annual Report, 1908*, 10; Johnston, "Notes on Binding," 14; University of Michigan Library, *Annual Report of the Director, 1894*, 8; *1896*, 9.

61. University of Michigan Library, *Annual Report of the Director, 1896*, 9; Minneapolis Public Library, *Annual Report, 1909*, 29; Virginia State Library, *Report, 1906*, 15-16.

62. "Binding in the Building," 345; "Binding," *Library Journal* 16, 83; "Binding," *Library Journal* 17, 62; Pittsburgh Carnegie Library, *Annual Report to the Board of Trustees, 1907-1908*, 8, 59, 64.

63. "Binding," *American Library Journal* 1, 124; "Paper Covers," 133; Braddock (Pa.) Carnegie Free Library, *Annual Report, 1909*, 14; Cleveland Public Library, *Annual Report, 1895*, 9; *1898*, 9-10; Minneapolis Public Library, *Annual Report, 1909*, 29; Washington, D.C., Public Library, *Annual Report, 1901*, 31; University of Michigan Library, *Annual Report of the Director, 1896-1897*, 9; Marx, "The Value of a Bindery in a Small Library," 796.

64. Melvil Dewey, "Bindery in Building," *Public Libraries* 8 (November 1903): 405; "Binding," *American Library Journal* 1, 124; Boston Public Library, *Annual Report of the Trustees, 1877*, 45.

65. Dewey, "Bindery in Building," 405; Boston Public Library, *Annual Report of the Trustees, 1881*, 44; Cleveland Public Library, *Annual Report, 1898*, 9-10; Washington, D.C., Public Library, *Annual Report, 1901*, 31; Library of Congress, *Report, 1899-1900*, 15; "Repair Slip," *Library Journal* 17 (July-August 1892): 30; Detroit Public Library, *Annual Report, 1886*, 92.

66. Washington, D.C., Public Library, *Annual Report, 1905-1906*, 44; New York State Library, *Annual Report of the Trustees, 1891*, 26; Detroit Public Library, *Annual Report, 1904*, 15; Bowerman, Cutter, and Bailey, "Report of the Committee on Bookbinding," 138.

67. Bowerman, Cutter, and Bailey, "Report of the Committee on Bookbinding," 138; Braddock (Pa.) Carnegie Free Library, *Annual Report, 1908*, 10; Cleveland Public Library, *Annual Report, 1895*, 8; Marx, "The Value of a Bindery in a Small Library," 796.

68. John C. Dana, "What Exhibitions Can Do," *Printing Art* 11 (June 1908): 220; Grace Ashley, "A Binding Exhibition," *Public Libraries* 10 (July 1905): 357; Newark (N.J.) Free Public Library, *Book Binding: An Exhibition of the Materials, Tools and Processes of Book Binding, with Examples of Plain and Ornamental Bindings. In the Free Public Library of*

Newark, New Jersey, February 6, to February 27, 1905 (Newark, N.J.: Free Public Library, 1905), 4-5, 8-10.

69. Ashley, "A Binding Exhibition," 357, 359; Dana, "What Exhibitions Can Do," 220; Newark (N.J.) Free Public Library, *Book Binding: An Exhibition.*

70. Dana, "What Exhibitions Can Do," 220; "Newark Binding Exhibit," *Library Journal* 31 (September 1906): 696; Queens Borough (N.Y.) Public Library, *Annual Report of the Board of Trustees, 1905,* 19; Washington, D.C., Public Library, *Annual Report, 1905-1906,* 25; Ashley, "A Binding Exhibition," 359; Wilde, "New York Library Club," 182.

71. "Western Massachusetts Library Club," *Library Journal* 30 (June 1905): 361; Lansing (Mich.) Public Library, *Annual Report, 1905-1906,* 9.

72. Johnston, "Binding and Binderies," 9; W. J. Eden Crane, *Book-Binding for Amateurs* (London, 1885); Zaehnsdorf, *The Art of Bookbinding: A Practical Treatise*; James B. Nicholson, *A Manual of the Art of Bookbinding* (Philadelphia: H.C. Baird, 1856; John Hanneth, *Bibliopegia; or, the Art of Bookbinding* (London: Simkin, Marshall, 1848.)

73. Cockerell, *Bookbinding and the Care of Books*; A. C. Potter, review of *Bookbinding and the Care of Books,* by Douglas Cockerell, in *Library Journal* 27 (April 1902): 213-14; Cockerell, "Note on Bookbinding."

74. Stephen and Coutts, *Manual of Library Bookbinding.*

75. American Library Association, Committee on Bookbinding, *Binding for Small Libraries*; John C. Dana, *Notes on Bookbinding for Libraries,* 2d ed. (Chicago: Library Bureau, 1910); Matthews, *Modern Bookbinding Practically Considered*; Emerson, *Bookbinding for Libraries*; Louis H. Kinder, *Formulas for Bookbinders* (East Aurora, N.Y.: Roycroft, 1905).

76. "Transactions of Council and Executive Board," *Library Journal* 29 (December 1904): 251; Bowerman, Cutter, and Bailey, "Report of the Committee on Bookbinding," 130; American Library Association, Committee on Bookbinding, *Binding for Small Libraries,* 6.

77. "Bookbinding for Libraries," 499; Bliss, review of *Report of the Committee on Leather for Bookbinding,* and *Notes on Bookbinding for Libraries,* 738-39; Stosskopf, "Library Bookbinding," 87.

78. Brown, *Mending and Repair of Books,* 22; Dana, *Notes on Bookbinding for Libraries*; review of *Notes on Bookbinding for Libraries,* by John C. Dana, in *Library World* 9 (December 1906): 221-22.

79. "Committee on Bookbuying," *Library Journal* 33 (February 1908): 58-59; "Bulletin of A.L.A. Committee on Bookbuying," *ALA Bulletin* 2 (January 1908): 6.

80. Dana, "What Exhibitions Can Do"; Wilde, "New York Library Club," 182; Rathbone, "A Trained Person in Charge of Condition of Books," 236.

81. "Notes and Queries," *Library Journal* 34 (January 1909): 40.

82. Frank E. Comparato, *Books for the Millions: A History of the Men Whose Methods and Machines Packaged the Printed Word* (Harrisburg, Pa.: Stackpole, 1971), 200; Bernard C. Middleton, *A History of English Craft Bookbinding Technique* (London and New York: Hafner, 1963), 25.

83. Comparato, *Books for the Millions*, 200; Bliss, "Better Bookbinding for Libraries," *Public Libraries*, 295; Bliss, "Better Bookbinding for Libraries," *Library Journal*, 850.

84. Bliss, "Better Bookbinding for Libraries," *Library Journal*, 850.

85. "Report of the Committee on Bookbuying," *ALA Bulletin* 2 (September 1908): 180.

86. "A New Method of Preserving Old Bookbindings, or of Rebinding Old Books," *Library*, n.s., 6 (July 1905): 208-11.

87. Bliss, review of *Report of the Committee on Leather for Bookbinding*, and *Notes on Bookbinding for Libraries*, 738; "Bookbinders Recommended by Indiana Librarians," *Library Occurrent* 2 (October 1908): 17; Rathbone, "A Trained Person in Charge of Condition of Books," 236; Brooklyn Public Library, *Annual Report of the Board of Directors, 1910*, 35; East Orange (N.J.) Free Public Library, *Annual Report of the Board of Directors, 1905*, 20; Haverhill (Mass.) Public Library, *Annual Report, 1906*, 27; Newark (N.J.) Free Public Library, *Annual Report of the Board of Trustees, 1903*, 37; Queens Borough (N.Y.) Public Library, *Annual Report of the Board of Trustees, 1905*, 19; St. Louis Public Library, *Annual Report, 1907-1908*, 33.

88. "Western Massachusetts Library Club," *Library Journal* 30, 361; Elizabeth Foote, "The New York Library Club," *Library Journal* 34 (April 1909): 178; Chivers, "The Paper and Binding of Lending Library Books," 231-59; "Library Bookbinding," 559; Chivers, *The Paper of Lending Library Books*; Chivers, *Bookbindings at the St. Louis Exhibition, 1904*.

89. "Book Binding Boycott in New York," *Library Journal* 33 (October 1908): 395-96.

90. "The Bookbinding Question Raised in New York," *Library Journal* 33 (November 1908): 428.

91. Cedric Chivers, "The Other Side of the Bookbinding Controversy," *Library Journal* 33 (November 1908): 444.

92. Ibid., 444-45.

93. "Notes and Queries," *Library Journal* 34, 40.

94. Philadelphia Free Library, *Annual Report, 1901*, 10; Newark (N.J.) Free Public Library, *Annual Report of the Board of Trustees, 1904*, 40-41; Emerson, *Bookbinding for Libraries*, 18-19.

95. "Bookbinders Recommended by Indiana Librarians," 17; Newark (N.J.) Free Public Library, *Bookbinding: An Exhibition*, 7; "Binding for Libraries," *Public Libraries* 12 (October 1907): 310.

96. East Orange (N.J.) Free Public Library, *Annual Report of the Board of Directors, 1905*, 20; Washington, D.C., Public Library, *Annual Report, 1906-1907*, 52.

97. Rathbone, "A Trained Person in Charge of Condition of Books," 236; Newark (N.J.) Free Public Library, *Annual Report of the Board of Trustees, 1904*, 40; *1906*, 15; East Orange (N.J.) Free Public Library, *Annual Report of the Board of Directors, 1906*, 24; Jacksonville (Fla.) Public Library, *Annual Report of the Board of Trustees, 1909*, 18; Queens Borough (N.Y.) Public Library, *Annual Report of the Board of Trustees, 1909*, 13.

98. "Wales' Improved Bookbinding," *Library Journal* 24 (January 1899): 38; Advertisement for Wales' Improved Bookbinding, *Library Journal* 25 (January 1900): 50; Stetson, "Bookbinding from the Librarian's Standpoint," 300.

99. Stosskopf, "Library Bookbinding," 87-89; St. Louis Public Library, *Annual Report, 1907-1908*, 33.

100. Los Angeles Public Library, *Annual Report of the Board of Directors and of the Librarian, 1907*, 21-31; Oakland (Calif.) Free Library and Reading Rooms, *Annual Report of the Board of Trustees, 1907-1908*, 15.

101. Davenport, "Library Bookbinding," 7; Wheatley, "Leather for Bookbinding," 313-14; Royal Society of Arts, Committee on Leather for Bookbinding, *Report*, 3; review of *Bookbinding and the Care of Books*, by Douglas Cockerell, in *Dial* 33 (1 February 1902): 90; Bowerman, Cutter, and Bailey, "Report of the Committee on Bookbinding," 130; Bliss, review of *Report of the Committee on Leather for Bookbinding*, and *Notes on Bookbinding for Libraries*, 738.

102. George F. Bowerman, "'Note on Bookbinding,'" *Library Journal* 31 (December 1906): 852; Arthur L. Bailey, "'Note on Bookbinding,'" *Library Journal* 32 (January 1907): 48; "Report of Committee on Bookbinding," 115.

103. Robert D. MacLeod, "The Preservation of Books in Libraries IV," *Library World*, n.s., 11 (May 1909): 422; Tobitt, "What a Librarian Should Know about Binding," 20; Zaehnsdorf, *The Art of Bookbinding*, 2d ed., rev. & enl.; A. W. Pollard, "Notes on Books and Work," *Library*, 2d ser., 1 (1 June 1900): 346.

104. Stephen, "Notes on Materials for Library Bookbinding," August 1906, 143-46; Stephen, "Notes on Materials for Library Bookbinding," September 1906, 162-64; Stephen, "Book-Cloths," 5-7; George A. Stephen, "Edition Binding," *Library Assistant* 6 (May 1909): 326-30; George A. Stephen, "Publishers' Binding," 9-13; Stephen, *Commercial Bookbinding*; George A. Stephen, *Machine Book-Sewing with Remarks on Publishers' Binding* (Aberdeen, Scotland: Aberdeen University Press, 1908); George A. Stephen, "Machine Book-Sewing, with Remarks on Publishers' Binding," *Library Association Record* 10 (June 1908): 261-80; George A. Stephen, "Publishers' Reinforced Bindings," *Library World*, n.s., 12 (April 1910): 380-81; "Report of the Committee on Bookbinding," *ALA Bulletin* 3 (September 1909): 222.

Chapter 9. Cleaning and Repair

1. Spofford, *A Book for All Readers*, 127.

2. Washington, D.C., Public Library, *Annual Report, 1901*, 20; Mary de Bure McCurdy, "Cleaning Books," *Library Occurrent* 1 (September 1907): 2; Flora H. Leighton, "Preparing New Books and Restoring Old," *Public Libraries* 10 (May 1905): 223; Wisconsin Free Library Commission, *Biennial Report, 1895-1896*, 65; "Hints from the Manchester Meeting," *Bulletin of the Vermont Library Commission* 3 (June 1907): 3; Queens Borough (N.Y.) Public Library, *Annual Report of the Board of Trustees, 1905*, 19; Dodd, "The Care of Books in a Children's Room," 84-85; "Fires – The Repair of Books," 23.

3. "How to Wash a Book without Injury," *Library Journal* 10 (August 1885): 184-85; Slater, *The Library Manual*, 9; Spofford, *A Book for All Readers*, 30.

4. Poole, review of *The Enemies of Books*, 65; Sawyer, "How to Care for Books in a Library," 6; "How to Wash a Book without Injury," 185; Water, "District of Columbia Library Association," 512; Library Association of the United Kingdom, Sound Leather Committee, *Leather for Libraries*, 47; Royal Society of Arts, Committee on Leather for Bookbinding, *Report*, 67; Elizabeth F. Purtill, "Formulas for Cleaning Books," *Library Occurrent* 2 (June 1910): 141; Maude W. Straight, "Repairing of Books," *Public Libraries* 5 (March 1900): 89; Lovina Knowlton, "Care of Leather Bindings," *Library Occurrent* 1 (March 1908): 5.

5. "How to Wash a Book without Injury," 185; Haslam, *Book of Trade Secrets*, 3; Spofford, *A Book for All Readers*, 128.

6. Woodard, "Notes on Bookbinding," 237; Haslam, *Book of Trade Secrets*, 3; Spofford, *A Book for All Readers*, 129.

7. Field, "Book Repairing," 107; "Repairing Books," 126; Queens Borough (N.Y.) Public Library, *Annual Report of the Board of Trustees, 1905*,

19; Brown, *Mending and Repair of Books*, 19; McCurdy, "Cleaning Books," 2; "Hints from the Manchester Meeting," 3; Purtill, "Formulas for Cleaning Books," 140; Sawyer, *How to Care for Books in a Library*, 5; Sawyer, "How to Care for Books in a Library," *Wisconsin Library Bulletin* 5 (January-February 1909): 6.

8. Leighton, "Preparing New Books and Restoring Old," 223.

9. Ibid.

10. Emma C. Beardsley, "More about Clean Books," *Public Libraries* 10 (May 1905): 224; Dodd, "The Care of Books in a Children's Room," 84-85; Cramer, "Methods for Keeping Books Clean," 66; Brown, *Mending and Repair of Books*, 19.

11. Field, "Book Repairing," 107; Brown, *Mending and Repair of Books*, 18; Zaehnsdorf, *The Art of Bookbinding*, 161; Dodd, "The Care of Books in a Children's Room," 85; Cramer, "Methods for Keeping Books Clean," 66; Sawyer, "How to Care for Books in a Library," 6; Queens Borough (N.Y.) Public Library, *Annual Report of the Board of Trustees, 1905*, 19; Purtill, "Formulas for Cleaning Books," 141.

12. Purtill, "Formulas for Cleaning Books," 141; Brown, *Mending and Repair of Books*, 18.

13. Javelle water was a fairly weak bleaching solution prepared either from sodium hypochlorite or potassium hypochlorite. See Roberts and Etherington, *Bookbinding and the Conservation of Books*, 144.

14. "Restoration of Books," *American Library Journal* 2 (September 1877): 24; "How to Wash a Book without Injury," 185; "Removal of Grease Spots from Books and Engravings," *Library Journal* 11 (April 1886): 123; Sharp, "Library Recipes," 212; Purtill, "Formulas for Cleaning Books," 140; Straight, "Repairing of Books," 89; Spofford, *A Book for All Readers*, 128; Wisconsin Free Library Commission, *Biennial Report, 1895-1896*, 65; "Restoring Leather Bindings," *Library Journal* 11 (November 1886): 454; "Ink Eraser," *Library Journal* 10 (November 1885): 385.

15. "Restoring Leather Bindings," 454; Purtill, "Formulas for Cleaning Books," 140; Robert D. MacLeod, "The Preservation of Books in Libraries II," *Library World*, n.s., 11 (March 1909): 332; Slater, *The Library Manual*, 10; Spofford, *A Book for All Readers*, 128; "Disinfection," *Library Journal* 13 (March-April 1888): 106; Brown, *Mending and Repair of Books*, 18; "How to Wash a Book without Injury," 338; Sharp, "Library Recipes," 209; Zaehnsdorf, *The Art of Bookbinding*, 162.

16. "How to Wash a Book without Injury," 184-85; Battershall, *Bookbinding for Bibliophiles*, 8-9; Slater, *The Library Manual*, 10-11; Zaehnsdorf, *The Art of Bookbinding*, 160.

17. Spofford, *A Book for All Readers*, 121.

18. Public Library of the City of Bangor (Maine), *Annual Reports, 1901*, 13; Portland (Maine) Public Library, *Annual Report, 1890-1891*, 5;

Yale University, *Report of the Librarian, 1907-1908*, 33; Pratt Institute, *Report of the Pratt Institute Free Library and School of Library Science, 1897-1898*, 9, 4.

19. Pratt Institute, *Report of the Pratt Institute Free Library and School of Library Science, 1896-1897*, 5; St. Louis Public Library, *Annual Report, 1890-1891*, 13; Boston Athenaeum, *Reports of the Library Committee and of the Librarian, 1905*, 3; Oakland (Calif.) Free Library and Reading Rooms, *Annual Report of the Board of Trustees, 1907-1908*, 15; *1910-1911*, 14; Worcester County (Mass.) Law Library, *Annual Report, 1910*, 10.

20. Rathbone, "A Trained Person in Charge of Condition of Books," 236; Sawyer, "How to Care for Books in a Library," 7; Brown, *Mending and Repair of Books*, 5-6; Wilmington (Del.) Institute, *Annual Report, 1894-1895*, 32; Library of Congress, *Report, 1903-1904*, 82.

21. "Western Massachusetts Library Club," 88; Marx, "The Value of a Bindery in a Small Library," 796-97; Bailey, Cutter, and Wire, "Rebinding Fiction and Juvenile Books," 10-11; Bailey, Cutter, and Wire, "Notes from A.L.A. Committee on Bookbinding," 186-87.

22. "Iowa State Library Association," *Library Journal* 25 (December 1900): 746; Knowlton, "Library Mending Kit," 5; "A.L.A. Library Primer (under revision)," 45; Marvin, "The Care of Books," 36; Detroit Public Library, *Annual Report, 1886*, 92; Dubuque (Iowa) Carnegie-Stout Free Public Library, *Annual Report, 1906*, 10; Seattle Public Library, *Report, 1896*, 15-16.

23. Cincinnati Public Library, *Annual Report of the Librarian and Treasurer, 1907-1908*, 18; Fletcher Free Library (Burlington, Vt.) *Annual Report of the Trustees, 1876*, 5; Providence Public Library, *Annual Report, 1902*, 15; Rockford (Ill.) Public Library, *Annual Report of the Board of Directors, 1908-1909*, 14; Springfield (Mass.) City Library Association, *Annual Report, 1902*, 28; Troy (N.Y.) Public Library, *Report, 1910*, 9-10.

24. Hartford (Conn.) Public Library, *Annual Report of the Directors, 1903*, 8; Wilmington (Del.) Institute, *Annual Report, 1903-1904*, 26-27; Rockford (Ill.) Public Library, *Annual Report of the Board of Directors, 1908-1909*, 14.

25. Somerville (Mass.) Public Library, *Annual Report, 1909*, 14-15; Rathbone, "A Trained Person in Charge of Condition of Books," 236; Boston Public Library, *Annual Report of the Trustees, 1877*, 45.

26. Braddock (Pa.) Carnegie Free Library, *Annual Report, 1903*, 41; Grand Rapids Public Library, *Annual Report, 1904-1905*, 36; Providence Public Library, *Annual Report, 1903*, 12-13; Evanston (Ill.) Public Library, *Annual Report, 1897*, 17; Pratt Institute, *Report of the Pratt Institute Free Library and School of Library Science, 1898-1899*, 7.

27. MacLeod, "The Preservation of Books in Libraries," 260; Davenport, "Library Bookbinding," 9; Crunden, "How Things are Done in One American Library," 25; Oakland (Calif.) Free Library and Reading Rooms, *Annual Report of the Board of Trustees, 1906-1907*, 17; *1907-1908*, 15; *1910-1911*, 13-14; Washington, D.C., Public Library, *Annual Report, 1905-1906*, 25.

28. Boston Public Library, *Annual Report of the Trustees, 1879*, 19; New York Yacht Club Library, *Report of Library Committee, 1905*, 2, and *1906*, 4; Grand Rapids Public Library, *Annual Report, 1904-1905*, 36; Woburn (Mass.) Public Library, *Annual Report, 1888*, 18.

29. Worcester County (Mass.) Law Library, *Annual Report, 1904*, 8; Braddock (Pa.) Carnegie Free Library, *Annual Report, 1903*, 41, 72; Dayton Public Library, *Annual Report of the Board of Managers and Librarian, 1905-1906*, 19; Scranton Public Library, *Annual Report, 1901*, 11; Boston Public Library, *Annual Report of the Trustees, 1905*, 10; Washington, D.C., Public Library, *Annual Report, 1908-1909*, 57; St. Louis Public Library, *Annual Report, 1910-1911*, 54; Cleveland Public Library, *Annual Report, 1907*, 72; Boston Athenaeum, *Reports of the Library Committee and of the Librarian, 1905*, 3; Grand Rapids Public Library, *Annual Report, 1901-1902*, 16; "Mutilating Books in Libraries," *Library Journal* 13 (June 1888): 182; Spofford, *A Book For All Readers*, 122.

30. Brown, *Mending and Repair of Books*, 9-11; Henry T. Coutts, "The Home Bindery or Repairing Department," *Library World* 9 (January 1907): 235-36; Knowlton, "Library Mending Kit," 5; Straight, "Repairing of Books," 88-89; Sawyer, "How to Care for Books in a Library," 8; Library Association of the United Kingdom, Committee on Leather for Bookbinding, *Leather for Libraries*, 51-52; Wisconsin Free Library Commission, *Biennial Report, 1895-1896*, 64-65; "Materials for Mending Books," 7-8.

31. Plummer, *Hints to Small Libraries*, 31-32; "Massachusetts Library Club," 172; Woodard, "Notes on Bookbinding," 237; W. C. Hollands, "Bookbinding," *Public Libraries* 9 (June 1904): 261; Reid, "Hints on Bookbinding," 64; Bailey, Cutter, and Wire, "Notes from A.L.A. Committee on Bookbinding," 187; Field, "Book Repairing," 106.

32. "Massachusetts Library Club," 172; Field, "Book Repairing," 8; Sawyer, "How to Care for Books in a Library," 8.

33. "Paste," *Library Journal* 3 (April 1878): 78; "Paste," *Library Journal* 17 (February 1892): 72; "A Good Paste," *Library World* 2 (May 1900): 301; Woodard, "Notes on Bookbinding," 237; Brown, *Mending and Repair of Books*, 11.

34. Karl A. Linderfelt, "Paste," *Library Journal* 8 (March-April 1883): 55; "Paste," *Library Journal* 17 (April 1892): 145; Wisconsin Free Library Commission, *Biennial Report, 1895-1896*, 64.

35. Sharp, "Library Recipes," 217; "Good Library Paste," *Library Occurrent* 2 (October 1908): 17; "A Good Recipe for Book Paste," *Bulletin of the Vermont Library Commission* 5 (December 1909): 8; S. M. Jacobus, "A Library Paste," *Public Libraries* 11 (June 1906): 310.

36. H. A. Homes, "Gum Tragacanth as a Library Paste," *Library Journal* 4 (31 March 1879): 93; Sharp, "Library Recipes," 216, 218.

37. Advertisement for the Holden System for Preserving Books, April 1895, 144, and April 1907, lxxi; Stosskopf, "Library Bookbinding," 87; Soldan, "Specifications for Binding," 106-107; "The Collection of Newspapers and Society Publications," *Library Journal* 18 (March 1893): 80-81; Spofford, *A Book for All Readers*, 122; Stearns, *Essentials in Library Administration*, 78.

38. "Mending Torn Leaves," *Library World* 2 (January 1900): 189; Brown, *Mending and Repair of Books*, 12; Library Association of the United Kingdom, Sound Leather Committee, *Leather for Libraries*, 52; Wisconsin Library Commission, *Biennial Report, 1895-1896*, 65.

39. Sharp, "Library Recipes," 213; Sawyer, "How to Care for Books in a Library," 6-7.

40. "Adhesive Paper," *Library Journal* 3 (May 1878): 135; Woodard, "Notes on Bookbinding," 237; Spofford, *A Book for All Readers*, 122; Brown, *Mending and Repair of Books*, 12.

41. Middleton, *A History of English Craft Bookbinding Technique*, 209-10; Chance, "Preservation of Bookbindings," 444; "Binding," *Library Journal* 17, 62.

42. Woodard, "Notes on Bookbinding," 236; Water, "District of Columbia Library Association," 512; Purtill, "Formulas for Cleaning Books," 141; Royal Society of Arts, Committee on Leather for Bookbinding, *Report*, 71; Washington, D.C., Public Library, *Annual Report, 1907-1908*, 27, 53; Worcester County (Mass.) Law Library, *Annual Report, 1907*, 13-14; *1908*, 15-16; *1910*, 10; *1911*, 19-26.

43. "Binding," *Library Journal* 17, 62; Moore, "The Art of Leather Making," 367; Knowlton, "Care of Leather Bindings," 5; Purtill, "Formulas for Cleaning Books," 141; Haslam, *Book of Trade Secrets*, 1; Samuel H. Ranck, "Softening Bindings," *Library Journal* 21 (May 1896): 218.

44. MacLeod, "The Preservation of Books in Libraries IV," 420; Davenport, "Library Bookbinding," 14; Royal Society of Arts, Committee on Leather for Bookbinding, *Report*, 72; Library Association of the United Kingdom, Sound Leather Committee, *Leather for Libraries*, 47.

45. Cloth bindings, especially on popular materials such as works of fiction and juvenile books, were also shellacked or varnished; this precaution kept them cleaner and made it easier to freshen them with a damp cloth. See McCurdy, "Cleaning Books," 2; Marvin, "The Care of Books," 36; "Oshkosh," *Wisconsin Library Bulletin* 3 (July-August 1907): 71; Worces-

ter County (Mass.) Law Library, *Annual Report, 1911*, 26; Brookline (Mass.) Public Library, *Annual Report of the Trustees, 1909*, 16; New Orleans Public Library, *Annual Report, 1910*, 14.

46. "Durability of Leather," *Scientific American* 100 (17 April 1909): 292; Davenport, "Library Bookbinding," 14; Field, "Book Repairing," 105; Brown, *Mending and Repair of Books*, 19; Dayton Public Library, *Annual Report of the Board of Managers and Librarian, 1902-1903*, 10.

47. "Book-Wash and Varnish," *Library Journal* 7 (June 1882): 111; "Preserving Bindings," 72; Flora F. Prince, "Book Repairing," *Bulletin of the Vermont Library Commission* 5 (September 1909): 7.

48. Water, "District of Columbia Library Association," 512; "Paste-Watering," *Book-Auction Records* 3 (1905-6): x; "Massachusetts Library Club," *Library Journal* 32 (February 1907): 83-84; Lutie E. Stearns, "Shellac for Book Covers," *Wisconsin Library Bulletin* 3 (July-August 1907): 64; Royal Society of Arts, Committee on Leather for Bookbinding, *Report*, 67.

49. "Paste-Watering," x; Purtill, "Formulas for Cleaning Books," 141.

50. "Book-Wash and Varnish," 111; Sharp, "Library Recipes," 213; C. P. Russell, "Note on the Preservation of Bindings," in *Transactions and Proceedings of the First Annual Meeting of the Library Association of the United Kingdom, Held at Oxford, October 1, 2, 3, 1878*, ed. Henry R. Tedder and Ernst C. Thomas (London, 1879), 100; Purtill, "Formulas for Cleaning Books," 141; Spofford, *A Book for All Readers*, 130-31.

51. Davenport, "Library Bookbinding," 14; Haslam, *Book of Trade Secrets*, 4; Royal Society of Arts, Committee on Leather for Bookbinding, *Report*, 71.

52. "Before Rebinding," *Library Journal* 5 (July-August 1880): 214-15; "Restoring Leather Bindings," 454; Sharp, "Library Recipes," 213; Haslam, *Book of Trade Secrets*, 4; Slater, *The Library Manual*, 13-14.

53. Comparato, *Books for the Millions*, 200; Middleton, *A History of English Craft Bookbinding Technique*, 146-47; "A New Method of Preserving Old Bookbindings, or of Rebinding Old Books," 208-9; Chivers, *Bookbindings at the St. Louis Exhibition, 1904*, 7, 28.

54. Trinity College Library, *Report of the Librarian, 1908*, 5-6.

55. Ibid., 7-8.

56. Ibid., 10.

57. "To Separate the Leaves of Charred Books or Deeds," *Library Journal* 12 (August 1887): 301; Haslam, *Book of Trade Secrets*, 9.

58. Milwaukee Public Library, *Annual Report of the Board of Trustees, 1894-1895*, 11, 13-14.

59. Philadelphia Mercantile Library Company, *Annual Report of the Board of Directors, 1877*, 5-6; "Fires – The Repair of Books," 23; Spofford, *A Book for All Readers*, 131-32.

Chapter 10. Publishers' Bindings

1. Lehmann-Haupt, *Bookbinding in America*, 132-34.

2. Stephen, *Machine Book-Sewing*, 1.

3. Poole, "Book-Binding Memoranda," 261-62; Stephen, "Edition Binding," 326-28; Spofford, *A Book for All Readers*, 62-63; Lehmann-Haupt, *Bookbinding in America*, 133.

4. Lehmann-Haupt, *Bookbinding in America*, 138; Johnston, "Notes on Binding," 14, 15; Dousman, "Methods of Inducing Care of Books – I," 60; Coutts, "The Home Bindery or Repairing Department," 233; Bliss, "Better Bookbinding for Libraries," *Public Libraries*, 294; Stephen, "Machine Book-Sewing, with Remarks on Publishers' Bindings," 274; Stephen, "Publishers' Bindings," 9; Salem (Mass.) Public Library, *Report of the Trustees, 1903*, 7.

5. Ellen D. Biscoe, "Bookbinding of Our American Publishers," *Library Journal* 24 (October 1899): 561; Stephen, *Machine Book-Sewing*, 14; Scranton Public Library, *Annual Report, 1899*, 12; Seattle Public Library, *Report, 1899*, 9; Salem (Mass.) Public Library, *Report of the Trustees, 1903*, 7.

6. "The Get-Up of Modern Books," *Library World* 4 (August 1901): 32; Stephen, "Publishers' Bindings," 9; Peoria (Ill.) Public Library, *Annual Report, 1898-1899*, 11.

7. Redwood Library and Athenaeum (Newport, R.I.), *Annual Report of the Directors, 1886*, 16; San Francisco Mercantile Library Association, *Annual Report of the President, Treasurer, and Librarian, 1876*, 21; Washington Heights (N.Y.) Free Library, *Annual Report, 1900*, 17-18; Bridgeport (Conn.) Public Library and Reading Room, *Annual Report, 1899*, 5; Brooklyn Public Library, *Annual Report of the Board of Directors, 1906*, 35; Fletcher Free Library (Burlington, Vt.) *Annual Report of the Trustees, 1902*, 5; Louisville (Ky.) Free Public Library, *Annual Report of the Board of Trustees, 1909-1910*, 20; Manchester (N.H.) City Library, *Annual Report of the Trustees, 1881*, 14; Rockford (Ill.) Public Library, *Annual Report of the Board of Directors, 1908-1909*, 14; San Francisco Public Library, *Report of the Board of Trustees, 1900*, 13; Silas Bronson Library (Waterbury, Conn.), *Annual Report of the Board of Agents, 1899-1900*, 8; Somerville (Mass.) Public Library, *Annual Report, 1902*, 12; Troy (N.Y.) Public Library, *Report, 1909*, 10; Wilmington (Del.) Institute, *Annual Report, 1894-1895*, 32.

8. Poole, "Elements of Good Binding," 15.

9. Biscoe, "Bookbinding of Our American Publishers," 563; Dousman, "Methods of Inducing Care of Books – I," 60.

10. Peoria (Ill.) Public Library, *Annual Report, 1898-1899*, 15; Scranton Public Library, *Annual Report, 1899*, 12; Seattle Public Library, *Report, 1899*, 9.

11. Washington, D.C., Public Library, *Annual Report, 1901*, 30.

12. Frederick M. Crunden, "Exclusion of Badly Made Books," *Library Journal* 24 (March 1899): 98; "Public Notice of Poor Editions," *Library Journal* 24 (October 1899): 574.

13. "Bulletins on Book Buying," *Library Journal* 31 (September 1906): 696; Dousman, "Methods of Inducing Care of Books – I," 60.

14. Lehmann-Haupt, *Bookbinding in America*, 152-53; Stephen, *Machine Book-Sewing*, 2-11; Stephen, "Machine Book-Sewing, with Remarks on Publishers' Binding," 264-73.

15. Stephen, *Machine Book-Sewing*, 11-13.

16. Lehmann-Haupt, *Bookbinding in America*, 143; Woodard, "Notes on Bookbinding," 233; Straight, "Repairing of Books," 88; E. Wyndham Hulme, "Machine Book-Sewing," *Library Association Record* 10 (January 1908): 8-9; Salem (Mass.) Public Library, *Report of the Trustees, 1903*, 7; Wisconsin Free Library Commission, *Biennial Report, 1895-1896*, 63.

17. Stephen, "Machine Book-Sewing, with Remarks on Publishers' Binding," 262-63; Library Association of the United Kingdom, Sound Leather Committee, *Leather for Libraries*, 42; Stephen, *Machine Book-Sewing*, 2.

18. Stephen, "Machine Book-Sewing, with Remarks on Publishers' Binding," 262-63; Stephen, *Machine Book-Sewing*, 2-3.

19. "Wire-Sewn Books," *Library Journal* 5 (July-August 1880): 213; "Objection to Wire Bookbinding," *Library Journal* 11 (December 1886): 490; Woodard, "Notes on Bookbinding," 233; "The Disadvantages of Wire-Sewing and the Necessity for Prohibiting It," *Library* 10 (1898): 255-57; Stephen, "Machine Book-Sewing, with Remarks on Publishers' Binding," 263-64.

20. Library Association of the United Kingdom, Sound Leather Committee, *Leather for Libraries*, 47; Stephen, *Machine Book-Sewing*, 3; "Libraries and Librarians," *Library World* 4 (March 1902): 249.

21. Emerson, *Bookbinding for Libraries*, 11; "The Get-Up of Modern Books," 33; "Notes on Books and Work," *Library*, n.s., 4 (1 July 1903): 336; "Ninth Meeting of German Librarians," *Library Journal* 33 (November 1908): 446-47; Stephen, *Machine Book-Sewing*, 4.

22. Roberts and Etherington, *Bookbinding and the Conservation of Books*, 6; Spofford, *A Book for All Readers*, 63.

23. Lehmann-Haupt, *Bookbinding in America*, 141-43, 155-57.

24. Spofford, *A Book for All Readers*, 64.

25. Ibid., 64; Stephen, *Machine Book-Sewing*, 14; Straight, "Repairing of Books," 88.

26. Lehmann-Haupt, *Bookbinding in America*, 151-56.

27. Biscoe, "Bookbinding of Our American Publishers," 561-63; Bowerman, Cutter, and Bailey, "Report of the Committee on Bookbinding," 134.

28. Biscoe, "Bookbinding of Our American Publishers," 561-62.

29. "American Library Association," *Library Journal* 30 (May 1905): 289, 291; Bowerman, "Committee on Bookbinding and Book Papers," 147.

30. Bowerman, "Report of the Committee on Bookbinding," 130-39; "Report of Committee on Bookbinding and Book Papers," *Library Journal* 31 (August 1906): 194; "Bookbindings and Book Papers," *Library Journal* 31 (August 1906): 281.

31. "Book-Binding Committee," *ALA Bulletin* 1 (January 1907): 8-9; "Report of Committee on Bookbinding," 110-16; Arthur L. Bailey, William P. Cutter, and George E. Wire, "Bookbinding Committee," *Library Journal* 33 (February 1908): 58.

32. Bailey, "Report of the Committee on Bookbinding," 173-76; "American Library Association Committee on Binding," *Library Journal* 34 (September 1909): 411-13; "American Library Association Committee on Binding," *Library Journal* 34 (October 1909): 452; "Bookbinding," 9; "Report of the Committee on Bookbinding," 220-22; Stephen, "Machine Book-Sewing, with Remarks on Publishers' Binding," 276-78; Stephen, "Publishers' Binding," 10; Stephen, *Commercial Bookbinding*, 55-56; Stephen, *Machine Book-Sewing*, 16-17.

Chapter 11. Library Editions and Binding Specifications

1. "Report of Committee on Bookbinding," 115; Bliss, "Better Bookbinding for Libraries," *Public Libraries*, 295; East Orange (N.J.) Free Public Library, *Annual Report of the Board of Directors, 1907*, 25; Washington, D.C., Public Library, *Annual Report, 1908-1909*, 25; Peoria (Ill.) Public Library, *Annual Report, 1910-1911*, 10.

2. Seattle Public Library, *Report, 1899*, 9.

3. John W. Singleton, "Bookbinding: A Suggestion," *Library World* 3 (May 1906): 289-90; Peoria (Ill.) Public Library, *Annual Report, 1910-1911*, 10.

4. "Bulletins on Book Buying," *Library Journal* 32 (January 1907): 48; Stephen, "Machine Book-Sewing, with Remarks on Publishers' Binding," 276; Stephen, *Machine Book-Sewing*, 16; Cockerell, "Note on Bookbinding," 98; Bliss, "Better Bookbinding for Libraries," *Library Jour-*

nal, 850; Peoria (Ill.) Public Library, *Annual Report, 1898-1899*, 12; "Special Library Bindings," *Library World* 2 (June 1900): 332.

5. American Library Association, Committee on Bookbinding, *Binding for Small Libraries*, 7; Salem (Mass.) Public Library, *Report of the Trustees, 1903*, 8; Stephen and Coutts, *Manual of Library Bookbinding*, 25.

6. Singleton, "Bookbinding: A Suggestion," 289; Philip, "Bookbinding for Lending Libraries," 72; Peoria (Ill.) Public Library, *Annual Report, 1910-1911*, 10; "Special Library Bindings," 332.

7. "Bulletins of the A. L. A. Committee on Book Prices," *Library Journal* 29 (August 1904): 425; Bowerman, Cutter, and Bailey, "Report of the Committee on Bookbinding," 138; Field, "Book Repairing," 105; Kirke H. Field, "Binding and Other Workroom Problems," *News Notes of California Libraries* 5 (July 1910): 372.

8. Roberts and Etherington, *Bookbinding and the Conservation of Books*, 83; "'Duro-Flexible' Bindings," *Library Journal* 11 (June 1886): 166; "Duro-Flexible Bookbinding," *Library Journal* 12 (January-February 1887): 70-71.

9. Field, "Book Repairing," 105; Cornelia Marvin, "Rebinding Made Unnecessary," *Wisconsin Library Bulletin* 1 (May 1905): 42; Silas Bronson Library (Waterbury, Conn.), *Annual Report of the Board of Agents, 1905-1906*, 6.

10. Advertisement for Chivers's Patent Bindings, *Library Journal* 30 (November 1905): 901; "Report of Committee on Bookbinding," 115; Pratt Institute, *Report of the Pratt Institute Free Library and School of Library Science, 1905-1906*, 15; Brockton (Mass.) Public Library, *Report of the Trustees, 1907*, 21-22; Dayton Public Library, *Annual Report of the Board of Managers and Librarian, 1905-1906*, 9; East Orange (N.J.) Free Public Library, *Annual Report of the Board of Directors, 1907*, 25; Brooklyn Public Library, *Annual Report of the Board of Directors, 1907*, 26; Hartford (Conn.) Public Library, *Annual Report of the Directors, 1906*, 9.

11. Advertisement for Cedric Chivers, Bookbinder, *Library Journal* 30 (May 1905): 317.

12. Stetson, "Bookbinding from the Librarian's Standpoint," 300; Dayton Public Library, *Annual Report of the Board of Managers and Librarian, 1905-1906*, 9; Dubuque (Iowa) Carnegie-Stout Free Public Library, *Annual Report, 1907*, 10; East Orange (N.J.) Free Public Library, *Annual Report of the Board of Directors, 1907*, 25; Rockford (Ill.) Public Library, *Annual Report of the Board of Directors, 1908-1909*, 14; Rosenberg Library (Galveston, Tex.), *Annual Report, 1906*, n.p.; St. Louis Public Library, *Annual Report, 1908-1909*, 69-70; Washington, D.C., Public Library, *Annual Report, 1905-1906*, 25; Wilmington (Del.) Institute, *Annual Report, 1906-1907*, 23; "Western Massachusetts Library Club," 88;

Brockton (Mass.) Public Library, *Report of the Trustees, 1907,* 21-22; Haverhill (Mass.) Public Library, *Annual Report, 1906,* 27; Thomas Crane Public Library (Quincy, Mass.), *Annual Report, 1909,* 10.

13. "Better Bookmaking for Libraries," *Library Journal* 18 (May 1893): 142.

14. Ibid.

15. Francis D. Tandy, "Special Editions of Library Books," *Library Journal* 18 (October 1893): 422.

16. Silas Bronson Library (Waterbury, Conn.), *Annual Report of the Board of Agents, 1898-1899,* 8-9.

17. Bliss, "Better Bookbinding for Libraries," *Library Journal,* 850; Bliss, "Better Bookbinding for Libraries," *Public Libraries,* 294.

18. Bowerman, Cutter, and Bailey, "Report of the Committee on Bookbinding," 134-35.

19. Ibid., 134-36.

20. "There Is Increasing Complaint as to the Bindings Furnished by Publishers for Popular Books," *Library Journal* 32 (February 1907): 49-50; "Committee on Bookbinding," 76; "Report of Committee on Bookbinding," 111-12, 116.

21. "Note from the A. L. A. Committee on Bookbinding," *Library Journal* 32 (April 1907): 168; "Report of Committee on Bookbinding," 111.

22. Bailey, Cutter, and Wire, "Bookbinding Committee," 58; Bailey, "Report of the Committee on Bookbinding," 174.

23. "Report of the A. L. A. Committee on Library Administration, 1908," 225-26.

24. "Committee on Bookbuying," 58-59.

25. "Committee on Bookbuying," *Library Journal* 33 (April 1908): 152.

26. Ibid.

27. "Report of the Committee on Bookbinding," 220.

28. "Committee on Binding," *Library Journal* 35 (March 1910): 122; "Bookbuying," 524-25; Arthur L. Bailey, "Committee on Bookbinding," *Library Journal* 35 (May 1910): 211; "The Library," *Book Buyer* (November 1910): 186-87.

29. "The Library," 187.

30. Ibid., 186.

31. East Orange (N.J.) Free Public Library, *Annual Report of the Board of Directors, 1908,* 26; Rockford (Ill.) Public Library, *Annual Report of the Board of Directors, 1908-1909,* 14; Salem (Mass.) Public Library, *Report of the Trustees, 1908,* 6; Wilmington (Del.) Institute, *Annual Report, 1905-1906,* 25; Buffalo Public Library, *Annual Report, 1908,* 15; Dubuque (Iowa) Carnegie-Stout Free Public Library, *Annual Report, 1908,* 10; Jacksonville (Fla.) Public Library, *Annual Report of the Board of*

Trustees, 1909, 15-16; Lynn (Mass.) Public Library, *Annual Report of the Trustees, 1908*, 19; Queens Borough (N.Y.) Public Library, *Annual Report of the Board of Trustees, 1910*, 22; Sedalia (Mo.) Public Library, *Annual Report, 1911*, 7; Woburn (Mass.) Public Library, *Annual Report, 1909*, 42; Atlantic City (N.J.) Free Public Library, *Annual Report, 1907*, 10-11.

32. Louisa M. Hooper, "Disadvantages of Reinforced Bindings," *Library Journal* 34 (October 1909): 437; Emerson, *Bookbinding for Libraries*, 19.

33. Antoinette Humphreys, "The Other Side," *Public Libraries* 14 (October 1909): 300; Mary K. Hasbrouck, "Reinforced Bindings Again," *Public Libraries* 14 (November 1909): 349.

34. "Committee on Bookbinding," 76; "Book-Binding Committee," 8-9; American Library Association, Committee on Bookbinding, *Binding for Small Libraries*, 6-8.

35. Marx, "The Value of a Bindery in a Small Library," 797; Scranton Public Library, *Annual Report, 1899*, 12.

36. Dayton Public Library, *Annual Report of the Board of Managers and Librarian, 1905-1906*, 9; Grand Rapids Public Library, *Annual Report, 1906-1907*, 58.

37. Annie M. Thayer, "Statistics of Re-Binding," *Library Journal* 31 (January 1906): 48; Bowerman, Cutter, and Bailey, "Report of the Committee on Bookbinding," 134; "American Library Association Committee on Binding," 412; Braddock (Pa.) Carnegie Free Library, *Annual Report, 1908*, 6; Bradford (Pa.) Carnegie Public Library, *Annual Report, 1904*, 7; Peoria (Ill.) Public Library, *Annual Report, 1910-1911*, 10.

38. "Report of the Committee on Bookbinding," 220-22.

39. Bailey, "Report of the Committee on Bookbinding," 174.

40. Brooklyn Public Library, *Annual Report of the Board of Directors, 1910*, 36; East Orange (N.J.) Free Public Library, *Annual Report of the Board of Directors, 1908*, 26.

41. "Report of Committee on Bookbinding," 112-13.

42. Brooklyn Public Library, *Annual Report of the Board of Directors, 1909*, 34; Philadelphia Free Library, *Annual Report, 1901*, 11.

43. Wilmington (Del.) Institute, *Annual Report, 1905-1906*, 20; *1906-1907*, 23-24; *1908-1909*, 23.

44. Wilde, "New York Library Club," 182.

45. "Association Bindings," 432.

46. Soldan, "Specifications for Binding," 106-7; Soldan, "Directions for Binding," 259-60; Growoll, *The Profession of Bookselling*, 3 vols., 2: 94.

47. San Francisco Public Library, *Report of the Board of Trustees, 1908*, 23; New York State Library, *Annual Report of the Trustees, 1898*, 11; Hertzberg, "Specifications for Library Bookbinding," 135-37; "Specifications for Binding," 66-67.

48. "Committee on Bookbinding," 76; "American Library Association Committee on Binding," 412; "Report of the Committee on Bookbinding," 220; "Committee on Binding," March 1910, 122; Oakland (Calif.) Free Library and Reading Rooms, *Annual Report of the Board of Trustees, 1907-1908*, 15-16.

49. Stephen, "Machine Book-Sewing, with Remarks on Publishers' Binding," 277-78; Stephen, *Commercial Bookbinding*, 55-56; Stephen, *Machine Book-Sewing*, 17-18.

50. Samuel H. Ranck, "Leather for Bookbinding," *Library Journal* 26 (September 1901): 683; Pollard, "Notes on Books and Work," 335-36; Royal Society of Arts, Committee on Leather for Bookbinding, *Report*, 34-36; Cockerell, *Bookbinding and the Care of Books*, 308-11.

51. Bowerman, Cutter, and Bailey, "Report of the Committee on Bookbinding," 133; Royal Society of Arts, Committee on Leather for Bookbinding, *Report*, 24-25; Pratt Institute, *Report of the Pratt Institute Free Library and School of Library Science, 1906-1907*, 17.

Chapter 12. Paper and Ink

1. Rossiter Johnson, "Inferior Paper a Menace to the Permanency of Literature," *Library Journal* 16 (August 1891): 242.

2. Fletcher Veitch, *Paper-Making Materials and Their Conservation* (Washington, D.C.: U.S. Bureau of Chemistry, 1908), 4.

3. "After All, the Library Must Depend upon the Book and the Book Must Be Made of Paper," *Library Journal* 34 (June 1909): 246; J. Franke, "Pressing Danger for Our Libraries," *Library Association Record* 10 (July 1908): 343.

4. Powell, "Book Production in Great Britain," 50.

5. Stosskopf, "Library Bookbinding," 87-88; Bliss, "Better Bookbinding for Libraries," *Public Libraries*, 294; Field, "Book Repairing," 105.

6. Veitch, "Suitable Paper for Permanent Records," 261.

7. Little, "The Durability of Paper," 115.

8. Chivers, "The Paper and Binding of Lending Library Books," 249; J. Y. W. MacAlister, "The Durability of Modern Book Papers," *Library* 10 (1898): 295-96.

9. Wilmington (Del.) Institute, *Annual Report, 1894-1895*, 32-33; Library of Congress, *Report, 1897-1898*, 45.

10. Johnson, "Inferior Paper a Menace," 242; William J. Manning, "Permanent Printed Records on Linen," *Scientific American* 98 (6 June 1908): 407.

11. Bliss, "Better Bookbinding for Libraries," *Public Libraries*, 294; MacAlister, "The Durability of Modern Book Papers," 298-303; Library of Congress, *Report, 1897-1898*, 45-46.

12. Butler Wood, "The Brittle Quality of Paper Used by Publishers," *Library* 2 (1890): 203.

13. "M900 + X050," *Library World*, n.s., 13 (December 1910): 170-71; Bliss, "Better Bookbinding for Libraries," *Public Libraries*, 294; Peoria (Ill.) Public Library, *Annual Report, 1898-1899*, 12; Salem (Mass.) Public Library, *Report of the Trustees, 1908*, 6.

14. Stosskopf, "Library Bookbinding," 87; Chivers, "Paper and Binding," 249.

15. Thomas Aldred, "An Appeal to Publishers," *Library* 7 (November 1895): 385; "Better Bookmaking for Libraries," 142; "December Meeting," 172.

16. The key word here is *properly*. Not all rag papers were strong and long-lasting. Inferior or "severely treated" rags sometimes yielded poorer paper than did some nonrag materials. See U.S. Department of Agriculture, *Durability and Economy in Papers for Permanent Records*, 14, 15; Veitch, "Suitable Paper for Permanent Records," 263; "Report of Committee on Bookbinding," 114.

17. Johnson, "Inferior Paper a Menace," 241; "New York Library Association," *Library Journal* 25 (March 1900): 128.

18. "Rebinding for General Circulation," 186; Straight, "Repairing of Books," 88.

19. Little, "The Durability of Paper," 116; Stephen and Coutts, *Manual of Library Bookbinding*, 79; U.S. Department of Agriculture, *Papers for Permanent Records*, 15.

20. Pennsylvania State Library, *Report of the State Librarian, 1898*, 3; U.S. Department of Agriculture, *Papers for Permanent Records*, 15; Stephen and Coutts, *Manual of Library Bookbinding*, 79; Library Association of the United Kingdom, Sound Leather Committee, *Leather for Libraries*, 41; MacAlister, "The Durability of Modern Book Papers," 296; Little, "The Durability of Paper," 115; Veitch, "Suitable Paper for Permanent Records," 264.

21. "Notes on Books and Work," 335; Chivers, "Paper and Binding," 234; U.S. Department of Agriculture, *Papers for Permanent Records*, 9-10.

22. "New York Library Association," 128; Powell, "Book Production in Great Britain," 50; Bliss, "Better Bookbinding for Libraries," *Public Libraries*, 294; Stephen and Coutts, *Manual of Library Bookbinding*, 78.

23. "Notes on Books and Work," 334; U.S. Department of Agriculture, *Papers for Permanent Records*, 11.

24. Little, "The Durability of Paper," 117; Veitch, "Suitable Paper for Permanent Records," 264; Stephen and Coutts, *Manual of Library Bookbinding*, 78; U.S. Department of Agriculture, *Papers for Permanent Records*, 18; "Report of Committee on Bookbinding," 114.

25. Veitch, "Suitable Paper for Permanent Records," 263; MacAlister, "The Durability of Modern Book Papers," 297; Blades, *The Enemies of Books*, 23; U.S. Department of Agriculture, *Papers for Permanent Records*, 15-16.

26. Little, "The Durability of Paper," 116.

27. Veitch, "Suitable Paper for Permanent Records," 263-64; MacAlister, "The Durability of Modern Book Papers," 297; Little, "The Durability of Paper," 117; U.S. Department of Agriculture, *Papers for Permanent Records*, 15.

28. Thomas L. Montgomery, "Report of the Co-Operation Committee," *Library Journal* 24 (July 1899): 94; Library of Congress, *Report, 1897-1898*, 45-46; Bowerman, Cutter, and Bailey, "Report of the Committee on Bookbinding," 132; Franke, "Pressing Danger for our Libraries," 343.

29. "Library Must Depend," 246; Chivers, "Paper and Binding," 233.

30. Chivers, *The Paper of Lending Library Books*, 3-6.

31. "Deterioration of Paper," *Library Journal* 22 (December 1897): 748.

32. Society for the Encouragement of Arts, Manufactures, & Commerce, Committee on the Deterioration of Paper, *Report*, 1-4, 41; Powell, "Book Production in Great Britain," 51.

33. H. W. Wiley, "The Government Leather and Paper Laboratory: Samples of Library Bindings Desired," *Library Journal* 31 (February 1906): 104; Bowerman, Cutter, and Bailey, "Report of the Committee on Bookbinding," 132-33.

34. U.S. Bureau of Chemistry, *Examination of Papers* (Washington, D.C., 1907), 7-8.

35. U.S. Bureau of Chemistry, *Examination of Papers*, 3-5, 9-10.

36. U.S. Department of Agriculture, *Papers for Permanent Records*, 4.

37. Ibid., 10-11.

38. Ibid., 18.

39. Ibid., 17.

40. Ibid., 33.

Chapter 13. Pamphlets, Periodicals, Newspapers, and Maps

1. Cutter, "The Preservation of Pamphlets," 51; Swift, "Pamphlets and Continuations of Serials," 351.

2. Cutter, "The Preservation of Pamphlets," 53; "Pamphlets," *American Library Journal* 1 (30 November 1876): 105; Brookline (Mass.) Public Library, *Annual Report of the Trustees, 1876*, 5.

3. Boston Athenaeum, *Reports of the Library Committee and of the Librarian, 1901*, 5; Harvard University, *Sixth Report of William Coolidge Lane, Librarian, 1903*, 215-16.

4. Bowdoin College Library, *Annual Report of the Librarian, 1891*, 33-34; Francis K. W. Drury, "Protecting Pamphlets," *Library Journal* 35 (March 1910): 118.

5. Cutter, "The Preservation of Pamphlets," 51; Swift, "Pamphlets and Continuations of Serials," 354; "What We Do with Pamphlets," *Library Journal* 14 (November 1889): 433; "What We Do with Pamphlets," *Library Journal* 14 (December 1889): 470-71.

6. Charlotte H. Foye, "The Care of Pamphlets," *Library Journal* 24 (January 1899): 14; Willard Austen, "Pamphlets–What to Do with Them," *Library Journal* 18 (May 1893): 143; Zaidee Brown, "What to Do with Pamphlets," *Library Journal* 32 (August 1907): 358; Columbia College Library, *Second and Third Annual Reports of the Chief Librarian, 1886*, 3.

7. Cutter, "The Preservation of Pamphlets," 51.

8. Ibid.; Brookline (Mass.) Public Library, *Annual Report of the Trustees, 1876*, 4.

9. "Pamphlet Holders," *Library Journal* 5 (September-October 1880): 291-92; Cutter, "The Preservation of Pamphlets," 51; Otis H. Robinson, "Pamphlets," *American Library Journal* 1 (30 November 1876): 102; "What We Do with Pamphlets," 433.

10. "On the Treatment of Pamphlets in Special Libraries," *Library Journal* 5 (June 1880): 167.

11. "Koch Spring Back Binders," *Library Journal* 3 (May 1878): 113; Advertisement for Common-Sense Binder, *Library Journal* 11 (August-September 1886): 397; Drury, "Protecting Pamphlets," 118-19.

12. Foye, "The Care of Pamphlets," 13.

13. Ibid.; East Orange (N.J.) Free Public Library, *Annual Report of the Board of Directors, 1910*, 19; George F. Bowerman, "Some Notes on Binding," *Library Journal* 35 (June 1910): 258-59; B. Pickmann Mann, "The Care of Pamphlets," *Science* 6 (6 November 1885): 407.

14. Robinson, "Pamphlets," 106; Boston Public Library, *Annual Report of the Trustees, 1877*, 61; H. A. Homes, "Unbound Volumes on Library Shelves," *Library Journal* 11 (August-September 1886): 214-15; Spofford, *A Book for All Readers*, 155.

15. Robinson, "Pamphlets," 101-2; Bowdoin College Library, *Annual Report of the Librarian, 1891*, 33-34; "University of Michigan Library (Report)," *Library Journal* 18 (January 1893): 24.

16. Swift, "Pamphlets and Continuations of Serials," 351; Woodard, "Notes on Bookbinding," 237.

17. "What We Do with Pamphlets," 434; Austen, "Pamphlets–What to Do with Them," 143-44; Harvard University, *Sixth Report of William*

Coolidge Lane, Librarian, 1903, 215-16; Robinson, "Pamphlets," 103; Boston Athenaeum, *Reports of the Library Committee and of the Librarian, 1901,* 5; Columbia College Library, *Second and Third Annual Reports of the Chief Librarian, 1886,* 3; Spofford, *A Book for All Readers,* 152.

18. Redwood Library and Athenaeum (Newport, R.I.), *Annual Report of the Directors, 1903,* 14; "A Substitute for Binding Periodicals," *News Notes of California Libraries* 3 (July 1908): 281.

19. Queens Borough (N.Y.) Public Library, *Annual Report of the Board of Trustees, 1904,* 26; *1905,* 18; *1909,* 12.

20. Advertisement for Von Laer's perfect binder, *Library Journal* 5 (January 1880): 30; Chicago Public Library, *Annual Report of the Board of Directors, 1873,* 21; Fanny R. Jackson, "The Care of Periodicals," *Public Libraries* 11 (November 1906): 494.

21. Minneapolis Public Library, *Annual Report, 1910,* 31; Thomas Crane Public Library (Quincy, Mass.), *Annual Report, 1909,* 10; Olin S. Davis, "Binders – Charging System," *Library Journal* 16 (August 1891): 232.

22. F. B. Perkins, "Transferable Book Covers," *Library Journal* 5 (May 1880): 146; "Magazine Punch," *Library Journal* 5 (September-October 1880): 292; Asa D. Dickinson, "A Magazine Campaign," *Public Libraries* 14 (June 1909): 216.

23. Hartford (Conn.) Public Library, *Annual Report of the Directors, 1909,* 10.

24. "Binding Materials," 246; Seattle Public Library, *Report, 1909,* 12; Springfield (Mass.) City Library Association, *Annual Report, 1899,* 31.

25. Wire, "Book Selection, Buying, and Binding," 65; American Library Association, Committee on Bookbinding, *Binding for Small Libraries,* 2; Milwaukee Public Library, *Annual Report of the Board of Trustees, 1878-1879,* 19-20; Pratt Institute, *Report of the Pratt Institute Free Library and School of Library Science, 1906-1907,* 16-17; Wilmington (Del.) Institute, *Annual Report, 1896-1897,* 15.

26. American Library Association, Committee on Bookbinding, *Binding for Small Libraries,* 2.

27. Perkins, "How to Bind Periodicals," 355-56; "Binding and Repair," 82-83; Spofford, *A Book for All Readers,* 85.

28. Hagey, "Binding," 271; Swift, "Pamphlets and Continuations of Serials," 353.

29. J. Schwartz, "Temporary vs. Eternal," *Library Journal* 14 (March 1889): 76.

30. "Preservation of Bound Newspapers," 161; Boston Athenaeum, *Reports of the Library Committee and of the Librarian, 1897,* 3.

31. "The Collection of Newspapers and Society Publications," 80-81; Library of Congress, *Report, 1897-1898,* 45; Pennsylvania State Library,

Report of the State Librarian, 1898, 2; Frank Hill, "The Deterioration of Newspaper Paper," *Library Journal* 35 (July 1910): 299.

32. "Notes on Books and Work," 335; Lawrence (Mass.) Free Public Library, *Annual Report of the Board of Trustees and Librarian, 1876*, 28; Montana Historical Society Library, *Biennial Report of the Librarian, 1903-1904*, 11; Hill, "The Deterioration of Newspaper Paper," 299.

33. Hill, "The Deterioration of Newspaper Paper," 299-301.

34. Jones, "Inaugural Address," 114; Cincinnati Public Library, *Annual Report of the Librarian and Treasurer, 1888-1889*, 9; Eames, "The Care of Special Collections," 51.

35. Utley, "Newspaper Volumes in a Library," 349; Hagey, "Binding," 272; Peabody Institute (Baltimore), *Annual Report of the Provost to the Trustees, 1880*, 9; Pratt Institute, *Report of the Pratt Institute Free Library and School of Library Science, 1902-1903*, 40; Providence Public Library, *Annual Report, 1900*, 21; "Care of Newspapers in the Massachusetts State Library," *Library Journal* 18 (November 1893): 472.

36. American Library Association, Committee on Bookbinding, *Binding for Small Libraries*, 3; Water, "District of Columbia Library Association," 512; Crunden, "How Things Are Done in One American Library," 25; Boston Public Library, *Annual Report of the Trustees, 1891*, 10.

37. Boston Public Library, *Annual Report of the Trustees, 1876*, 10; Harvard University, *Second Report of William Coolidge Lane, Librarian, 1899*, 208.

38. Cincinnati Public Library, *Annual Report of the Librarian and Treasurer, 1886-1887*, 8.

39. Utley, "Newspaper Volumes in a Library," 349; Boston Athenaeum, *Reports of the Library Committee and of the Librarian, 1897*, 3; Brookline (Mass.) Public Library, *Annual Report of the Trustees, 1898*, 18.

40. "Care of Newspapers in the Massachusetts State Library," 472; St. Joseph (Mo.) Free Public Library, *Annual Report, 1901-1902*, 30; Indiana State Library, *Report, 1905-1906*, 24; Boston Public Library, *Annual Report of the Trustees, 1896*, 19.

41. While Harvard typically placed maps in portfolios, Justin Winsor reported binding a group of maps into one hundred volumes. See Harvard University, *Seventh Report of Justin Winsor, Librarian, 1884*.

42. "Notes and Queries," June 1883, 111; Francis H. Parsons, "The Care of Maps," *Library Journal* 20 (June 1895): 199; Francis K. W. Drury, "The Care of Maps," *ALA Bulletin* 2 (September 1908): 348; "How We Keep Unbound Maps," *Library Journal* 16 (March 1891): 72.

43. "How We Keep Unbound Maps," 72-73; "Mounting of Maps," *Library Journal* 18 (January 1893): 25; Sharp, "Library Recipes," 214; Boston Athenaeum, *Reports of the Library Committee and of the Librar-*

ian, 1905, 3; New York Yacht Club Library, *Report of Library Committee, 1905*, 1; Drury, "The Care of Maps," 352.

44. "Varnish for Maps," *Library Journal* 16 (July 1891): 223.

45. "How We Keep Unbound Maps," 72; Drury, "The Care of Maps," 349.

46. Drury, "The Care of Maps," 348; McFarlane, *Library Administration*, 228; J. N. Larned, "Arrangement of Maps," *Library Journal* 17 (July-August 1892): 44; P. Lee Phillips, "Preservation and Record of Maps in the Library of Congress," *Library Journal* 25 (January 1900): 15; Library of Congress, *Report, 1897-1898*, 26; Indiana State Library, *Report, 1901-1902*, 11.

47. "How We Keep Unbound Maps," 72-73; Thomas Letts, "Maps, from the Romantic and Prosaic Standpoints," *Library Journal* 25 (January 1900): 6; Sarah B. Ball, "Maps and Atlases: Their Selection and Care," *Public Libraries* 15 (January 1910): 13; Boston Public Library, *Annual Report of the Trustees, 1899*, 33-34; Bowerman, "Some Notes on Binding," 258-59.

48. "How We Keep Unbound Maps," 72; Larned, "Arrangement of Maps," 44; Drury, "The Care of Maps," 348.

49. Letts, "Maps," 6; Drury, "The Care of Maps," 348; Harvard University Library, *Annual Report, 1907*, 6.

50. "How We Keep Unbound Maps," 74; Boston Public Library, *Annual Report of the Trustees, 1899*, 33.

51. Parsons, "The Care of Maps," 200; Phillips, "Maps in the Library of Congress," 15; Drury, "The Care of Maps," 348, 350-51; P. L. Windsor, "A New Vertical File for Maps," *Public Libraries* 15 (November 1910): 388-89.

52. Parsons, "The Care of Maps," 200; Larned, "Arrangement of Maps," 44; "How We Keep Unbound Maps," 72; Drury, "The Care of Maps," 348; Ball, "Maps and Atlases," 12.

53. Drury, "The Care of Maps," 348-49.

54. Larned, "Arrangement of Maps," 44-45; McFarlane, *Library Administration*, 228; Ball, "Maps and Atlases," 12; Phillips, "Maps in the Library of Congress," 15.

Chapter 14. The Influence of Rare Books, Documents, Manuscripts, and Works of Art on Paper

1. Battershall, *Bookbinding for Bibliophiles*, 6, 8-9; "A New Method of Preserving Old Bookbindings, or of Rebinding Old Books," 208; Spofford, "Binding and Preservation of Books," 677.

2. Davenport, "Bookbinding and Book-Production," 553-55.

3. James L. Gear, "The Repair of Documents–American Beginnings," *American Archivist* 26 (October 1963): 469-72; Marwick, "An Historical Study of Paper Document Restoration Methods," 57, 68, 81-82.

4. Harvard University, *Third Report of William Coolidge Lane, Librarian, 1900,* 237; Herbert Friedenwald to Francis W. R. Emery, 1 May 1899, letter no. 258, Letter Book 1, 1898-1900, 26 April-7 May, Manuscripts Division, Library of Congress.

5. Massachusetts Commission of Public Records, *Third Report on the Custody and Condition of the Public Records of Parishes, Towns, and Counties, 1891,* 111-37; Robert T. Swan, "Paper and Ink," *Library Journal* 20 (May 1895): 163-67; Herbert Friedenwald to Robert T. Swan, 17 April 1899, letter no. 221, Letter Book 1, 1898-1900, 26 April-7 May, Manuscripts Division, Library of Congress; Friedenwald to Swan, 21 December 1899, letter no. 243, Letter Book 1, 1898-1900, 26 April-7 May, Manuscripts Division, Library of Congress.

6. "Specifications for Book Cloths," 120-21; Bailey, "Report of the Committee on Bookbinding," 175-76; "Report of the Committee on Bookbinding," September 1909, 222.

7. In 1906 the Laboratory encouraged librarians to follow the Royal Society of Arts' standard for binding leathers until a U.S. specification might become available (see Bowerman, Cutter, and Bailey, "Report of the Committee on Bookbinding," 133). The laboratory, however, apparently never worked seriously to develop such a specification; it considered paper research its most important work. This is not surprising, since leather had fallen out of favor as a binding material (see Bailey, Cutter, and Wire, "Points Worth Remembering in Rebinding Fiction and Juvenile Books," 11; Post, "Report of the Committee on Public Documents," 138), and the Bureau of Standards had begun to develop its specifications for a book cloth that would replace leather for binding government publications.

8. Wiley, "The Government Leather and Paper Laboratory," 104; Bowerman, Cutter, and Bailey, "Report of the Committee on Bookbinding," 132-33; "Report of Committee on Bookbinding," 114.

9. U.S. Department of Agriculture, *Durability and Economy in Papers for Permanent Records,* 10-11, 13, 18, 30-44; U.S. Bureau of Chemistry, *Examination of Papers*; Veitch, *Paper-Making Materials and Their Conservation.*

10. Montgomery, "Report of the Co-operation Committee," 94.

11. Otto Posse, ed., *Handschriften-Konservirung nach den Verhandlungen der St. Gallener internationalen Konferenz zur Erhaltung und Ausbesserung alter Handschriften von 1898, sowie der dresdener Konferenz deutscher Archivare von 1899* (Dresden: Apollo, 1899), 37; Bowerman, Cutter, and Bailey, "Report of the Committee on Bookbinding," 132; Society for the Encouragement of Arts, Manufactures, & Commerce, Committee on the Deterioration of Paper, *Report,* 4-39; Library of Congress, *Report, 1897-1898,* 45-46, 58-62.

12. For a description of simple cleaning, repair, and mounting techniques, see J. B. Fitzpatrick, *Notes on the Care, Cataloging, Calendaring and Arranging of Manuscripts* (Washington, D.C.: Government Printing Office, 1913).

13. Fitzpatrick, *Notes on Care,* 5, 37; Herbert Friedenwald, "The Care of Manuscripts: A Paper Presented before the American Library Association, Philadelphia, June 25, 1897," 1, Manuscripts Division, Library of Congress.

14. Edward W. B. Nicholson, "Report by Bodley's Librarian to the Curators of the Bodleian, on the Conference Held at St. Gallen, Sept. 30 and Oct. 1, 1898, upon the Preservation and Repair of Old MSS.," The St. Gallen Conference 1898, Library Records c.1429, 22 December 1898, 3, Bodleian Library, Oxford University.

15. Jones, "Inaugural Address," 114; H. J. Plenderleith, *The Conservation of Prints, Drawings, and Manuscripts* (Oxford: Oxford University Press, 1937), 4; Fitzpatrick, *Notes on Care,* 40; Posse, *Handschriften-Konservirung,* 35.

16. Posse, *Handschriften-Konservirung,* 8, 14, 30.

17. "The St. Gall Library Conference of 1898," *Library Journal* 24 (February 1899): 61; Herbert Friedenwald to Franz Ehrle, 1 November 1898, letter no. 124, Letter Book 1, 1898-1900, 26 April-7 May, Manuscripts Division, Library of Congress; Friedenwald to Ehrle, 20 December 1898, letter no. 157, Letter Book 1, 1898-1900, 26 April-7 May, Manuscripts Division, Library of Congress; Friedenwald to Edward W. B. Nicholson, 23 March 1899, letter no. 216, Letter Book 1, 1898-1900, 26 April-7 May, Manuscripts Division, Library of Congress; Friedenwald to Nicholson, 17 April 1899, letter no. 222, Letter Book 1, 1898-1900, 26 April-7 May, Manuscripts Division, Library of Congress.

18. Although Zapon was publicly presented as a paper preservative for the first time at the International Conference for the Preservation and Restoration of Manuscripts, it was initially used for this purpose by the Saxony Royal War Ministry to keep maps and documents dry in the field. Thus, nitrocellulose could be said to have originated as a substance for use in document preservation. See Posse, *Handschriften-Konservirung,* 15.

19. Nicholson, "Report by Bodley's Librarian," 16-17, 9-10.

20. David G. Vaisey, "E. W. B. Nicholson and the St. Gall Conference, 1898," *Bodleian Library Record* 9 (March 1974): 107; Nicholson, "Report by Bodley's Librarian," 10; Posse, *Handschriften-Konservirung,* 35.

21. Posse, *Handschriften-Konservirung,* 35-36, 50-51.

22. "Preservation of Manuscripts," 64; "Paper Preservation," 528; Nicholson, "Report by Bodley's Librarian," 12-13; Arnold J. F. Van Laer,"The Work of the International Congress of Archivists and Librarians

at Brussels, August 28-31, 1910," in *Annual Report of the American Historical Association, 1910* (Washington, D.C.: Government Printing Office, 1912), 291; Herbert Friedenwald to H. O. Collins, 10 December 1900, letter no. 450, Letter Book 1, 1898-1900, 26 April-7 May, Manuscripts Division, Library of Congress; Marwick, "An Historical Study of Paper Document Restoration Methods," 64-65; Vaisey, "Nicholson and the St. Gall Conference," 113.

23. Marwick, "An Historical Study of Paper Document Restoration Methods," 53, 64-65, 99-103; Nicholson, "Report by Bodley's Librarian," 11-12; Fitzpatrick, *Notes on Care*, 39; C. H. Lincoln to the Librarian of Congress, letter no. 149, "The Repair of Manuscripts," Memorandums to Librarian, vol. 2, 1900-1902, 20 April-11 October, Manuscripts Division, Library of Congress; "Proceedings of the Seventh Annual Conference of Historical Societies," in *Annual Report of the American Historical Association, 1910* (Washington, D.C.: Government Printing Office, 1912), 248-50.

24. Boston Public Library, *Annual Report of the Trustees, 1896*, 440; Waldo G. Leland, "The Application of Photography to Archive and Historical Work," in *Annual Report of the American Historical Association, 1908* (Washington, D.C.: Government Printing Office, 1909), 159-60.

25. Henry Wilson, "Remarks on Facsimile Reproduction," *Monthly Notes of the Library Association* 1 (15 May 1880): 40; John Fretwell, "Photographic Copying in Libraries," *Library Journal* 33 (June 1908): 224; McFarlane, *Library Administration*, 200-203.

26. "The Loan of Rare Books," *Library Journal* 5 (July-August 1880): 217-18; O. Hartwig, "The Interchange of Manuscripts between Libraries," *Library Journal* 18 (December 1893): 505; "The Autotype Reproduction of Greek, Latin, and Other Manuscripts," *Library Journal* 20 (March 1895): 87-88; "The Autotype Reproduction of Greek, Latin, and Other Manuscripts," *Library Journal* 20 (June 1895): 205; "Facsimiles of Rare Manuscripts," *Library Journal* 21 (March 1896): 91-92; W. Du Rieu, "For the Reproduction of Rare Manuscripts," *Library Journal* 21 (March 1896): 92; "Pennsylvania Library Association," *Library Journal* 21 (March 1896): 108; "Autotype Reproduction of Rare Manuscripts," *Library Journal* 21 (May 1896): 230; Charles M. Gayley, "An Account of the Proceedings of the International Congress for the Reproduction of Manuscripts," in *Report of the Commisioner of Education, 1905*, 2 vols. (Washington, D.C.: Government Printing Office, 1907), 1: 133-34.

27. Gayley, "International Congress," 135-36; "Reproductions of Ancient Manuscripts," *Library Journal* 24 (July 1899): 125-26.

28. Gayley, "International Congress," 1: 137; "The St. Gall Library Conference of 1898," 61; "Reproductions of Ancient Manuscripts," 125-26; Vaisey, "Nicholson and the St. Gall Conference," 101.

29. Gayley, "International Congress," 1:138; Biagi, "The Library," 13.

30. Gayley, "International Congress," 1:131, 136, 138-40; "International Congress on Facsimiles," *New York Evening Post,* 6 September 1905, Saturday Supplement sec., 6.

31. Gayley, "International Congress," 1:141-42; "International Congress on Facsimiles," 6; "Reproduction of Manuscripts," *Library Journal* 30 (December 1905): 929.

32. "Cards for Photographic Reprints," *ALA Bulletin* 2 (March 1908): 17; Vaisey, "Nicholson and the St. Gall Conference," 108.

33. Plenderleith, *The Conservation of Prints, Drawings, and Manuscripts,* 1.

34. Ibid., 2-3.

35. Joseph Meder, *The Mastery of Drawing,* 2 vols. (New York: Abaris Books, 1978), 1:495; Plenderleith, *The Conservation of Prints, Drawings, and Manuscripts,* 21-27; Alexander, *Museums in Motion,* 9, 151-52; Norman S. Brommelle, "Material for a History of Conservation," *Studies in Conservation* 2 (October 1956): 177.

36. Haslam, *The Book of Trade Secrets*; Plenderleith, *The Conservation of Prints, Drawings, and Manuscripts*; Alfred Bonnardot, *Essai sur l'art de restaurer les estampes et les livres, ou traité sur les meilleurs procédés pour blanchir, détacher, décolorier, réparer et conserver les estampes, livres et dessins* (Paris, 1858); "Removal of Grease Spots from Books and Engravings," 123.

37. Plenderleith, *The Conservation of Prints, Drawings, and Manuscripts,* 40; Haslam, *Book of Trade Secrets,* 10; Meder, *The Mastery of Drawing,* 1:505.

38. "Removal of Grease Spots," 123; "Cleaning Prints and Printed Papers," *Library Journal* 13 (July 1888): 228; "Removing Stains from Prints," *Library Journal* 27 (October 1902): 910; "Cleaning Old Prints," *Wisconsin Library Bulletin* 3 (December 1907): 97-98; Meder, *The Mastery of Drawing,* 1:507; Plenderleith, *The Conservation of Prints, Drawings, and Manuscripts,* 45-54; Haslam, *Book of Trade Secrets,* 10-11, 21-22.

39. Meder, *The Mastery of Drawing,* 1:507, 509; Plenderleith, *The Conservation of Prints, Drawings, and Manuscripts,* 55-56.

40. Meder, *The Mastery of Drawing,* 1:508; Plenderleith, *The Conservation of Prints, Drawings, and Manuscripts,* 34-39.

41. Marilyn K. Weidner, "Damage and Deterioration of Art on Paper Due to Ignorance and the Use of Faulty Materials," *Studies in Conservation* 12 (February 1967): 5.

42. The Louvre was fully opened in 1801. It was followed by the National Gallery (London), established in 1824; the Berlin museum center (developed between 1830 and 1930); and the Metropolitan Museum of Art (New York) and the Museum of Fine Arts (Boston), 1870. The Philadelphia

Museum of Art and the Art Institute (Chicago) were also established in the 1870s. See Alexander, *Museums in Motion*, 23-31, 141.

43. Brommelle, "Material for a History of Conservation," 184; Alexander, *Museums in Motion*, 148.

44. Nicholson, "Report by Bodley's Librarian," 11.

45. Weidner, "Damage and Deterioration of Art on Paper," 5.

Chapter 15. Looking Forward, Looking Back: 1910

1. R. Kathleen Molz, *The Knowledge Institutions in the Information Age: The Special Case of the Public Library: An Engelhard Lecture on the Book, Presented on April 7, 1987, at the Library of Congress*, Center for the Book Viewpoint Series, no. 2 (Washington, D.C.: Library of Congress, 1988), 12.

2. See the Appendix to this book, a timeline of milestones in preservation from 1842 to 1910.

3. "Verein deutscher Bibliothekare: Verhandlungen und Vorträge auf der 2. Jahres-Versammlung, Gotha, den 30. und 31. Mai 1901," *Zentralblatt für Bibliothekswesen* 18 (August-September 1901): 337-80; Montgomery, "Report of the Co-operation Committee," 94.

4. Chivers, "The Other Side of the Bookbinding Controversy," 444-45; Chivers, "The Paper and Binding of Lending Library Books," 231-59; Nicholson, "On Buckram as a Binding Material," *American Library Journal*, 207-9; Nicholson, "The Use of Buckram, Linoleum, and Cretonne for Binding," 304-5.

5. "The Autotype Reproduction of Greek, Latin, and Other Manuscripts," March 1895, 87-88; Fretwell, "Photographic Copying in Libraries," 223-24; "The Zapon Conference in Dresden," *Library Journal* 25 (January 1900): 19; Hill, "The Deterioration of Newspaper Paper," 299-301; "Preservation of Manuscripts," 64; "Paper Preservation," *Library Journal* 35 (November 1910): 528; Hartwig, "The Interchange of Manuscripts between Libraries," 503-505.

6. Biagi, "A Note on Italian Library Affairs," 57-60; Biagi, "The Library: Its Past and Future," 8-15; "Turin, Italy. National L.," 308.

7. Edward B. Nicholson and Henry R. Tedder, eds., *Transactions and Proceedings of the Conference of Librarians Held in London October, 1877* (London: printed at Chiswick Press by Charles Whittingham, 1878); "International Congress on Facsimiles," 6; Gayley, "An Account of the Proceedings of the International Congress for the Reproduction of Manuscripts," 1:131-42; Van Laer, "The Work of the International Congress of Archivists and Librarians at Brussels, August 28-31, 1910," 282-92.

8. Blades, *The Enemies of Books*; Cockerell, *Bookbinding and the Care of Books*; Coutts and Stephen, *Manual of Library Bookbinding*; Zaehnsdorf, *The Art of Bookbinding*.

9. Lehmann-Haupt, *Edition Bookbinding in America*, 137, 163-68. Interestingly, America later gained the ascendancy as British librarians requested that English manufacturers meet the cloth standards established by the U.S. Bureau of Standards. See Stephen, "Book-Cloths," 5-7; Stephen, "Publishers' Binding," 12-13; Stephen, *Commercial Bookbinding*, 57.

10. "Notes and Queries," 40; Bliss, "Better Bookbinding for Libraries," *Public Libraries*, 299; Rathbone, "A Trained Person in Charge of Condition of Books," 236; Brooklyn Public Library, *Annual Report of the Board of Directors, 1905*, 24-25, 38; East Orange (N.J.) Free Public Library, *Annual Report of the Board of Directors, 1905*, 20; Haverhill (Mass.) Public Library, *Annual Report, 1906*, 27; Newark (N.J.) Free Public Library, *Annual Report of the Board of Trustees, 1903*, 37; Queens Borough (N.Y.) Public Library, *Annual Report of the Board of Trustees, 1905*, 19; St. Louis Public Library, *Annual Report, 1907-1908*, 33.

11. "The Birmingham Fire," 19-20; "The Prevention of Fires in Libraries," 52-54; Spofford, *A Book for All Readers*, 107; Boston Public Library, *Annual Report of the Trustees, 1879*, 19.

12. Seymour-Jones, "On the Glazing of Libraries," 641-46; Royal Society of Arts, Committee on Leather for Bookbinding, *Report*, 69-70; Library of Congress, *Report, 1901-1902*, 31-32; Green, "Library Buildings and Book Stacks," 55.

13. "British Museum: Further Reforms," 101-2; "Electric Light," *Library Journal* 4 (31 March 1879): 102.

14. Royal Society of Arts, Committee on Leather for Bookbinding, *Report*; Ranck, "Leather for Bookbinding," 681-84; Powell, "Book Production in Great Britain," 50-54; Pratt Institute, *Report of the Pratt Institute Free Library and School of Library Science, 1906-1907*, 17; Library Association of the United Kingdom, Sound Leather Committee, *Leather for Libraries*; "Bookbinding," *Library Journal* 30 (November 1905): 848.

15. "Deterioration of Paper," 748; Society for the Encouragement of Arts, Manufactures, & Commerce, Committee on the Deterioration of Paper, *Report*; "After All, the Library Must Depend upon the Book and the Book Must Be Made of Paper," 246; Chivers, "The Paper and Binding of Lending Library Books," 231-59; Chivers, *The Paper of Lending Library Books*.

16. Royal Society of Arts, Committee on Leather for Bookbinding, *Report*, 34-36; Pollard, "Notes on Books and Work," 330-36; Cockerell, *Bookbinding and the Care of Books*, 308-11.

17. Atkinson, "Fire-Proof Wood," 26.

18. Biagi, "The Library," 13.

19. Gould, "Co-ordination, or Method in Co-operation," 122-28.

20. Charles A. Cutter, "The Buffalo Public Library in 1983," *Library Journal* 8 (September-October 1883): 211-12.

21. Ibid., 215.

22. Ibid., 215-16.

23. Biagi, "The Library," 8-15.

24. Henderson and Krupp, "The Librarian as Conservator," 178; A. E. Kimberley and B. W. Scribner, *Summary Report of Bureau of Standards Research on Preservation of Records* (Washington, D.C.: Government Printing Office, 1934); "Specifications for Library Binding," *Library Journal* 60 (1 January 1935): 18-20.

25. Randolph G. Adams, "Librarians as Enemies of Books," *Library Quarterly* 7 (July 1937): 317-31; W. H. Gordon, "The Preservation of Books," *Librarian and Book World* 21 (July 1932): 315-16; "Preservation of Records in Libraries," *Librarian and Book World* 24 (September 1934): 11-12; D. B. Gilchrist, "Death and Destruction on Library Shelves," *Medical Library Association Bulletin* 24 (December 1935): 100-104.

26. Fussler, *Photographic Reproduction for Libraries*; William J. Barrow, "Barrow Method of Laminating Documents," *Journal of Documentary Reproduction* 2 (June 1939): 147-51.

27. Archibald MacLeish, "Library of Congress Protects Its Collections," *ALA Bulletin* 36 (February 1942): 74-75; J. Orne, "Library of Congress Prepares for Emergencies," *ALA Bulletin* 35 (June 1941): 341-48; J. Foley, "Preservation of Cultural Resources in a Time of War," *Maine Library Association Bulletin* 3 (May 1942): 9-10.

28. Pelham Barr, "Book Conservation and University Library Administration," *College and Research Libraries* 7 (July 1946): 214-19.

29. Gwinn, "CLR and Preservation," 105-7; Howard S. White and Herbert L. Hanna, "Library Technology Program," *Encyclopaedia of Library and Information Science* (1975), vol. 16, 96-100; Darling and Ogden, "From Problems Perceived to Programs in Practice," 11; Gordon Williams, *The Preservation of Deteriorating Books: An Examination of the Problems with Recommendations for a Solution* (Washington, D. C.: Association of Research Libraries, 1964); Church, *Deterioration of Book Stock: Causes and Remedies: Two Studies on the Permanence of Book Paper Conducted by W. J. Barrow*.

30. Edmond L. Applebaum, "Implications of the National Register of Microform Masters as Part of a National Preservation Program," *Library Resources and Technical Services* 9 (Fall 1965): 489-94.

31. "Salvaging Miles of Sodden Books," *Life* 61 (16 December 1966): 34-35; "Disaster Aid Made Available to Flood-Stricken Libraries," *Library Journal* 97 (1 November 1972): 3528-30; "Temple University Library Destroyed by Fire," *Library Journal* 97 (15 September 1972): 2796-97;

D. Dempsey, "Operation Booklift: Restoring the Library at the Jewish Theological Seminary of America," *Saturday Review* 50 (15 April 1969): 39-41.

32. Pamela W. Darling, "Our Fragile Inheritance: The Challenge of Preserving Library Materials," in *ALA Yearbook, 1978* (Chicago: American Library Association, 1978), xxxii.

33. Norman J. Shaffer, "Library of Congress Pilot Preservation Project," *College and Research Libraries* 30 (January 1969): 5-11; Warren J. Haas, *Preparation of Detailed Specifications for a National System for the Preservation of Library Materials* (Washington: Association of Research Libraries, 1972).

34. Darling and Ogden, "From Problems to Programs," 20, 22; Walter Brahm, "A Regional Approach to Conservation: The New England Document Conservation Center," *American Archivist* 40 (October 1977): 421-27.

35. George Kelly, "Mass Deacidification," Conference on the Preservation of Library Materials, Rutgers University, 20-21 July 1979.

36. Paul N. Banks, "Preservation of Library Materials," in *Encyclopaedia of Library and Information Science* (1978), vol. 23, 181.

37. Stange, "Millions of Books Are Turning to Dust," 38.

38. Council on Library Resources, *The Commission on Preservation and Access*; "An Appeal to Preserve Old Books," C28.

39. "An Appeal," C28.

40. Hosmer, *Presence of the Past*, 22, 25, 35-36, 41-62, 103-6; John S. Pyke, Jr., *Landmark Preservation*, 2d ed. (New York: Citizens Union Research Foundation, Inc., of the City of New York, 1972), 7-11.

41. Pyke, *Landmark Preservation*, 7.

Bibliography

Primary Sources

Journals, Newspapers, Proceedings, and Reports

"A. L. A. Library Primer (under revision)." *Public Libraries* 1 (June 1896): 39-45.

"Action of Electric Lights on Paper." *Library Journal* 12 (September-October 1887): 428-29.

Adams, Randolph G. "Librarians as Enemies of Books." *Library Quarterly* 7 (July 1937): 317-31.

"Adhesive Paper." *Library Journal* 3 (May 1878): 135.

Advertisement for Adjustable Book Covers. *Library Journal* 20 (April 1895): 152.

Advertisement for Cedric Chivers, Bookbinder. *Library Journal* 30 (May 1905): 317.

Advertisement for Chivers's Patent Bindings. *Library Journal* 30 (November 1905): 901.

Advertisement for Common-Sense Binder. *Library Journal* 11 (August-September 1886): 397.

Advertisement for Library Bureau Book Support. *Library Journal* 19 (February 1894): 40.

Advertisement for Library Bureau Steel Stack. *Library Journal* 20 (April 1895): 146-47.

Advertisement for the Boston Stack. *Library Journal* 21 (April 1896): 199.

Advertisement for the Holden System for Preserving Books. *Library Journal* 20 (April 1895): 144.

Advertisement for the Holden System for Preserving Books. *Library Journal* 32 (April 1907): lxxi.

Advertisement for the Yale Book Support. *Library Journal* 23 (October 1898): 595.

Advertisement for Von Laer's Perfect Binder. *Library Journal* 5 (January 1880): 30.

Advertisement for Wales' Improved Bookbinding. *Library Journal* 25 (January 1900): 50.

"After All, the Library Must Depend upon the Book and the Book Must Be Made of Paper." *Library Journal* 34 (June 1909): 246.

Aldred, Thomas. "An Appeal to Publishers." *Library* 7 (November 1895): 385.

"American Libraries: Chicago, Ill. John Crerar L." *Library Journal* 34 (April 1909): 183-84.

"American Library Association." *Library Journal* 30 (May 1905): 289-94.

"American Library Association Committee on Binding." *Library Journal* 34 (September 1909): 411-13.

"American Library Association Committee on Binding.: *Library Journal* 34 (October 1909): 452.

"Appeal of a State Librarian." *Library Journal* 8 (May 1883): 72.

"An Appeal to Preserve Old Books." *New York Times*, 5 March 1987, sec. C, 28.

Applebaum, Edmond L. "Implications of the National Register of Microform Masters as Part of a National Preservation Program." *Library Resources and Technical Services* 9 (Fall 1965): 489-94.

Ashley, Grace. "A Binding Exhibition." *Public Libraries* 10 (July 1905): 357-59.

Askew, Sarah B. "Problems of a Small Town Library." *Library Journal* 31 (October 1906): 705-8.

"Association Bindings." *American Library Journal* 2 (31 August 1877): 432.

Atkinson, E. "Fire-Proof Wood." *American Architect and Building News* 77 (6 September 1902): 75-78.

Austen, Willard. "Bookworms in Fact and Fancy." *Popular Science Monthly* 55 (June 1899): 240-48.

_____. "Pamphlets–What to Do with Them." *Library Journal* 18 (May 1893): 143-44.

"The Autotype Reproduction of Greek, Latin, and Other Manuscripts." *Library Journal* 20 (March 1895): 87-88.

"The Autotype Reproduction of Greek, Latin, and Other Manuscripts." *Library Journal* 20 (June 1895): 205.

"Autotype Reproduction of Rare Manuscripts." *Library Journal* 21 (May 1896): 230.

Bailey, Arthur L. "Committee on Bookbinding." *Library Journal* 35 (May 1910): 211.

_____. "'Note on Bookbinding.'" *Library Journal* 32 (January 1907): 48.

_____. "Report of the Committee on Bookbinding." *ALA Bulletin* 2 (September 1908): 173-76.

Bailey, Arthur L.; Cutter, William P.; and Wire, George E. "Bookbinding Committee." *Library Journal* 33 (February 1908): 58.

_____. "Notes from A. L. A. Committee on Bookbinding." *Public Libraries* 12 (May 1907): 186-87.

_____. "Points Worth Remembering in Rebinding Fiction and Juvenile Books." *ALA Bulletin* 1 (March 1907): 10-12.

Bailey, J. B. "The Library of the Royal College of Surgeons of England." *Library* 1 (1889): 249-61.

Ball, Sarah B. "Maps and Atlases: Their Selection and Care." *Public Libraries* 15 (January 1910): 11-15.

Barr, Pelham. "Book Conservation and University Library Administration." *College and Research Libraries* 7 (July 1946): 214-19.

Barrett, Francis T. "Note on the Manner of Binding Adopted by the Mitchell Library." *Library Association Transactions* 4-5 (1881-1882): 185-86.

Barrow, William J. "Barrow Method of Laminating Documents," *Journal of Documentary Reproduction* 2 (June 1939): 147-51.

Barry, Redmond. "On Binding." *American Library Journal* 2 (November-December 1877): 203-7.

Beardsley, Emma C. "More about Clean Books." *Public Libraries* 10 (May 1905): 224.

"Before Rebinding." *Library Journal* 5 (July-August 1880): 214-15.

"Best Light for Libraries." *Library Journal* 17 (December 1892): 501.

"Better Bookmaking for Libraries." *Library Journal* 18 (May 1893): 142.

Biagi, Guido. "The Library: Its Past and Future." *Library Journal* 29 (December 1904): 8-15.

_____. "A Note on Italian Library Affairs." *Library Journal* 29 (December 1904): 57-60.

"Bindery Notes." *Library Journal* 20 (August 1895): 280.

"Binding." *American Library Journal* 1 (30 November 1876): 124.

"Binding." *Library Journal* 11 (August-September 1886): 373-76.

"Binding." *Library Journal* 16 (December 1891): 83-85.

"Binding." *Library Journal* 17 (July-August 1892): 62.

"Binding and Repair." *Library Journal* 18 (September 1893): 82-83.

"Binding: Digest of Answers to a Circular." *Library Association Transactions* 4-5 (1881-82): 243-50.

"Binding for Libraries." *Public Libraries* 12 (October 1907): 310-11.

"Binding in Building." *American Library* Journal 2 (January-February 1878): 308-9.

"Binding in Duck." *Library Journal* 10 (September-October 1885): 346-47.

"Binding in the Building." *Library Journal* 10 (September-October 1885): 345-50.

"Binding Kit." *Public Libraries* 12 (June 1907): 237.

"Binding Materials." *Library Journal* 31 (May 1906): 246.

"The Birmingham Fire." *Library Journal* 4 (January 1879): 19-20.

"The Birmingham Library." *Athenaeum*, 18 January 1879, 89.

Biscoe, Ellen D. "Bookbinding of Our American Publishers." *Library Journal* 24 (October 1899): 561-63.

Bliss, Henry E. "Better Bookbinding for Libraries." *Library Journal* 30 (November 1905): 849-57.

_____. "Better Bookbinding for Libraries." *Public Libraries* 11 (June 1906): 294-99.

_____. Review of *Report of the Committee on Leather for Bookbinding*, by the Royal Society of Arts' Committee on Leather for Bookbinding, and *Notes on Bookbinding for Libraries*, by John C. Dana. In *Library Journal* 31 (October 1906): 737-39.

"Book Binding Boycott in New York." *Library Journal* 33 (October 1908): 395-96.

"Book-Binding Committee." *ALA Bulletin* 1 (January 1907): 8-9.

"A Book-Dusting Machine." *Library Journal* 29 (February 1904): 99.

"Book Mark." *Public Libraries* 11 (January 1906): 21.

"Book Support." *Library Journal* 3 (March 1878): 35.

"Book Supports." *Library Journal* 3 (July 1878): 192.

"Book Supports." *Library Journal* 10 (September-October 1885): 311-12.

"Book Surgery in Libraries." *Public Libraries* 11 (June 1906): 311-12.

"Book-Wash and Varnish." *Library Journal* 7 (June 1882): 111.

"A Book Worm." *Library Journal* 10 (June 1885): 131.

"Bookbinders Recommended by Indiana Librarians." *Library Occurrent* 2 (October 1908): 17.

"Bookbinding." *ALA Bulletin* 3 (January 1909): 9.

"Bookbinding." *Library Journal* 30 (November 1905): 848.

"Bookbinding for Libraries." *Library Journal* 30 (August 1905): 499.

"The Bookbinding Question Raised in New York." *Library Journal* 33 (November 1908): 428.

"Bookbindings and Book Papers." *Library Journal* 31 (August 1906): 281.

"Bookbuying." *ALA Bulletin* 4 (May 1910): 524-25.

"Bookworms." *Library Journal* 11 (July 1886): 191.

"Bookworms." *Library Journal* 12 (April 1887): 174.

Bowerman, George F. "Committee on Bookbinding and Book Papers." *Library Journal* 30 (September 1905): 146-47.

_____. "'Note on Bookbinding.'" *Library Journal* 31 (December 1906): 852.

_____. "Some Notes on Binding." *Library Journal* 35 (June 1910): 258-59.

Bowerman, George F.; Cutter, William P.; and Bailey, Arthur L. "Report of the Committee on Bookbinding." *Library Journal* 31 (August 1906): 130-39.

Boyer, Jacques. "The Insect Enemies of Books." *Scientific American* 98 (6 June 1908): 413-14.

Brahm, Walter. "A Regional Approach to Conservation: The New England Document Conservation Center." *American Archivist* 40 (October 1977): 421-27.

"British Museum: Further Reforms." *Library Journal* 4 (31 March 1879): 101-2.

Brown, Zaidee. "What to Do with Pamphlets." *Library Journal* 32 (August 1907): 358-60.

Browne, Frank. "The Preservation of Books in Hot Climates." *Scientific American,* suppl. 56 (15 August 1903): 23095.

Browne, William H. "Bindings Deteriorated without Gas." *Library Journal* 5 (February 1880): 50.

"Buckram Bindings." *American Library Journal* 1 (31 July 1877): 410.

"Buckram for Bindings." *American Library Journal* 2 (September 1877): 34.

"Bulletin of A. L. A. Committee on Bookbuying." *ALA Bulletin* 2 (January 1908): 5-6.

"Bulletins of the A. L. A. Committee on Book Prices." *Library Journal* 29 (August 1904): 424-25.

"Bulletins on Book Buying." *Library Journal* 31 (September 1906): 696.

"Bulletins on Book Buying." *Library Journal* 32 (January 1907): 48.

"Cards for Photographic Reprints." *ALA Bulletin* (March 1908): 17.

"Care of Newspapers in the Massachusetts State Library." *Library Journal* 18 (November 1893): 472.

Carney, Frank. "Some Problems of a Shelf Department." *Library Journal* 33 (November 1908): 433-37.

Carr, Henry J. "Fixtures, Furniture, and Fittings." In *U.S. Office of Education Annual Report, 1892-1893*, 733-43.

Carroll, Annie. "Library Membership as a Civic Force." *Library Journal* 7 (July 1908): 269-74.

Chance, F. "Preservation of Bookbindings." *Notes and Queries*, 7th ser., 2 (4 December 1886): 444.

"A Children's Book Mark." *Library Journal* 22 (April 1897): 199.

"The Children's 'Story' Bookmark." *Library Journal* 22 (May 1897): 257.

Chivers, Cedric. "How to Open a New Book." *Library*, 2d ser., 1 (1 June 1900): 323-26.

_____. "The Other Side of the Bookbinding Controversy." *Library Journal* 33 (November 1908): 444-45.

_____. "The Paper and Binding of Lending Library Books." *ALA Bulletin* 3 (September 1909): 231-59.

Church, A. H. "Destruction of Leather by Gas." *Chemical News* 36 (19 October 1877): 179.

Clark, George T. "Lessons as to Construction from the San Francisco Fire." *Public Libraries* 12 (July 1907): 255-57.

"Cleaning Old Prints." *Wisconsin Library Bulletin* 3 (December 1907): 97-98.

"Cleaning Prints and Printed Papers." *Library Journal* 13 (July 1888): 228.

"Cloth as a Book Binding Material." *Library Journal* 31 (January 1906): 43.

Cockerell, Douglas. "Leather for Bookbinding." *Journal of the Society of Arts* 48 (30 March 1900): 401-11.

"The Collection of Newspapers and Society Publications." *Library Journal* 18 (March 1893): 80-81.

"Colors in Binding." *Library Journal* 10 (September-October 1885): 339-41.

"Committee on Binding." *Library Journal* 34 (May 1909): 223-34.

"Committee on Binding." *Library Journal* 35 (March 1910): 122.

"Committee on Bookbinding." *Library Journal* 32 (February 1907): 76.

"Committee on Bookbuying." *Library Journal* 33 (February 1908): 58-59.

"Committee on Bookbuying." *Library Journal* 33 (April 1908): 152-53.

"Corrugated Paper Boxes." *Library Journal* 21 (July 1896): 342.

Coutts, Henry T. "The Home Bindery or Repairing Department." *Library World* 9 (January 1907): 233-36.

"Covering Paper." *Library Journal* 4 (January 1879): 14.

Cramer, Katharine D. "Methods for Keeping Books Clean." *Wisconsin Library Bulletin* 1 (June 1905): 66.

"Crocker Book-Support." *Library Journal* 12 (January-February 1887): 85.

"The Croton Bug as a Library Pest." *Library Journal* 4 (September-October 1879): 376-77.

Crunden, Frederick M. "Exclusion of Badly Made Books." *Library Journal* 24 (March 1899): 98.

_____. "How Things Are Done in One American Library." *Library*, n.s., 2 (1 January 1901): 20-43.

Cutter, Charles A. "The Buffalo Public Library in 1983." *Library Journal* 8 (September-October 1883): 211-17.

_____. "The Preservation of Pamphlets." *American Library Journal* 1 (30 November 1876): 51-54.

Dana, John C. "Binding for a Public Library." *Public Libraries* 7 (April 1902): 147-48.

_____. "What Exhibitions Can Do." *Printing Art* 11 (June 1908): 215-24.

"Dangers from Electric Light." *Library Journal* 5 (May 1880): 153.

Davenport, Cyril. "Bookbinding and Book-production." *Library Association Record* 7 (November 1905): 553-55.

_____. "Leather as Used in Bookbinding." *Library* 10 (1898): 15-19.

_____. "Leathers Used in Bookbinding." *Transactions of the Bibliographical Society* 5 (1899): 161-62.

_____. "Library Bookbinding." *Library Association Record* 5 (January 1903): 5-15.

Davis, Cecil T. "Insurance of Public Libraries." *Library World* 2 (November 1899): 121-22.

Davis, Olin S. "Binders – Charging System." *Library Journal* 16 (August 1891): 232.

"December Meeting." *Library Assistant* 1 (January 1901): 171-73.

"Defacing of Books." *American Library Journal* 1 (31 January 1877): 194.

Dempsey, D. "Operation Booklift: Restoring the Library at the Jewish Theological Seminary of America." *Saturday Review* 50 (15 April 1969): 39-41.

"Destruction of San Francisco and Other California Libraries." *Library Journal* 31 (May 1906): 213-15.

"The Deterioration of Bindings." *Library Journal* 3 (August 1878): 229.

"Deterioration of Paper." *Library Journal* 22 (December 1897): 748.

Dewey, Melvil. "Bindery in Building." *Public Libraries* 8 (November 1903): 405.

_____. "Book Braces, Supports, or Props." *Library Notes* 1 (December 1886): 214-23.

_____. "Buckram and Morocco." *Library Journal* 11 (June 1886): 161-62.

_____. "Doors on Bookcases." *Library Notes* 2 (September 1887): 112-14.

_____. "Heating Libraries." *Library Journal* 6 (April 1881): 93-96.

_____. "Pamphlets Ruined by Rolling." *Library Journal* 16 (July 1891): 202.

_____. "School of Library Economy at Columbia College." *Library Journal* 9 (July 1884): 117-20.

Dickinson, Asa D. "A Magazine Campaign." *Public Libraries* 14 (June 1909): 215-16.

"The Disadvantages of Wire-Sewing and the Necessity for Prohibiting It." *Library* 10 (1898): 255-58.

"Disaster Aid Made Available to Flood-Stricken Libraries." *Library Journal* 97 (1 November 1972): 3528-30.

"Disinfection." *Library Journal* 13 (March-April 1888): 105-6.

Dodd, Helen P. "The Care of Books in a Children's Room." *Public Libraries* 12 (March 1907): 83-86.

Dousman, Mary E. "Children's Departments." *Library Journal* 21 (September 1896): 406-8.

_____. "Methods of Inducing Care of Books–I." *Library Journal* 25 (August 1900): 60-62.

Drury, Francis K. W. "The Care of Maps." *ALA Bulletin* 2 (September 1908): 347-55.

_____. "Labor Savers in Library Service." *Library Journal* 35 (December 1910): 538-44.

_____. "Protecting Pamphlets." *Library Journal* 35 (March 1910): 118-19.

Du Rieu, W. "For the Reproduction of Rare Manuscripts." *Library Journal* 21 (March 1896): 92.

"Durability of Leather." *Scientific American* 100 (17 April 1909): 292.

"'Duro-Flexible' Bindings." *Library Journal* 11 (June 1886): 166.

"Duro-Flexible Bookbinding." *Library Journal* 12 (January-February 1887): 70-71.

"Dust." *Library Journal* 4 (April 1893): 122.

"The Dust Problem in Libraries." *Library World*, n.s., 9 (January 1907): 242.

Eames, Wilberforce. "The Care of Special Collections." *Library Journal* 22 (October 1897): 48-52.

Eastman, Linda. "The Library and the Children; An Account of the Children's Work in the Cleveland Public Library." *Library Journal* (April 1898): 142-44.

Editorial. *Library Journal* 7 (March 1882): 43.

"The Effect of Illuminating Gas on Leather." *Scientific American*, suppl. 67 (1 May 1909): 287.

"Electric Light." *Library Journal* 4 (31 March 1879): 102.

"The Electric Light at the British Museum." *Library Journal* 5 (June 1880): 171.

"The Electric Light in the British Museum Reading Room." *Chemical News* 39 (7 March 1879): 101-102.

"Electric Lighting." *Library Journal* 12 (July 1887): 270.

"Electric Lights." *Library Journal* 10 (September-October 1885): 333-35.

Eliot, Charles W. "The Division of a Library into Books in Use, and Books Not in Use, with Different Storage Methods for the Two Classes of Books." *Library Journal* 27 (July 1902): 51-56.

Emands, John. "Report on Library Architecture." *Library Journal* 8 (September-October 1883): 201-3.

"The Enemies of Books." *Scientific American*, suppl. 6 (24 August 1878): 2200-2201, 2282.

"Enforcing Cleanliness in Public Libraries." *Library Journal* 15 (September 1890): 260.

"Facsimiles of Rare Manuscripts." *Library Journal* 21 (March 1896): 91-92.

Field, Clara. "Book Repairing." *News Notes of California Libraries* 2 (February 1907): 105-8.

Field, Kirke H. "Binding and Other Workroom Problems." *News Notes of California Libraries* 5 (July 1910): 371-72.

"Fire Protection of Public Libraries." *American Architect* 30 (11 October 1890): 26.

"Fires – The Repair of Books." *American Library Journal* 2 (September 1877): 22-23.

Fletcher, William I. "Economy of Shelf Room." *Library Journal* 15 (May 1890): 134-35.

_____. "The Proper Lighting of Library Rooms." *Library Journal* 15 (December 1890): 9-11.

_____. "Some Library Superstitions." *Library Journal* 14 (May-June 1889): 155-59.

Foley, J. "Preservation of Cultural Resources in a Time of War." *Maine Library Association Bulletin* 3 (May 1942): 9-10.

Foote, Elizabeth. "The New York Library Club." *Library Journal* 34 (April 1909): 178.

Foster, William E. "Methods of Inducing Care of Books – II." *Library Journal* 25 (August 1900): 63-64.

Foye, Charlotte H. "The Care of Pamphlets." *Library Journal* 24 (January 1899): 13-14.

Franke, J. "Pressing Danger for Our Libraries." *Library Association Record* 10 (July 1908): 343.

"French Prizes for Essays on Insects Destructive to Books." *Library Journal* 27 (December 1902): 1026.

"French Prizes for Monographs on Bookworms." *Library Journal* 26 (July 1901): 388-89.

Fretwell, John. "Photographic Copying in Libraries." *Library Journal* 33 (June 1908): 223-34.

Fuller, Edith D. "United States, State, and Town Documents in Small Libraries." *Library Journal* 23 (October 1898): 564-66.

"Gas and Bindings Again." *Library Journal* 12 (November 1887): 522.

Gayley, Charles M. "An Account of the Proceedings of the International Congress for the Reproduction of Manuscripts." In *Report of the Commissioner of Education, 1905*, 1: 131-42. Washington, D.C.: Government Printing Office, 1907.

"The Get-Up of Modern Books." *Library World* 4 (August 1901): 32-33.

Gilchrist, D. B. "Death and Destruction on Library Shelves." *Medical Library Association Bulletin* 24 (December 1935): 100-104.

Gladstone, W. E. "On Books and the Housing of Them." *Nineteenth Century* 27 (March 1890): 384-96.

"Good Library Paste." *Library Occurrent* 2 (October 1908): 17.

"A Good Paste." *Library World* 2 (May 1900): 301.

"A Good Recipe for Book Paste." *Bulletin of the Vermont Library Commission* 5 (December 1909): 8.

Gordon, W. H. "The Preservation of Books." *Librarian and Book World* 21 (July 1932): 315-16.

Gould, Charles H. "Co-ordination, or Method in Co-operation." *ALA Bulletin* 3 (September 1909): 122-28.

Green, Bernard R. "Library Book Stacks without Daylight." *Science*, n.s., 29 (9 April 1909): 592.

_____. "Library Buildings and Book Stacks." *Library Journal* 31 (August 1906): 52-56.

_____. "The New Building for the Library of Congress." *Library Journal* 21 (December 1896): 13-20.

_____. "Planning and Construction of Library Buildings." *Library Journal* 25 (November 1900): 677-83.

Green, Samuel S. "The Elevator in the Worcester Public Library – Precautions against Fire." *Library Journal* 4 (30 June 1879): 201-202.

Greenhough, William H. "On the Ventilation, Heating, and Lighting, Especially Electric Lighting, of Public Libraries and Reading Rooms." *Library* 2 (1890): 421-33.

"Green's Book-Stack and Shelving for Libraries." *Library Journal* 18 (May 1893): 154-55.

Gwinn, Nancy E. "CLR and Preservation." *College and Research Libraries* 42 (March 1981): 105-107.

Hagen, H. A. "Insect Pests in Libraries." *Library Journal* 4 (July-August 1879): 251-54.

_____. "On a New Library Pest." *Boston Weekly Transcript*, 16 March 1886, 6.

Hagey, Joanna. "Binding." *Public Libraries* 9 (June 1904): 268-72.

Hartwig, O. "The Interchange of Manuscripts between Libraries." *Library Journal* 18 (December 1893): 503-5.

Hasbrouck, Mary K. "Reinforced Bindings Again." *Public Libraries* 14 (November 1909): 349.

Hathaway, F. P. "Bindings for a Public Library." *Library Journal* 4 (July-August 1879): 248-49.

Hepburn, William M. "Selection and Preservation of Agricultural Periodicals." *Library Journal* 35 (July 1910): 309-11.

Hertzberg, Edward C. J. "Specifications for Library Bookbinding." *Library Occurrent* 2 (June 1910): 135-37.

Hill, Frank "The Deterioration of Newspaper Paper." *Library Journal* 35 (July 1910): 299-301.

_____. "Storage Libraries." *ALA Bulletin* 3 (September 1909): 140-45.

"Hints from the Manchester Meeting." *Bulletin of the Vermont Library Commission* 3 (June 1907): 3.

Hollands, W. C. "Bookbinding." *Public Libraries* 9 (June 1904): 260-62.

Homes, H. A. "Deterioration of Bindings." *Library Journal* 5 (July-August 1880): 213-14.

_____. "Gum Tragacanth as a Library Paste." *Library Journal* 4 (31 March 1879): 93.

_____. "Unbound Volumes on Library Shelves." *Library Journal* 11 (August-September 1886): 214-15.

Hooper, Louisa M. "Disadvantages of Reinforced Bindings." *Library Journal* 34 (October 1909): 437.

Hooper, W. D. "Dirt in the City Library." *Indianapolis Journal*, 14 December 1886, 3.

"How to Wash a Book without Injury." *Library Journal* 10 (August 1885): 184-85.

"How We Keep Unbound Maps." *Library Journal* 16 (March 1891): 72-75.

"How We Protect Rare and Illustrated Books." *Library Journal* 15 (April 1890): 104.

"How We Protect Rare and Illustrated Books II." *Library Journal* 15 (May 1890): 133-34.

"How We Treat New Books." *Library Journal* 14 (April 1889): 109-11.

Hulme, E. Wyndham. "Decay in Leather Bindings." *Library Association Record* 3 (April 1901): 231-32.

_____. "Insect Book-Pests: A Review of the Recent Literature." *Library Association Record* 1 (June 1899): 369-72.

_____. "Machine Book-Sewing." *Library Association Record* 10 (January 1908): 8-9.

Humphreys, Antoinette. "The Other Side." *Public Libraries* 14 (October 1909): 300.

"In Cutting a Book with a Paper Knife." *Public Libraries* 1 (May 1896): 10.

"Injuries from Gas and Heat." *American Library Journal* 1 (30 November 1876): 124-25.

"Ink Eraser." *Library Journal* 10 (November 1885): 385.

"The Insect Enemies of Books." *Library Journal* 11 (December 1886): 484.

"Insects." *Library Journal* 11 (April 1886): 123.

"Insects Which Injure Books." *Zoologist* 3 (October 1879): 430.

"International Congress of Librarians, Paris, August 20-23, 1900." *Library Journal* 25 (September 1900): 580-82.

"International Congress on Facsimiles." *New York Evening Post*, 6 September 1905, Saturday Supplement sec., 6.

"Iowa State Library Association." *Library Journal* 25 (December 1900): 745-48.

Jackson, Fanny R. "The Care of Periodicals." *Public Libraries* 11 (November 1906): 493-94.

Jacobus, S. M. "A Library Paste." *Public Libraries* 11 (June 1906): 310.

Johnson, Rossiter. "Inferior Paper a Menace to the Permanency of Literature." *Library Journal* 16 (August 1891): 241-42.

Johnston, D. V. R. "Binding and Binderies." *Library Journal* 16 (December 1891): 9-16.

_____. "Elements in Library Binding." In *U.S. Office of Education Annual Report, 1892-1893*, 907-16.

_____. "Notes on Binding." *Library Journal* 17 (July-August 1892): 13-15.

Jones, Gardner M., and Green, H. E. "Linen Bindings." *Library Journal* 17 (July-August 1892): 29.

Jones, John W. "Inaugural Address." *American Library Journal* 2 (November-December 1877): 99-119.

Keen, W. W. "Library Book-Stacks without Daylight." *Science*, n.s., 29 (18 June 1909): 973-74.

"Keeping Books Upright." *American Library Journal* 1 (30 September 1876): 24.

"Keeping Books Upright." *American Library Journal* 1 (28 February 1877): 233.

"Keeping Books Upright." *American Library Journal* 1 (31 March 1877): 267.

Klett, Harold. "Don't." *Library Journal* 11 (April 1886): 117-18.

Knowlton, Lovina. "Care of Leather Bindings." *Library Occurrent* 1 (March 1908): 5.

_____. "Library Mending Kit." *Library Occurrent* 1 (December 1907): 4-5.

"Koch Spring Back Binders." *Library Journal* 3 (May 1878): 113.

Kroeger, Alice B. "The Care of Books." *Public Libraries* 8 (July 1903): 319-21.

Lamb, M. Charles. "Colors in Bookbinding Leathers." *Library World* 7 (March 1905): 256.

Larned, J. N. "Arrangement of Maps." *Library Journal* 17 (July-August 1892): 44-45.

Leighton, Flora H. "Preparing New Books and Restoring Old." *Public Libraries* 10 (May 1905): 223-24.

Leland, Waldo G. "The Application of Photography to Archive and Historical Work." In *Annual Report of the American Historical Association, 1908*, 154-60. Washington, D.C.: Government Printing Office, 1909.

Letts, Thomas. "Maps, from the Romantic and Prosaic Standpoints." *Library Journal* 25 (January 1900): 5-7.

"Libraries and Librarians." *Library World* 4 (March 1902): 248-49.

"Libraries and Librarians." *Library World* 6 (June 1904): 330.

"The Library." *Book Buyer* (November 1910): 186-87.

"Library Architecture." *Library Journal* 7 (July-August 1882): 196-97.

"Library Architecture." *Library Journal* 8 (September-October 1883): 269-74.

"Library Bookbinding." *Library Association Record* 7 (November 1905): 559-62.

"Library Buildings." *Library Journal* 6 (April 1881): 123-26.

"Library Handicraft at Colorado State Normal School." *Library Journal* 25 (July 1900): 335.

"A Library in Ruins." *Library Journal* 8 (December 1883): 337-38.

"The Library of the Athenaeum Club." In *Transactions and Proceedings of the Conference of Librarians Held in London October, 1877*, edited by Edward B. Nicholson and Henry R. Tedder, 231-32. London: printed at Chiswick Press by Charles Whittington, 1878.

Linderfelt, Karl A. "Paste." *Library Journal* 8 (March-April 1883): 55.

Little, Arthur D. "The Durability of Paper." *Printing Art* 1 (June 1903): 115-18.

"The Loan of Rare Books." *Library Journal* 5 (July-August 1880): 217-18.

"Local Records." *Library World* 2 (June 1900): 313-16.

Lord, Isabel E. "Open Shelves and Public Morals." *Library Journal* 26 (February 1901): 65-70.

"The Lowell Book Support." *Library Journal* 9 (January 1884): 16.

"M900 + X050." *Library World*, n.s., 13 (December 1910): 170-71.

MacAlister, J. Y. W. "The Durability of Modern Book Papers." *Library* 10 (1898): 295-304.

McCurdy, Mary de Bure. "Cleaning Books." *Library Occurrent* 1 (September 1907): 2.

MacLeish, Archibald. "Library of Congress Protects Its Collections." *ALA Bulletin* 36 (February 1942): 74-75.

MacLeod, Robert D. "The Preservation of Books in Libraries." *Library World*, n.s., 11 (January 1909): 256-61.

_____. "The Preservation of Books in Libraries II." *Library World*, n.s., 11 (March 1909): 331-35.

_____. "The Preservation of Books in Libraries III." *Library World*, n.s., 11 (April 1909): 368-71.

_____. "The Preservation of Books in Libraries IV." *Library World*, n.s., 11 (May 1909): 417-22.

"Magazine Punch." *Library Journal* 5 (September-October 1880): 292.

Mann, B. Pickman. "The Care of Pamphlets." *Science* 6 (6 November 1885): 407.

Manning, William J. "Permanent Printed Records on Linen." *Scientific American* 98 (6 June 1908): 407.

Marsden, Henry. "Bookbinders and Paper Rulers' Forum on the Premature Decay of Leather Used in Modern Bookbinding, Part II." *International Bookbinder* (October 1905): 356-59.

_____. "Decay of Leather Bindings." *Public Libraries* 11 (June 1906): 312-13.

Martins, Charlotte. "Intricacies of Binding." *Library Journal* 27 (June 1902): 312-13.

Marvin, Cornelia. "The Care of Books." *Wisconsin Library Bulletin* 1 (May 1905): 35-37.

_____. "Rebinding Made Unnecessary." *Wisconsin Library Bulletin* 1 (May 1905): 42.

Marx, Henry F. "The Value of a Bindery in a Small Library." *Library Journal* 30 (October 1905): 796-97.

"Mason's Book Support." *Library Journal* 11 (December 1886): 491.

"Massachusetts Library Club." *Library Journal* 19 (May 1894): 171-74.

Bibliography

"Massachusetts Library Club." *Library Journal* 32 (February 1907): 83-84.

"Materials for Mending Books." *Bulletin of the Vermont Library Commission* 5 (September 1909): 7-8.

Mathews, E. R. Norris. "Library Binderies." *Library Association Record* 8 (15 March 1906): 73-78.

"Menasha." *Wisconsin Library Bulletin* 1 (June 1905): 67.

"Mending Torn Leaves." *Library World* 2 (January 1900): 189.

"Mercantile L., N. Y." *Library Journal* 8 (July 1883): 129-30.

"Michigan Library Association." *Library Journal* 25 (December 1900): 748-49.

"Michigan Library Association." *Library Journal* 27 (November 1902): 954-56.

"Miss Hewins' 'Goop' Verse." *Wisconsin Library Bulletin* 1 (September 1905): 79.

Montgomery, Thomas L. "Report of the Co-operation Committee." *Library Journal* 24 (July 1899): 92-94.

Moore, Fred N. "The Art of Leather Making." *Library Journal* 32 (August 1907): 367-70.

"Mounting of Maps." *Library Journal* 18 (January 1893): 25.

"Mutilating Books in Libraries." *Library Journal* 13 (June 1888): 182.

Neumann Brothers, Bookbinders. "Notes on Bookbinding: The Bookbinder's Side of the Question." *Library Journal* 23 (September 1898): 526.

"New Method of Preserving Old Bookbindings, or of Rebinding Old Books." *Library*, n.s., 6 (July 1905): 208-11.

"New York Library Association." *Library Journal* 25 (March 1900): 126-30.

"Newark Binding Exhibit." *Library Journal* 31 (September 1906): 696.

"The Newberry Library: Dr. Poole's Plans for the New Structure Examined." *Chicago Tribune*, 29 December 1889, 6.

Nichols, William R. "On the Deterioration of Library Bindings." *Library Journal* 4 (December 1879): 435-38.

Nicholson, Edward W. B. "On Buckram as a Binding Material." *American Library Journal* 2 (November-December 1877): 207-9.

Bibliography

_____. "On Buckram as a Binding Material." In *Transactions and Proceedings of the Conference of Librarians Held in London October 1877*, edited by Edward B. Nicholson and Henry R. Tedder, 124-26. London: Printed at the Chiswick Press by Charles Whittingham, 1878.

_____. "The Use of Buckram, Linoleum, and Cretonne for Binding." *Library Journal* 5 (November-December 1880): 304-5.

Nicholson, James B. "What a Librarian Should Know about Binding." *Library Journal* 9 (June 1884): 102.

"Ninth Meeting of German Librarians." *Library Journal* 33 (November 1908): 446-47.

"Note from the A. L. A. Committee on Bookbinding." *Library Journal* 32 (April 1907): 168.

"Notes." *Library Journal* 10 (December 1885): 406.

"Notes and Queries." *Library Journal* 8 (June 1883): 111.

"Notes and Queries." *Library Journal* 34 (January 1909): 40.

"Notes on Books and Work." *Library*, n.s., 4 (1 July 1903): 328-36.

"Objection to Wire Bookbinding." *Library Journal* 11 (December 1886): 490.

"On Binding Books for Public Libraries." *American Library Journal* 2 (January-February 1878): 271.

"On Binding of Books for Public and Private Libraries; and on Shelf-Arrangement as Associated Therewith (Discussion)." *American Library Journal* 2 (January-February 1878): 271.

"On Buckram as a Binding Material." *American Library Journal* 2 (January-February 1878): 271-72.

"On Library Buildings." *American Library Journal* 2 (January-February 1878): 251-55.

"On Library Buildings." In *Transactions and Proceedings of the Conference of Librarians Held in London October 1877*, edited by Edward B. Nicholson and Henry R. Tedder, 147-51. London: Printed at Chiswick Press by Charles Whittingham, 1878.

"On the Treatment of Pamphlets in Special Libraries." *Library Journal* 5 (June 1880): 166-67.

Orne, J. "Library of Congress Prepares for Emergencies." *ALA Bulletin* 35 (June 1941): 341-48.

"Oshkosh." *Wisconsin Library Bulletin* 3 (July-August 1907): 71.

"Pamphlet Holders." *Library Journal* 5 (September-October 1880): 291-92.

"Pamphlets." *American Library Journal* 1 (30 November 1876): 101-6.

"Paper Covers." *American Library Journal* 1 (30 November 1876): 131-33.

"Paper Preservation." *Library Journal* 35 (November 1910): 528.

Parker, J. Gordon. "Leather for Bookbinding." *Journal of the Society of Arts* 50 (29 November 1901): 25-35.

_____. "The Leather Question." *Library Association Record* 8 (October 1906): 489-91.

Parsons, Francis H. "The Care of Maps." *Library Journal* 20 (June 1895): 199-201.

"Paste." *Library Journal* 3 (April 1878): 78.

"Paste." *Library Journal* 17 (February 1892): 72.

"Paste." *Library Journal* 17 (April 1892): 145.

"Paste-Watering." *Book-Auction Records* 3 (1905-6): x.

Patton, Normand S. "Heating, Ventilation, and Lighting of Libraries." In *U.S. Office of Education Annual Report, 1892-1893*, 718-24.

_____. "Light, Heat, and Ventilation." *Library Journal* 18 (September 1893): 28-30.

Pendleton, A. M. "How to Start Libraries in Small Towns, IV." *American Library Journal* 1 (31 May 1877): 313-14.

_____. "How to Start Libraries in Small Towns, V." *American Library Journal* 1 (30 June 1877): 355-59.

"Pennsylvania Library Association." *Library Journal* 21 (March 1896): 108.

"Perforating Punch." *Library Journal* 19 (February 1894): 66-67.

Perkins, F. B. "Transferable Book Covers." *Library Journal* 5 (May 1880): 146.

Perkins, Norman C. "How to Bind Periodicals." *Library Journal* 12 (September-October 1887): 354-56.

"Philadelphia Mercantile Library." *American Library Journal* 1 (31 March 1877): 269.

Philip, Alexander J. "Bookbinding for Lending Libraries." *Library Assistant* 4 (1903): 70-74.

Phillips, P. Lee. "Preservation and Record of Maps in the Library of Congress." *Library Journal* 25 (January 1900): 15-16.

"Pig-Skins for Bookbinding." *Library Journal* 11 (June 1886): 166.

Pollard, A. W. "Notes on Books and Work." *Library*, 2d ser., 1 (1 June 1900): 337-47.

_____. "Notes on Books and Work." *Library*, n.s., 2 (1 July 1901): 330-36.

Poole, Reuben B. "Book-Binding Memoranda." *Library Journal* 14 (May-June 1889): 261-64.

_____. "Elements of Good Binding." *Library Journal* 17 (July-August 1892): 15-18.

_____. "Fires, Protection, Insurance." *Library Journal* 18 (July 1893): 224.

_____. "Fires, Protection, Insurance." In *U.S. Office of Education Annual Report, 1892-1893*, 724-33.

Poole, William F. "The Construction of Library Buildings." *Library Journal* 6 (April 1881): 69-77.

_____. "The Organization and Management of Public Libraries." In *Public Libraries in the United States of America: Their History, Condition, and Management: Special Report*, 476-504. Washington, D.C.: U.S. Bureau of Education, 1876.

_____. "Progress of Library Architecture." *Library Journal* 7 (July-August 1882): 130-36.

_____. Review of *The Enemies of Books*, by William Blades. *Dial* 9 (July 1888): 64.

_____. "Small Library Buildings." *Library Journal* 10 (September-October 1885): 250-56.

_____. "Three Libraries More Destroyed by Fire." *Library Journal* 6 (May 1881): 163-64.

_____. "Why Wood Shelving Is Better than Iron." *Library Notes* 2 (September 1887): 95.

Post, William L. "Report of the Committee on Public Documents: Address of Mr. Post." *ALA Bulletin* 1 (July 1907): 135-45.

Potter, A. C. Review of *Bookbinding and the Care of Books*, by Douglas Cockerell. *Library Journal* 27 (April 1902): 213-14.

Powell, Walter. "Book Production in Great Britain." *Library Journal* 29 (December 1904): 50-54.

_____. "Library Bookbinding." *Library World* 5 (January 1903): 171-77.

"Practical Notes." *Library Journal* 16 (July 1891): 223.

"Practical Notes." *Library Journal* 28 (June 1903): 319.

"The Preservation of Books from Fire." *Academy* 26 (26 July 1884): 61.

"Preservation of Books in Libraries." *Librarian and Book World* 24 (September 1934): 11-12.

"Preservation of Bound Newspapers." *Library Journal* 22 (March 1897): 161.

"Preservation of Manuscripts." *Library Journal* 35 (February 1910): 64.

"Preserving Bindings." *Library Journal* 17 (February 1892): 72.

"The Prevention of Fires in Libraries." *Library Journal* 4 (28 February 1879): 52-54.

Prince, Flora F. "Book Repairing." *Bulletin of the Vermont Library Commission* 5 (September 1909): 7.

"Proceedings of the Seventh Annual Conference of Historical Societies." In *Annual Report of the American Historical Association, 1910*, 243-55. Washington, D.C.: Government Printing Office, 1912.

"Proposed Charging System." *Library Journal* 25 (July 1900): 350.

"Public Notice of Poor Editions." *Library Journal* 24 (October 1899): 574.

Purtill, Elizabeth F. "Formulas for Cleaning Books." *Library Occurrent* 2 (June 1910): 140-41.

Pyle, Walter. "The Durability of Leather in Bookbinding." *Library Journal* 26 (July 1901): 386-87.

"The Question of Publishers' Bindings." *Quarterly of the Iowa Library Commission* 2 (April 1902): 33-34.

"Quicklime." *Library Journal* 13 (February 1888): 56.

R. D. "Dirt in the City Library." *Indianapolis Journal*, 12 December 1886, 6.

Rae, W. S. "A Conference of Books." *Library World* 2 (January 1900): 187-88.

"Ragged Books." *New York Libraries* 1 (January 1909): 185.

Ranck, Samuel H. "Leather for Bookbinding." *Library Journal* 26 (September 1901): 681-84.

_____. "Softening Bindings." *Library Journal* 21 (May 1896): 218.

"Rapid Discoloration of Paper." *Library Journal* 11 (November 1886): 442.

Rathbone, Frances L. "A Trained Person in Charge of Condition of Books." *Public Libraries* 12 (June 1907): 236-37.

"The Ravages of Bookworms." *Library Journal* 19 (July 1894): 230-31.

"Rebinding for General Circulation." *Library Journal* 18 (June 1893): 186-87.

Reid, H. W. "Hints on Bookbinding." *Public Libraries* 12 (February 1907): 63-64.

Reinick, William R. "Insects Destructive to Books." *Scientific American,* suppl. 70 (24 December 1910): 408-10.

"Removal of Grease Spots from Books and Engravings." *Library Journal* 11 (April 1886): 123.

"Removing Stains from Prints." *Library Journal* 27 (October 1902): 910.

"Repair Slip." *Library Journal* 17 (July-August 1892): 29-30.

"Repairing Books." *Public Libraries* 12 (April 1907): 124-26.

"Report of Committee on Bookbinding." *ALA Bulletin* 1 (July 1907): 110-16.

"Report of Committee on Bookbinding and Book Papers." *Library Journal* 31 (August 1906): 194.

"Report of the A. L. A. Committee on Library Administration, 1908." *ALA Bulletin* 2 (September 1908): 222-31.

"Report of the Committee on Bookbinding." *ALA Bulletin* 3 (September 1909): 220-22.

"Report of the Committee on Bookbuying." *ALA Bulletin* 2 (September 1908): 179-80.

"Reproduction of Manuscripts." *Library Journal* 30 (December 1905): 929.

Bibliography

"Reproductions of Ancient Manuscripts." *Library Journal* 24 (July 1899): 125-26.

"Resolutions." *Library Journal* 7 (July-August 1882): 203.

"Restoration of Books." *American Library Journal* 2 (September 1877): 24-25.

"Restoring Leather Bindings." *Library Journal* 11 (November 1886): 454.

Review of *Bookbinding and the Care of Books*, by Douglas Cockerell. *Dial* 33 (1 February 1902): 90.

Review of *Notes on Bookbinding for Libraries*, by John C. Dana. *Library World* 9 (December 1906): 221-22.

Robinson, Otis H. "College Library Administration." In *Public Libraries in the United States of America: Their History, Condition, and Management: Special Report*, 504-25. Washington, D.C.: U.S. Bureau of Education, 1876.

_____. "Pamphlets." *American Library Journal* 1 (30 November 1876): 101-106.

"Roller Shelves for Large Volumes." *Library Journal* 11 (December 1886): 491-92.

Ropes, W. L. "'Evaporation.'" *Library Journal* 10 (May 1885): 104-5.

Russell, C. P. "Note on the Preservation of Bindings." In *Transactions and Proceedings of the First Annual Meeting of the Library Association of the United Kingdom, Held at Oxford, October 1, 2, 3, 1878*, edited by Henry R. Tedder and Ernst C. Thomas (London, 1879), 99-100.

"The St. Gall Library Conference of 1898." *Library Journal* 24 (February 1899): 61.

"Salvaging Miles of Sodden Books." *Life* 61 (16 December 1966): 34-35.

Sargent, M. E. "Binding for Library Use." *Library Journal* 19 (July 1894): 262.

Sawyer, Harriet P. "How to Care for Books in a Library." *Wisconsin Library Bulletin* 5 (January-February 1909): 6-8.

Schwartz, J. "Temporary vs. Eternal." *Library Journal* 14 (March 1889): 76.

Seymour-Jones, A. "On the Glazing of Libraries, with Reference to the Chemical Action of Light on Leather." *Library Association Record* 8 (December 1906): 641-46.

Shaffer, Norman J. "Library of Congress Pilot Preservation Project." *College and Research Libraries* 30 (January 1969): 5-11.

Sharp, Katharine L. "Library Recipes." *Library Notes* 4 (July 1895): 205-23.

"Shelves for Heavy Books." *Library Journal* (August-September 1886): 355.

"Shelving on the Fore-Edge." *American Library Journal* 1 (30 June 1877): 377.

"Shelving on the Fore-Edge (Response)." *American Library Journal* 2 (January-February 1878): 309.

"The Siemens Light at the British Museum." *Chemical News* 40 (31 October 1897): 212-13.

Singleton, John W. "Bookbinding: A Suggestion." *Library World* 3 (May 1906): 289-90.

Soldan, F. J. "Directions for Binding." *Public Libraries* 9 (June 1904): 259-60.

_____. "Specifications for Binding." *Library Journal* 8 (June 1883): 106-7.

"Special Library Bindings." *Library World* 2 (June 1900): 332.

"Specifications for Binding." *Wisconsin Library Bulletin* 3 (July-August 1907): 66-67.

"Specifications for Book Cloths." *Library Journal* 34 (March 1909): 120-21.

"Specifications for Library Binding." *Library Journal* 60 (1 January 1935): 18-20.

Spofford, Ainsworth R. "Binding and Preservation of Books." In *Public Libraries in the United States of America: Their History, Condition, and Management: Special Report*, 673-78. Washington, D.C.: U.S. Bureau of Education, 1876.

"Spring Book Supports." *Library Journal* 11 (April 1886): 122.

Stearns, Lutie E. "Shellac for Book Covers." *Wisconsin Library Bulletin* 3 (July-August 1907): 62-63.

Stephen, George A. "Book-Cloths." *Library Association Record* 11 (January 1909): 5-7.

_____. "Edition Binding." *Library Assistant* 6 (May 1909): 326-30.

_____. "Machine Book-Sewing, with Remarks on Publishers' Binding." *Library Association Record* 10 (June 1908): 261-80.

_____. "Notes on Materials for Library Bookbinding." *Library Assistant* 5 (August 1906): 143-46.

_____. "Notes on Materials for Library Bookbinding." *Library Assistant* 5 (September 1906): 162-64.

_____. "Publishers' Binding." *Library Association Record* 12 (January 1910): 9-13.

_____. "Publishers' Reinforced Bindings." *Library World*, n.s., 12 (April 1910): 380-81.

Stetson, W. K. "Bookbinding from the Librarian's Standpoint." *Public Libraries* 11 (June 1906): 300-1.

Stosskopf, George. "Library Bookbinding." *Public Libraries* 14 (March 1909): 87-89.

Straight, Maude W. "Repairing of Books." *Public Libraries* 5 (March 1900): 88-89.

"Study of the Hygiene of Libraries: Methods of Preserving Books against Their Enemies Suggested by the International Congress of Librarians – Suffocation the Best." *Public Opinion* 36 (18 February 1904): 213.

"A Substitute for Binding Periodicals." *News Notes of California Libraries* 3 (July 1908): 280-81.

"Suggestions to Readers on the Care of Books." *Monthly Bulletin of the Providence Public Library* 4 (February 1898): 43-44.

Swan, Robert T. ""Paper and Ink." *Library Journal* 20 (May 1895): 163-67.

Swift, Lindsay. "Pamphlets and Continuations of Serials." *Library Journal* 12 (September-October 1887): 350-54.

Tandy, Francis D. "Special Editions of Library Books." *Library Journal* 18 (October 1893): 422.

"Temple University Library Destroyed by Fire." *Library Journal* 97 (15 September 1972): 2796-97.

Thayer, Annie M. "Statistics of Re-binding." *Library Journal* 31 (January 1906): 48.

"There Is Increasing Complaint as to the Bindings Furnished by Publishers for Popular Books." *Library Journal* 32 (February 1907): 49-50.

Thwaites, Reuben G. "Ten Years of American Library Progress." *Library Journal* 25 (August 1900): 1-7.

"To Separate the Leaves of Charred Books or Deeds." *Library Journal* 12 (August 1887): 301.

Tobitt, Edith. "What a Librarian Should Know about Binding." *Iowa Library Quarterly* 5 (April 1905): 18-21.

"Transactions of Council and Executive Board." *Library Journal* 29 (December 1904): 249-51.

"Turin, Italy. National L." *Library Journal* (May 1905): 308.

Tyler, Anna C. "A Live Bookworm–A Nature Study." *Library Journal* 33 (August 1908): 311-12.

"United Kingdom Association." *Library Journal* 6 (July 1881): 204.

"University of Michigan Library (Report)." *Library Journal* 18 (January 1893): 23-24.

Utley, H. M. "Newspaper Volumes in a Library." *Library Journal* 12 (September-October 1887): 349-50.

_____. "Newspaper Volumes in a Library (Discussion)." *Library Journal* 12 (September-October 1887): 438-40.

Van Laer, Arnold J. F. "The Work of the International Congress of Archivists and Librarians at Brussels, August 28-31, 1910." In *Annual Report of the American Historical Association, 1910*, 282-92. Washington, D.C.: Government Printing Office, 1912.

"Varnish for Maps." *Library Journal* 16 (July 1891): 223.

Veitch, Fletcher P. "Suitable Paper for Permanent Records." In *U.S. Department of Agriculture Yearbook, 1908*, 261-66. Washington, D.C.: Government Printing Office, 1909.

"Verein deutscher Bibliothekare: Verhandlungen und Vorträge auf der 2. Jahres-Versammlung, Gotha, den 30. und 31 Mai 1901." *Zentralblatt für Bibliothekswesen* 18 (August-September 1901): 383-87.

"Wales' Improved Bookbinding." *Library Journal* 24 (January 1899): 38.

Walford, Cornelius. "The Destruction of Libraries by Fire Considered Practically and Historically." *Library Association Transactions* 2 (1879): 65-70.

_____. "On Binding of Books for Public and Private Libraries; and On Shelf-Arrangement as Associated Therewith." *American Library Journal* 2 (November-December 1877): 201-3.

Warren, S. R., and Clark, S. N. "Library Reports and Statistics." In *Public Libraries in the United States of America: Their History, Condition, and Management: Special Report*, 745-83. Washington, D.C.: U.S. Bureau of Education, 1876.

Water, Willard O. "District of Columbia Library Association." *Library Journal* 33 (December 1908): 511-12.

Wellman, Hiller C. "Some Points about Library Bookbindings." *Bulletin of the New Hampshire Public Libraries*, n.s., 4 (n.d.): 23-25.

"Western Massachusetts Library Club." *Library Journal* 26 (February 1901): 87-88.

"Western Massachusetts Library Club." *Library Journal* 30 (June 1905): 361-62.

"What We Do with Pamphlets." *Library Journal* 14 (November 1889): 433-34.

"What We Do with Pamphlets." *Library Journal* 14 (December 1889): 470-71.

Wheatley, H. B. "Leather for Bookbinding." *Library*, n.s., 2 (1 July 1901): 311-20.

Wilde, Alice. "New York Library Club." *Library Journal* 31 (April 1906): 182-83.

Wiley, H. W. "The Government Leather and Paper Laboratory: Samples of Library Bindings Desired." *Library Journal* 31 (February 1906): 104.

Wilson, Henry. "Remarks on Facsimile Reproduction." *Monthly Notes of the Library Association* 1 (15 May 1880): 33-40.

Windsor, P. L. "A New Vertical File for Maps." *Public Libraries* 15 (November 1910): 388-89.

Winsor, Justin. "Library Buildings." In *Public Libraries in the United States of America: Their History, Condition, and Management: Special Report*, 465-75. Washington, D.C.: U.S. Bureau of Education, 1876.

_____. "Library Memoranda." In *Public Libraries in the United States of America: Their History, Condition, and Management: Special Report*, 711-14. Washington, D.C.: U.S. Bureau of Education, 1876.

Wire, George E. "Book Selection, Buying, and Binding." *Library Journal* 24 (July 1899): 63-65.

"Wire-Sewn Books." *Library Journal* 5 (July-August 1880): 213.

Wood, Butler. "The Brittle Quality of Paper Used by Publishers." *Library* 2 (1890): 203.

Woodard, Gertrude E., "Notes on Bookbinding." *Library Journal* 23 (June 1898): 231-37.

Woodbine, H. "Essay on Modern Methods of Book Storage." *Library Association Record* 12 (September 1910): 446-54.

Woodward, C. J. "The Action of Gas on Leather Bookbindings: A Preliminary Experimental Enquiry." *Library Chronicle* 5 (1888): 25-29.

_____. "A Preliminary Experimental Inquiry as to the Action of Burning-gas on Leather Used for Book-binding." *Library Journal* 12 (September-October 1887): 321-22.

Zaehnsdorf, Joseph. "Practical Suggestions in Bookbinding." *Library Chronicle* 4 (September 1887): 107-11.

"The Zapon Conference in Dresden." *Library Journal* 25 (January 1900): 19.

Monographs

American Library Association. Committee on Bookbinding. *Binding for Small Libraries; Suggestions*. Chicago: American Library Association, 1909.

Barrow, W. J., Research Laboratory. *Permanence/Durability of the Book*. 5 vols. Richmond, Va.: W. J. Barrow Research Laboratory, 1963-76.

Barrow, William J. *The Barrow Method of Restoring Deteriorated Documents*. Richmond, Va.: Barrow, 1965.

Blades, William. *The Enemies of Books*. London: E. Stock, 1896.

Battershall, Fletcher. *Bookbinding for Bibliophiles: Being Notes on the Technical Features of the Well-Bound Book for the Aid of Connoisseurs; With a Sketch of Gold Tooling, Ancient and Modern*. Greenwich, Conn.: Library Collector Press, 1905.

Bonnardot, Alfred. *Essai sur l'art de restaurer les estampes et les livres, ou traité sur les meilleurs procédés pour blanchir, détacher, décolorier, réparer et conserver les estampes, livres et dessins*. Paris, 1858.

Brown, Margaret W. *Mending and Repair of Books*. Chicago: American Library Association, 1910.

Chivers, Cedric. *Bookbindings at the St. Louis Exhibition, 1905, by Cedric Chivers, Bath, England.* New York: Chivers, 1904 or 1905.

_____. *The Paper of Lending Library Books.* New York: Baker & Taylor, 1909 or 1910.

Church, R. W., ed. *Deterioration of Book Stock: Causes and Remedies, Two Studies on the Permanence of Book Paper Conducted by W. J. Barrow.* Richmond: Virginia State Library, 1959.

_____. *The Manufacture and Testing of Durable Book Papers, Based on the Investigations of W. J. Barrow.* Richmond: Virginia State Library, 1960.

Cockerell, Douglas. *Bookbinding and the Care of Books: A Text-book for Bookbinders and Librarians.* New York: Appleton, 1902.

_____. "Note on Bookbinding." In his *Some Notes on Bookbinding*, 94-105. Oxford: Oxford University Press, 1929.

Council on Library Resources. *The Commission on Preservation and Access.* Washington, D.C.: Council on Library Resources, 1987.

Crane, W. J. Eden. *Book-binding for Amateurs.* London, 1885.

Dana, John C. *Notes on Bookbinding for Libraries.* 2d ed. Chicago: Library Bureau, 1910.

Emerson, Gilbert D. *Bookbinding for Libraries.* Philadelphia: Emerson, 1909.

Fitzpatrick, J. B. *Notes on the Care, Cataloging, Calendaring and Arranging of Manuscripts.* Washington, D.C.: Government Printing Office, 1913.

Freeman, Sarah J. *Syllabus of a Course on Elementary Bookmaking and Bookbinding.* New York: Teachers College of Columbia University, 1910.

Growoll, Adolf. *The Profession of Bookselling.* 3 vols. New York: Publishers' Weekly, 1893-1913.

Haas, Warren J. *Preparation of Detailed Specifications for a National System for the Preservation of Library Materials.* Washington, D.C.: Association of Research Libraries, 1972.

Hannett, John. *Bibliopegia; or, the Art of Bookbinding.* London: Simkim, Marshall, 1848.

Bibliography

Haslam, W. *Book of Trade Secrets: Receipts and Instructions for Renovating, Repairing, Improving and Preserving Old Books and Prints*. New York: Scribner, 1909.

Humphreys, Arthur L. *The Private Library: What We Do Know, What We Don't Know, What We Ought to Know about Our Books*. New York: J. W. Bouton, 1897.

Jewett, Charles C. *Notices of Public Libraries in the United States of America*. Washington, D.C.: Printed for the House of Representatives, 1851.

Kimberley, A. E. and Scribner, B. W. *Summary Report of Bureau of Standards Research on Preservation of Records*. Washington, D.C.: Government Printing Office, 1934.

Kinder, Louis H. *Formulas for Bookbinders*. East Aurora, N.Y.: Roycroft, 1905.

Library Association of the United Kingdom. Sound Leather Committee. *Leather for Libraries*. By E. Wyndham Hulme, J. Gordon Parker, A. Seymour-Jones, Cyril Davenport, and F. J. Williamson. London: Library Supply Co., 1905.

McFarlane, John. *Library Administration*. London: G. Harper; New York: F. Harper, 1898.

Matthews, William. *Modern Bookbinding Practically Considered*. New York: Grolier Club, 1889.

Newark (N.J.) Free Public Library. *Book Binding: An Exhibition of the Materials, Tools and Processes of Book Binding, with Examples of Plain and Ornamental Bindings. In the Free Public Library of Newark, New Jersey, February 6, to February 27, 1905*. Newark: Free Public Library, 1905.

Nicholson, Edward W. B., and Tedder, Henry R., eds. *Transactions and Proceedings of the Conference of Librarians Held in London October, 1877*. London: printed at Chiswick Press by Charles Whittingham, 1878.

Nicholson, James B. *A Manual of the Art of Bookbinding*. Philadelphia: H. C. Baird, 1856.

O'Conor, J. F. X. *Facts about Bookworms: Their History in Literature and Work in Libraries*. New York: F. Harper, 1898.

Plenderleith, H. J. *The Conservation of Prints, Drawings, and Manuscripts*. Oxford: Oxford University Press, 1937.

Plummer, Mary W. *Hints to Small Libraries*. 2d ed., rev. & enl. New York: Truslove & Comba, 1898.

Posse, Otto, ed. *Handschriften-Konservirung nach den Verhandlungen der St. Gallener internationalen Konferenz zur Erhaltung und Ausbesserung alter Handschriften von 1898, sowie der dresdener Konferenz deutscher Archivare von 1899*. Dresden: Apollo, 1899.

Proceedings of the Librarians' Convention Held in New York City, September 15, 16, and 17, 1853. Cedar Rapids, Iowa: Torch Press, 1915.

Royal Society of Arts. Committee on Leather for Bookbinding. *Report of the Committee on Leather for Bookbinding*. Edited by Viscount Cobham and Sir Henry Trueman Wood. London: Bell & Sons, 1905.

Sawyer, Harriet P. *How to Care for Books in a Library*. Madison: Wisconsin Free Library Commission, 1910.

Slater, Herbert J. *The Library Manual: A Guide to the Formation of a Library, and the Valuation of Books*. 3d ed. enl., London: Gill, n.d.

Society for the Encouragement of Arts, Manufactures, & Commerce. Committee on the Deterioration of Paper. *Report of the Committee on the Deterioration of Paper. With Two Appendixes: 1. Abstracts of Papers on German Official Tests, 1885-96. 2. Précis of Correspondence*. London: Society, 1898.

Spofford, Ainsworth R. *A Book for All Readers: Designed as an Aid to the Collection, Use, and Preservation of Books and the Formation of Public and Private Libraries*. 2d ed. New York: Putnam, 1900.

Stearns, Lutie E. *Essentials in Library Administration*. Boston: A.L.A. Publishing Board, 1905.

Stephen, George A. *Commercial Bookbinding*. London: Stonhill & Co., 1910.

_____. *Machine Book-Sewing with Remarks on Publishers' Binding*. Aberdeen (Scotland): Aberdeen University Press, 1908.

Stephen, George A., and Coutts, Henry T. *Manual of Library Bookbinding*. London: Libraco Ltd., 1911.

U.S. Bureau of Chemistry. *Examination of Papers*. Washington, D.C.: U.S. Bureau of Chemistry, 1907.

U.S. Congress. House. Committee on Education and Labor. *Oversight Hearing on the Problem of "Brittle Books" in Our Nation's Libraries*.

Hearing before the Subcommittee on Postsecondary Education. 100th Cong., 1st sess., 1987.

U.S. Department of Agriculture. *Durability and Economy in Papers for Permanent Records: A Report Submitted by H. W. Wiley, Chief of Bureau of Chemistry, and C. Hart Merriam, Chief of Bureau of Biological Survey, Committee on Paper for Departmental Use. Including 'Paper Specifications,' by F. P. Veitch, Chief, Leather and Paper Laboratory, Bureau of Chemistry.* Washington, D.C.: Government Printing Office, 1909.

Veitch, Fletcher P. *Paper-making Materials and Their Conservation.* Washington, D.C.: U.S. Bureau of Chemistry, 1908.

Williams, Gordon. *The Preservation of Deteriorating Books: An Examination of the Problems with Recommendations for a Solution.* Washington, D.C.: Association of Research Libraries, 1964.

Zaehnsdorf, Joseph W. *The Art of Bookbinding: A Practical Treatise.* 2d ed., rev. & enl. London: Bell & Sons, 1890.

Library Annual Reports

Adriance Memorial Library of the City of Poughkeepsie, (N.Y.). *Annual Report, 1903.*

Alameda (Calif.) Free Library and Reading Room. *Annual Report of the Board of Trustees, 1894.*

Andover (Mass.) Memorial Hall Library. *Annual Report, 1907.*

Astor Library (New York City). *Annual Report of the Trustees, 1878, 1879, 1880, 1882, 1890.*

Atlantic City (N.J.) Free Public Library. *Annual Report, 1907.*

Boston Athenaeum. *Reports of the Library Committee and of the Librarian, 1882, 1897, 1899, 1901, 1904, 1905, 1906, 1908.*

Boston Public Library. *Annual Report of the Trustees, 1875, 1876, 1877, 1878, 1879, 1880, 1881, 1882, 1883, 1885, 1886, 1887, 1888, 1889, 1891, 1894, 1896, 1897, 1898, 1899, 1900, 1902, 1903, 1905, 1907, 1908, 1909, 1910.*

Bowdoin College Library. *Annual Report of the Librarian, 1891, 1895, 1903, 1904.*

Braddock (Pa.) Carnegie Free Library. *Annual Report, 1903, 1908, 1909.*

Bradford (Pa.) Carnegie Public Library. *Annual Report, 1901, 1903, 1904, 1905.*

Bridgeport (Conn.) Public Library and Reading Room. *Annual Report, 1899.*

Brockton (Mass.) Public Library. *Report of the Trustees, 1907.*

Brookline (Mass.) Public Library. *Annual Report of the Trustees, 1876, 1877, 1878, 1879, 1887, 1889, 1898, 1899, 1905, 1909.*

Brooklyn Mercantile Library Association. *Annual Report of the Board of Directors, 1883, 1885.*

Brooklyn Public Library. *Annual Report of the Board of Directors, 1905, 1906, 1907, 1909, 1910.*

Buffalo Public Library. *Annual Report, 1899, 1900, 1907, 1908.*

California State Library. *Biennial Report of the Trustees, 1904-1906.*

Cambridge (Mass.) Public Library. *Annual Report of the Trustees, 1889.*

Chicago Public Library. *Annual Report of the Board of Directors, 1873, 1886, 1908-1909.*

Cincinnati Public Library. *Annual Report of the Librarian and Treasurer, 1886-1887, 1888-1889, 1889-1890, 1903-1904, 1905-1906, 1907-1908.*

Cleveland Public Library. *Annual Report of the Library Board and Librarian, 1878, 1885, 1887, 1891, 1894, 1895, 1898, 1899, 1900, 1905, 1907.*

Columbia College Library. *Annual Report of the Chief Librarian, 1884, 1886, 1887.*

Connecticut State Library. *Report of the State Librarian, 1905-1906, 1907-1908.*

Cooper Union. *Annual Report of the Trustees, 1896, 1910.*

Cornell University Library. *Report of the Librarian, 1902-1903.*

Council Bluffs (Iowa) Free Public Library. *Annual Report, 1892, 1895, 1906.*

Dayton Public Library. *Annual Report of the Board of Managers and Librarian, 1898-1899, 1902-1903, 1905-1906.*

Dedham (Mass.) Public Library. *Annual Report of the Trustees, 1888.*

Detroit Public Library. *Annual Report, 1882, 1886, 1887, 1895, 1904.*

Dover (N.H.) Public Library. *Annual Report of the Trustees, 1891, 1897.*

Dubuque (Iowa) Carnegie-Stout Free Public Library. *Annual Report, 1906, 1907, 1908.*

Duluth Public Library. *Annual Report of the Public Library Board, 1903.*

East Orange (N.J.) Free Public Library. *Annual Report of the Board of Directors, 1905, 1906, 1907, 1908, 1909, 1910.*

Evanston (Ill.) Public Library. *Annual Report, 1897, 1899.*

Fitchburg (Mass.) Public Library. *Annual Report, 1907, 1910.*

Fletcher Free Library (Burlington, Vt.). *Annual Report of the Trustees, 1876, 1878, 1879, 1880, 1885, 1886, 1894, 1898, 1902.*

Forbes Library (Northampton, Mass.). *Annual Report of the Trustees, 1910.*

General Theological Library (New York City). *Annual Report of the Directors and Treasurer, 1875.*

Gloversville (N.Y.) Free Library. *Annual Report of the Librarian, 1898, 1899.*

Grand Rapids Public Library. *Annual Report, 1901-1902, 1904-1905, 1906-1907, 1909-1910.*

Hartford (Conn.) Public Library. *Annual Report of the Directors, 1903, 1906, 1909.*

Harvard University. *First Report of Justin Winsor, Librarian, 1878.*

_____. *Seventh Report of Justin Winsor, Librarian, 1884.*

_____. *Twelfth Report of Justin Winsor, Librarian, 1889.*

_____. *Second Report of William Coolidge Lane, Librarian, 1899.*

_____. *Third Report of William Coolidge Lane, Librarian, 1900.*

_____. *Sixth Report of William Coolidge Lane, Librarian, 1903.*

_____. *Seventh Report of William Coolidge Lane, Librarian, 1904.*

Harvard University Library. *Annual Report, 1905, 1907, 1908, 1909.*

Haverhill (Mass.) Public Library. *Annual Report, 1906.*

Howard Memorial Library (New Orleans). *Annual Report of the Librarian, 1889-1890.*

Indiana State Library. *Report, 1901-1902, 1905-1906.*

Iowa Library Commission. *Report, 1900-1903.*

Iowa State Library. *Report of the Librarian, 1880-1881, 1886-1887, 1908-1910.*

Jacksonville (Fla.) Public Library. *Annual Report of the Board of Trustees, 1908, 1909.*

John Crerar Library (Chicago). *Annual Report, 1896, 1901.*

Johns Hopkins University Library. *Report of the Librarian, 1908-1909, 1909-1910.*

Kansas City (Mo.) Public Library. *Annual Report, 1897-1898.*

Lansing (Mich.) Public Library. *Annual Report, 1880, 1905-1906.*

Lawrence (Mass.) Free Public Library. *Annual Report of the Board of Trustees and Librarian, 1876, 1877, 1878, 1880, 1886, 1893, 1900.*

Library of Congress. *Report, 1881, 1897-1898, 1899-1900, 1900-1901, 1901-1902, 1903-1904, 1905-1906, 1909-1910.*

Los Angeles Public Library. *Annual Report of the Board of Directors and the Librarian, 1907.*

Louisville (Ky.) Free Public Library. *Annual Report of the Board of Trustees, 1905-1906, 1909-1910.*

Lowell (Mass.) City Library. *Annual Report of the Directors, 1891.*

Lynn (Mass.) Public Library. *Annual Report of the Trustees, 1908.*

Maine State Library. *Annual Report of the Librarian, 1885-1886.*

Malden (Mass.) Public Library. *Annual Report, 1879.*

Manchester (N.H.) City Library. *Annual Report of the Trustees, 1881, 1882, 1884, 1885, 1908.*

Marlborough (Mass.) Public Library. *Annual Report of the Library Committee, 1902.*

Massachusetts Commission of Public Records. *Third Report on the Custody and Condition of the Public Records of Parishes, Towns, and Counties, 1891.*

Medford (Mass.) Public Library. *Report of the Trustees, 1899.*

Mercantile Library Association of the City of New York. *Annual Report of the Board of Direction, 1882-1883.*

Milwaukee Public Library. *Annual Report of the Board of Trustees, 1878-1879, 1894-1895.*

Minneapolis Public Library. *Annual Report, 1895, 1897, 1898, 1909, 1910.*

Montana Historical Society Library. *Biennial Report of the Librarian, 1903-1904.*

Nebraska State Library. *Report, 1905-1906.*

New Bedford (Mass.) Free Public Library. *Annual Report of the Trustees, 1892, 1902, 1906.*

New Hampshire State Library. *Report, 1896-1898, 1908-1910.*

New Haven (Conn.) Free Public Library. *Annual Report of the Board of Directors, 1901, 1903, 1904.*

New Orleans Public Library. *Annual Report, 1901, 1908, 1910.*

New York Society Library. *Annual Report, 1899.*

New York State Library. *Annual Report of the Trustees, 1891, 1898, 1899.*

New York Yacht Club Library. *Report of Library Committee, 1898, 1905, 1906.*

Newark (N.J.) Free Public Library. *Annual Report of the Board of Trustees, 1889-1890, 1891, 1893, 1895, 1902, 1903, 1904, 1906.*

Newberry Library (Chicago). *Report of the Trustees, 1889.*

North Adams (Mass.) Public Library. *Annual Report, 1905.*

North Carolina State Library. *Biennial Report, 1903-1904.*

Oakland (Calif.) Free Library and Reading Rooms. *Annual Report of the Board of Trustees, 1906-1907, 1907-1908, 1910-1911.*

Ohio State Library. *Annual Report, 1876.*

Omaha Public Library. *Annual Report of the Board of Directors, 1896-1897.*

Otis Library (Norwich, Conn). *Annual Report, 1897-1898.*

Paterson (N.J.) Free Public Library. *Report, 1888-1889, 1890-1891, 1901-1902.*

Peabody Institute (Baltimore). *Annual Report of the Provost to the Trustees, 1876, 1879, 1880, 1882, 1891.*

Peabody Institute (Danvers, Mass.). *Annual Report of the Trustees, 1887.*

Bibliography

Pennsylvania State Library. *Report of the State Librarian, 1888, 1898*.

Peoria (Ill.) Public Library. *Annual Report, 1892-1893, 1893-1894, 1898-1899, 1910-1911*.

Philadelphia Free Library. *Annual Report, 1900, 1901*.

Philadelphia Mercantile Library Company. *Annual Report of the Board of Directors, 1877, 1881*.

Pittsburgh Carnegie Library. *Annual Report to the Board of Trustees, 1907-1908*.

Portland (Maine) Public Library. *Annual Report, 1890-1891, 1894-1895*.

Portland (Oreg.) Library Association. *Annual Report, 1900-1901*.

Poughkeepsie (N.Y.) City Library. *Report, 1896*.

Pratt Institute. *Report of the Pratt Institute Free Library and School of Library Science, 1896-1897, 1897-1898, 1898-1899, 1902-1903, 1903-1904, 1905-1906, 1906-1907, 1910-1911*.

Providence Athenaeum. *Annual Report of the Directors, 1876, 1883, 1884, 1886, 1894, 1895, 1897, 1899, 1904, 1906*.

Providence Public Library. Annual Report, *1889, 1891, 1900, 1902, 1903*.

Public Library of the City of Bangor (Maine). *Annual Reports, 1890, 1891, 1892, 1893, 1896, 1901, 1910*.

Queens Borough (N.Y.) Public Library. *Annual Report of the Board of Trustees, 1904, 1905, 1908, 1909, 1910*.

Redwood Library and Athenaeum (Newport, R.I.). *Annual Report of the Directors, 1878, 1879, 1880, 1882, 1884, 1885, 1886, 1887, 1888, 1889, 1891, 1892, 1894, 1896, 1898, 1899, 1900, 1902, 1903, 1909*.

Reynolds Library (Rochester, N.Y.). *Annual Report, 1890-1891*.

Rhode Island State Library. *Annual Report, 1902*.

Rockford (Ill.) Public Library. *Annual Report of the Board of Directors, 1908-1909*.

Rosenberg Library (Galveston, Tex.). *Annual Report, 1906*.

St. Joseph (Mo.) Free Public Library. *Annual Report, 1901-1902, 1909-1910*.

St. Louis Mercantile Library Association. *Annual Report of the Board of Directors, 1876, 1892*.

St. Louis Public Library. *Annual Report, 1880-1881, 1887-1888, 1888-1889, 1890-1891, 1891-1892, 1894-1895, 1895-1896, 1907-1908, 1908-1909, 1910-1911.*

Salem (Mass.) Public Library. *Report of the Trustees, 1889, 1900, 1903, 1908.*

San Francisco Mercantile Library Association. *Annual Report of the President, Treasurer, and Librarian, 1876.*

San Francisco Public Library. *Report of the Board of Trustees, 1882-1883, 1890, 1900, 1906, 1908, 1909.*

Scranton Public Library. *Annual Report, 1899, 1901.*

Seattle Public Library. *Report, 1896, 1897, 1899, 1908, 1909.*

Sedalia (Mo.) Public Library. *Annual Report, 1911.*

Silas Bronson Library (Waterbury, Conn.). *Annual Report of the Board of Agents, 1878-1879, 1879-1880, 1898-1899, 1899-1900, 1905-1906, 1909-1910.*

Somerville (Mass.) Public Library. *Annual Report, 1895, 1902, 1909.*

Southbridge (Mass.) Public Library. *Annual Report, 1878-1879.*

Springfield (Mass.) City Library Association. *Annual Report, 1888, 1889, 1892, 1899, 1902, 1904.*

Syracuse Public Library. *Yearbook, 1893-1894 and 1894-1895, 1899.*

Thomas Crane Public Library (Quincy, Mass.). *Annual Report, 1878, 1909.*

Trinity College Library. *Report of the Librarian, 1900, 1906, 1908.*

Troy (N.Y.) Public Library. *Report, 1909, 1910.*

University of Michigan Library. *Annual Report of the Director, 1890, 1891, 1892, 1894, 1896, 1896-1897, 1897-1898.*

University of Pennsylvania Library. *Report, 1901-1902.*

Virginia State Library. *Report, 1906.*

Washington, D.C., Public Library. *Annual Report, 1900, 1901, 1905-1906, 1906-1907, 1907-1908, 1908-1909, 1909-1910.*

Washington Heights (N.Y.) Free Library. *Annual Report, 1900.*

Washington State Library. *Biennial Report of the State Librarian, 1906.*

Washington Territory Library. *Report of the Librarian, 1889.*

Bibliography

Watertown (Mass.) Free Public Library. *Annual Report, 1880, 1882, 1883, 1892.*

Wilmington (Del.) Institute. *Annual Report, 1885-1886, 1894-1895, 1895-1896, 1896-1897, 1903-1904, 1905-1906, 1906-1907, 1908-1909, 1909-1910.*

Wisconsin Free Library Commission. *Biennial Report, 1895-1896.*

Woburn (Mass.) Public Library. *Annual Report, 1888, 1889, 1892, 1894, 1909, 1910.*

Worcester County (Mass.) Law Library. *Annual Report, 1902, 1903, 1904, 1906, 1907, 1908, 1909, 1910, 1911.*

Yale University. *Report of the Librarian, 1902-1903, 1907-1908, 1908-1909.*

Unpublished and Manuscript Material

Kelly, George. "Mass Deacidification." Conference on the Preservation of Library Materials, Rutgers University, 20-21 July 1979. Unpublished speech.

Oxford, U.K. Bodleian Library. Library Records c1429, The St. Gallen Conference, 1898. Nicholson, Edward W. B. "Report by Bodley's Librarian to the Curators of the Bodleian, on the Conference Held at St. Gallen, Sept. 30 and Oct. 1, 1898, upon the Preservation and Repair of Old M.S.S.," 22 December 1898, p. 3.

Washington, D.C. Library of Congress. Manuscripts Division. "The Care of Manuscripts: A Paper Read before the American Library Association, Philadelphia, June 25, 1897."

_____. Letter Book 1, 1898-1900, 26 April-7 May. Letter no. 124, Herbert Friedenwald to Franz Ehrle, 1 November 1898.

_____. Letter Book 1, 1898-1900, 26 April-7 May. Letter no. 157, Herbert Friedenwald to Franz Ehrle, 20 December 1898.

_____. Letter Book 1, 1898-1900, 26 April-7 May. Letter no. 216, Herbert Friedenwald to Edward W. B. Nicholson, 23 March 1899.

_____. Letter Book 1, 1898-1900, 26 April-7 May. Letter no. 221, Herbert Friedenwald to Robert T. Swan, 17 April 1899.

_____. Letter Book 1, 1898-1900, 26 April-7 May. Letter no. 222, Herbert Friedenwald to Edward W. B. Nicholson, 17 April 1899.

_____. Letter Book 1, 1898-1900, 26 April-7 May. Letter no. 258, Herbert Friedenwald to Francis W. R. Emery, 1 May 1899.

Bibliography

_____. Letter Book 1, 1898-1900, 26 April-7 May. Letter no. 243, Herbert Friedenwald to Robert T. Swan, 21 December 1899.

_____. Letter Book 1, 1898-1900, 26 April-7 May. Letter no. 450, Herbert Friedenwald to H. O. Collins, 10 December 1900.

_____. Memorandums to Librarian, vol. 2, 1900-1902, 20 April-11 October. Letter no. 149, "The Repair of Manuscripts," C. H. Lincoln to the Librarian of Congress.

Secondary Sources

Journals, Newspapers, Yearbooks, Encyclopedias, and Proceedings

Banks, Paul N. "Preservation of Library Materials." In _Encyclopaedia of Library and Information Science_ 23 (1978): 181.

Brommelle, Norman S. "Material for a History of Conservation." _Studies in Conservation_ 2 (October 1956): 176-85.

_____. "The Russell and Abney Report on the Action of Light on Water Colours." _Studies in Conservation_ 9 (1984): 140-52.

Darling, Pamela W. "Our Fragile Inheritance: The Challenge of Preserving Library Materials." In _ALA Yearbook, 1978_, xxxii. Chicago: American Library Association, 1978.

Darling, Pamela W., and Ogden, Sherelyn. "From Problems Perceived to Programs in Practice: The Preservation of Library Resources in the U.S.A., 1956-1980." _Library Resources and Technical Services_ 25 (January-March 1981): 9-29.

Gear, James L. "The Repair of Documents–American Beginnings." _American Archivist_ 26 (October 1963): 469-75.

Gwinn, Nancy E. "CLR and Preservation." _College and Research Libraries_ 42 (March 1981): 105-7.

Henderson, James W., and Krupp, Robert G. "The Librarian as Conservator." In _Deterioration and Preservation of Library Materials: The Thirty-fourth Annual Conference of the Graduate Library School, August 4-6, 1969_, edited by Howard W. Winger and Richard D. Smith, 176-92. Chicago: University of Chicago Press, 1970.

Santucci, Ludovico. "The Application of Chemical and Physical Methods to Conservation of Archival Materials." _Bolletino dell'Istituto di Patologia del Libro_ 20 (January 1961): 85-111.

Bibliography

Stange, Eric. "Millions of Books are Turning to Dust—Can They be Saved?" *New York Times Book Review*, 29 March 1987, 3, 38.

Vaisey, David G. "E. W. B. Nicholson and the St. Gall Conference, 1898." *Bodleian Library Record* 9 (March 1974): 101-13.

Weidner, Marilyn K. "Damage and Deterioration of Art on Paper Due to Ignorance and the Use of Faulty Materials." *Studies in Conservation* 12 (February 1967): 5-25.

White, Howard S., and Hanna, Herbert L. "Library Technology Program." In *Encyclopaedia of Library and Information Science* 16 (1975): 96-100.

Williams, Edwin. "Deterioration of Library Collections Today." In *Deterioration and Preservation of Library Materials: The Thirty-fourth Annual Conference of the Graduate Library School, August 4-6, 1969*, edited by Howard W. Winger and Richard D. Smith, 3-17. Chicago: University of Chicago Press, 1970.

Monographs

Alexander, Edward P. *Museums in Motion: An Introduction to the History and Functions of Museums*. Nashville: American Association for State and Local History, 1979.

Caldwell, Frank C. *Modern Lighting*. New York: Macmillan, 1930.

Comparato, Frank E. *Books for the Millions: A History of the Men Whose Methods and Machines Packaged the Printed Word*. Harrisburg: Stackpole, 1971.

Cunha, George M., and Cunha, Dorothy G. *Conservation of Library Materials: A Manual and Bibliography on the Care, Repair, and Restoration of Library Materials*. 2d ed. 2 vols. Metuchen, N.J.: Scarecrow Press, 1971.

Fussler, Herman H. *Photographic Reproduction for Libraries: A Study of Administrative Problems*. Chicago: University of Chicago Press, 1942.

Hosmer, Charles B., Jr. *Presence of the Past: A History of the Preservation Movement in the United States before Williamsburg*. New York: Putnam, 1965.

Lehmann-Haupt, Helmut, ed. *Bookbinding in America: Three Essays*. Portland, Maine: Southworth-Anthoensen Press, 1941.

Meder, Joseph. *The Mastery of Drawing*. 2 vols. New York: Abaris Books, 1978.

Bibliography

Middleton, Bernard C. *A History of English Craft Bookbinding Technique*. London and New York: Hafner, 1963.

Molz, R. Kathleen. *The Knowledge Institutions in the Information Age: The Special Case of the Public Library: An Engelhard Lecture on the Book Presented on April 7, 1987, at the Library of Congress*. Center for the Book Viewpoint Series, no. 2. Washington, D.C.: Library of Congress, 1988.

Pyke, John S. *Landmark Preservation*. 2d ed. New York: Citizens Union Research Foundation, Inc., of the City of New York, 1972.

Roberts, Matt T., and Etherington, Don. *Bookbinding and the Conservation of Books: A Dictionary of Descriptive Terminology*. Washington, D.C.: Library of Congress, 1982.

Shera, Jesse H. *Foundations of the Public Library Movement in New England, 1629-1855*. Hamden, Conn.: Shoestring Press, 1965.

Wiegand, Wayne A. *The Politics of an Emerging Profession: The American Library Association, 1876-1917*. New York: Greenwood Press, 1986.

Theses and Dissertations

Crowe, William J. "Verner W. Clapp as Opinion Leader and Change Agent in the Preservation of Library Materials." Ph.D. thesis, Indiana University, 1986.

Manley, Keith A. "E. W. B. Nicholson (1849-1912) and His Importance to Librarianship." D.Phil. thesis, Trinity College, Oxford, 1977.

Marwick, Claire S. "An Historical Study of Paper Document Restoration Methods." Master's thesis, American University, 1964.

Ogden, Sherelyn. "A Study of the Impact of the Florence Flood on the Development of Library Conservation in the United States: 1966-1976." Master's thesis, University of Chicago, 1978.

Smith, Richard. "Non-Aqueous Deacidification of Paper and Books." Ph.D. thesis, University of Chicago, 1971.

Index